Basics of Autodesk Inventor Nastran 2027

By

Gaurav Verma
Matt Weber
(CADCAMCAE Works)

ISBN # 978-1-77459-218-2

NOTICE TO THE READER

Publisher does not warrant or guarantee any of the products described in the text or perform any independent analysis in connection with any of the product information contained in the text. Publisher does not assume, and expressly disclaims, any obligation to obtain and include information other than that provided to it by the manufacturer.

The reader is expressly warned to consider and adopt all safety precautions that might be indicated by the activities herein and to avoid all potential hazards. By following the instructions contained herein, the reader willingly assumes all risks in connection with such instructions.

The Publisher makes no representation or warranties of any kind, including but not limited to, the warranties of fitness for a particular purpose or merchantability, nor are any such representations implied with respect to the material set forth herein, and the publisher takes no responsibility with respect to such material. The publisher shall not be liable for any special, consequential, or exemplary damages resulting, in whole or part, from the reader's use of, or reliance upon, this material.

DEDICATION

To teachers, who make it possible to disseminate knowledge
to enlighten the young and curious minds
of our future generations

To students, who are the future of the world

THANKS

To my friends and colleagues

To my family for their love and support

Table of Contents

Preface iv
About Author vi

Chapter 1 : Introduction to Simulation

Simulation **1-2**
Types of Analyses performed in Autodesk Inventor Nastran **1-2**
Static Analysis 1-2
Normal Modes Analysis 1-4
Buckling Analysis 1-4
Transient Response Analysis 1-6
Frequency Response Analysis 1-7
Impact Analysis 1-8
Random Response Analysis 1-8
Shock/Response Spectrum Analysis 1-8
Multi-Axial Fatigue Analysis 1-8
Vibrational Fatigue Analysis 1-9
Thermal analysis 1-9
Explicit Analysis 1-9
Installing and Activating Inventor Nastran **1-10**
Performing Analysis (Overview) **1-13**
Applying Material 1-13
Applying Constraint 1-14
Applying Loads 1-15
Running Analysis 1-16
Self Assessment **1-17**

Chapter 2 : Basics of Analysis

Introduction **2-2**
Default Settings **2-2**
General Options 2-2
Setting Display Options 2-3
Nodes 2-4
Elements 2-4
Post-Processing 2-4
Report Generation 2-6
Starting A New Study **2-6**
Options tab 2-7
Model State 2-8
Editing Analysis **2-9**
Importing from Stress Analysis **2-9**
Applying Materials **2-10**
Creating New Material 2-11
Material Properties 2-13
Idealization **2-19**
Solid Idealization 2-20
Shell Idealization 2-20
Line Idealization 2-25

Using Concentrated Masses **2-29**
Applying Connections between Assembly Components **2-30**
Applying Rod Connection 2-31
Applying Cable Connection 2-32
Applying Spring Connection 2-33
Applying Rigid Body Connection 2-34
Applying Bolt Connection 2-36
Offsetting Surface for Creating Shell Components **2-38**
Finding Thin Bodies **2-39**
Creating Midsurface **2-39**
Managing Structural Members **2-41**
Applying Constraints **2-41**
Applying Loads **2-43**
Applying Force 2-44
Applying Moment Load 2-46
Applying Distributed Load 2-47
Applying Hydrostatic Load 2-47
Applying Pressure and Gravity 2-49
Applying Remote Force 2-49
Applying Bearing Load 2-50
Applying Rotational Force 2-51
Applying Enforced Motion Load 2-52
Applying Initial Condition 2-52
Applying Body Temperature 2-53
Applying Temperature 2-53
Applying Thermal Convection 2-54
Applying Thermal Radiation 2-56
Applying Heat Generation 2-57
Applying Heat Flux 2-57
Applying Loads based on Analysis Results 2-58
Applying Rigid Motion (Explicit) 2-59
Defining Contact Sets **2-60**
Applying Automatic Contact Sets 2-60
Applying Manual Contacts 2-61
Defining Solver Settings 2-65
Meshing **2-66**
Defining Mesh Settings 2-66
Mesh Table Parameters 2-68
Generating Mesh 2-68
Setting Mesh Control 2-69
Adaptive Meshing using Convergence Settings 2-70
Mesh Troubleshooting 2-71
Running Analysis **2-72**
Setting Plot Options **2-73**
Contour Options 2-74
Deform Options 2-74
Section View Options 2-74
Setting Part View Options 2-75
Vector Options 2-76
Animation Options 2-76

Visibility Options 2-77
Using Probe to Check Node Results 2-78
Result Options 2-79
Loading Results 2-79
Toggling Contour Shape 2-79
Deformed Shape 2-80
Stress Linearization 2-80
Generating Animation File of Results 2-82
Object Visibility Options 2-82
Self Assessment 2-83

Chapter 3 : Static Analyses

Introduction 3-2
Performing Linear Static Analysis on Part 3-2
Applying Material 3-3
Applying Idealizations 3-4
Applying Constraints 3-5
Applying Force 3-5
Creating Mesh 3-6
Running Analysis 3-6
Performing Linear Static Analysis on an Assembly 3-7
Starting Linear Static Analysis 3-7
Applying Material 3-8
Applying Contacts 3-8
Applying Constraint 3-8
Applying Loads 3-9
Mesh Setting 3-9
Running Analysis 3-10
Performing Analysis on Frame Model 3-11
Performing Prestress Static Analysis 3-13
Non Linear Static Analysis 3-14
Theory Behind Non-Linear Analysis 3-15
Role of Time in Non-Linear Analysis 3-17
Performing Non Linear Static Analysis 3-18
Nonlinear Setup Parameters 3-19
Material Orientation 3-22
Sub-Cases 3-23
Nastran Solver Parameters 3-24
Practical 1 3-26
Practical 2 3-31
Practical 3 3-34
Self Assessment 3-40

Chapter 4 : Normal Modes Analyses

Introduction 4-2
Performing Normal Modes Analysis 4-3
Modal Setup Options 4-3
Performing Prestress Normal Modes Analysis 4-7
Adding Concentrated Mass 4-9
Practical 1 4-12

Practical 2 4-15
Practice 4-21
Self Assessment 4-21

Chapter 5 : Buckling Analysis

Introduction 5-2
Performing Linear Buckling Analysis 5-3
Performing Non-Linear Buckling Analysis 5-5
Practical 1 5-7
Practice 1 5-10
Practice 2 5-10
Self Assessment 5-11

Chapter 6 : Transient Response Analysis

Introduction 6-2
Performing Direct Transient Response 6-3
Setting Damping Values 6-3
Dynamic Setup Parameters 6-4
Performing Modal Transient Response Analysis 6-5
Performing Nonlinear Transient Response Analysis 6-7
Practical 6-8
Practice 6-16
Self Assessment 6-17

Chapter 7 : Impact Analysis

Introduction 7-2
Performing Impact Analysis 7-2
Defining Impact Parameters 7-4
Manual Impact Analysis 7-7
Practice 7-12
Self Assessment 7-12

Chapter 8 : Frequency Response Analysis

Introduction 8-2
Performing Direct Frequency Response Analysis 8-2
Performing Modal Frequency Response Analysis 8-7
Practical 8-10
Self Assessment 8-14

Chapter 9 : Random Response Analysis

Introduction 9-2
Performing Random Response Analysis 9-2
Performing Shock/Response Spectrum Analysis 9-4
Self Assessment 9-8

Chapter 10 : Fatigue Analyses

Introduction 10-2
Performing Multi-axial Fatigue Analysis 10-2
Fatigue Parameters 10-3

Performing Vibration Fatigue Analysis 10-5
Self Assessment 10-7

Chapter 11 : Heat Transfer Analyses

Introduction 11-2
Important terms related to Thermal Analysis 11-2
Performing Linear Steady State Heat Transfer Analysis 11-5
Performing Nonlinear Steady State Heat Transfer Analysis 11-8
Performing Nonlinear Transient Heat Transfer Analysis 11-9
Practice 11-10
Problem 1 11-11
Problem 2 11-11
Self Assessment 11-12

Chapter 12 : Explicit Analyses

Introduction 12-2
Performing Explicit Dynamics Analysis 12-2
Applying Shell Idealization 12-3
Applying Impulse Load 12-4
Performing Explicit Quasi-Static Analysis 12-6
Practice 12-8
Self Assessment 12-8

Chapter 13 : Fundamentals of FEA and Nastran

Introduction 13-2
General Description Of The Method 13-2
A Brief Explanation Of FEA For A Stress Analysis Problem 13-3
Finite Element Method V/S Classical Methods 13-5
Fem Vs Finite Difference Method (FDM) 13-6
Need For Studying FEA 13-7
Warning To FEA Package Users 13-8
Geometric Discontinuities 13-8
Discontinuity of Loads 13-9
Discontinuity of Boundary conditions 13-10
Material Discontinuity 13-10
Refining Mesh 13-11
Use Of Symmetry 13-11
Higher Order Elements V/S Refined Mesh 13-11
FEA in Nastran 13-12
Input Geometry and Parameters 13-12
Conversion to Nastran Cards 13-13
Element Stiffness Matrix Formation 13-16
Nastran Cards for Elemental Stiffness Matrix 13-22
Force Matrix 13-22
Global Matrix 13-24
Applying Constraints to Global Matrix 13-25
Solution 13-26
Summary 13-26
Self Assessment 13-26

Practice Questions

Problem 1 P-2
Problem 2 P-2
Problem 3 P-3
Problem 4 P-3
Problem 5 P-4
Problem 6 P-4

Index I-1
Ethics of an Engineer I-6
Other Books by CADCAMCAE Works I-6

Preface

Autodesk Inventor® Nastran® software is a general purpose finite element analysis (FEA) tool embedded in Autodesk® Inventor. It is powered by the Autodesk® Nastran® solver and offers simulation capabilities that span across multiple analysis types, such as linear and nonlinear stress, dynamics, and heat transfer.

Autodesk Inventor® Nastran® is available as a network license and serves multiple CAD platforms to provide a consistent user experience and eliminate the need for multiple single-platform simulation technologies. It delivers high-end simulation technology in a CAD-embedded workflow so you can make great products.

The **Basics of Autodesk Inventor Nastran 2027**, 7th edition, is a book to help professionals as well as students in learning basics of Finite Element Analysis via Autodesk Inventor Nastran. The book follows a step by step methodology. This book explains the background work running behind your simulation analysis screen. The book starts with introduction to simulation and goes through all the analysis tools of Autodesk Inventor Nastran with practical examples of analysis. Chapter on manual FEA ensure the firm understanding of FEA concepts. In this edition, we have added new topics that explain how Nastran works in background to solve analyses. Some of the salient features of this book are:

In-Depth explanation of concepts

Every new topic of this book starts with the explanation of basic concepts. In this way, the user becomes capable of relating the things with real world.

Topics Covered

Every chapter starts with a list of topics being covered in that chapter. In this way, the user can easy find the topic of his/her interest easily.

Instruction through illustration

The instructions to perform any action are provided by maximum number of illustrations so that the user can perform the actions discussed in the book easily and effectively. There are about 400 illustrations that make the learning process effective.

SIMULATION

Simulation is the study of effects caused on an object due to real-world loading conditions. Computer Simulation is a type of simulation which uses CAD models to represent real objects and it applies various load conditions on the model to study the real-world effects. Autodesk Inventor Nastran is one of the Computer Simulation programs available in the market. In Autodesk Inventor Nastran, we apply loads on a constrained model under predefined environmental conditions and check the result(visually and/or in the form of tabular data). The types of analyses that can be performed in Autodesk Inventor Nastran are given next.

TYPES OF ANALYSES PERFORMED IN AUTODESK INVENTOR NASTRAN

Autodesk Inventor Nastran performs almost all the mechanical analyses that are generally performed in Industries. These analyses and their uses are given next.

Static Analysis

This is the most common type of analysis we perform. In this analysis, loads are applied to a body due to which the body deforms and the effects of the loads are transmitted throughout the body. To absorb the effect of loads, the body generates internal forces and reactions at the supports to balance the applied external loads. These internal forces and reactions cause stress and strain in the body. Static analysis refers to the calculation of displacements, strains, and stresses under the effect of external loads, based on some assumptions. The assumptions are as follows.

- All loads are applied slowly and gradually until they reach their full magnitudes. After reaching their full magnitudes, load will remain constant (i.e. load will not vary against time).
- Linearity assumption: The relationship between loads and resulting responses is linear. For example, if you double the magnitude of loads, the response of the model (displacements, strains and stresses) will also double. You can make linearity assumption if:

1. All materials in the model comply with Hooke's Law that is stress is directly proportional to strain.
2. The induced displacements are small enough to ignore the change in stiffness caused by loading.
3. Boundary conditions do not vary during the application of loads. Loads must be constant in magnitude, direction, and distribution. They should not change while the model is deforming.

Linear Static Analysis

If the above assumptions are valid for your analysis, then you can perform **Linear Static Analysis**. For example, a cantilever beam fixed at one end and force applied on other end; refer to Figure-1.

Chapter 1

Introduction to Simulation

Topics Covered

The major topics covered in this chapter are:

- ***Simulation***
- ***Types of Analyses performed in Autodesk Inventor Nastran***
- ***FEA***
- ***Activating Autodesk Inventor Nastran***

About Author

Gaurav Verma is a Mechanical Design Engineer with deep knowledge of CAD, CAM and CAE field. He has an experience of more than 15 years on CAD/CAM/CAE packages. He has delivered presentations in Autodesk University Events on AutoCAD Electrical and Autodesk Inventor. He is an active member of Autodesk Knowledge Share Network. He has provided content for Autodesk Design Academy. He is also working as technical consultant for many Indian Government organizations for Skill Development sector. He has authored books on SolidWorks, Mastercam, Creo Parametric, Autodesk Inventor, Autodesk Fusion, and many other CAD-CAM-CAE packages. He has developed content for many modular skill courses like Automotive Service Technician, Welding Technician, Lathe Operator, CNC Operator, Telecom Tower Technician, TV Repair Technician, Casting Operator, Maintenance Technician and about 50 more courses. He has his books published in English, Russian and Hindi worldwide.

He has trained many students on mechanical, electrical, and civil streams of CAD-CAM-CAE. He has trained students online as well as offline. He also owns a small workshop of 20 CNC and VMC machines where he tests his CAM skills on different Automotive components. He is providing consultant services to more than 15 companies worldwide. You can contact the author directly at cadcamcaeworks@gmail.com

Tutorial point of view

The book explains the concepts through the tutorial to make the understanding of users firm and long lasting. Each chapter of the book has tutorials that are real world projects.

Project

Projects and exercises are provided to students for asking for more practice.

For Faculty

If you are a faculty member, then you can ask for video tutorials on any of the topic, exercise, tutorial, or concept. As faculty, you can register on our website to get electronic desk copies of our latest books, self-assessment, and solution of practical. Faculty resources are available in the **Faculty Member** page of our website (**cadcamcaeworks**) once you login. Note that faculty registration approval is manual and it may take upto two days for approval before you can access the faculty website.

Formatting Conventions Used in the Text

All the key terms like name of button, tool, drop-down etc. are kept bold.

Free Resources

Link to the resources used in this book are provided to the users via email. To get the resources, mail us at ***cadcamcaeworks@gmail.com*** or ***info@cadcamcaeworks.com*** with your contact information. With your contact record with us, you will be provided latest updates and informations regarding various technologies. The format to write us e-mail for resources is as follows:

Subject of E-mail as ***Application for resources of ....Book***.
You can give your information below to get updates on the book.
Name:
Course pursuing/Profession:
Contact Address:
E-mail ID:

For Any query or suggestion

If you have any query or suggestion please let us know by mailing us on ***cadcamcaeworks@gmail.com*** or ***info@cadcamcaeworks.com***. Your valuable constructive suggestions will be incorporated in our books and your name will be addressed in special thanks area of our books.

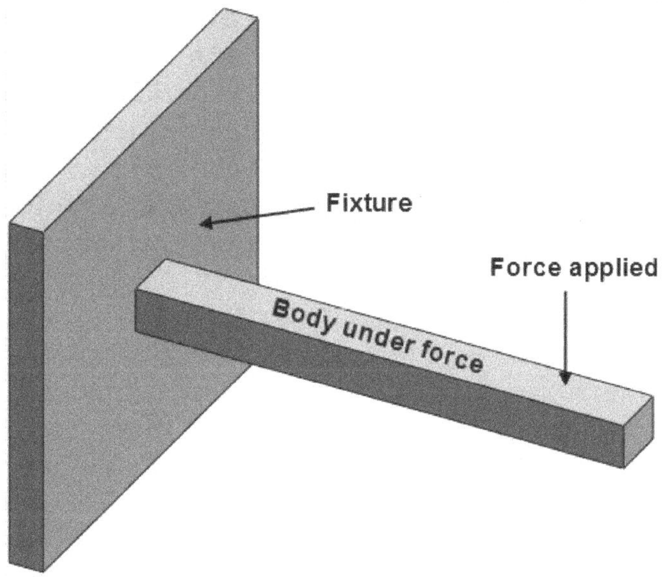

Figure-1. Linear static analysis example

Nonlinear Static Analysis

If the above assumptions are not valid, then you need to perform the **Non-Linear Static analysis**. For example, an object attached with a spring being applied under forces; refer to Figure-2. There are many other conditions of non-linearity like material non-linearity, load changes with time, and so on.

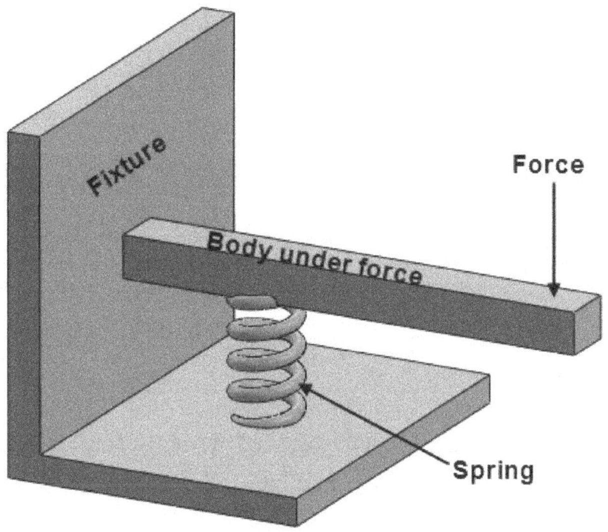

Figure-2. Non-linear static analysis example

Prestress Static Analysis

The Prestress static analysis is performed when you have model already prestressed and want to apply additional loads.

Normal Modes Analysis

The Normal Modes Analysis also called harmonic analysis is used to find natural frequencies. By its very nature, vibration involves repetitive motion. Each occurrence of a complete motion sequence is called a "cycle." Frequency is defined as so many cycles in a given time period. "Cycles per seconds" or "Hertz". Individual parts have what engineers call "natural" frequencies. For example, a violin string at a certain tension will vibrate only at a set number of frequencies, which is why you can produce specific musical tones. There is a base frequency at which the entire string is going back and forth in a simple bow shape.

Harmonics and overtones occur because individual sections of the string can vibrate independently within the larger vibration to form different shapes. These various shapes are called "modes". The base frequency is said to vibrate in the first mode, and so on up the ladder. Each mode shape will have an associated frequency. Higher mode shapes have higher frequencies. The most disastrous kinds of consequences occur when a power-driven device such as a motor for example, produces a frequency at which an attached structure naturally vibrates. This event is called "resonance." If sufficient power is applied, the attached structure will be destroyed. Note that ancient armies, which normally marched "in step," were taken out of step when crossing bridges. Should the beat of the marching feet align with a natural frequency of the bridge, it could fall down. Engineers must design in such a way that resonance does not occur during regular operation of machines. This is a major purpose of Normal Modes Analysis. Ideally, the first mode has a frequency higher than any potential driving frequency. Frequently, resonance cannot be avoided, especially for short periods of time. For example, when a motor comes up to speed it produces a variety of frequencies. It may pass through a resonant frequency.

Buckling Analysis

The Buckling Analysis is performed to check sudden failure of structure. If you press down on an empty soft drink can with your hand, not much will seem to happen. If you put the can on the floor and gradually increase the force by stepping down on it with your foot, at some point it will suddenly squash. This sudden scrunching is known as "buckling."

Models with thin parts tend to buckle under axial loading. Buckling can be defined as the sudden deformation, which occurs when the stored membrane(axial) energy is converted into bending energy with no change in the externally applied loads. Mathematically, when buckling occurs, the total stiffness matrix becomes singular.

In the normal use of most products, buckling can be catastrophic if it occurs. The failure is not one because of stress but geometric stability. Once the geometry of the part starts to deform, it can no longer support even a fraction of the force initially applied. The worst part about buckling for engineers is that buckling usually occurs at relatively low stress values for what the material can withstand. So, they have to make a separate check to see if a product or part thereof is okay with respect to buckling.

Slender structures and structures with slender parts loaded in the axial direction buckle under relatively small axial loads. Such structures may fail in buckling while their stresses are far below critical levels. For such structures, the buckling load becomes a critical design factor. Stocky structures, on the other hand, require large loads to buckle, therefore buckling analysis is usually not required.

Buckling almost always involves compression; refer to Figure-3. In mechanical engineering, designs involving thin parts in flexible structures like airplanes and automobiles are susceptible to buckling. Even though stress can be very low, buckling of local areas can cause the whole structure to collapse by a rapid series of 'propagating buckling'. Buckling analysis calculates the smallest (critical) loading required buckling a model. Buckling loads are associated with buckling modes. Designers are usually interested in the lowest mode because it is associated with the lowest critical load. When buckling is the critical design factor, calculating multiple buckling modes helps in locating the weak areas of the model. This may prevent the occurrence of lower buckling modes by simple modifications.

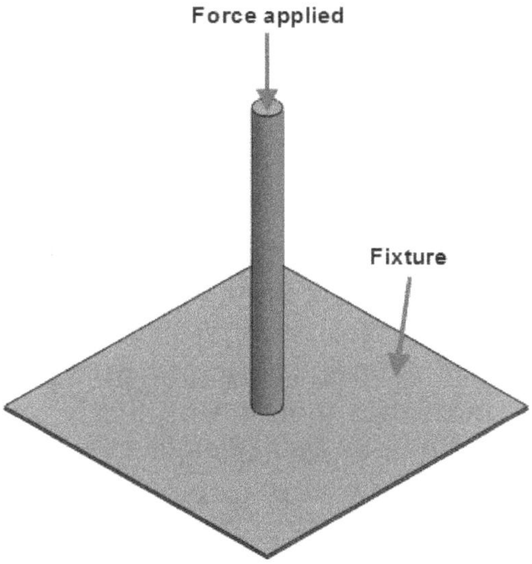

Figure-3. Buckling example

Linear Buckling Analysis

Linear-buckling analysis (also called eigenvalue-based buckling analysis) is in many ways similar to modal analysis. Linear buckling is the most common type of analysis and is easy to execute, but it is limited in the results it can provide.

Linear-buckling analysis calculates buckling load magnitudes that cause buckling and associated buckling modes. FEA programs provide calculations of a large number of buckling modes and the associated buckling-load factors (BLF). The BLF is expressed by a number which the applied load must be multiplied by (or divided — depending on the particular FEA package) to obtain the buckling-load magnitude.

The buckling mode presents the shape the structure will assume when it buckles in a particular mode, but says nothing about the numerical values of the displacements or stresses. The numerical values can be displayed, but are merely relative. This is in close analogy to modal analysis, which calculates the natural frequency and provides qualitative information on the modes of vibration (modal shapes), but not on the actual magnitude of displacements.

Nonlinear Buckling Analysis

The nonlinear-buckling analysis requires a load to be applied gradually in multiple steps rather than in one step as in a linear analysis. Each load increment changes the structure's shape, and this, in turn, changes the structure's stiffness. Therefore, the structure stiffness must be updated at each increment. In this approach, which is called the load control method, load steps are defined either by the user or automatically so the difference in displacement between the two consecutive steps is not too large.

Although the load-control method is used in most types of nonlinear analyses, it would be difficult to implement in a buckling analysis. When buckling happens, the structure undergoes a momentary loss of stiffness and the load control method would result in numerical instabilities. Nonlinear buckling analysis requires another way of controlling load application — the arc length control method. Here, points corresponding to consecutive load increments are evenly spaced along the load-displacement curve, which itself is constructed during load application.

In contrast to linear-buckling analysis, which only calculates the potential buckling shape with no quantitative values of importance, nonlinear analysis calculates actual displacements and stresses. To better understand the inner workings of nonlinear-buckling analysis, first consider what happens in running a nonlinear-buckling analysis on an idealized structure. Imagine a perfectly round and perfectly straight column under a perfectly aligned compressive load. Theoretically, buckling will never happen, but in actuality, buckling will take place because of imperfections in the geometry, loads, and supports.

Transient Response Analysis

Transient response analysis is the most general method for computing forced dynamic response. The purpose of a transient response analysis is to determine the behavior of a structure subjected to time-varying excitation. The transient excitation is explicitly defined in the time domain. The loads applied to the structure are known at each instant in time. Loads can be in the form of applied forces and enforced motions. The results obtained from a transient response analysis are typically displacements, velocities, and accelerations of grid points, and forces and stresses in elements, at each output time step. Depending upon the structure and the nature of the loading, two different numerical methods can be used for a transient response analysis:

Direct Transient Response Analysis

Direct Transient Response Analysis calculates the response of a system to a load over time. The load applied to the system can vary over time or simply be an initial condition that is allowed to evolve over time. This method may be more efficient for models where high-frequency excitation require the extraction of a large number of modes. Also, if structural damping is used, the direct method should be used.

Modal Transient Response Analysis

Modal Transient Response Analysis is an alternate technique available for dynamics that utilizes the mode shapes of the structure, reduces the solution degrees of freedom, and can significantly impact the run time. This approach replaces the physical degrees of freedom with a reduced number of modal degrees of freedom. Fewer degrees of freedom mean a faster solution. This can be a big time saver for transient models with a large number of time steps. Because modal transient response analysis uses the mode shapes of a structure, this analysis is a natural extension of normal modes analysis.

Nonlinear Transient Response Analysis

A nonlinear transient analysis requires both dynamic and nonlinear setup steps. Autodesk Inventor Nastran solves both analyses essentially simultaneously, making it one of the most complex yet exciting solution types in FEA.

An important element to having a stable nonlinear transient (NLT) solution is to provide damping in the model. There are two types of damping that can be applied in NLT solutions:

`Global damping value` is specified using a PARAM,G followed by a PARAM,W3 which defines the frequency at which to apply the damping.

`Material based damping` is defined on each material card directly. PARAM,W4 is needed to define the frequency at which to apply the material based damping. Note that the units of W3 and W4 are radians per unit time.

Frequency Response Analysis

The frequency response analysis is used to compute structural response of model to steady-state oscillatory excitation. In frequency response analysis, the excitation is explicitly defined in the frequency domain. Excitations can be in the form of applied forces and enforced motions (displacements, velocities, or accelerations). There are two types of frequency response analysis:

Direct Frequency Response Analysis

In Direct Frequency Response Analysis the structural response is computed at discrete excitation frequencies by solving a set of coupled matrix equations using complex algebra. The direct method may be more efficient for models where high-frequency excitation require the extraction of a large number of modes.

Modal Frequency Response Analysis

Modal Frequency Response Analysis is an alternate method to compute frequency response. This method uses the mode shapes of the structure to uncouple the equations of motion (when no damping or only modal damping is used) and, depending on the number of modes computed and retained, reduce the problem size. Both of these factors tend to make modal frequency response analysis computationally more efficient than direct frequency response analysis. It is used for large models where a large number of solution frequencies are specified. This method replaces the physical degrees of freedom (DOF) with a reduced number of modal degrees of freedom. Fewer degrees of freedom mean a faster solution. Because modal frequency response analysis uses the mode shapes of a structure, modal frequency response analysis is a natural extension of normal modes analysis.

Impact Analysis

The Impact analysis is used to perform drop-test and projectile impact studies. This study simulates the effect of dropping a part or an assembly on a rigid or flexible floor. To perform this study, the floor is considered as planar and flat. The forces that are considered automatically for this study are gravity and impact reaction.

Random Response Analysis

Engineers use this type of analysis to find out how a device or structure responds to steady shaking of the kind you would feel riding in a truck, rail car, rocket (when the motor is on), and so on. Also, things that are riding in the vehicle, such as on-board electronics or cargo of any kind, may need Random Vibration Analysis. The vibration generated in vehicles from the motors, road conditions, etc. is a combination of a great many frequencies from a variety of sources and has a certain “random” nature. Random Vibration Analysis is used by mechanical engineers who design various kinds of transportation equipment.

Shock/Response Spectrum Analysis

Engineers use this type of analysis to find out how a device or structure responds to sudden forces or shocks. It is assumed that these shocks or forces occur at boundary points, which are normally fixed. An example would be a building, dam or nuclear reactor when an earthquake strikes. During an earthquake, violent shaking occurs. This shaking transmits into the structure or device at the points where they are attached to the ground (boundary points).

Mechanical engineers who design components for nuclear power plants must use response spectrum analysis as well. Such components might include nuclear reactor parts, pumps, valves, piping, condensers, etc. When an engineer uses response spectrum analysis, he is looking for the maximum stresses or acceleration, velocity and displacements that occur after the shock. These in turn lead to maximum stresses.

Multi-Axial Fatigue Analysis

The Multi-Axial Fatigue Analysis is used to check the effect of continuous loading and unloading of forces on a body. The base element for performing fatigue analysis are results of static, nonlinear, or time history linear dynamic studies.

Vibrational Fatigue Analysis

The Vibrational Fatigue Analysis is used to check the effect of vibrational loading and unloading on the body.

Thermal analysis

There are three mechanisms of heat transfer. These mechanisms are Conduction, Convection, and Radiation. Thermal analysis calculates the temperature distribution in a body due to some or all of these mechanisms. In all three mechanisms, heat flows from a higher-temperature medium to a lower temperature one. Heat transfer by conduction and convection requires the presence of an intervening medium while heat transfer by radiation does not.

There are two modes of heat transfer analysis.

Steady State Thermal Analysis

In this type of analysis, we are only interested in the thermal conditions of the body when it reaches thermal equilibrium, but we are not interested in the time it takes to reach this status. The temperature of each point in the model will remain unchanged until a change occurs in the system. At equilibrium, the thermal energy entering the system is equal to the thermal energy leaving it. Generally, the only material property that is needed for steady state analysis is the thermal conductivity.

Transient Thermal Analysis

In this type of analysis, we are interested in knowing the thermal status of the model at different instances of time. A thermos designer, for example, knows that the temperature of the fluid inside will eventually be equal to the room temperature(steady state), but he is interested in finding out the temperature of the fluid as a function of time. In addition to the thermal conductivity, we also need to specify density, specific heat, initial temperature profile, and the period of time for which solutions are desired.

Explicit Analysis

The explicit analysis solve for acceleration value at nodal points by multiplying inverse of diagonal mass matrix with net nodal force. In this way, explicit analysis is faster in solving problems with contact and material non-linearities. Like force applied on a rubber band. There are two types of explicit analyses available in Inventor Nastran; Explicit Dynamics and Explicit Quasi-Static. Explicit dynamics analysis is performed when severe load is applied on the model for very short time (in milli- or micro-seconds) causing large deformation. The Explicit quasi-static analysis is used to analyze linear or nonlinear problems with time-dependent material changes like swelling in material, creep, viscoelasticity, and so on.

Till this point, we have learned the basic types of analyses that can be performed in Inventor Nastran. Now, we will discuss the procedure of activating Inventor Nastran and starting a basic analysis.

INSTALLING AND ACTIVATING INVENTOR NASTRAN

The procedure to install and activate Inventor Nastran tool in Autodesk Inventor is given next.

- Open the link **https://www.autodesk.com/education/edu-software/overview** in your default web browser. The web page will be displayed as shown in Figure-4.

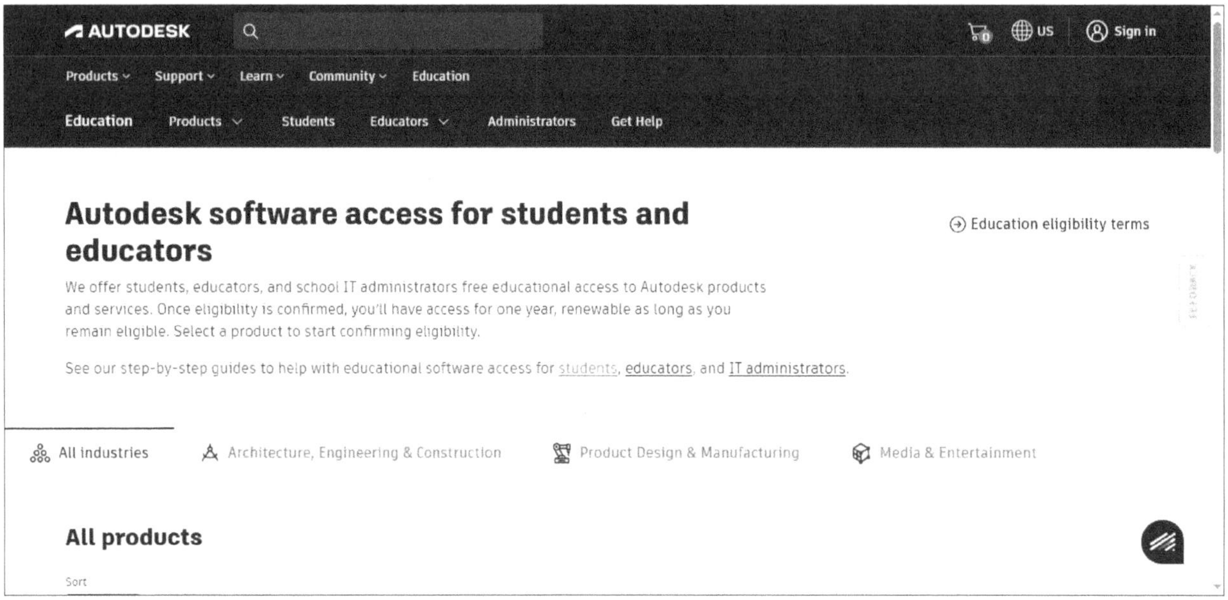

Figure-4. Inventor Nastran web page

- Click on the **Sign in** button. A webpage to enter your autodesk account credentials will be displayed; refer to Figure-5.

Figure-5. Sign in page

- Enter your credentials if you have an autodesk student/educator account already created otherwise click on the **Create account** button, create an educator/student account and then sign in. A web page to access software with educational license will be displayed. Scroll down on the displayed page and click on the **Select** link button for **Inventor Nastran**; refer to Figure-6. The web page to get access to the software will be displayed; refer to Figure-7.

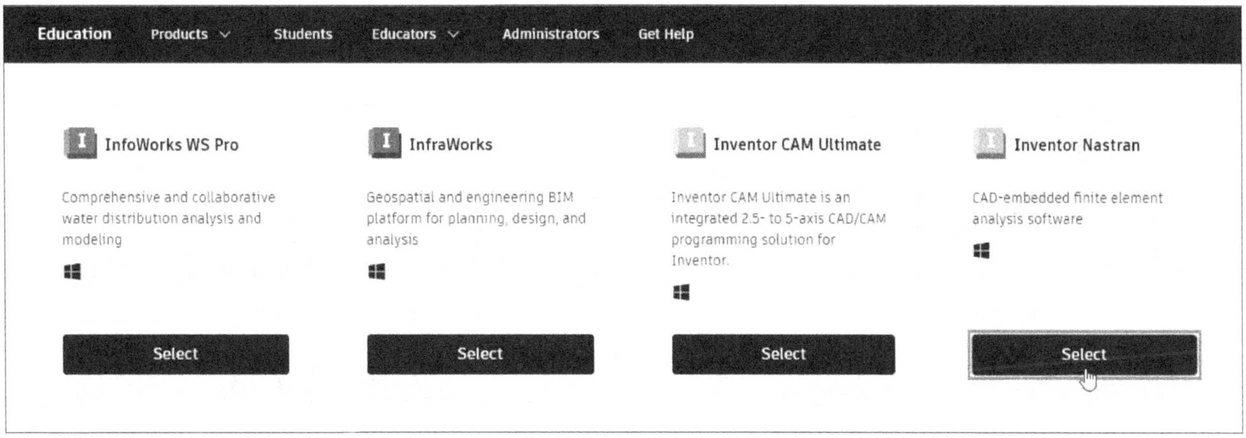

Figure-6. Select button for Inventor Nastran

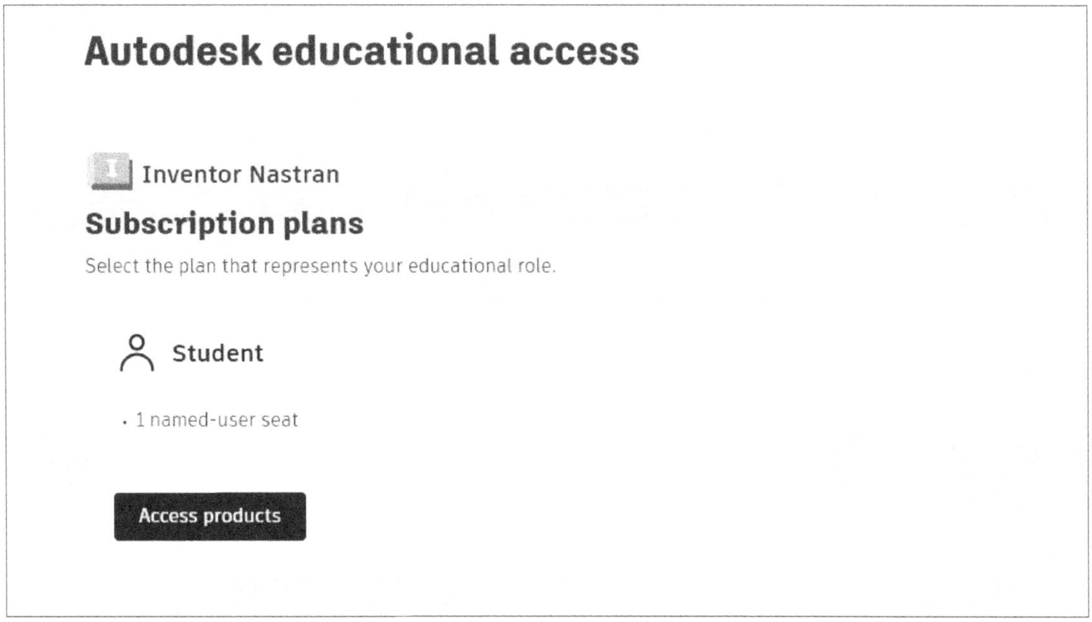

Figure-7. Webpage for accessing subscription

- Click on the **Access products** link button from the web page. The web page will be displayed as shown in Figure-8.

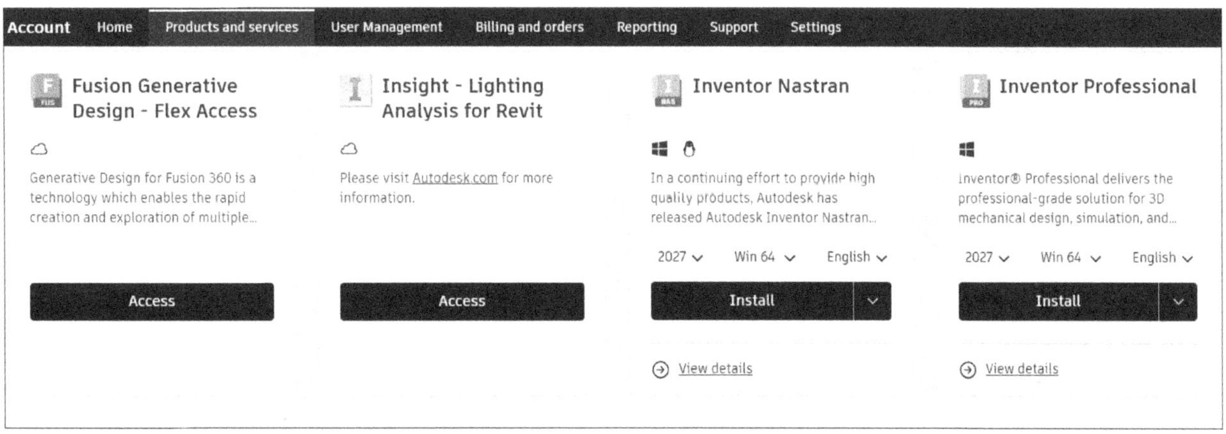

Figure-8. Webpage for downloading Inventor Nastran

- Click on the **INSTALL** button for Inventor Nastran software and then select the **Accept** button from pop-up displayed. After downloading, installation of software will start.

- Accept the license terms of software and install software at desired location.

You can also use custom installation option to create installation package with desired features as discussed next.

- Select the **Custom Install** option from the drop-down next to **Install** button at the web page for downloading the software; refer to Figure-9. The **New package** web page will be displayed; refer to Figure-10. Select check box for **Inventor Nastran** to customize the software.

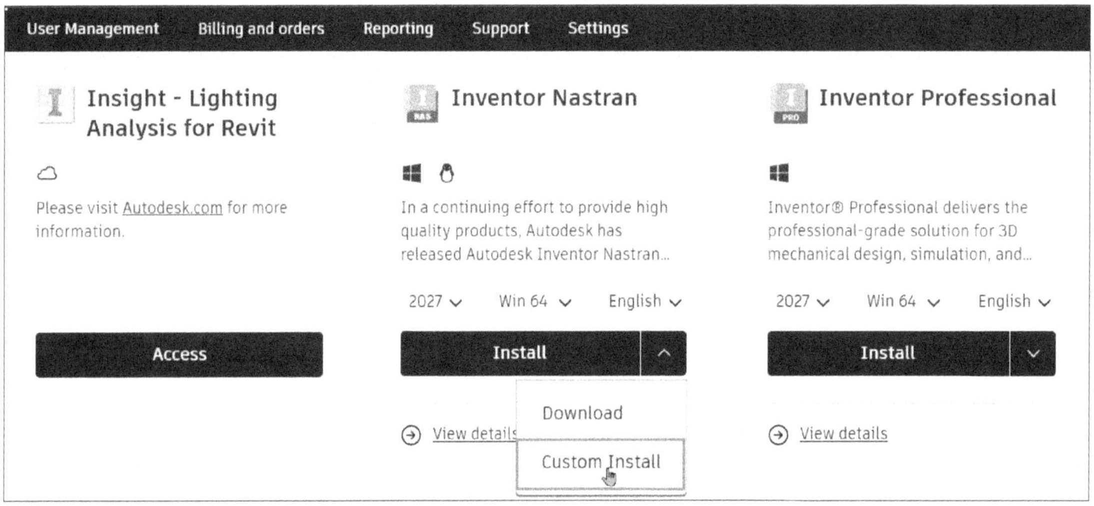

Figure-9. Custom Install option

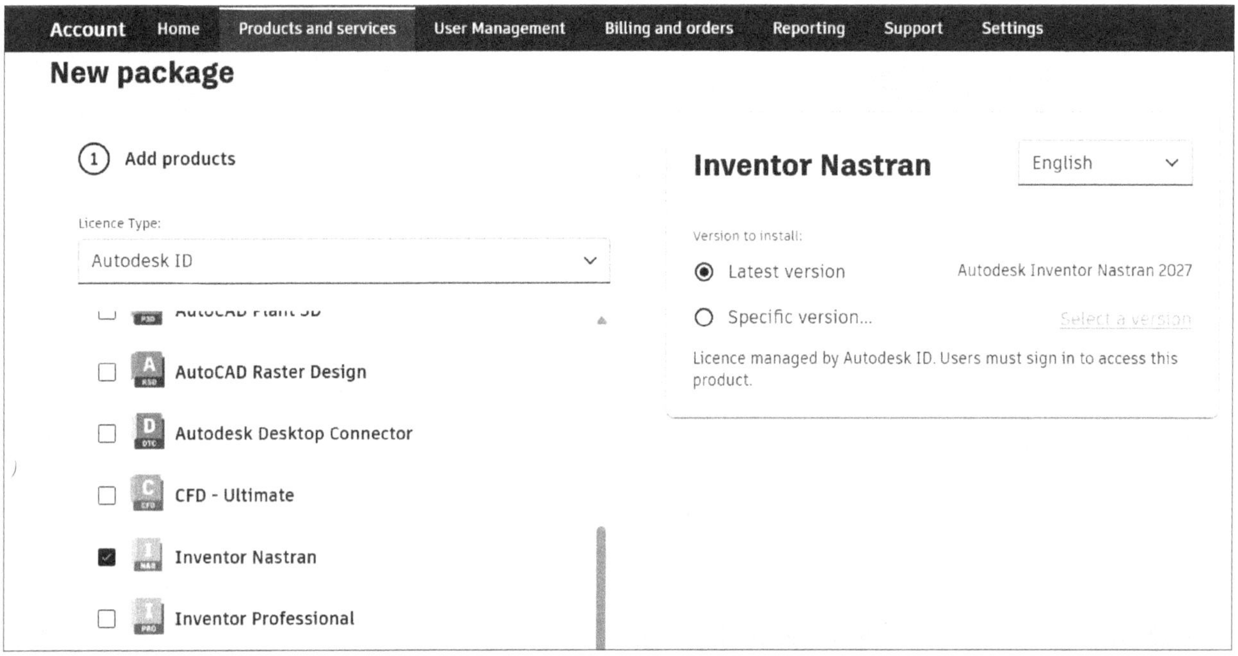

Figure-10. Custom Install page

- After setting desired parameters, click on the **Next** button from the web page. You will be asked to specify installation location for the software. Set desired path location in **Installation Path** field and select the **I agree to the Terms of Use** check box. The **Download** button will become active on page.
- Save the file at desired location and run it. Once the files have been downloaded, install the software.

- Once installation is complete, start **Autodesk Inventor** and open the model on which you want to perform analysis. Click on the **Autodesk Inventor Nastran** tool from the **Begin** panel in the **Environments** tab of **Ribbon**. The **Autodesk Inventor Nastran** tab will be added in the **Ribbon**; refer to Figure-11 and you will be asked specify license detail. Specify the license detail for the software.

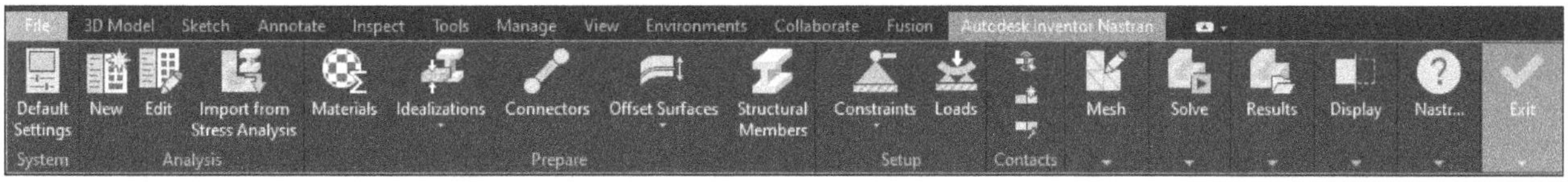

Figure-11. Autodesk Inventor Nastran tab

PERFORMING ANALYSIS (OVERVIEW)

There are various steps involved in performing analysis like applying material, assigning constraints, applying loads, applying mesh settings, and performing analysis. These steps are given next.

Applying Material

Applying material is an important step in analysis. Material properties can affect the result of analysis to a great extent. The procedure to apply material is given next.

- Click on the **Materials** tool from the **Prepare** panel in the **Autodesk Inventor Nastran** tab of **Ribbon**. The **Material** dialog box will be displayed; refer to Figure-12.

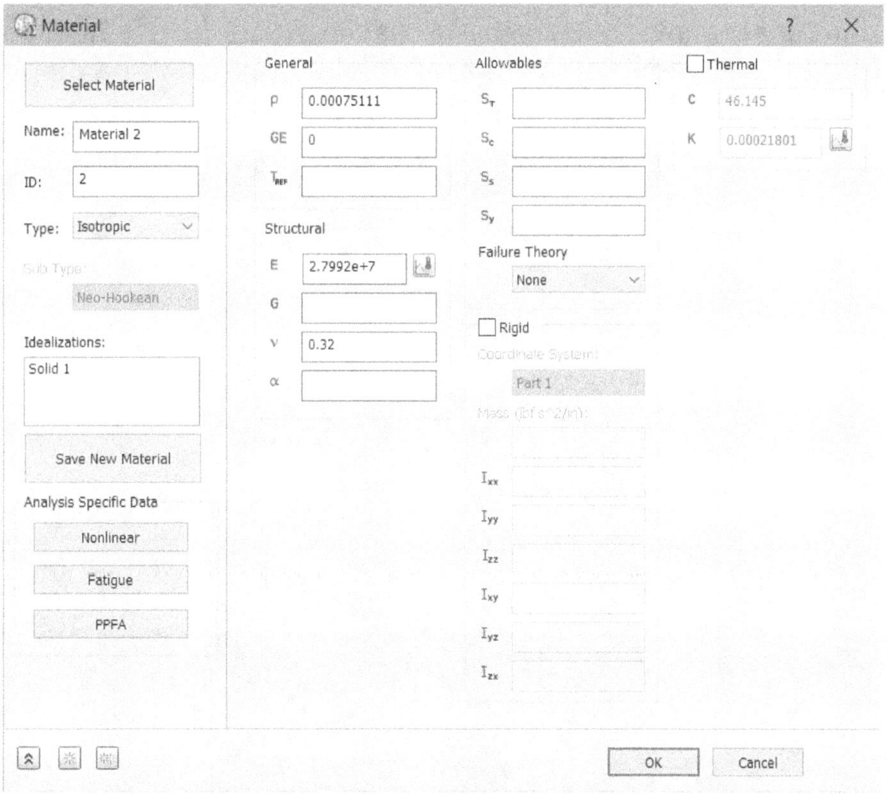

Figure-12. Material dialog box

- Set desired parameters in the dialog box for material properties. You will learn about material properties later in this book.
- If you want to select the material from library then click on the **Select Material** button. The **Material DB** dialog box will be displayed; refer to Figure-13.

Figure-13. Material DB dialog box

- Expand the node and select desired material. After selecting material, click on the **OK** button. The **Material** dialog box will be displayed again.
- Click on the **OK** button to apply material.

Applying Constraint

The constraints are used to restrict the motion of part during an analysis. The procedure to apply constraint is given next.

- Click on the **Constraints** tool from the **Setup** panel in the **Autodesk Inventor Nastran** tab of the **Ribbon**. The **Constraint** dialog box will be displayed; refer to Figure-14.

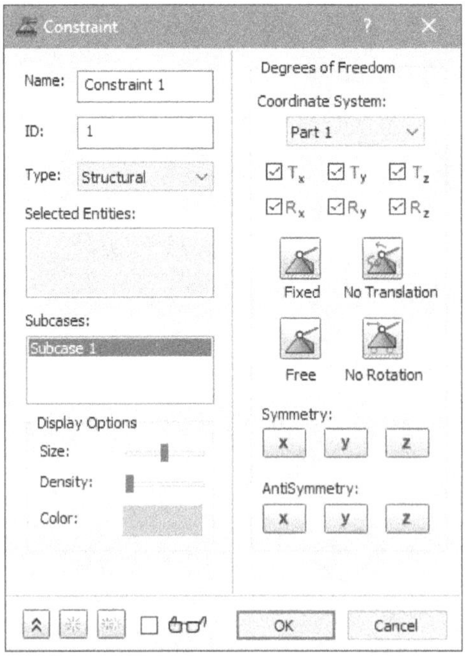

Figure-14. Constraint dialog box

- Select desired option from the **Type** drop-down. The options in this drop-down are **Structural**, **Pin, Frictionless, Response Spectrum, Thermal, Rigid(Explicit)**. Select the **Structural** option if you want to apply structural constraints like restricting translation and rotation of selected object. Select the **Pin** option if you want to apply the constraint only to cylindrical faces. Select the **Frictionless** option if you want to apply the constraint to the parallel flat faces or concentric cylindrical faces whose surfaces are in contact to each other. Select the **Response Spectrum** option if you want to restrict moment or reaction force for selected objects. Select the **Thermal** option if you want to apply temperature to selected face. Select the **Rigid(Explicit)** option if you want to apply the constraint only to a body that has a rigid material idealization. This constraint requires zero displacements or zero rotations.
- Click in the **Selected Entities** selection box and select the faces/edges/vertices that you want to be constrained.
- Select desired option from the **Degrees of Freedom** area.
- Set desired display options from the **Display Options** area of the dialog box.
- After setting desired parameters, click on the **OK** button.

Applying Loads

Loads are applied on the model to represent real load conditions for analysis. The procedure to apply loads is given next.

- Click on the **Loads** tool from the **Setup** panel in the **Autodesk Inventor Nastran** tab of **Ribbon**. The **Load** dialog box will be displayed; refer to Figure-15.

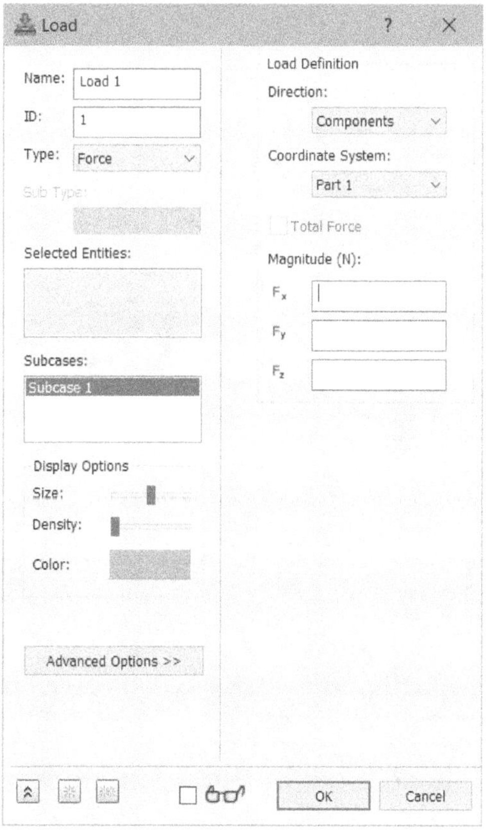

Figure-15. Load dialog box

- Select desired option from the **Type** drop-down. There are various options like force, moment, pressure, distributed load, and so on to define different types of loads.

- Select the **Force** option from the drop-down and set desired value of force in the **Magnitude (N)** edit box(es).
- Click in the **Selected Entities** selection box and select the faces/edges/vertices to apply load.
- Select the **Preview** check box to display direction of the load on model.
- Click on the **OK** button to apply load.

Running Analysis

- Click on the **Generate Mesh** tool from the **Mesh** panel in the **Autodesk Inventor Nastran** tab of **Ribbon**. The preview of mesh will be displayed; refer to Figure-16.

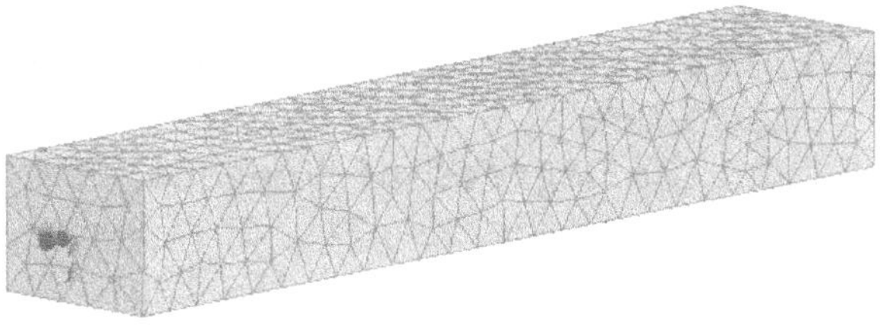

Figure-16. Meshing created

Click on the **Run** tool from the **Solve** panel in **Autodesk Inventor Nastran** tab of the **Ribbon**. A message box will be displayed telling you that analysis solution has been generated. If you have not saved the file then **Save As** dialog box will be displayed. Save the file at desired location. Once the analysis is complete, the results of analysis will be displayed. Click on the **OK** button from the dialog box; refer to Figure-17.

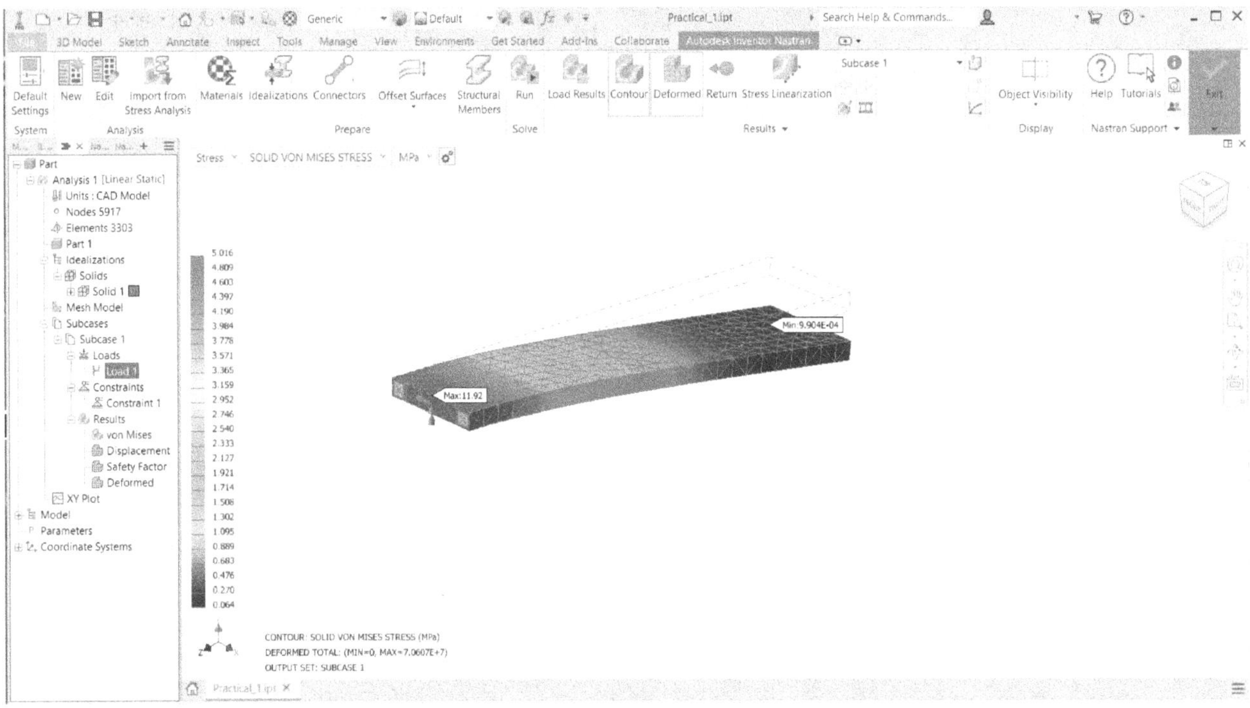

Figure-17. Result of analysis

You will learn more about these tools in the next chapter.

SELF ASSESSMENT

Q1. What do you mean by Simulation? Describe briefly.

Q2. Discuss the types of analyses performed in Autodesk Inventor Nastran.

Q3. Which of the following analyses is also called Harmonic Analysis?

a) Static Analysis
b) Buckling Analysis
c) Normal Modes Analysis
d) Impact Analysis

Q4. In which of the following mechanism, the heat transfer requires the presence of an intervening medium?

a) Conduction
b) Convection
c) Radiation
d) Both a and b

Q5. When a power driven device such as a motor produces a frequency at which an attached structure naturally vibrates. This phenomena is called ....

Q6. .... is also called eigenvalue-based buckling analysis.

Q7. An important element for having a stable nonlinear transient (NLT) solution is to provide .... in the model.

Q8. **Random Vibration Analysis** is used by Civil engineers who design various kinds of transportation equipment. (True/False)

Q9. **Pin** option should be selected to apply the constraint only to cylindrical faces of the material. (True/False)

Q10. Loads are applied on the model to represent real load conditions for analysis. (True/False)

Q11. What does simulation study in mechanical engineering primarily focus on?

A. Designing CAD models
B. Visualizing internal features of materials
C. Effects on an object due to real-world loading conditions
D. Manufacturing processes of materials

Q12. What is the main assumption in a Linear Static Analysis regarding loads?

A. Loads increase exponentially over time
B. Loads are applied randomly
C. Loads are constant in magnitude, direction, and distribution
D. Loads change with temperature

Q13. When is Nonlinear Static Analysis required?

A. When all materials comply with Hooke's law
B. When displacements are negligible
C. When assumptions of linearity are not valid
D. When loads are constant

Q14. What kind of analysis should be performed if a model is already prestressed and additional loads are to be applied?

A. Static Analysis
B. Prestress Static Analysis
C. Nonlinear Static Analysis
D. Modal Analysis

Q15. What does Normal Modes Analysis determine?

A. Buckling loads
B. Static displacements
C. Natural frequencies
D. Material strength

Q16. What is the phenomenon called when a structure vibrates at its natural frequency due to an external force?

A. Buckling
B. Resonance
C. Compression
D. Oscillation

Q17. In which situation is buckling most likely to occur?

A. Tensile loading on thick structures
B. Axial loading on slender structures
C. Torsional loading on short beams
D. Lateral loading on wide plates

Q18. Which of the following statements about linear buckling analysis is true?

A. It gives actual displacement values during buckling
B. It does not provide buckling modes
C. It gives a qualitative prediction of buckling modes
D. It is used only for nonlinear structures

Q19. What is the purpose of the Arc Length Control Method in nonlinear buckling analysis?

A. To stabilize temperature variation
B. To apply loads in one step
C. To manage loss of stiffness during buckling
D. To simplify the stiffness matrix

Q20. What is the primary purpose of a transient response analysis?

A. To calculate fatigue due to cyclic loads
B. To determine behavior under steady-state excitation
C. To find the maximum stress in an earthquake simulation
D. To determine the behavior of a structure under time-varying excitation

Q21. Which of the following methods is more efficient for high-frequency excitation and structural damping in transient analysis?

A. Modal Transient Response Analysis
B. Frequency Response Analysis
C. Direct Transient Response Analysis
D. Random Response Analysis

Q22. What does Modal Transient Response Analysis primarily utilize?

A. Applied forces in physical space
B. Direct degrees of freedom
C. Mode shapes of the structure
D. Explicit analysis of contact

Q23. In a nonlinear transient analysis, which element is important to ensure a stable solution?

A. Reduced degrees of freedom
B. Modal uncoupling
C. Damping
D. Frequency domain excitation

Q24. What is the unit of W3 and W4 damping parameters in nonlinear transient analysis?

A. Degrees per second
B. Hertz
C. Radians per unit time
D. Newtons per meter

Q25. What type of excitation is used in Frequency Response Analysis?

A. Time-varying excitation
B. Step input excitation
C. Random domain excitation
D. Steady-state oscillatory excitation

Q26. Which method is more efficient in computing structural response when a large number of solution frequencies are specified?

A. Direct Frequency Response Analysis
B. Modal Frequency Response Analysis
C. Nonlinear Transient Analysis
D. Explicit Quasi-Static Analysis

Q27. Which analysis simulates the dropping of a part or assembly on a surface?

A. Shock Spectrum Analysis
B. Impact Analysis
C. Explicit Analysis
D. Fatigue Analysis

Q28. What kind of excitation does Random Response Analysis consider?

A. High-frequency oscillations only
B. Single frequency oscillation
C. Combination of many frequencies from multiple sources
D. Direct step force application

Q29. What is the primary goal of Multi-Axial Fatigue Analysis?

A. Check vibrational displacements
B. Evaluate thermal equilibrium
C. Assess effect of repeated loading/unloading
D. Measure conduction heat transfer

Q30. Which analysis is used to evaluate the effect of vibrational loading on a structure?

A. Transient Response Analysis
B. Vibrational Fatigue Analysis
C. Random Vibration Analysis
D. Modal Frequency Response Analysis

Q31. What type of heat transfer does not require a medium?

A. Conduction
B. Convection
C. Radiation
D. Thermal conduction

Q32. What is true about Explicit Dynamics Analysis?

A. Solves problems over long durations
B. Uses modal degrees of freedom
C. Solves severe loads applied for very short times
D. Assumes linear elasticity

Q33. Which analysis is ideal for time-dependent material behavior like swelling or creep?

A. Explicit Dynamics
B. Modal Frequency Response
C. Explicit Quasi-Static
D. Impact Analysis

Q34. What is the first step in performing an analysis in Autodesk Inventor Nastran?

A. Applying mesh settings
B. Assigning constraints
C. Applying material
D. Performing analysis

Q35. When should you use the 'Pin' constraint type?

A. To apply thermal constraints
B. To apply constraints to flat faces
C. To apply constraints to cylindrical faces
D. To restrict temperature

Q36. What is required for the Rigid(Explicit) constraint to work correctly?

A. Only curved faces selected
B. Zero loads applied
C. Rigid material idealization
D. Frictionless surfaces

Q37. What is the purpose of applying loads during analysis?

A. To reduce the model size
B. To restrict motion
C. To define material properties
D. To simulate real load conditions

FOR STUDENT NOTES

Chapter 2

Basics of Analysis

Topics Covered

The major topics covered in this chapter are:

- ***Introduction***
- ***Starting Analysis***
- ***Default Settings***
- ***Starting New Study***
- ***Editing Analysis Parameters***
- ***Importing Data from Stress Analysis***
- ***Applying and Editing Material***
- ***Idealization***
- ***Applying Connections to Components in Assemblies***
- ***Generating Surfaces for Shell Components***
- ***Managing Structural Members***
- ***Applying Loads and Constraints***
- ***Defining Contacts***
- ***Generating Meshes***
- ***Running Analyses and Generating Plots***

INTRODUCTION

In previous chapter, you learned the basic process of performing analysis in Autodesk Inventor Nastran. Now, you will learn about basic operation of each of the tool in **Autodesk Inventor Nastran** tab.

DEFAULT SETTINGS

The **Default Settings** tool is used to set display options and other basic settings of the dialog box. The procedure to use this tool is given next.

- Click on the **Default Settings** tool from the **System** panel in **Autodesk Inventor Nastran** tab of the **Ribbon**. The **Default Settings** dialog box will be displayed; refer to Figure-1.

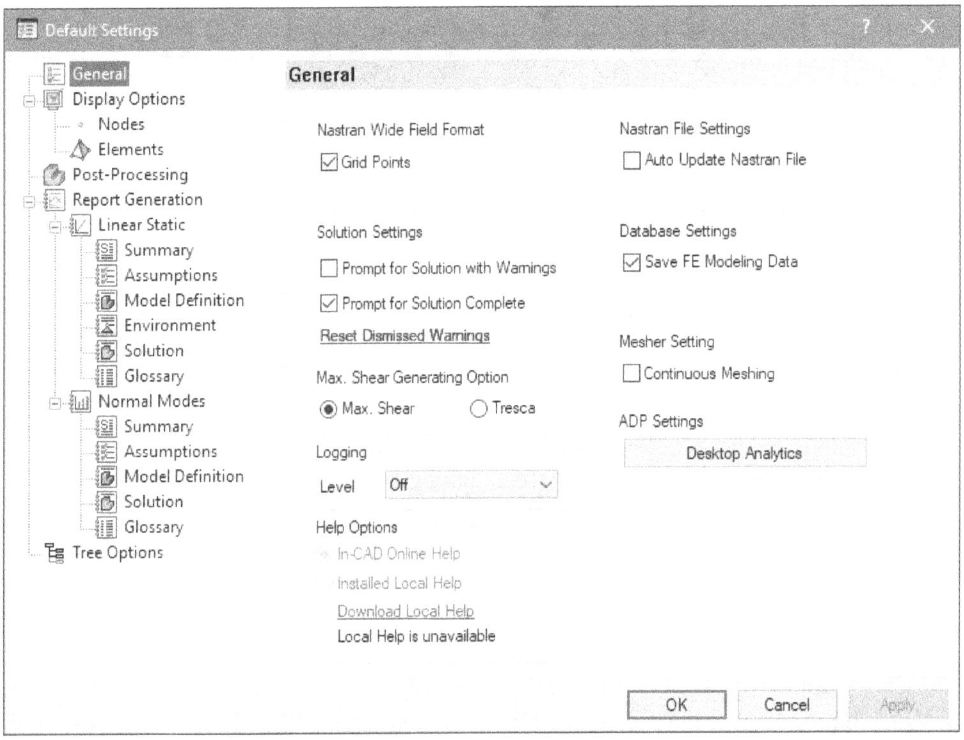

Figure-1. Default Settings dialog box

General Options

- Click on the **General** option from the left area to set default display options. The options will be displayed as shown in above figure.
- Select the **Grid Points** check box to display grid points of the model.
- Select the **Prompt for Solution with Warnings** check box to let system prompt for solutions if there are any warnings.
- Select the **Prompt for Solution Complete** check box to let system prompt you with solution when analysis is complete. Select the **Reset Dismissed Warnings** link button to set all the warning messages to default.
- Select the **Max. Shear** radio button if you want to find maximum shear stress of the model in result. Select the **Tresca** radio button if you want to find out shell/ solid tresca results.
- Select the **Auto Update Nastran File** check box to automatically update the nastran files based on specified parameters.

- Select the **Save FE Modeling Data** check box to save finite element data separately in organized structure.
- Select the **Continuous Meshing** check box to mesh shell objects automatically during editing. This will increase processing load during editing.
- Select desired option from the **Level** drop-down in the **Logging** area. Select **Crash** option if you want the system to generate log of software events when the software crashes. Select the **Verbose** option if you want the system to generate log of all events of the software.
- Select the **Installed Local Help** radio button from **Help Options** area of dialog box if you have installed local copy of help and want to use it for reference. If you have not downloaded location copy of help documentation then select the **Download Local Help** link button from the **Help Options** area.
- Click on the **Desktop Analytics** button from the dialog box if you want to enable or disable data collection by Autodesk. On clicking this button, the **Data collection and use** dialog box will be displayed. Select the check box in the dialog box if you want to enable data collection and click on the **OK** button.

Setting Display Options

- Click on the **Display Options** node from the left area of the dialog box. The options in the dialog box will be displayed as shown in Figure-2.

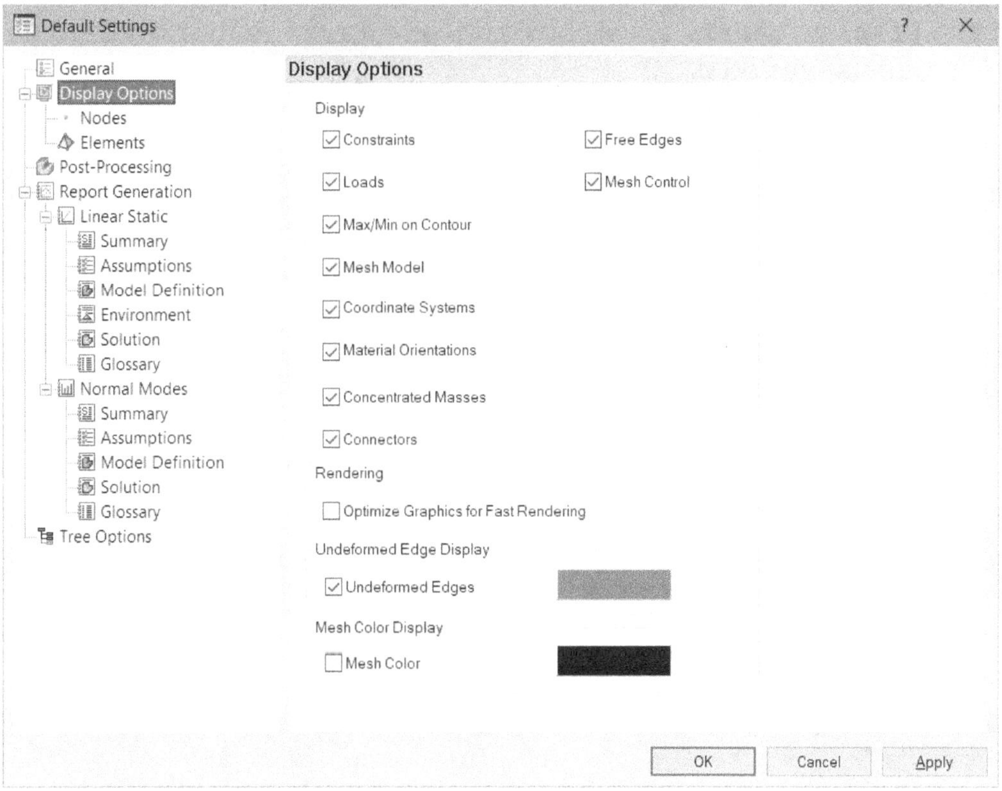

Figure-2. Display Options page

- Select desired check boxes from the **Display Options** area of the dialog box to set which entities of model to be displayed in the graphics area.
- Select the **Optimize Graphics for Fast Rendering** check box to generate faster rendering of results by optimizing graphics.
- Set desired colors for mesh and undeformed edges using respective color buttons.

Nodes

- Select the **Nodes** option from the left area of the dialog box. The dialog box will be displayed as shown in Figure-3.

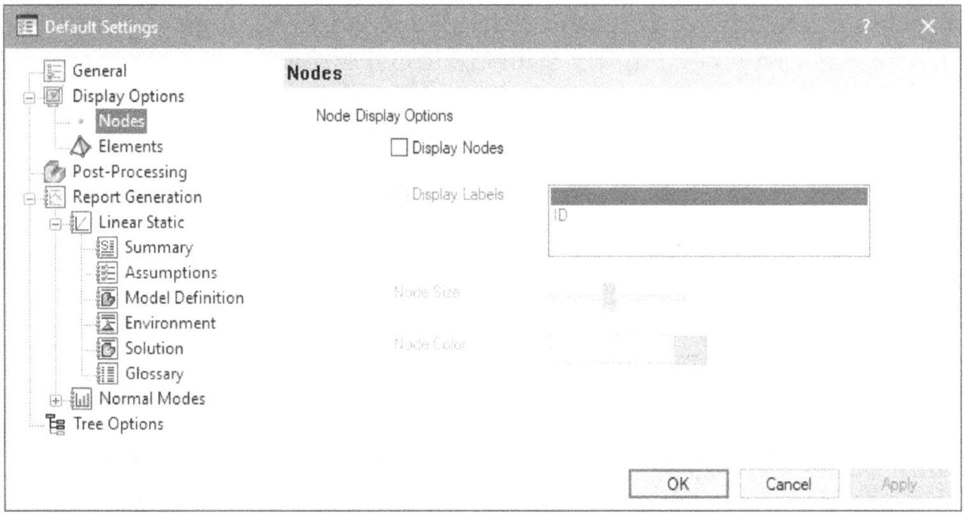

Figure-3. Nodes display options

- Select the **Display Nodes** check box to display nodes in the model when mesh or results are displayed.
- Select the **Display Labels** check box and select desired option from the list box to display labels on nodes.
- Set desired parameters for node size and color from this page.

Elements

- Select the **Elements** option from the **Default Settings** dialog box to set options for display of element labels. The dialog box will be displayed as shown in Figure-4.

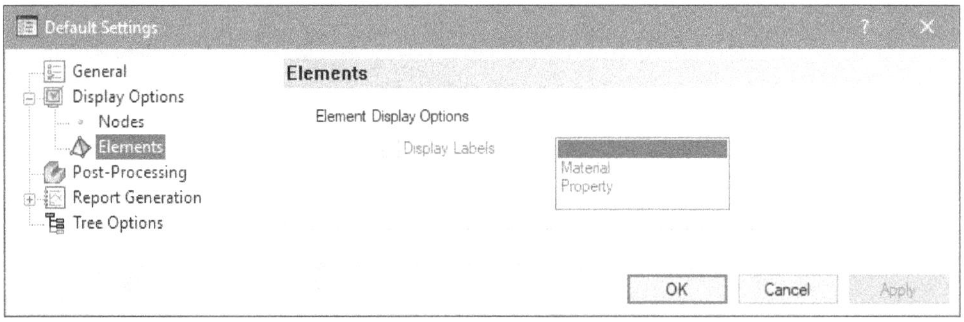

Figure-4. Elements display options

- Select the **Display Labels** check box and select the label types to be displayed.

Note that if **Display Labels** check boxes of **Nodes** and **Elements** page in the dialog box are not active in your case then do not worry, we are in the same boat!! Autodesk has disabled these check boxes although they are still shown in the dialog box. They say it causes longer time to display results.

Post-Processing

- Select the **Post-Processing** option from the left area of the dialog box. The options in the dialog box will be displayed as shown in Figure-5.

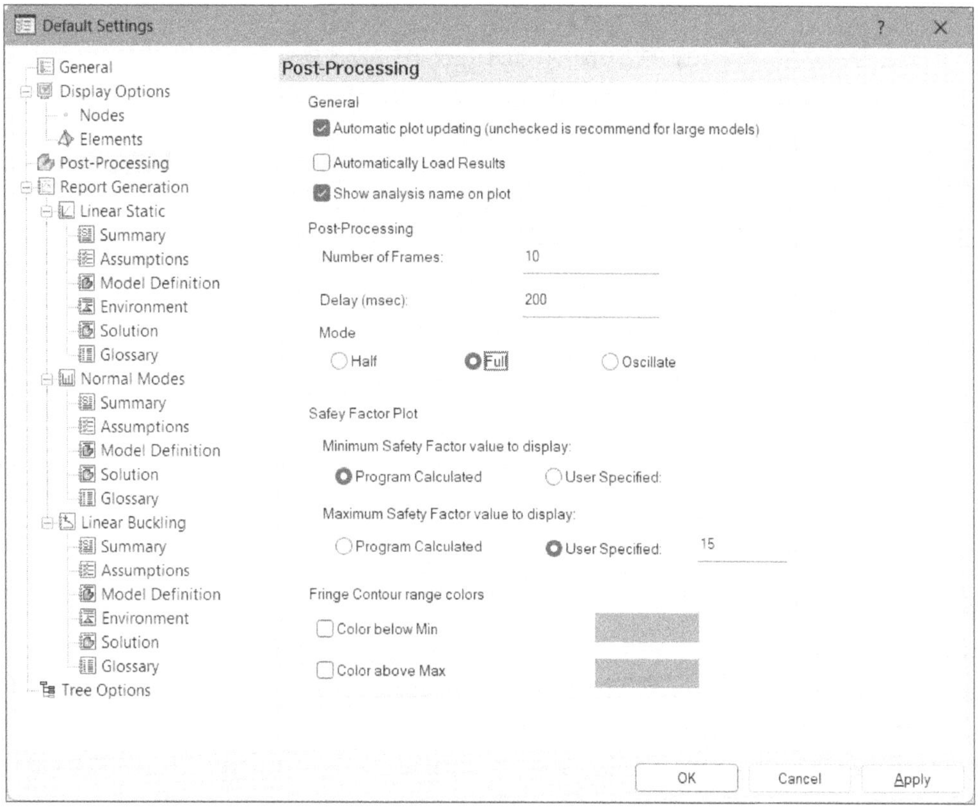

Figure-5. Post Processing display options

- Select the **Automatic plot updating** check box to automatically update all plots after performing analysis if you have modified the study parameters.
- Select the **Automatically Load Results** check box to automatically load the results after solving analysis.
- Select the **Show analysis name on plot** check box to display name of analysis on plot generated after running analysis.
- Specify the number of frames to be created per second for animation in the **Number of Frames** edit box.
- Specify desired value of microseconds delay between frames of animation in the **Delay (msec)** edit box.
- Select desired option from the **Mode** area. If you select the **Half** option then the animation will start at unloaded/undeformed state, gradually advance to the fully loaded/deformed results, and then stop. If you select the **Full** option then animation will start at the unloaded/undeformed state, gradually advancing to the fully loaded/deformed results, and then reversing (gradually returning to the unloaded/undeformed state). If you select the **Oscillate** option then first half of the animation is identical to the **Full** option. After that, a second full-cycle is added using a mirror image of the calculated deformed shape. This option is useful for visualizing vibration modes. For example, if the top of a tower bends to the right when determining the mode shape, it will also bend to the left for the second half of a full oscillation cycle.
- Set desired option for minimum and maximum safety factor value in the **Safety Factor Plot** area of the dialog box.
- Select the **Color below Min** and **Color above Max** check boxes from the **Fringe Contour range colors** section of the dialog box to define color for sections of result which are below minimum value and above maximum value of the result parameter.

Report Generation

- Click on the **Report Generation** option from the left area of the dialog box. The options in the dialog box will be displayed as shown in Figure-6.

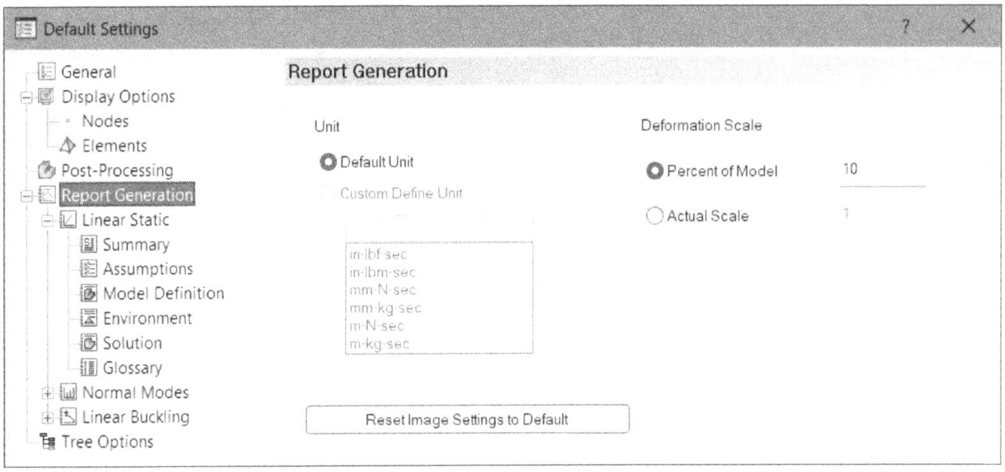

Figure-6. Report Generation options

- Select desired unit system from the dialog box.
- Set desired scale of deformation to be applied to the result plot using radio buttons in the **Deformation Scale** area.
- Set the options for current analysis as required by using the nodes from the left box.
- After setting desired parameters, click on the **OK** button.

STARTING A NEW STUDY

The **New** tool in the **Analysis** panel of **Autodesk Inventor Nastran** tab is used to create new simulation study. The procedure to use this tool is given next.

- Click on the **New** tool from the **Analysis** panel in the **Autodesk Inventor Nastran** tab of the **Ribbon**. The **Analysis** dialog box will be displayed; refer to Figure-7.

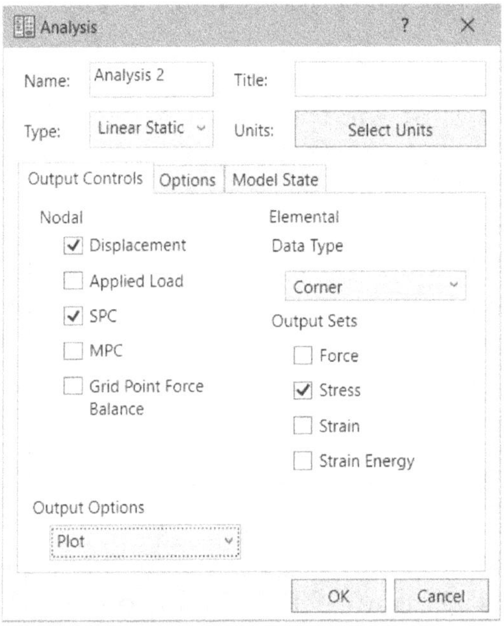

Figure-7. Analysis dialog box

- Specify desired name of analysis in **Name** edit box and specify desired title for documentation of current analysis in the **Title** edit box.
- Select desired type of analysis from the **Type** drop-down like Linear Static, Normal Modes, and so on.
- Click on the **Select Units** button to set units for the analysis. The **Units** dialog box will be displayed; refer to Figure-8. Select desired option from the **Unit System** drop-down and click on the **OK** button. The selected unit will be set and the **Analysis** dialog box will be displayed again.

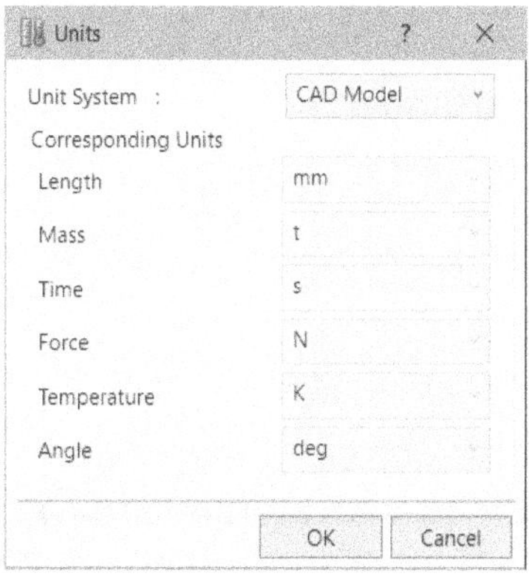

Figure-8. Units dialog box

- Select desired check box(es) from the **Nodal** area of the dialog box to set as output control parameter. The selected parameter will be plotted in output files. For example, select the **Displacement** check box to use displacement as controlling parameter for analysis. So, apart from general data model with grid points and elements for analysis, there will also be a matrix of displacement for solving the equations. You can find the equations in .nas file generated after solving analysis in the same folder where your model file is stored.
- Select desired option from the **Output Options** drop-down to define how output of analysis will be generated. Select the **Plot** option to generate nastran plot file (.NAS file) for result. Select the **Print** option if you want to generate additional result output file(.OUT file). Select the **Punch** option if you want to generate a punch file (.PCH) for results. Select the **Punch and Plot** option if you want to generate both punch(.PCH) and nastran output (.NAS) files for results.
- Select desired option from the **Data Type** drop-down to define what elemental data will be generated. Select the **Corner** option to use results at the nodes of elements for calculating final result. Select the **Centroidal** option from the drop-down to use results calculated at centroids of elements for calculating final result.
- From the **Output Sets** area, select desired check boxes for parameters you want to be generated in result files. Select the **Force** check box to control elemental force output. Select the **Stress** check box to control elemental stress output. Select the **Strain** check box to control elemental strain output. Select the **Strain Energy** check box to control elemental strain energy output. Select the **Heat Flux** check box to control elemental heat flux output.

Options tab

- Click on the **Options** tab in the dialog box. The options will be displayed as shown in Figure-9.

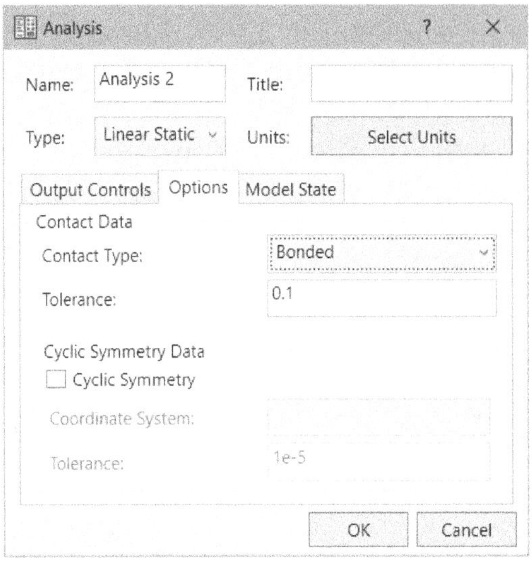

Figure-9. Options tab

- Select desired option from the **Contact Type** drop-down to define the way two or more bodies will be joined for the analysis. The option set here will be default for the analysis. Note that you can later modify contacts between various components. You will learn more about these options later in this book.
- Set desired tolerance value in the **Tolerance** edit box. If two components have separation distance within specified tolerance range then the selected contact type will be applied automatically.
- Select the **Cyclic Symmetry** check box if you want to system to search for cyclic symmetry in analysis when solving the problem. Note that system will search for cyclic constraints and cylindrical coordinate system to confirm cyclic symmetry so after creating cylindrical coordinate system and cyclic constraints, you need to edit properties of analysis for enabling cyclic symmetry; refer to Figure-10.

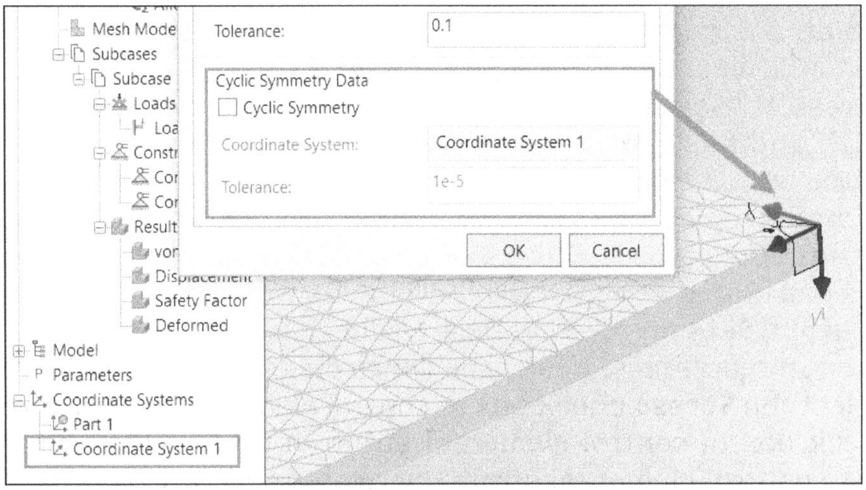

Figure-10. Cyclic symmetry data

- After selecting this check box, select desired coordinate system from the **Coordinate System** drop-down and specify related tolerance of measurement in the **Tolerance** edit box.

Model State

- Click on the **Model State** tab from the dialog box to select the orientation and state of model. The options in the dialog box will be displayed as shown in Figure-11.

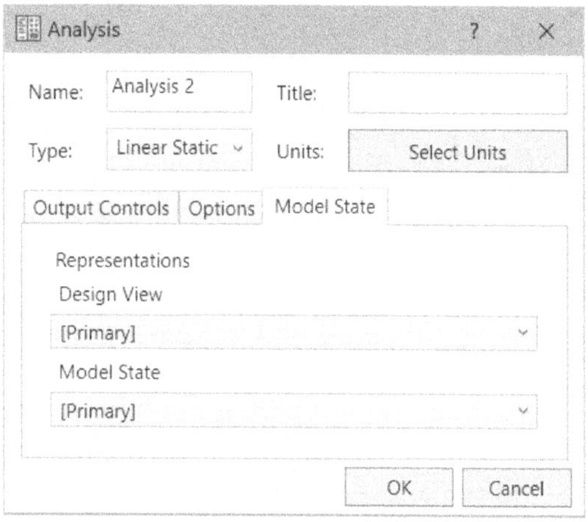

Figure-11. Model State tab

- Select desired option from the **Design View** drop-down to define which view of model will be used by default.
- Select desired option from the **Model State** drop-down to define which state (configuration) of model is used for analysis.
- Click on the **OK** button from the dialog box to apply parameters.

EDITING ANALYSIS

The **Edit** tool in the **Analysis** panel is used to edit general parameters specified for the analysis. The procedure to use this tool is given next.

- Click on the **Edit** tool from the **Analysis** panel in the **Autodesk Inventor Nastran** tab of **Ribbon**. The **Analysis** dialog box will be displayed. The options of this dialog box have already been discussed.

IMPORTING FROM STRESS ANALYSIS

The **Import from Stress Analysis** tool is used to import the study parameters from Autodesk Inventor Stress Analysis. The procedure to use this tool is given next.

- Open a part in Autodesk Inventor on which you have earlier performed stress analysis.
- Activate the Autodesk Inventor Nastran environment as discussed earlier.
- Click on the **Import from Stress Analysis** tool from the **Analysis** panel in the **Autodesk Inventor Nastran** tab of the **Ribbon**. The analysis will be added as current study; refer to Figure-12.

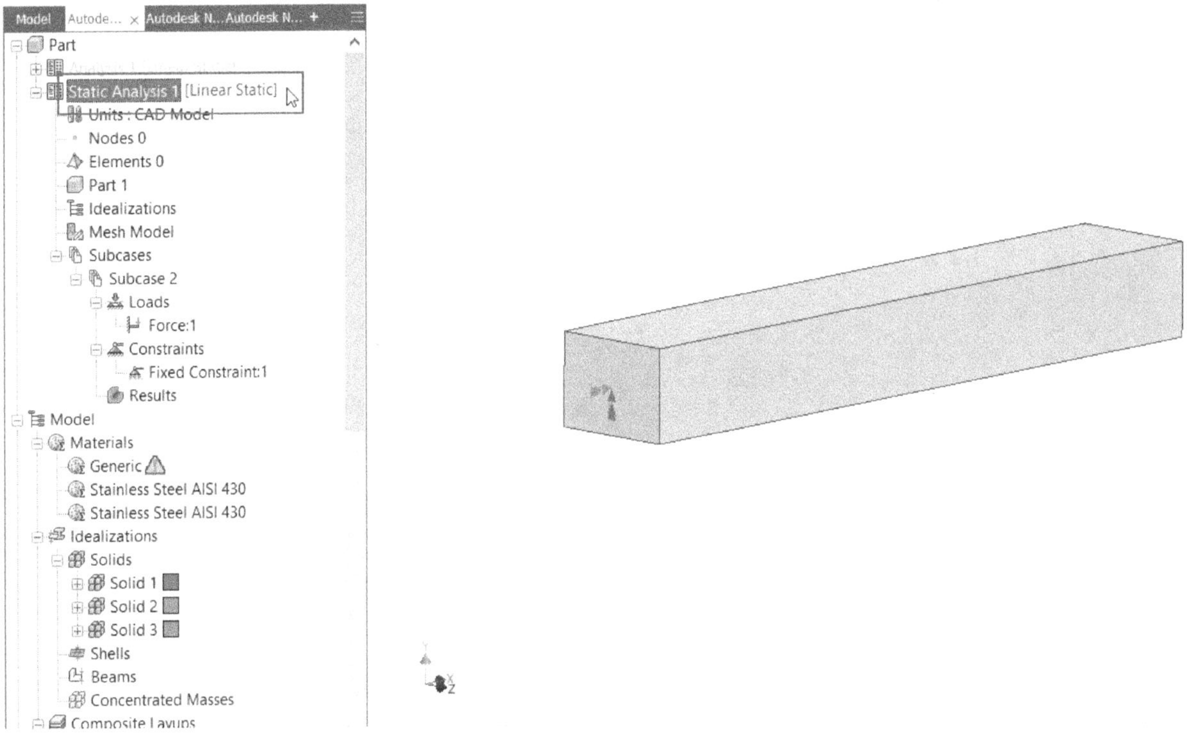

Figure-12. New analysis added by importing

APPLYING MATERIALS

The **Materials** tool is used to create, edit, and assign materials to objects for analysis. The procedure to use this tool is given next.

- Click on the **Materials** tool from the **Prepare** panel in the **Autodesk Inventor Nastran** tab. The **Material** dialog box will be displayed; refer to Figure-13.

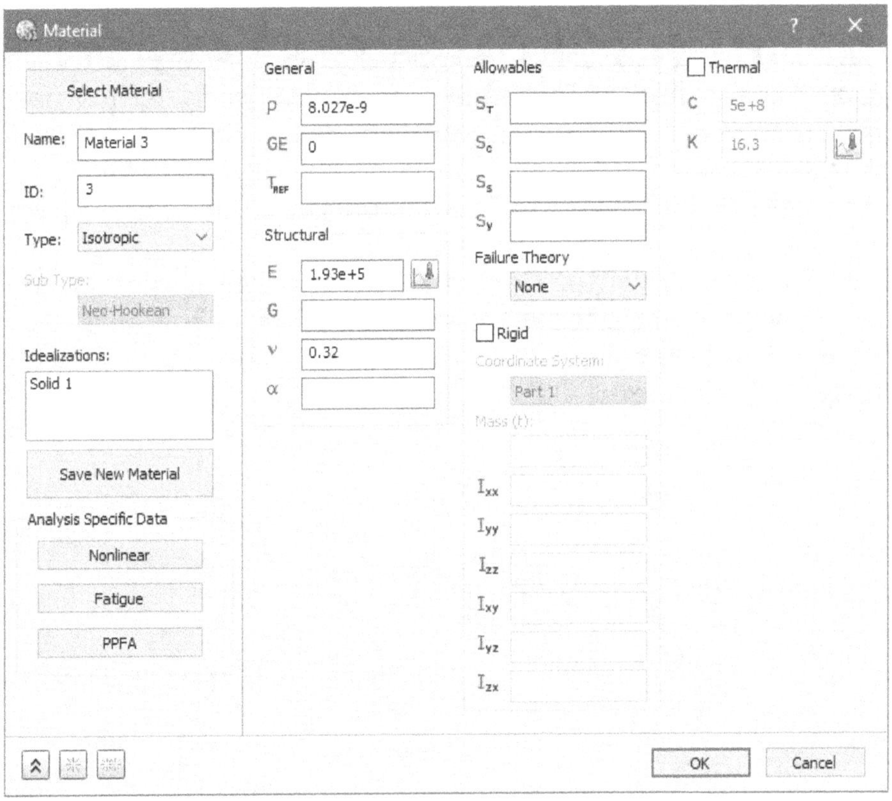

Figure-13. Material dialog box

- To select a material, click on the **Select Material** tool from the **Material** dialog box. The **Material DB** dialog box will be displayed.
- Select desired material from the dialog box and click on the **OK** button from the **Material DB** dialog box.

Creating New Material

Although, you can use the directory of materials provided by Autodesk but there is always a requirement of new materials in engineering. If you want to add a new material which is not available by default then the procedure is given next.

- After activating the **Materials** tool, specify desired parameters in the edit boxes of the dialog box like name of material, general parameters, structural parameters, allowables, and so on.
- Select desired option from the **Type** drop-down; refer to Figure-14. The options of this dialog box are discussed later in this chapter.

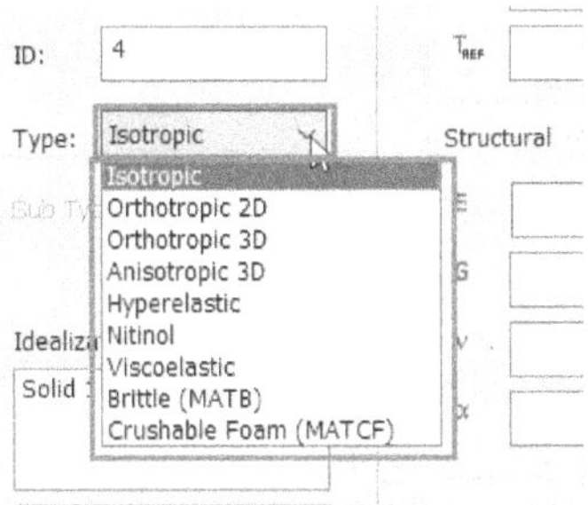

Figure-14. Type drop-down

- The options to specify analysis specific properties are available in the **Analysis Specific Data** area; like Nonlinear, Fatigue, and PPFA.
- Click on the **Nonlinear** button to specify material data for nonlinearity. The **Nonlinear Material Data** dialog box will be displayed; refer to Figure-15.

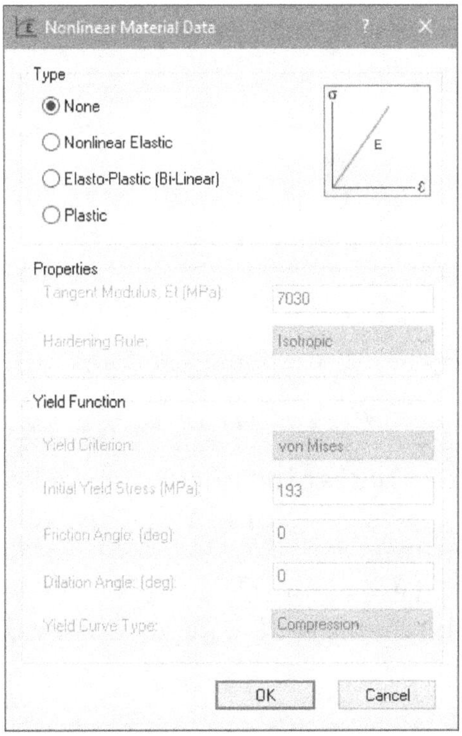

Figure-15. Nonlinear Material Data dialog box

- Select the **Nonlinear Elastic** radio button to apply nonlinear elastic property to material. Select the **Elasto-Plastic (Bi-Linear)** radio button to specify tangent modulus and initial yield stress values. Select the **Plastic** radio button to apply plastic nonlinearity to the material. After setting desired parameters, click on the **OK** button.
- Click on the **Fatigue** button from the **Analysis Specific Data** area. The **Fatigue** dialog box will be displayed; refer to Figure-16.

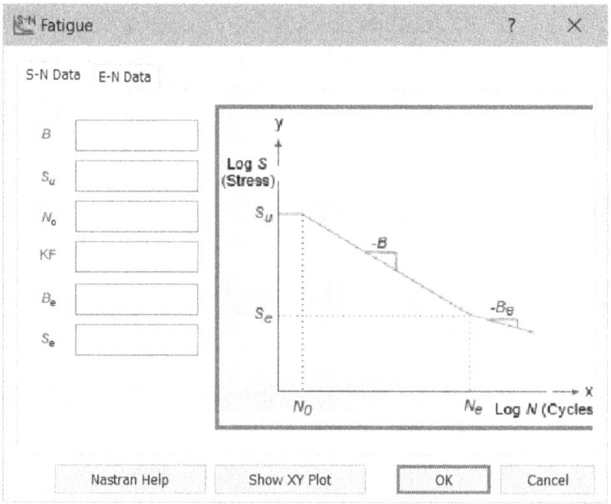

Figure-16. Fatigue dialog box

- Specify desired parameters in the edit boxes of the dialog box and click **OK** button to define S-N Data. Click on the **E-N Data** tab from the dialog box if you want to define E-N data parameters for fatigue.
- Click on the **PPFA** button from the **Analysis Specific Data** area to create progressive ply failure analysis data. The **PPFA** dialog box will be displayed; refer to Figure-17.

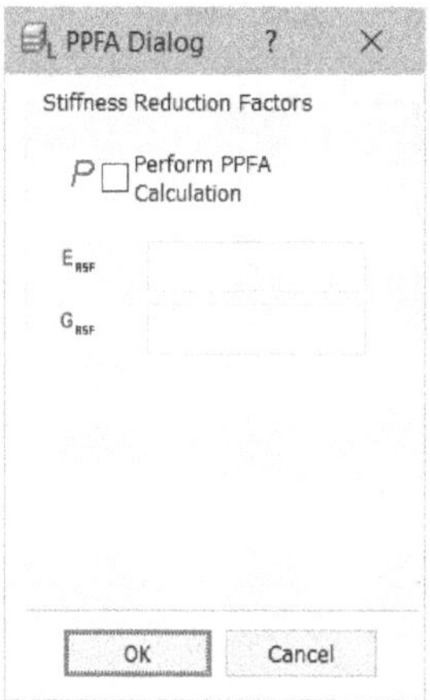

Figure-17. PPFA dialog box

- Select the **Perform PPFA Calculation** check box to specify Young's modulus and Shear modulus reduction scale factors in respective edit boxes. After setting the values, click on the **OK** button.
- Click on the **Save New Material** button to save the newly created material. The **Save As** dialog box will be displayed; refer to Figure-18.

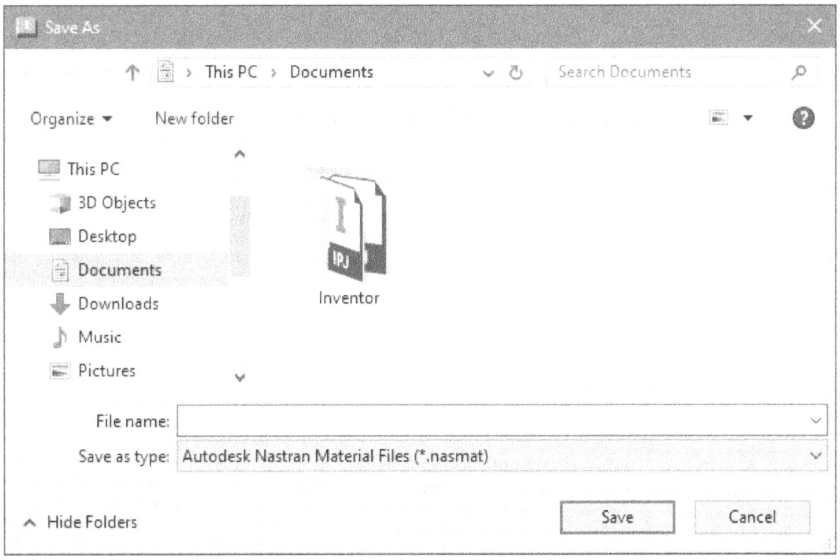

Figure-18. Save As dialog box

- Specify desired name of material property and click on the **Save** button. The material will be created.
- After setting desired parameters, click on the **OK** button from the dialog box to exit.

Material Properties

For different type of materials, there are different property parameters to be defined for the material. The material properties for different type of materials types are discussed next.

Isotropic Material

Select the **Isotropic** option from the **Type** drop-down in **Material** dialog box to create a material which has same properties in all directions. It means you can apply 100 N load in any direction (X, Y, or Z) of material and it will cause same stress in the material in that direction because Young's Modulus is same in all directions. On selecting this option, the parameters in the dialog box will be displayed as shown in Figure-19.

- Specify desired value in the **Mass density** edit box ρ to define mass of per unit volume of the material.
- Specify desired value in the **Damping Coefficient** edit box GE to define dimensionless ratio value by which oscillations decay. Mathematically, damping ratio is the ratio of actual damping to critical damping. You get actual damping by experiments and critical damping is given by formula

$$c_c = 2\sqrt{km} \quad \text{or} \quad c_c = 2m\sqrt{\frac{k}{m}} = 2m\omega_n$$

- Specify desired value in the **Reference Temperature** edit box to define room temperature for the material at which properties of material are measured.
- Specify desired value in the **Elastic Modulus (MPa)** edit box E to define resistance of material against elastic deformation. Young's modulus is also referred to as elastic modulus, tensile modulus, or modulus of elasticity. Mathematically, elastic modulus is given by ratio of stress to strain.

- Specify desired value in the **Shear Modulus (MPa)** edit box G to define resistance of the material against elastic deformation when load applied is parallel to the model surface. Shear Modulus is also referred to as Modulus of rigidity. Mathematically, shear modulus is ratio of shear stress to shear strain.

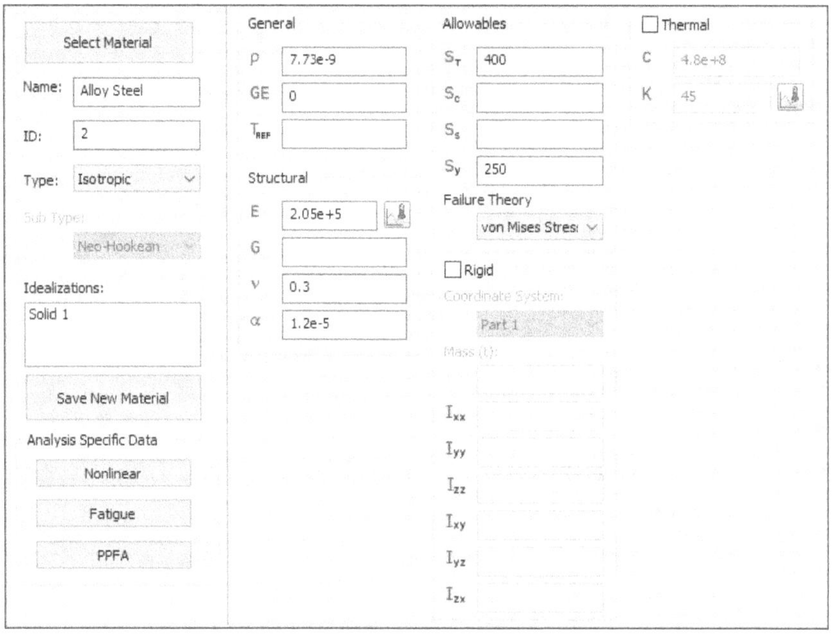

Figure-19. Isotropic material properties

- Specify desired value in the **Poisson's Ratio** edit box ν to define ratio of longitudinal strain to lateral strain. Poisson's ratio is the ratio of transverse contraction strain to longitudinal extension strain in the direction of stretching force. Tensile deformation is considered positive and compressive deformation is considered negative. The definition of Poisson's ratio contains a minus sign so that normal materials have a positive ratio. Poisson's ratio, also called Poisson ratio or the Poisson coefficient, or coefficient de Poisson, is usually represented as a lower case Greek nu, ν.
- Specify desired value in the **Thermal Exp. Coeff.** edit box to define the amount of change in size that occurs in the material due to change in temperature at constant pressure.
- The edit boxes in **Allowables** area of the **Material** dialog box are used to define different strength parameters for the material. Strength parameters define maximum limit of load that material can sustain without failure. Specify desired value in the **Tensile Limit (MPa)** edit box to define maximum tensile force that material can sustain without failure. Specify desired value in the **Compressive Limit (MPa)** edit box to define maximum compression force that material can sustain without failure. Specify desired value in the **Shear Limit (MPa)** edit box to define maximum shear force that can be applied to the material without failure. Specify desired value in the **Yield Limit (MPa)** edit box to define maximum stress after which material undergoes plastic deformation.
- Select desired option from the **Failure Theory** drop-down to define criteria for calculating factor of safety for the part using this material. Select the **None** option if you do not want to define the criteria. Select the **von Mises Stress** option to use von Mises stress as the failure criteria for factor of safety calculation. Select the **Principal Stress** option to use principal stress as the failure criteria for factor of safety calculation.

Note: Principal stresses are the stresses acting along main three axes on the model. So, selecting Principal Stress is useful when looking for fatigue or stress in major directions usually in simple loading cases. For simple major directional loading, selecting **Principal stress** option gives more accurate results. Select the **Von mises Stress** option if there is a complex case of loading like shear stress, compression stress and tension occurring the model simultaneously.

- Select the **Rigid** check box to mark current material is rigid type. In a rigid type material, there is zero strain (deformation) due to any amount of stress which means their Young's Modulus value is infinite. The options in **Rigid** area of the dialog box will become active on selecting this check box. Select desired option from the **Coordinate System** drop-down to define reference coordinate system for material rigidity. Specify desired value in the **Mass(t)** edit box to define mass to be added to computed mass of rigid body. Specify desired values of inertia along different axes to be added to the computed inertia of rigid body in respective edit boxes of the **Rigid** area in the dialog box.
- Select the **Thermal** check box to define thermal properties of the material. On selecting the check box, options below it will become active. Specify desired values of specific heat and thermal conductivity in respective edit boxes in the **Thermal** area.

Orthotropic 2D Material

Select the **Orthotropic 2D** option from the drop-down to specify separate values of material properties along the plane and perpendicular to the plane. On selecting this option, the **Material** dialog box will be displayed as shown in Figure-20. Specify the parameters as discussed earlier for each direction.

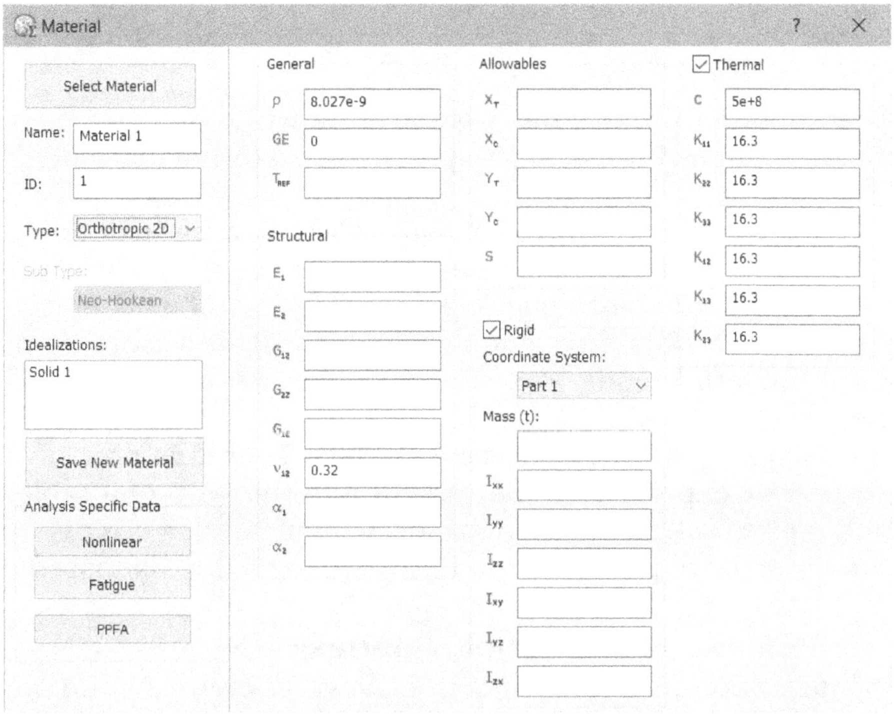

Figure-20. Orthotropic 2D material type

Orthotropic 3D

Select the **Orthotropic 3D** option from the drop-down to specify values of material properties separately for each directions. On selecting this option, you will be asked to specify material parameters separately for each direction.

Anisotropic 3D

Select the **Anisotropic 3D** option from the drop-down to specify parameters for material matrix. The properties of anisotropic materials are direction dependent. You need to define the material properties in various planes along different directions.

Hyperelastic Material

Select the **Hyperelastic** option from the drop-down to define properties of a material like rubber. The options for hyperelastic material as shown in Figure-21.

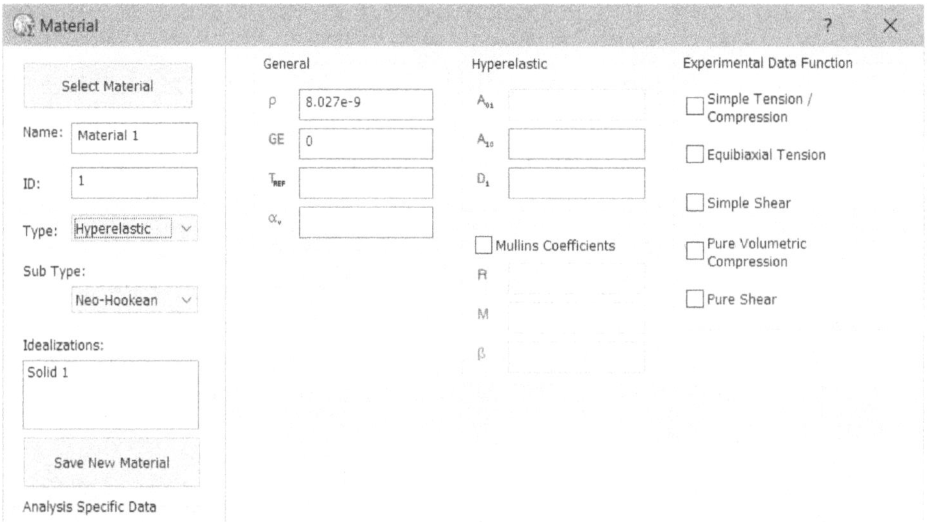

Figure-21. Hyperelastic material options

- Select desired option from the **Sub type** drop-down to define the equations used by hyperelastic material for defining properties. We have selected **Neo-Hookean** option in our case.
- Specify desired values in edit boxes of **Hyperelastic** area to define constant A01, A10, and Volumetric deformation constant D1.
- Select the **Mullins Coeficients** check box to define Mullins coefficients for stress softening of material. Note that when cyclic loading is performed on rubber like materials, the material tends to soften at some key areas which is defined by Mullins effect.
- Select check boxes from the **Experimental Data Function** area of the dialog box to define respective experimental data results in the form of a table. Click on the **Table** button next to selected check box for invoking dialog box of respective table.
- Other parameters for hyperelastic material are same as discussed earlier.

Nitinol Material

Select the **Nitinol** option from the **Type** drop-down to create Nitinol material which a metal alloy of nickel and titanium, where the two elements are present in roughly equal atomic percentages. Nitinol can deform 10-30 times as much as ordinary metals and return to its original shape. Note that this material is applicable for Nonlinear analyses only. Specify the parameters of material as discussed earlier.

Viscoelastic Material

Select the **Viscoelastic** option from the **Type** drop-down to create polymer like materials. Generally, viscoelastic materials are used for damping vibrations and noises. After selecting this option, specify the parameters as discussed earlier in the dialog box.

Brittle Material

Select the **Brittle** option from the **Type** drop-down to create materials like glass, cast iron, and so on. Brittle material tend to shatter under loads rather than bending. You can specify the parameters as discussed earlier.

Crushable Foam Material

Select the **Crushable Foam** option from the **Type** drop-down to create materials which can be compressed under load to confined space. Crushable foam materials are used to model the enhanced ability of a foam material to deform in compression due to cell wall buckling processes (it is assumed that the resulting deformation is not recoverable instantaneously and can, thus, be idealized as being plastic for short duration events). Specify the parameters for material as discussed earlier in the dialog box.

Analysis Specific Data

There are three buttons available in **Analysis Specific Data** area to define properties of material related to specific analyses. For example, **Nonlinear** button is used to specify non-linear properties of material for the nonlinear analysis. The use of these buttons is given next.

Nonlinear Property of Material

- Click on the **Nonlinear** button from the **Analysis Specific Data** area of the **Material** dialog box. The **Nonlinear Material Data** dialog box will be displayed; refer to Figure-22.

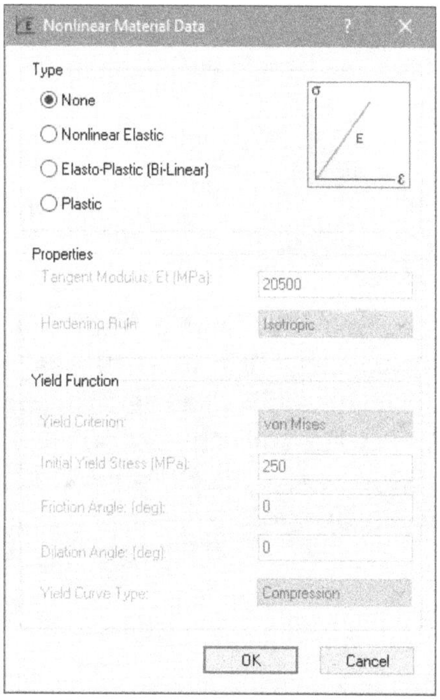

Figure-22. Nonlinear Material Data dialog box

- Select desired radio button from the **Type** area to define type of nonlinearity for the material. Select the **Nonlinear Elastic** radio button from the dialog box to define nonlinear elastic properties of the material. A nonlinear elastic material does not yield which means that however high the load will be, after taking that load away the material will return to initial state without any permanent deformations. It also does not show strain hardening even after several times of loading – unloading cycles. Select the **Elasto-Plastic (Bi-Linear)** radio button to define nonlinear behavior of material in which strain hardening occurs on several loading cycles. After selecting this radio button, select desired option from the **Hardening Rule** drop-down to define how hardening will occur in the material and select desired option from the **Yield Criterion** drop-down to define method for calculating yield strength. Select the **Plastic** radio button to define material which undergoes plastic deformation after specified strain point.
- After specifying parameters, click on the **Show XY Plot** button to check plot of material properties in Stress vs Strain graph.
- After setting desired parameters, click on the **OK** button.

Fatigue

The **Fatigue** button is used to define fatigue data for the material. On clicking this button, the **Fatigue** dialog box will be displayed; refer to Figure-23. Select the **S-N** tab from the dialog box to define fatigue data for material using stress amplitude against number of cycles. Select the **E-N** tab from the dialog box to define fatigue data for material using strain amplitude against number of cycles. Specify the experimental data of fatigue in edit boxes of the dialog box and click on the **OK** button.

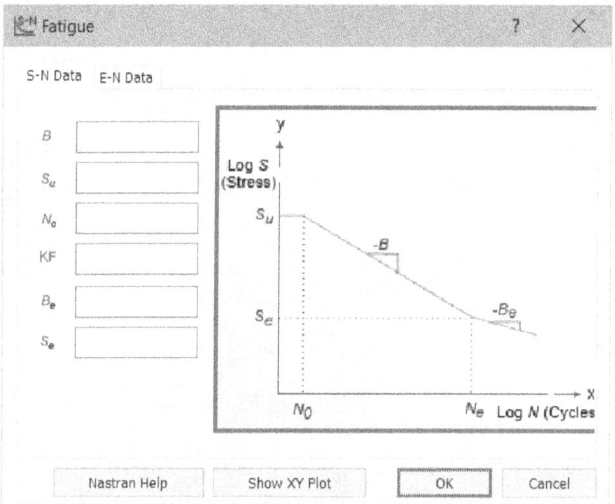

Figure-23. Fatigue dialog box

Progressive Ply Failure Analysis Data

The **PPFA** button is used to define reduction in stiffness of material due to continuous loading. On clicking this button, the **PPFA Dialog** will be displayed; refer to Figure-24. Select the **Perform PPFA Calculation** check box and specify desired values of reduction factor for Young's Modulus and Shear Modulus in respective edit boxes. Click on the **OK** button to apply changes.

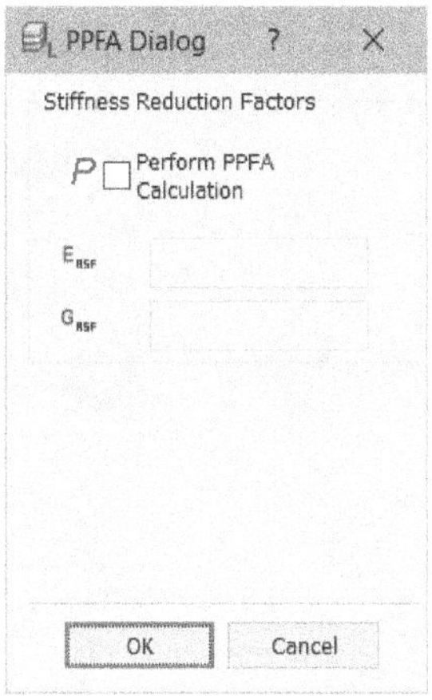

Figure-24. PPFA dialog box

IDEALIZATION

Idealization is used to idealize the model based on simple assumptions like assuming shell elements as quadrilaterals. The procedure to perform idealization is given next.

- Click on the **Idealizations** tool from the **Prepare** panel in the **Autodesk Inventor Nastran** tab of the **Ribbon**. The **Idealizations** dialog box will be displayed; refer to Figure-25.

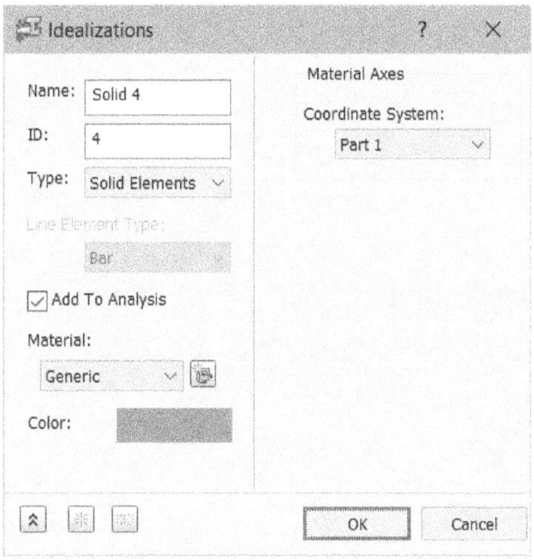

Figure-25. Idealizations dialog box

- Specify desired name for idealization in the **Name** edit box and specify id number in the **ID** edit box to give identification code.
- From the **Type** drop-down, select desired type of idealization to be performed on the model.
- Select the **Add To Analysis** check box to add idealization to current analysis.
- From the **Material** drop-down, select desired material.
- Click on the colored button for **Color** field and select desired color from the **Color** dialog box.
- To specify coordinate system for material, select desired coordinate system from the **Coordinate System** drop-down.
- Click on the **OK** button from the dialog box to set idealization. The options for different idealizations are discussed next.

Solid Idealization

- Select the **Solid** option from the **Type** drop-down to apply solid elements idealization to the model; refer to Figure-26. In Solid Idealization, there are two types of elements available: Solid Parabolic Tetrahedral element and Solid Tetrahedral element; refer to Figure-27.

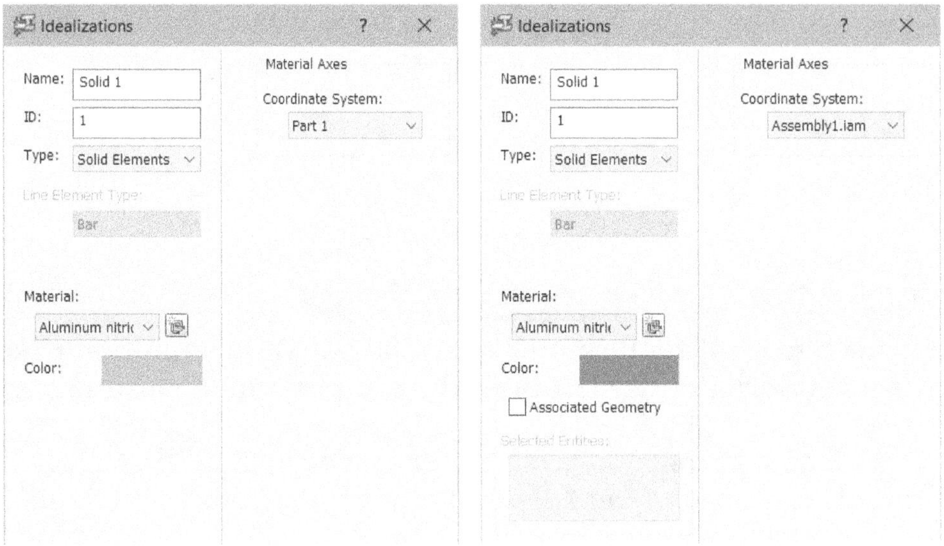

For Part Model **For Assembly Model**

Figure-26. Solid Idealizations

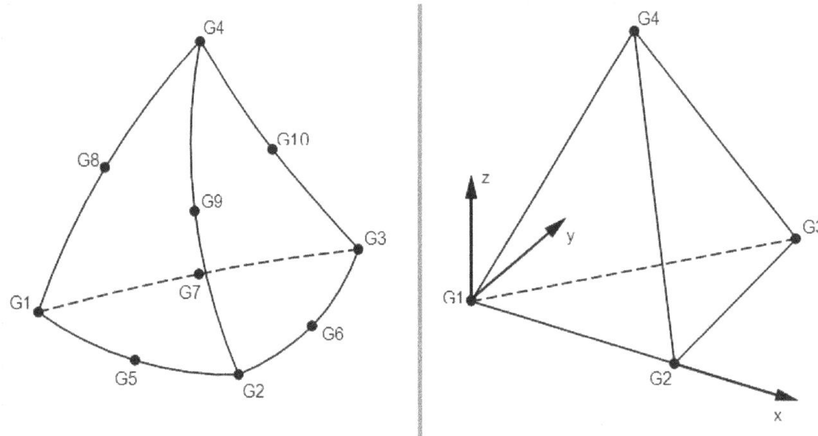

Parabolic Tetrahedral Element **Tetrahedral Element**

Figure-27. Solid elements

- Select the **Associated Geometry** check box if you are working on an assembly and want to select the parts from assembly to which current idealization will be applied.
- Similarly, you can select desired part option from the **Coordinate System** drop-down to use it as coordinate system for material axes.
- Specify the other parameters as discussed earlier and click on the **OK** button.

Shell Idealization

- Select the **Shell Elements** option from the **Type** drop-down to create shell idealization of the surface or sheetmetal parts. The options in the dialog box will be displayed; refer to Figure-28.

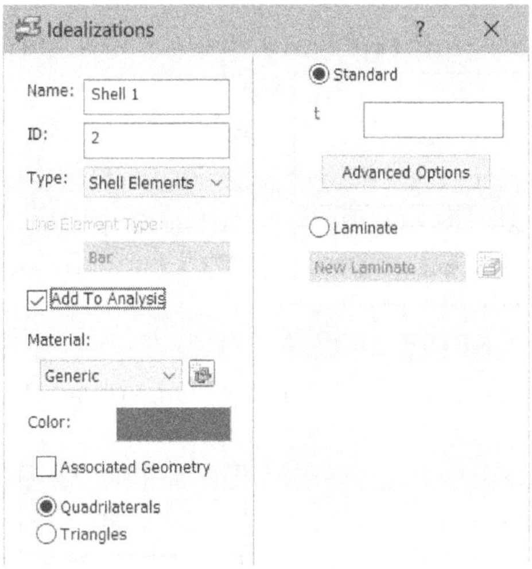

Figure-28. Shell element idealizations

- If there is a part model in graphics area then you do not need to select the geometry, it will be automatically converted to shell elements. If you are working on an assembly then select the part model as discussed earlier for solid idealization.
- Select the **Quadrilaterals** radio button from the dialog box to create 2D quadrilateral elements. Select the **Triangles** radio button to create 2D triangular elements for the shell object; refer to Figure-29.

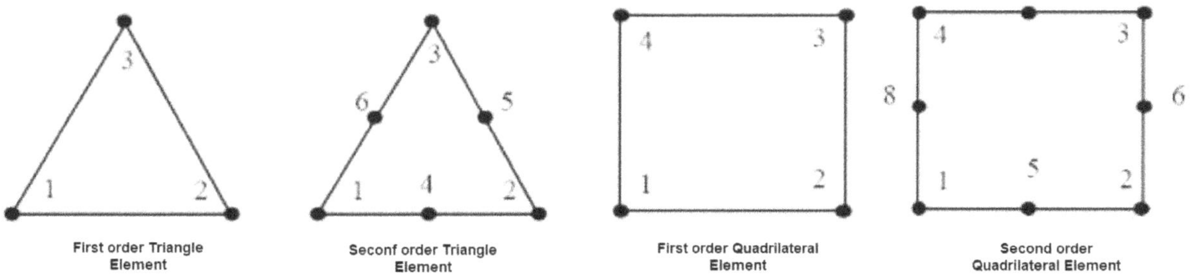

Figure-29. Shell elements

- You can associate a specific type of shell element to selected geometry by selecting the **Associated Geometry** check box. On selecting this check box, two different selection boxes will become active for selecting quadrilateral geometries and triangle geometries. Click in desired selected box and select respective geometry from the model.
- Select the **Standard** radio button from the dialog box to specify thickness of the shell element. Note that a uniform thickness will be applied to shell model by using this option. After selecting this radio button, specify desired value of thickness in the **Thickness** edit box t .

- Click on the **Advanced Options** button to specify advanced parameters for standard shell elements. The **Advanced Options** dialog box will be displayed as shown in Figure-30. Specify desired values in the **Top Fiber** and **Bottom Fiber** edit boxes to define upper boundary face and lower boundary face of the model using selected shell surface/face as reference. Note that by default half of thickness value specified earlier will be applied automatically to top fiber and bottom fiber. Select the **MidPlane Offset Distance (mm)** check box to move mid plane of shell mesh from selected face/surface by value specified in edit box below the check box. Select the **Include Drilling DOF (CQUADR/CTRIAR)** check box if you want to include drilling axis (normal to shell plane) movements in calculations of analysis. Generally, translation and rotation in plane of shell elements is considered for shell analysis. Note that this check box can be selected only if you are working with linear shell elements (First order). Click in the **NSM** edit box to define amount of non-structural mass to be added to the shell model. Non-structural mass represents external mass attached to the model. Select the **Use Plane Strain Element Type** check box to check strain on elements in current shell plane only. In this case, the bending and transverse shear of membrane of elements will be disabled. Specify desired values of bending stiffness and transverse shear/membrane thickness in respective edit boxes if the **Use Plane Strain Element Type** check box is not selected. Note that when this check box is selected then options of **Material** area in the dialog box will be disabled. Select the **Bending** check box from the **Material** area to define material used for defining bending properties. Similarly, select the **Transverse Shear** and **Membrane-Bending** check boxes to define material for respective parameters. After setting desired parameters, click on the **OK** button to apply advanced properties to elements.

Figure-30. Advanced Options dialog box

- Select the **Laminate** radio button from **Idealizations** dialog box to create a composite laminate of different materials stacked one over other. After selecting this radio button, click on the **New Laminate** button below it. The **Laminate** dialog box will be displayed; refer to Figure-31. The options of this dialog box are discussed next.

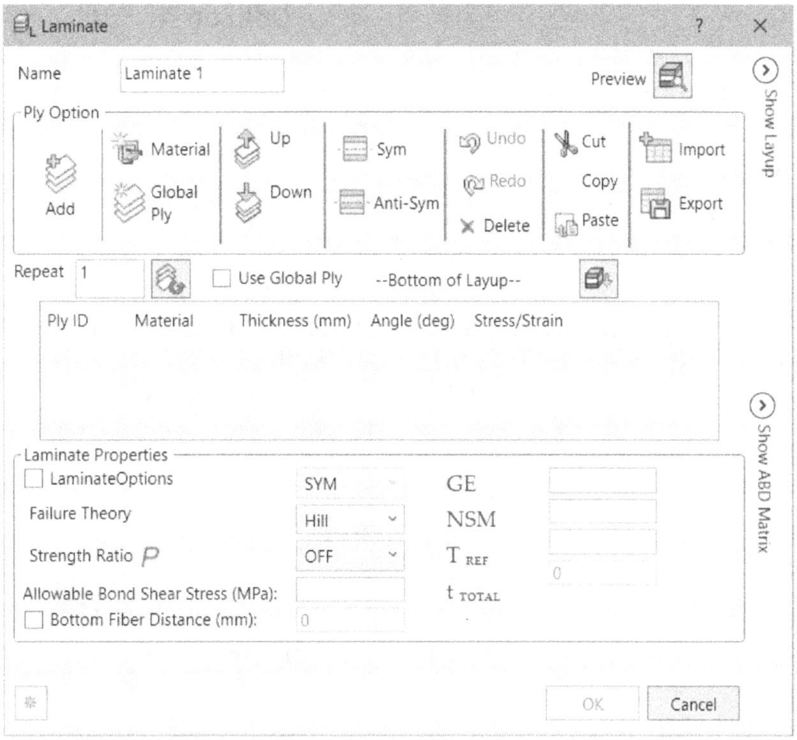

Figure-31. Laminate dialog box

Laminate Options

- Specify the name of laminate in the **Name** edit box of the dialog box.
- Click on the **Add** button from the **Ply Option** area of the dialog box to create a new layer (Ply) in the laminate. The options in the table will be displayed as shown in Figure-32.

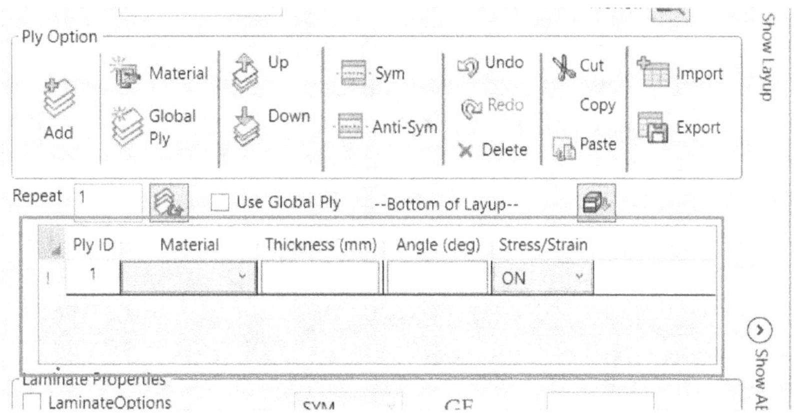

Figure-32. Table for defining layer

- Set the material, thickness, angle, and Stress/Strain status in respective fields of the table. Note that the **Angle** edit box in table is used to define rotation of layer with respect to material orientation. Repeat the above steps to create multiple layers (plies) of the laminate.
- If desired material is not available in the drop-down of table then click on the **Material** button from **Ply Option** area of the dialog box. The familiar **Material** dialog box will be displayed. Select desired material as discussed earlier and click on the **OK** button. The selected material will now be available in **Material** drop-down of the table.

- Click on the **Global Ply** button from the **Ply Option** area to create a general ply parameter set which will be applied if no properties are applied plies to laminate.
- Select the **Up** or **Down** buttons to move the laminate layers up or down in the stack.
- Select the **Sym** button from the **Ply Option** area to create symmetric copy of selected ply in the table.
- Select the **Anti-Sym** button from the **Ply Option** area to create a copy of selected ply with negative sign to angle of selected ply.
- You can use other buttons in the **Ply Option** area to perform general operations like delete, undo, redo, import, export, and so on.
- Select the **LaminateOptions** check box and set different forms of laminates in the drop-down next to the check box. If **SYM** option is selected then only plies on one side of the element center line are specified. The plies are numbered starting with 1 for the bottom layer. If an odd number of plies is desired in SYM form then the center ply thickness (Ti) should be half the actual thickness. If **HCS**, **FCS**, or **ACS** option is selected then a composite sandwich is defined for the purpose of face sheet stability index output. **HCS** specifies a honeycomb core material, **FCS** specifies a form core material, and **ACS** selects either HCS or FCS based on the core material specified. If the **SME** option is selected then the ply effects are smeared and the stacking sequence is ignored. If the **SMC** option is selected then a composite sandwich is defined using equivalent orthotropic properties.
- Select desired option from the **Failure Theory** drop-down to define which failure theory will be used for checking failure of model. Select the **HILL** option from the drop-down to check failure of orthotropic materials with equal strengths in tension and compression. Select the **HOFF** option from the drop-down to check failure of orthotropic materials under a general state of plane stress with unequal tensile and compressive strengths. Select the **TSAI** option from the drop-down to check failure of orthotropic materials under a general state of plane stress with unequal tensile and compressive strengths. Select the **Max. Stress** option from the drop-down to check maximum stress of the model for failure. Select the **Max. Strain** option from the drop-down to check maximum strain of the model for failure. Select the **NASA LaRC** or **LARC02** option to check failure of orthotropic materials comprised of unidirectional plies under a general state of plane stress. Select the **PUCK** option from the drop-down to use Puck PCP theory for checking failure of orthotropic materials comprised of unidirectional plies under a general stare of plane stress. Select the **MCT** option from the drop-down to use Multicontinuum theory for checking failure of orthotropic materials comprised of unidirectional plies or plain weave fabric under general state of plane stress.
- Select the **ON** option from the **Strength Ratio** drop-down to consider strength ratio as failure parameter in comparison to Failure Index.
- Specify desired value in the **Allowable Bond Shear Stress (MPa)** edit box to define inter-laminar shear stress of a bonded material.
- Select the **Bottom Fiber Distance (mm)** check box and specify bottom thickness of the shell.
- Specify desired value in the **Damping coefficient** edit box to define coefficient of damping for laminates.
- Similarly, specify other parameters in edit boxes like NSM and T_{REF}.
- After setting desired parameters, click on the **OK** button from the **Laminate** dialog box.
- Click on the **OK** button from the **Idealizations** dialog box to apply the idealization.

Note that there are various technical parameters involved with laminate shell idealization like failure theory and laminate forms so make sure to check the parameters in reference books or Internet to know more about them.

Line Idealization

Select the **Line Elements** option from the **Type** drop-down in the **Idealizations** dialog box to apply 1 dimensional line elements to the model for meshing. On selecting the option, the parameters in dialog box will be displayed as shown in Figure-33. Line element is one of the most capable and versatile elements in the finite element library. It is very commonly used in the aerospace stress analysis industry and also in many other industries such as marine, automotive, and civil engineering structures. The options to create a line element are discussed next.

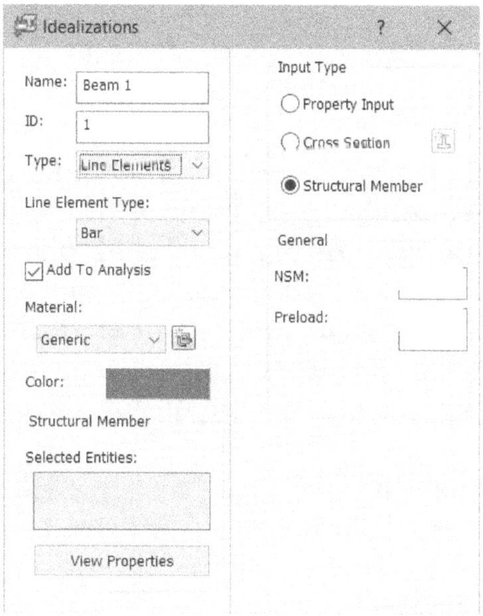

Figure-33. Idealizations dialog box with line elements

- Select desired option from the **Line Element Type** drop-down to define type of 1D element. Select the **Bar** option if the structural member will undergo axial loading only (tension and compression). A bar element cannot be used under transverse or torsional loading. Rod is also a category in bar elements. Select the **Beam** option if structural member will undergo torsional/transverse loading along with axial loading. Select the **Pipe** option to represent straight, slender to moderately stubby/thick pipe structures. The elements are especially useful in the offshore drilling industry, as their cross-section data includes interior fluid and outside insulation. Although, the above explanation of different line elements is just a surface of deep topic. This can help you decide the elements fast.

Note: Difference between Beam, Bar, and Pipe Elements

- Beam elements can have tightened segments, which means one end can be littler/bigger/more extensive/smaller/more slender/thicker than the other; however, the shape cannot be entirely unexpected.
- Beam components are fit for representing enormous avoidances and differential solidness because of massive diversions.

- Beam components can have three unique balances—one for sheer focus, one for the nonpartisan pivot, and one for the non-structural mass hub. While bar components have just a single-center, every one of the three is a similar unbiased hub.
- For a bar component, the network focuses are situated at the area centroidal nonpartisan pivot. For beam components, they are consistently at the shear place hub, and the impartial axle is counterbalanced from the shear community hub.
- Bar components are best for doubly even segments with the load applied along centroidal planes. They are not fit for representing bowing or winding, or distorting of the areas because of hub or cross overburden. This is just conceivable with Beam components.
- A pipe element is a special form of beam element. Pipe cross-section is normally axis-symmetric so that the bending resistance is the same in both directions. Element orientation (via an orientation node) is still necessary, however, as the element loads can differ in the y and z directions.
- Pipe can account for both internal and external pressures.

- After selecting line element type, select desired radio button from the **Input Type** area of the dialog box to define properties of line element. Select the **Property Input** radio button to define shape, size, and physical properties of element manually. Select the **Cross Section** radio button to draw the cross section of element manually. Select the **Structural Member** radio button to select structural member from the model. Note that the structural members are frame members of Inventor assembly. Various input type options are discussed next.

Property Input Type for Line Element

- Select the **Property Input** radio button from the **Input Type** area of the dialog box to define parameters for line element. The options of the dialog box will be displayed as shown in Figure-34.

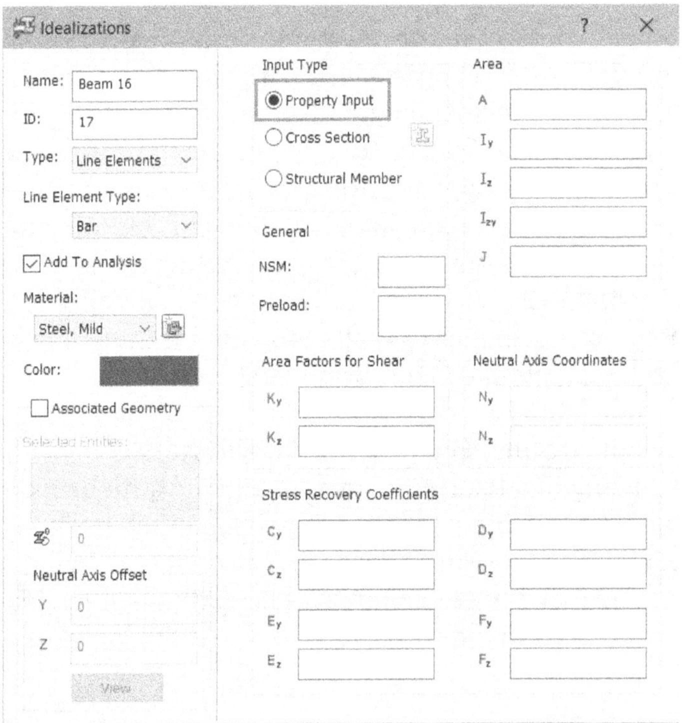

Figure-34. Property Input options

- Specify desired non structural mass value in the **NSM** edit box as discussed earlier.
- Specify desired value in the **Preload** edit box to define additional load already applied on the element apart from simulation load.
- Specify desired values of cross-sectional area (A), Inertia for bending along various axes (I) and Saint-Venant torsional constant (J) in respective edit boxes.
- Specify the values of shear area factor along y and z axes in respective edit boxes of the **Area Factors for Shear** area of the dialog box. Shear area factor defines the amount of cross-section of element which is effective in resisting shear deformation. In other words, its the amount of cross-section area where shear stress/strain will be calculated by Nastran.
- Similarly, specify desired distance values in edit boxes of **Stress Recovery Coefficients** area to define the distance of stress/strain calculation points from center of the element; refer to Figure-35. Note that the y and z subscripts in various edit boxes represent two ends of the bar element.
- Select the **Associated Geometry** check box and then select the model geometry to be idealized as bar element; refer to Figure-36.

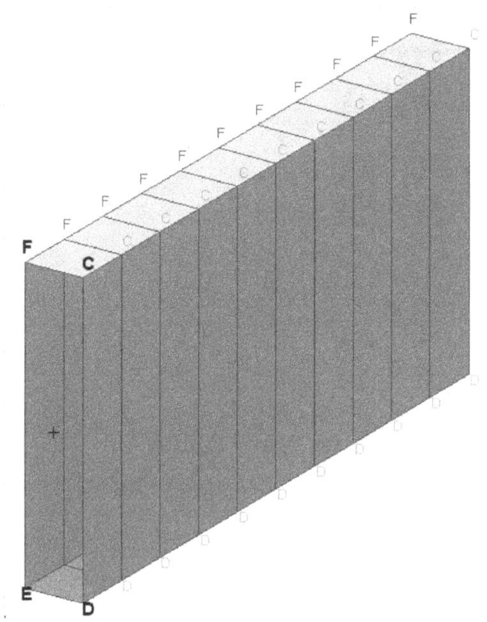

Figure-35. Stress recovery points

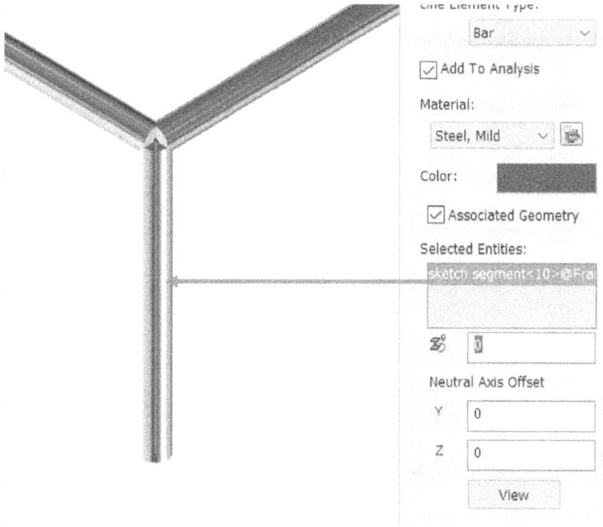

Figure-36. Geometry selected for bar element

- By default the neutral axis is at center of the bar but if you want to move it then specify desired distance values in **Y** and **Z** edit boxes of the **Neutral Axis Offset** area of the dialog box. You can also rotate the bar about its neutral axis by specifying angle value in the **Rotation Angle** edit box.
- Specify other parameters as discussed earlier.

Cross Section Type for Line Element

- Select the **Cross Section** radio button to select desired cross section for the line element. The options in the dialog box will be displayed as shown in Figure-37.
- Click on the button next to **Cross-Section** radio button. The **Cross Section Definition** dialog box will be displayed; refer to Figure-38.
- Select desired option from the **Shape** drop-down to define shape of the bar element and specify related size parameters in the edit boxes.
- Click on the **Draw End A** button at the bottom in the dialog box to check preview of the bar and properties.

- Click on the **OK** button from the dialog box to define cross section. You will return **Idealizations** dialog box.
- Select desired option from the **Offset To** drop-down to move center point of the cross-section to centroid or reference point specified by you.

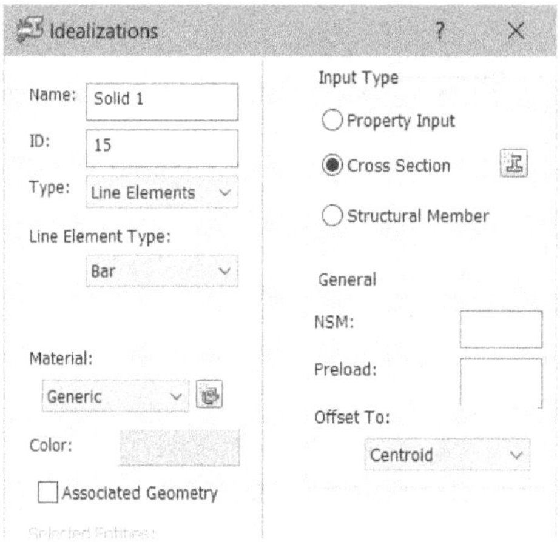

Figure-37. Cross Section input type

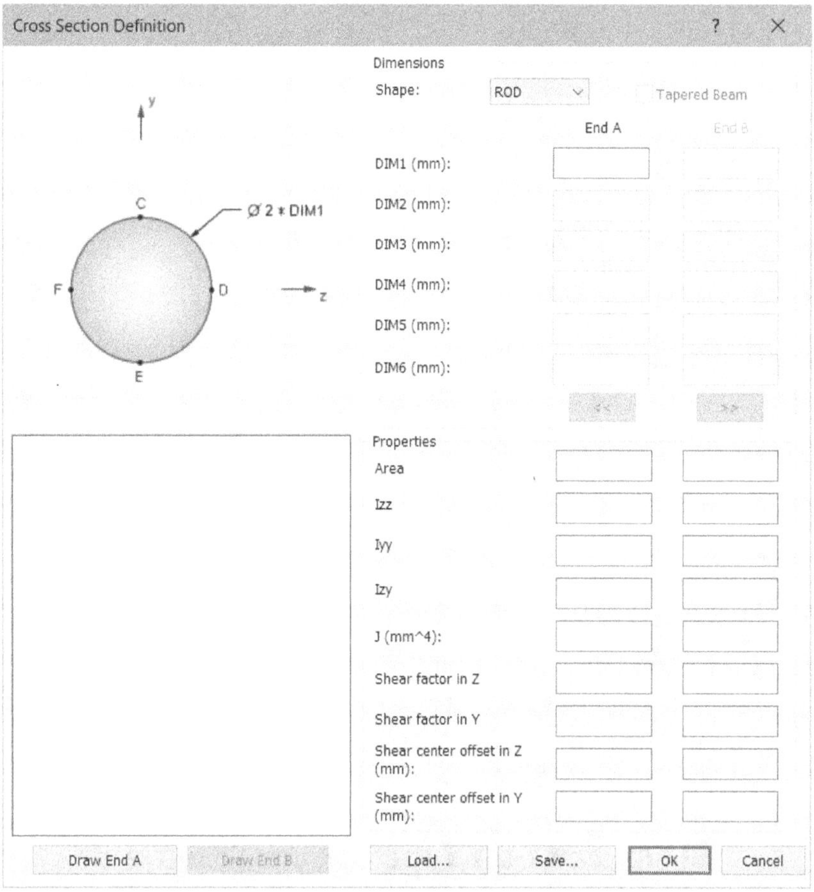

Figure-38. Cross Section Definition dialog box

Structural Member Type for Line Element

- Select the **Structural Member** radio button to convert selected member to a line type element specified in the **Line Element Type** drop-down.
- Click in the **Selected Entities** selection box and then select the frame member from the graphics area.

- If you have selected **Pipe** option from the **Line Element Type** drop-down then **End Condition** section will be displayed. Select the **Both Ends Closed** radio button or **Both Ends Open** radio button to define condition of end points of pipe elements as closed or open, respectively. Specify the pressure value in **Internal Pressure** (P) edit box of **End Conditions** section.
- After setting desired parameters, click on the **New** button to save the current idealization and start a new idealization. Click on the **Create Duplicate** button to copy current idealization and start a new idealization. Click on the **OK** button to create the element.

USING CONCENTRATED MASSES

The **Concentrated Masses** tool is used to replace selected assembly part with a mass point of specified properties. The procedure to use this tool is given next.

- Click on the **Concentrated Masses** tool from the **Idealizations** drop-down in the **Prepare** panel of **Autodesk Inventor Nastran** tab in the **Ribbon**. The **Concentrated Mass** dialog box will be displayed; refer to Figure-39.

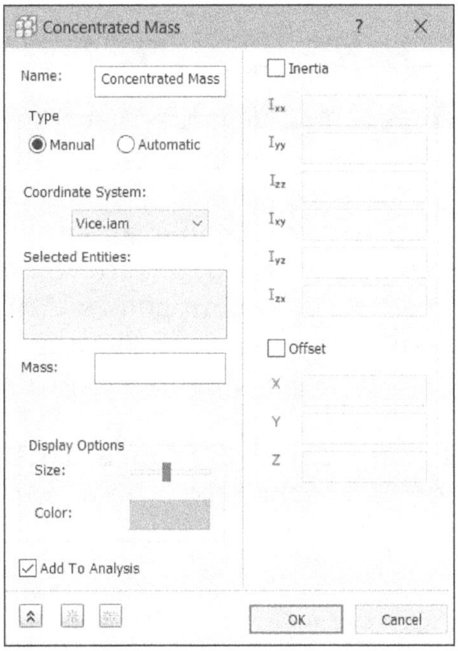

Figure-39. Concentrated Mass dialog box

- Specify desired name of concentrated mass in the **Name** edit box.
- Select the **Manual** radio button to specify point of concentrated mass at desired location in the model. This option is useful when you know exact mass of concentrated mass object. After selecting this radio button, specify mass of point in the **Mass** edit box.
- Select the **Automatic** radio button to replace selected assembly part from the graphics area to a point mass of specified density. After selecting this radio button, select the part to be replaced by concentrated mass; refer to Figure-40.
- Set the other parameters as discussed earlier and click on the **OK** button to create the concentrated mass object.

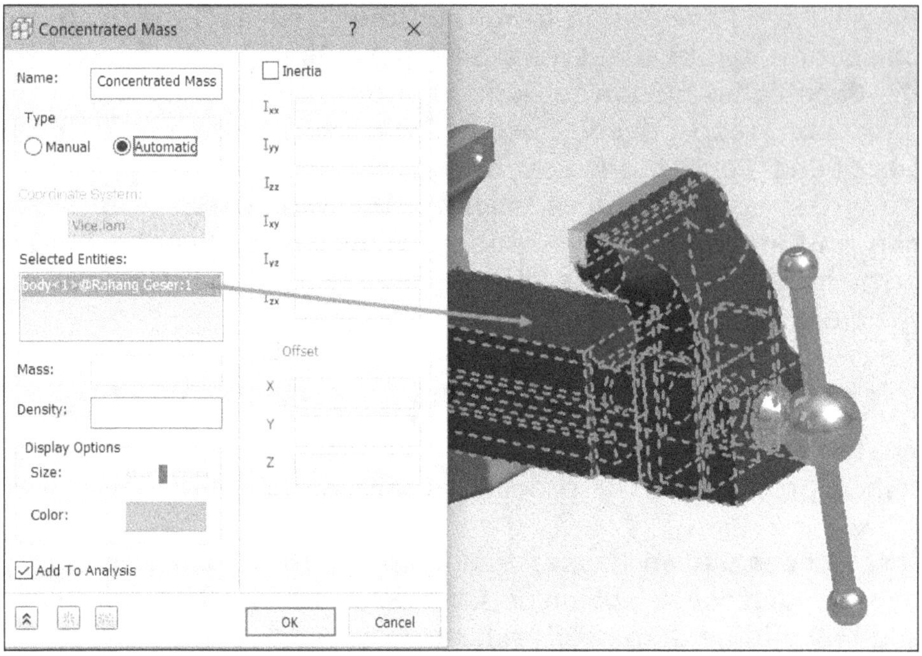

Figure-40. Selecting part for concentrated mass

APPLYING CONNECTIONS BETWEEN ASSEMBLY COMPONENTS

The **Connectors** tool is used to apply connections between various components of the assembly. You can create a solid model of connector to link the components of assembly/design or you can use the **Connectors** tool to create representation of real connector between the components. Using the **Connectors** tool gives benefit of easily checking result parameters on the connectors. Also, using connectors reduces the processing time of analysis significantly if there are multiple connectors in the assembly/design. The procedure to use this tool is given next.

- Click on the **Connectors** tool from the **Prepare** panel of the **Autodesk Inventor Nastran** tab in the **Ribbon**. The **Connector** dialog box will be displayed; refer to Figure-41.

Figure-41. Connector dialog box

There are five different types of connections; Rod, Cable, Spring, Rigid Body, and Bolt. The procedures to apply these connections are given next.

Applying Rod Connection

- Select the **Rod** option from the **Type** drop-down if you are concerned with compression and tension displacements in the connected points of the model. A rod connection do not capture bending in the model. On selecting the **Rod** option, the **Connectors** dialog box will be displayed as shown in Figure-41.
- Click in the first **End point of connector** selection box and select the point on one end face connector.
- Click in the second **End point of connector** selection box and select the point on another end face of connector. Note that you can also use sketch points to create rod connector; refer to Figure-42.
- Specify desired value of cross-section area of the rod in **A** edit box. Similarly, specify the torsion constant and coefficient of torsion stress in the **J** and **C** edit boxes respectively.
- You can use the **Size** slider to increase or decrease the representation size of the rod connector.
- Specify the other parameters as discussed earlier and click on the **Next** button to create next connector.
- Click on the **OK** button to create connectors and exit the dialog box.

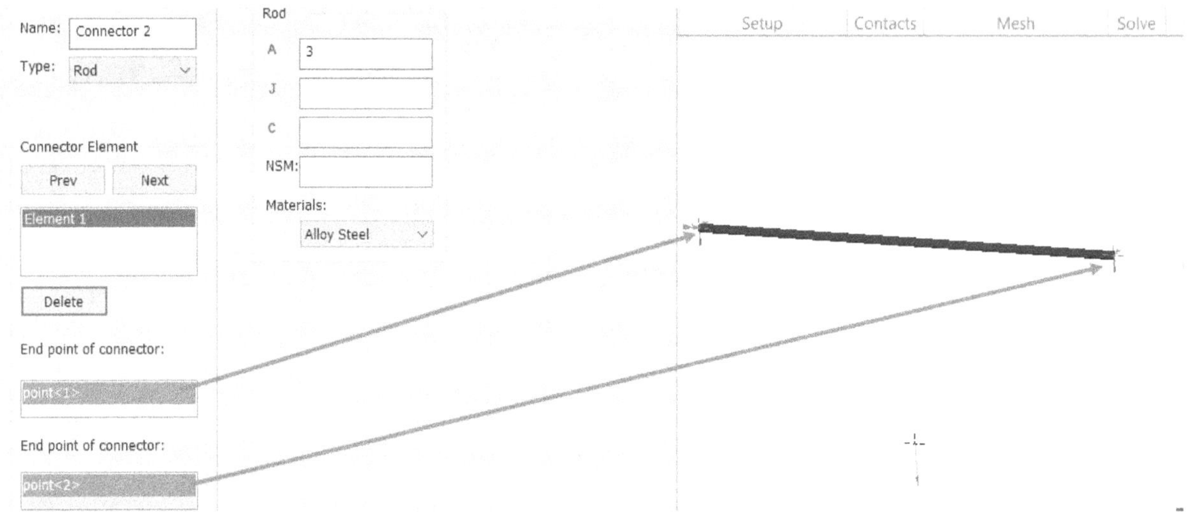

Figure-42. Specifying points for rod connector

Applying Cable Connection

- Select the **Cable** option from the **Type** drop-down to create a cable connection between selected points for analysis. A cable connection is similar to rod connection but slack parameter. The options in the dialog box for cable connector are displayed as shown in Figure-43.

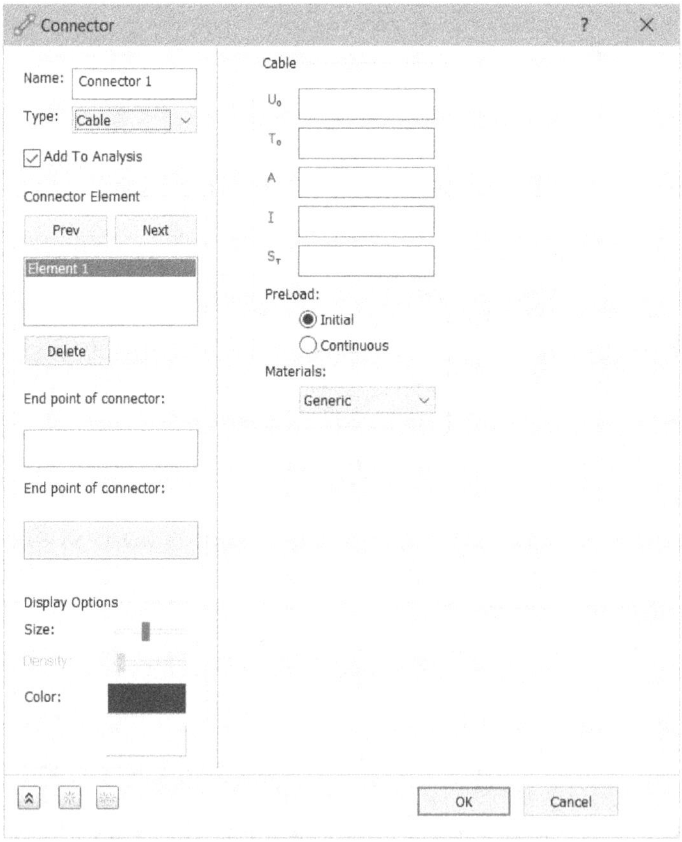

Figure-43. Connector dialog box with Cable options

- Click in the **End point of connector** selection boxes and select desired points on the model as discussed for rod connection. A cable connection will be applied between the points.
- Specify desired value of initial cable slack in the U_0 edit box.
- Specify desired value of initial cable tension in the T_0 edit box.

- Specify the cross section area, area of moment of inertia, and allowable tensile stress in respective edit boxes as discussed earlier.
- Select the **Initial** radio button from **Preload** area to apply preload only at the beginning of analysis. Select the **Continuous** radio button to keep applying preload for full duration of the analysis.
- Specify other parameters as discussed earlier and click on the **Next** button to create next connector.
- Click on the **OK** button to create connectors and exit the dialog box.

Applying Spring Connection

The spring connection is used to define a connection that represents spring of specified damping and stiffness coefficient between selected points. The procedure to use this option is given next.

- Select the **Spring** option from the **Type** drop-down in **Connector** dialog box. The options in the dialog box will be displayed as shown in Figure-44.

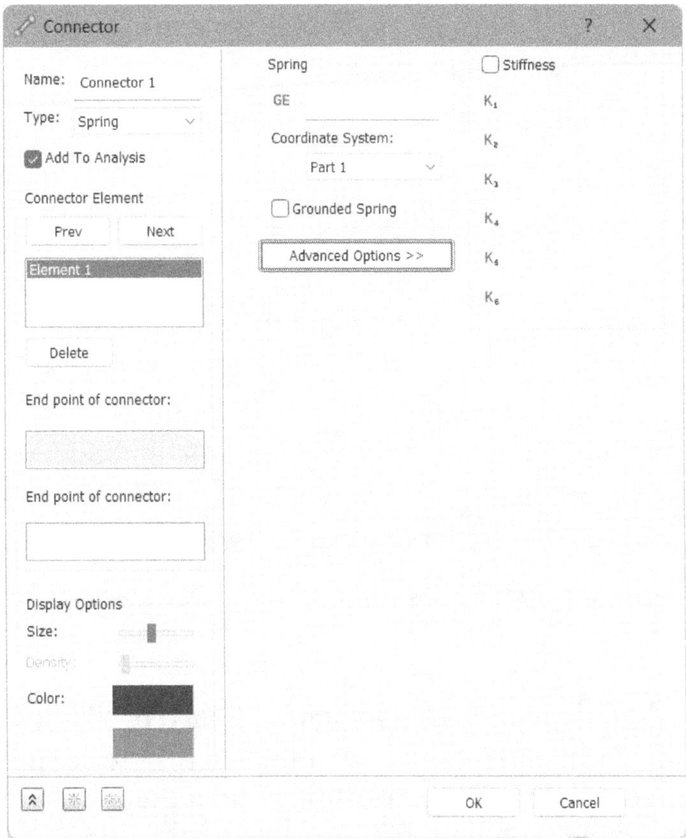

Figure-44. Connector dialog box with Spring options

- Select the connector points as discussed earlier.
- Specify the value of damping coefficient in **GE** edit box. Damping coefficient define resistance to vibrations and oscillations in the connection.
- Select the **Stiffness** check box and specify desired value of stiffness of spring in the edit box below it.
- Select the **Grounded Spring** check box if one end of spring is grounded. Selecting this check box means the point at which spring connector is being applied is attached to a fixed block with specified spring properties.
- Click on the **Advanced Options** button to define recovery coefficient and vector components of stiffness & damping. Note that the value specified in **K_1** edit box

is meant for stiffness in X direction so if you want to define stiffness in any other direction then you need to work with advanced options. On selecting **Advanced Options** button, the options in dialog box will be displayed as shown in Figure-45.

- Specify desired values in the **Damping** and **Stiffness** areas to define damping coefficient and stiffness values in various directions. The subscripts 1, 2, and 3 in edit boxes correspond to translational X, Y, and Z directions. The subscripts 4, 5, and 6 correspond to rotation about X, Y, and Z axes.
- The Stress and Strain recovery coefficients define the factor by which spring will recover to original shape after unloading. Generally, the default values are 1 as we always perform analysis on new springs. But, if your spring is older or a special one then after experiments you can get the factor by which spring recovers in translational and rotational directions. If half of your spring returns to original shape after unloading then specify the coefficient value as 0.5.

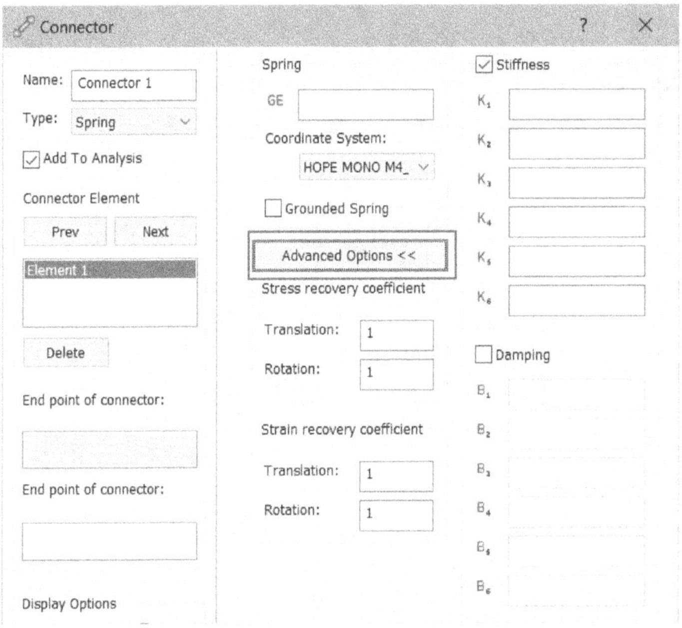

Figure-45. Advanced options for spring connection

- Specify other parameters as discussed earlier and click on the **OK** button to create the connector.

Applying Rigid Body Connection

Rigid body connection is used to make selected component rigid so that the object do not deform or deflect in any direction unless specified. It is a link from one node to one or more other nodes, where the motion of the node(s) is governed by the "degrees of freedom" you choose to connect. A rigid element is an equation rather than connection. Some of the examples where rigid connection is applied in analysis are:

1. An engine of a vehicle removed from the analysis scope and in place of engine a rigid element (RBE2) is connected to the vehicle body if we are concerned about deformation in vehicle body.
2. Passengers of a vehicle replaced by rigid element (RBE3) to check effects of masses of passengers during the analysis of vehicle body.

The procedure to apply rigid connection is given next.

- Select the **Rigid Body** option from the **Type** drop-down in the **Connector** dialog box. The options in the dialog box will be displayed as shown in Figure-46.

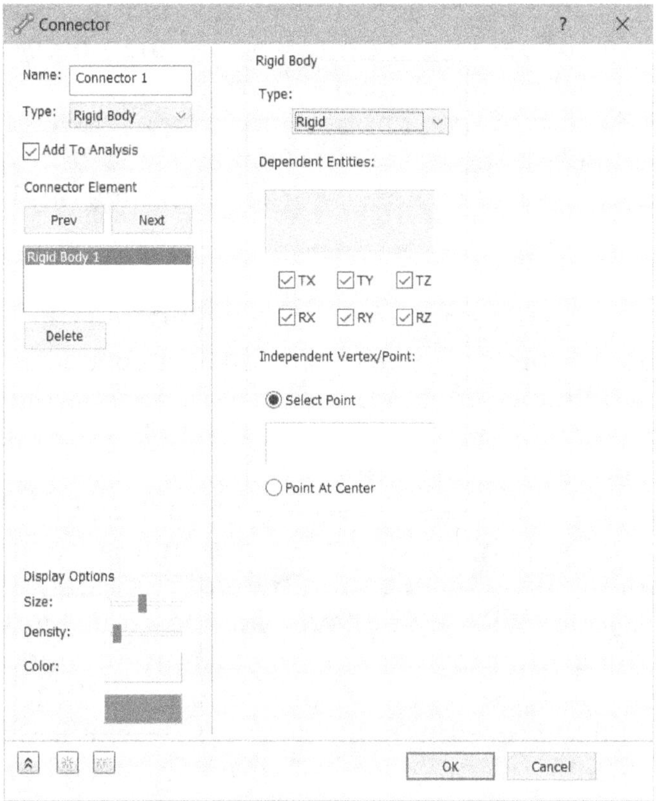

Figure-46. Connector dialog box with Rigid Body options

- Select the **Rigid** option from the **Type** drop-down in **Rigid Body** area to create a link with infinite stiffness. On selecting this option, you will be asked to select dependent entities and independent vertex/point from the model. Select the Interpolation option from the drop-down if you want to distribute loads on the connected nodes without adding any stiffness. On selecting this option, you will be asked to select entities on which load will be distributed and reference point/ vertex for rigid connection. Figure-47 shows the difference in selecting two types when a lateral load is applied on plates connected by rigid connection to same point of load.

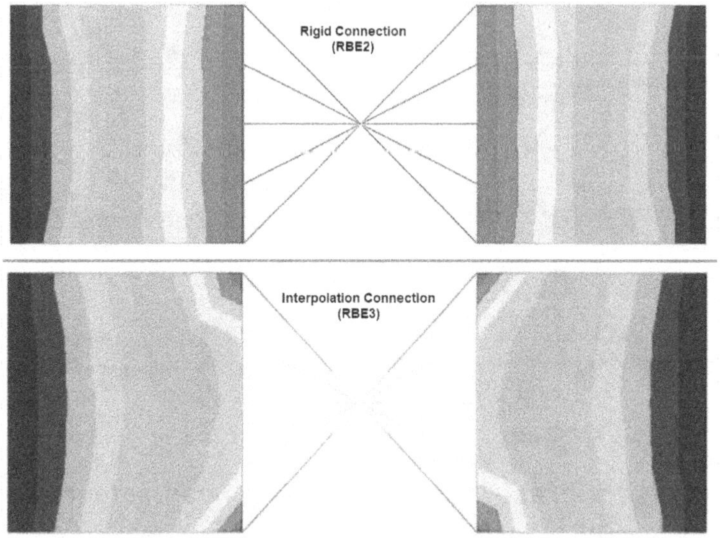

Figure-47. Rigid connection types

- Click in the **Dependent Entities** selection box for rigid type or click in the **Entities to Average** selection box for interpolation type rigid connection and select the faces/edges/vertices that you want to be connected by rigid link.
- Select the **Select Point** radio button to specify the point/vertex on which load is being applied and select desired point/vertex.
- If you want the load point of rigid connection to be at the center of selected faces/ edges/vertices then select the **Point At Center** radio button.
- Specify other parameters as discussed earlier and click on the **OK** button to create the connection.

Applying Bolt Connection

- Select the **Bolt** option from the **Type** drop-down in **Connector** dialog box to create representation of a bolted connection. Note that effects of deformation of shank in the bolt are not transferred to side walls of the holes through which bolt passes to create connection. If you are concerned about such deformation then you should use model of bolt instead. Also, you cannot use symmetry feature in the model if bolt connection is applied as they may not generate the symmetric bolt connections automatically. On selecting the **Bolt** option in **Type** drop-down, the options in the dialog box will be displayed as shown in Figure-48.
- Select the **Bolt** radio button to create a bolt with nut connection or select the **Cap Screw** radio button to create a screw connection which does not need nut. The options will be modified accordingly in the dialog box. For Cap Screw connection, you are asked to specify useful length of screw in place of nut washer height in case of Bolt connection in the dialog box.

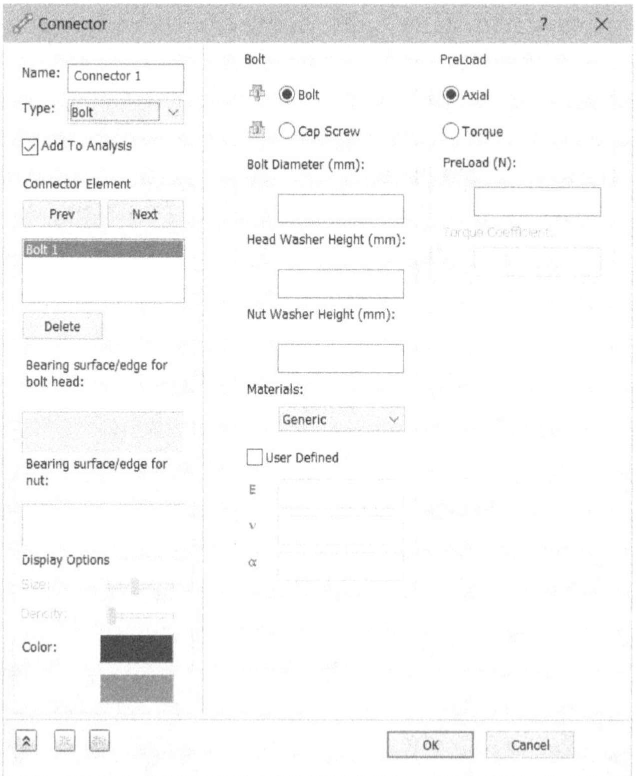

Figure-48. Connector dialog box with Bolt options

- Click in the **Bearing surface/edge for bolt head** selection box and select the edge/face on which bolt head will rest.

- Click in the **Bearing surface/edge for nut** selection box if the **Bolt** radio button is selected or click in the **Surface(s) for threaded region** selection box if the **Cap Screw** radio button is selected and select the edge/face on which nut will rest. Preview of the bolt will be displayed; refer to Figure-49 for bolted connection and Figure-50 for cap screw connection.

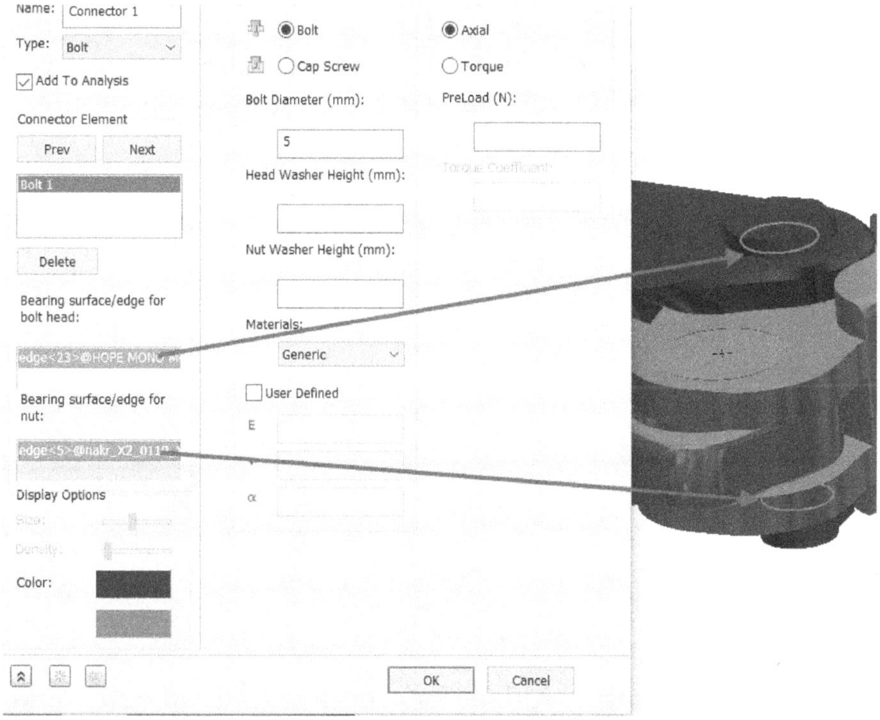

Figure-49. Edges selected for bolt

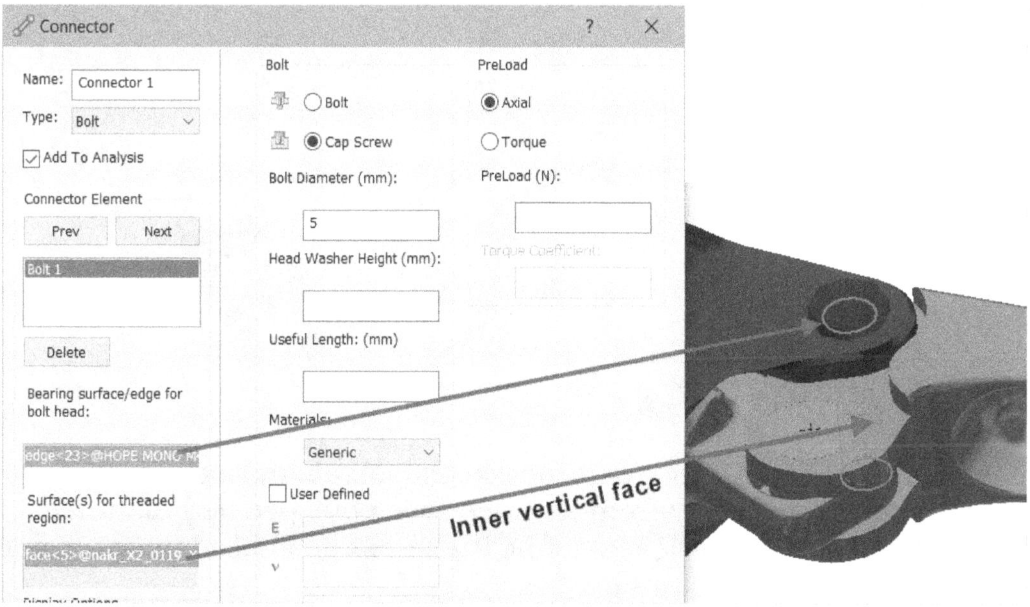

Figure-50. Edge and face selected for screw

- Specify desired dimensions and parameters for the bolt/screw in the edit boxes of **Bolt** area in the dialog box.
- Select desired radio button from the **PreLoad** area to define whether you want to specify axial preload or torque preload on the bolt.
- Specify other parameters as discussed earlier and click on the **OK** button to apply connection.

OFFSETTING SURFACE FOR CREATING SHELL COMPONENTS

The **Offset Surfaces** tool in the **Prepare** panel is used to create a surface copy of selected faces of the part at specified distance to form shell component. The procedure to use this tool is given next.

- Click on the **Offset Surfaces** tool from the **Prepare** panel in the **Autodesk Inventor Nastran** tab of **Ribbon**. The **Offset Surface** dialog box will be displayed; refer to Figure-51.

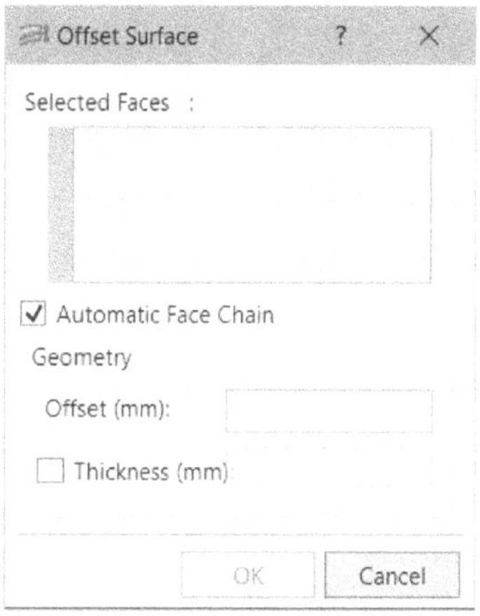

Figure-51. Offset Surface dialog box

- Select the faces that you want to offset for creating shell objects; refer to Figure-52.

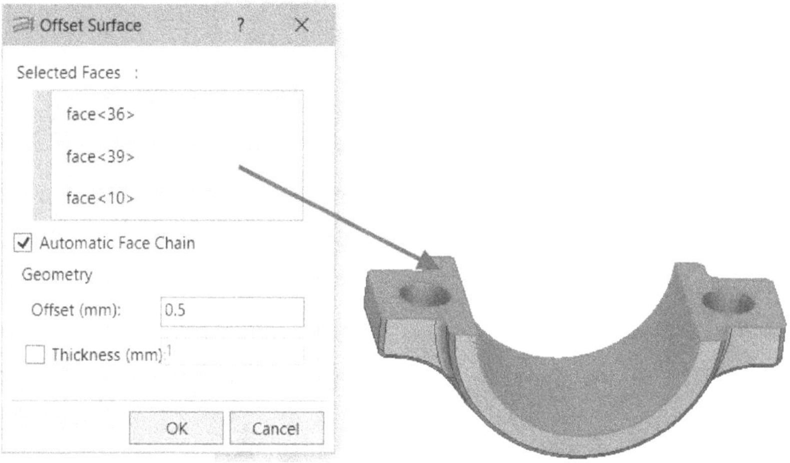

Figure-52. Faces selected

- Specify desired value of offset distance in the **Offset(mm)** edit box. Note that the surface will be created away from selected faces by specified distance
- Select the **Thickness** check box to define thickness of shell component and specify desired value in adjacent edit box.
- After setting desired parameters, click on the **OK** button to create shell component; refer to Figure-53.

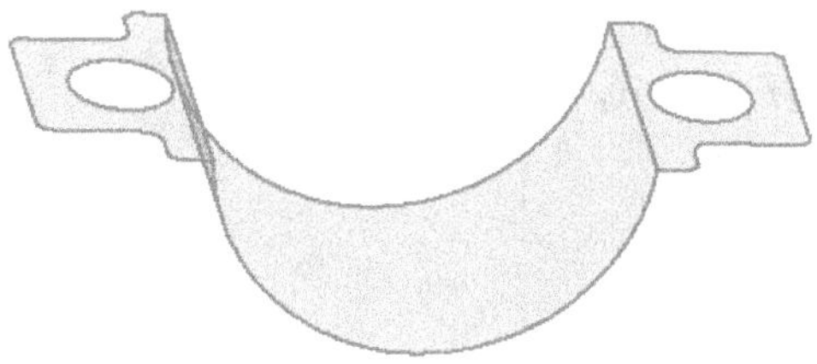

Figure-53. Shell component created

FINDING THIN BODIES

The **Find Thin Bodies** tool is used to find sections which have low thickness as compared to rest of the model. For example for a plate if the ratio of thickness to length of its sides is less than 0.05 then it will be considered thin body. Note that the body should have uniform thickness for being considered by this tool. The procedure to use this tool is given next.

- After opening the model and starting **Autodesk Inventor Nastran**, click on the **Find Thin Bodies** tool from the **Offset Surfaces** drop-down in the **Prepare** panel of the **Autodesk Inventor Nastran** tab in the **Ribbon**. If one or more thin bodies are found then **Autodesk Inventor Nastran** information box will be displayed; refer to Figure-54.

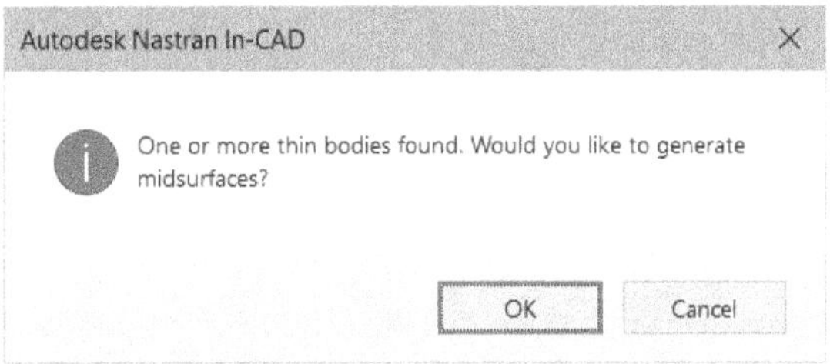

Figure-54. Autodesk Inventor Nastran information box

- If you want to generate mid surfaces then click on the **OK** button. The **Midsurface** dialog box will be displayed; refer to Figure-55.

Figure-55. Midsurface dialog box

- If you want to remove any body from the list then right-click on it and select the **Delete** option from the shortcut menu.
- Click on the **OK** button from the dialog box to create the mid surfaces.

CREATING MIDSURFACE

The **Midsurfaces** tool is used to create shell objects at the mid location of selected solid bodies. The procedure to use this tool is given next.

- Click on the **Midsurfaces** tool from the **Offset Surfaces** drop-down in the **Prepare** panel of the **Autodesk Inventor Nastran** tab in the **Ribbon**. The **Midsurface** dialog box will be displayed; refer to Figure-55.
- Select the bodies for which you want to create midsurface; refer to Figure-56.

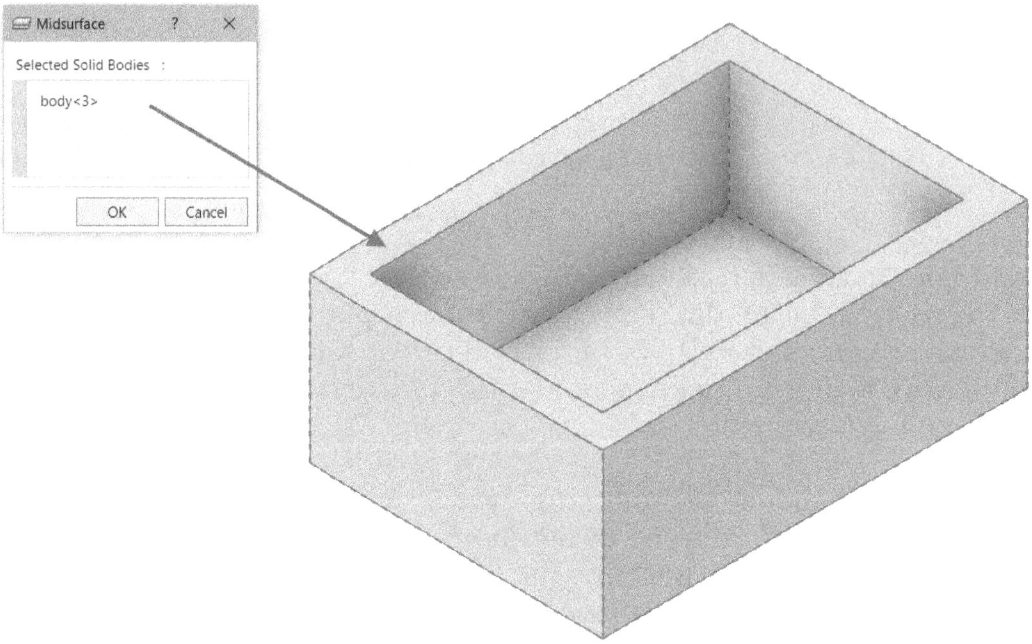

Figure-56. Body selected for midsurface

- Click on the **OK** button from the dialog box. The midsurface will be created; refer to Figure-57.

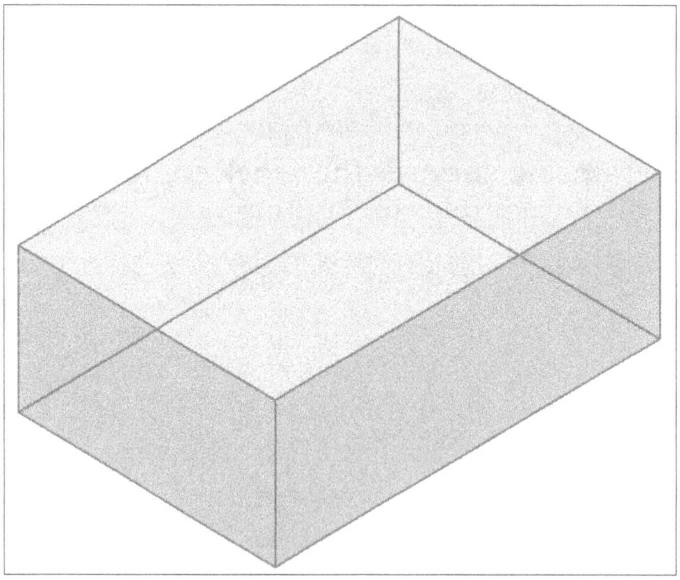

Figure-57. Midsurface generated

MANAGING STRUCTURAL MEMBERS

The **Structural Members** tool is used to manage whether the structural members in model are to be used as solids or 1D beams in analysis. Note that structural members are generated by Frame Generator environment of Autodesk Inventor. The procedure to use this tool is given next.

- Click on the **Structural Members** tool from the **Prepare** panel of **Autodesk Inventor Nastran** tab in the **Ribbon**. The **Structural Members** dialog box will be displayed; refer to Figure-58.

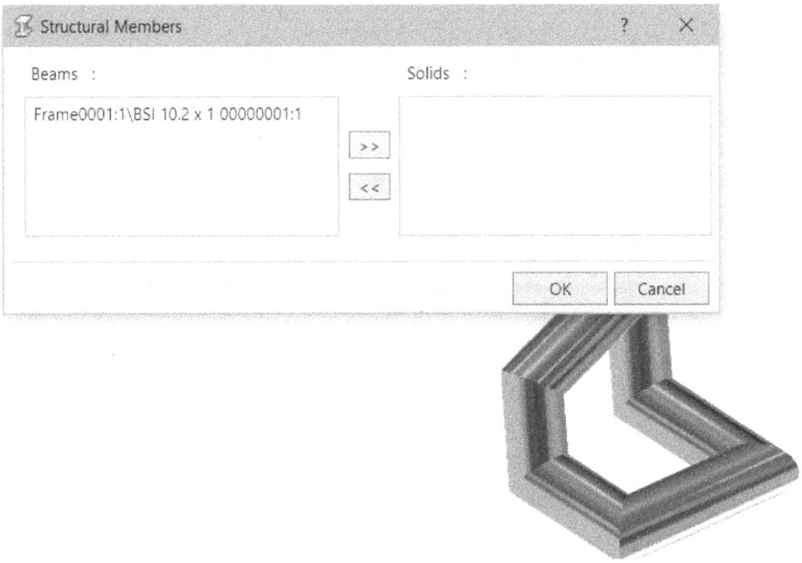

Figure-58. Structural Members dialog box

- Select desired frame members from the **Beams** list box and click on the **Forward(>>)** button to use them as solid members in analysis. Similarly, select desired frame members from the **Solids** list box and click on the **Backward (<<)** button to use them as beam members in analysis.
- After setting desired parameter, click on the **OK** button from the dialog box.

APPLYING CONSTRAINTS

The **Constraints** tool in **Setup** panel is used to apply restrictions to translation and rotation of selected objects in specified directions. The procedure to apply constraint is given next.

- Click on the **Constraints** tool from the **Setup** panel in the **Autodesk Inventor Nastran** tab of the **Ribbon**. The **Constraint** dialog box will be displayed; refer to Figure-59.

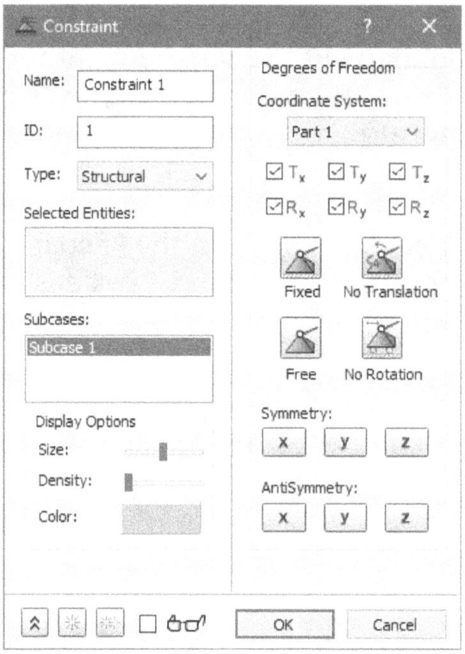

Figure-59. Constraint dialog box

- Select desired type of constraint from the **Type** drop-down. The options will be modified accordingly in the dialog box. Select the **Structural** option from **Type** drop-down if you want apply translation and rotation of a point/edge/face/vertex in X, Y, and/or Z directions.
- Select the **Pin** option from the drop-down if you have cylindrical body and you want to restrict its movements in radial, axial, and/or tangential directions. On selecting **Pin** option, the options in the dialog box will be displayed as shown in Figure-60.
- Select the **Frictionless** option from the **Type** drop-down if you want to allow free movement of bodies along plane of selected face. (You can assume it as a soap placed on wet floor and someone step on it. So the soap will move on floor without friction but it will not move above or below the floor. Although, the person on soap will feel like flying!!).
- Select the **Response Spectrum** option from **Type** drop-down if you want to restrict movements of vertices of the body for shock/response spectrum analysis. Note that you cannot select edge or face for constraining body during response spectrum analysis because it will defeat the whole purpose of doing the analysis.
- Select the **Thermal** option from the **Type** drop-down if you want to specify temperature on selected faces/edges/vertices. On selecting this option, the dialog box will be displayed as shown in Figure-61. Note that thermal constraint is applicable only for Heat Transfer analysis.

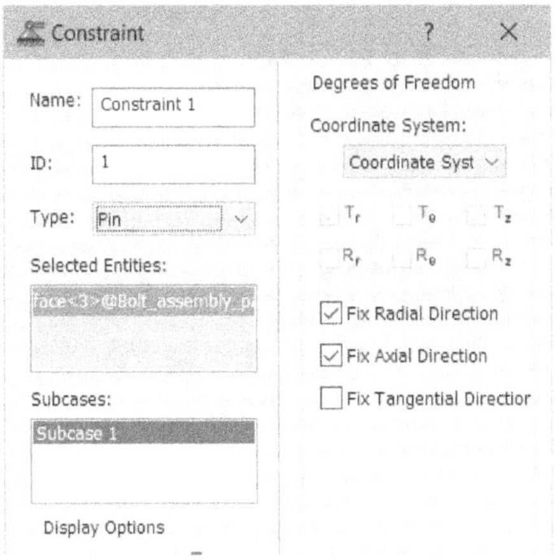

Figure-60. Pin constraint options

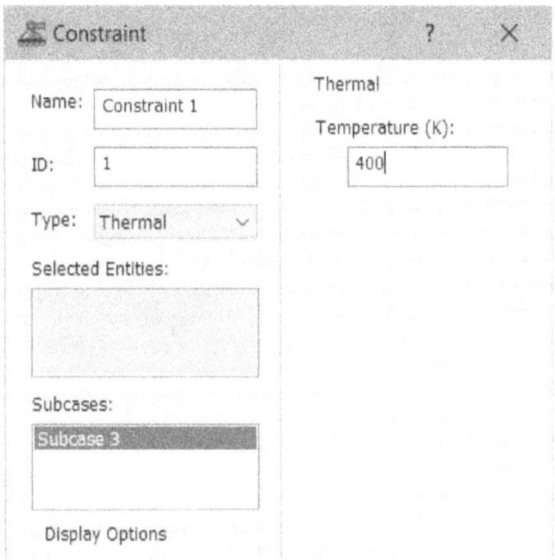

Figure-61. Thermal constraint options

- Select the **Rigid(Explicit)** option from the **Type** drop-down if you are working on an Explicit type analysis and want to restrict the motion of a body. Note that you will not be able to select points for Rigid(Explicit) constraint. Selecting this constraint means no rotation and translation for the rigid body idealization (solid, shell, or line) in graphics area.
- Select the faces/edges/vertices depending on the constraint type selected to apply constraint.
- Select desired check boxes from T_x, T_y, T_z, R_x, R_y, and R_z from the **Degrees of Freedom** area. Here, T designates translation along subscripted direction and R designates rotation along subscripted direction. You can also use the **Fixed** button to restrict translation and rotation of selected objects, **No Translation** button to restrict only translation of selected objects, **Free** button to allow free movement of selected objects, and **No Rotation** button to restrict only rotation of selected objects. Note that directions X, Y, and Z are based on coordinate system selected in the **Coordinate System** drop-down of the dialog box. These check boxes are available only when **Structural**, **Response Spectrum**, or **Rigid(Explicit)** option is selected in the **Type** drop-down of the dialog box.
- Select desired button from the **Symmetry** area to make the object symmetric along axis of selected button. Similarly, you can use the buttons in **AntiSymmetry** area. Note that these buttons are available for Structural and Rigid (Explicit) constraints only.
- Set desired option from the **Display Options** area like display size, display density, and color of constraint.
- Click on the **New** button at the bottom of the dialog box to create another constraint.
- After setting desired parameters, click on the **OK** button.

APPLYING LOADS

The **Loads** tool is used to apply different type of loads on selected faces/edges/vertices. The procedure to apply different type of loads is discussed next.

- Click on the **Loads** tool from the **Setup** panel in the **Autodesk Inventor Nastran** tab of **Ribbon**. The **Load** dialog box will be displayed; refer to Figure-62.

Figure-62. Load dialog box when Direct Transient Response analysis performed

- Specify desired load name and id in respective edit boxes.
- Set desired display options in **Display Options** area.

Applying Force

- Select the **Force** option from the **Type** drop-down to apply physical force on selected face/edge/vertex.
- Select the faces on which you want to apply force.
- Specify desired values in different components of force in the F_x, F_y, and F_z edit boxes of the **Magnitude** area if the **Components** option is selected in **Direction** drop-down.
- Select the **Normal to Surface** option from the **Direction** drop-down to apply force perpendicular to selected face and specify the magnitude in **Magnitude** edit box.
- Select the **Geometric Entity** option from the **Direction** drop-down to apply force along selected direction reference; refer to Figure-63.

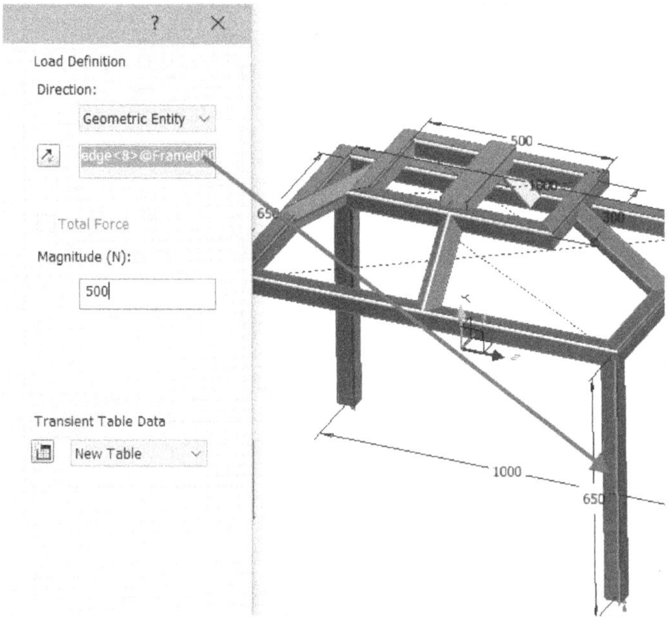

Figure-63. Edge selected for direction

- Click on the **Advanced Options** button from the dialog box to set variable load. The options of the dialog box will be displayed as shown in Figure-64.

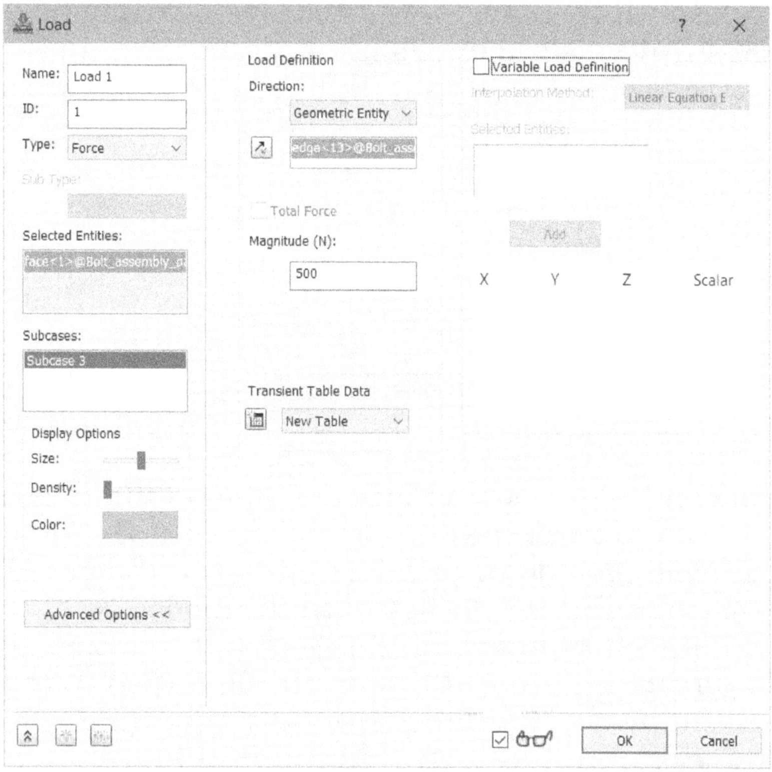

Figure-64. Advanced options for force load

- Select the **Variable Load Definition** check box to create variable loading. The options below the check box will become active.
- Select the **Linear** option if you want the load to vary linearly along selected point. Minimum four points are required for a face. Select the **Linear Equation Based** option to vary load linearly based on standard plane equation. Minimum 3 points are required for a face load. Select the **Quadratic** option to vary load based on parabolic equation. Figure-65 shows the difference between load distributions of these options.

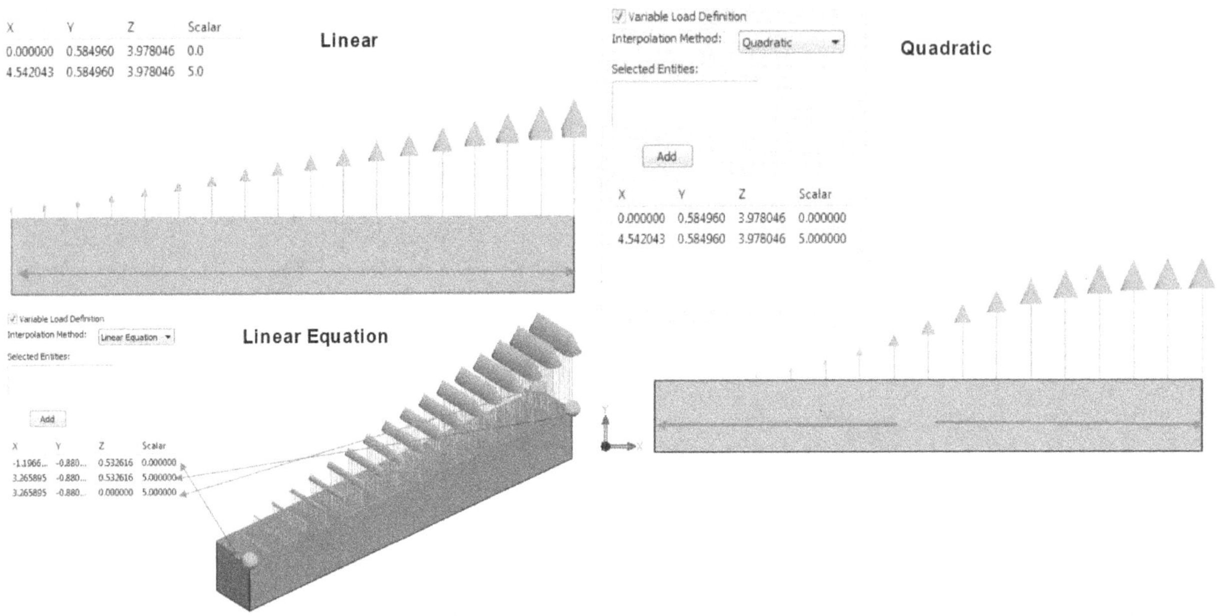

Figure-65. Variable load distribution

- Click on the **Define New Table** button from the dialog box to specify transient data of load when performing transient response analyses. Using this table, you can generate a load which changes with time. On clicking the **Define New Table** button, the **Table Data** dialog box will be displayed; refer to Figure-66.

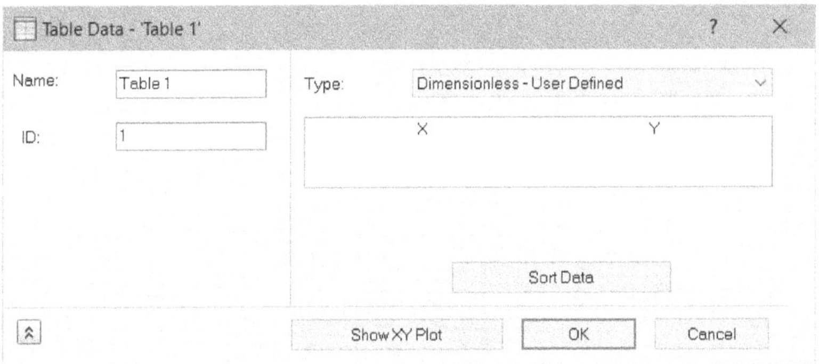

Figure-66. Table Data dialog box

- Select the **Dimensionless - User Defined** option from the **Type** drop-down to use a dimensionless table of parameters. Select the **Load Scale Factor vs. Time** option from the **Type** drop-down to define load scale factor and respective time duration for which the load will be active on the model.
- Specify desired parameters in the table and click on the **Show XY Plot** button to check plot of load factor vs time. Click on the **OK** button from the dialog box to create the transient plot.

Applying Moment Load

- Moment is load applied on part which rotates or tends to rotate the part. After activating the **Load** dialog box, select the **Moment** option from the **Type** drop-down. The options in the dialog box will be displayed as shown in Figure-67.

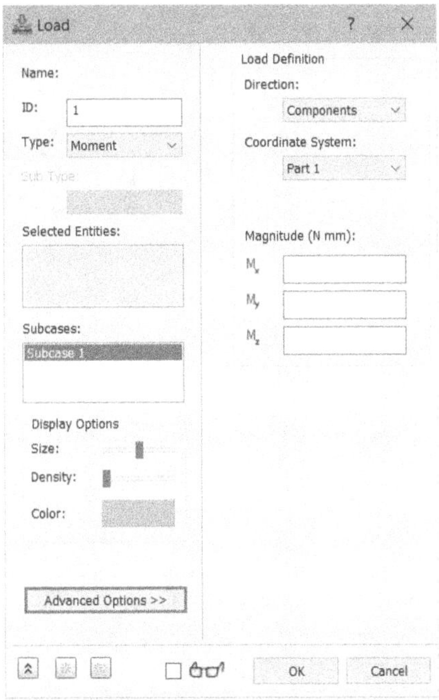

Figure-67. Load dialog box with Moment options

- Most of the options in this dialog box are same as discussed for the **Force** option. Specify the value of moment in place of force and click on the **OK** button to apply changes.

Applying Distributed Load

Distributed load is applied when you need to specify the force or moment per unit length of the object; refer to Figure-68. To apply distributed load, select the **Distributed Load** option from the **Type** drop-down. The options in this dialog box are same as discussed earlier. Select desired option from the **Sub Type** drop-down. The other options are same as discussed earlier.

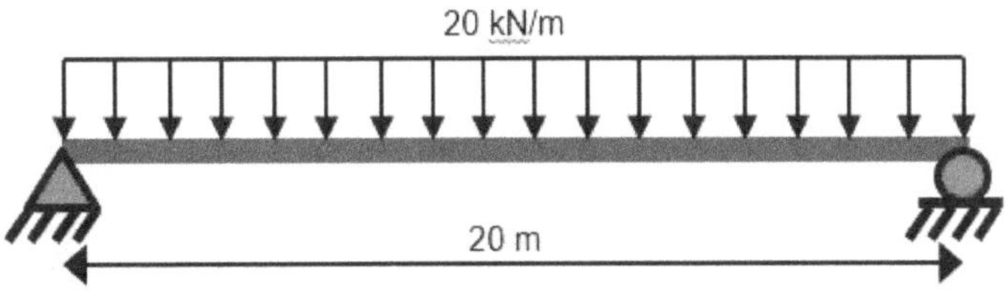

Figure-68. Distributed load

Applying Hydrostatic Load

The hydrostatic load is applied when you need to define force exerted by fluid (at rest) on a surface. In simple words, hydrostatic force is equal to force exerted due to pressure of fluid at rest. Hydrostatic pressure is calculated as fluid density x depth of fluid. Hydrostatic force is maximum at bottom and minimum on top of wall if fluid is filled in a vertical standing hollow cylinder. The procedure to apply this load is given next.

- Select the **Hydrostatic Load** option from the **Type** drop-down in the dialog box. The options will be displayed as shown in Figure-69.
- Select the face/surface on which you want to apply the load.

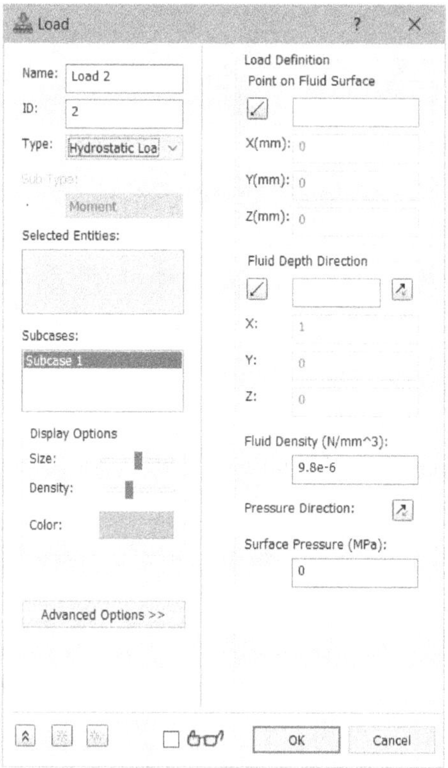

Figure-69. Options for hydrostatic load

- Click on the button in **Point on Fluid Surface** area of the dialog box and select the top point up to which fluid is exerting pressure.
- Click on the button in **Fluid Depth Direction** area and select the direction reference (edge or axis).
- Specify desired values of fluid density and surface pressure in respective fields. Preview of hydrostatic load will be displayed; refer to Figure-70.

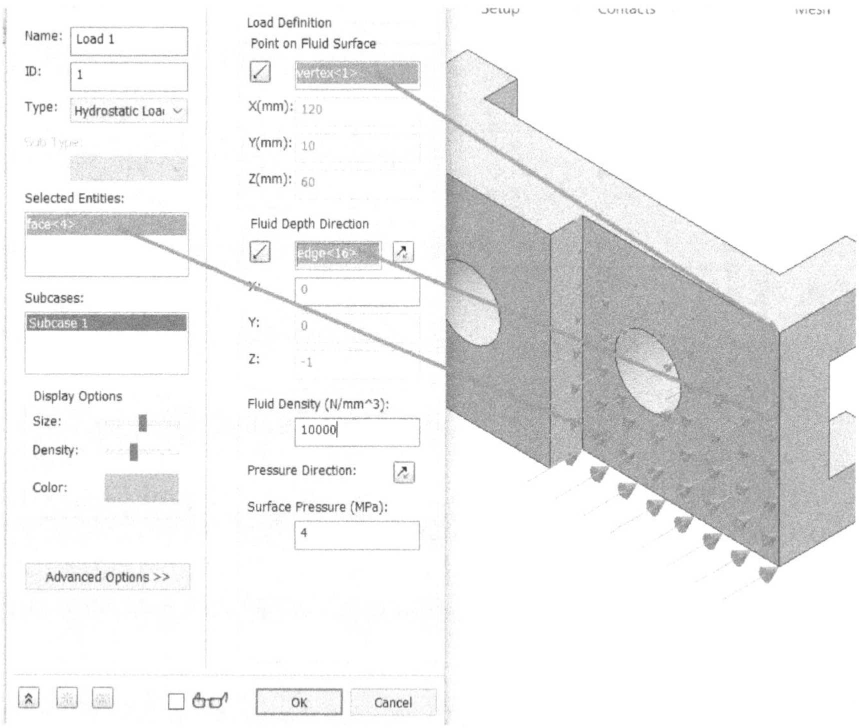

Figure-70. Preview of hydrostatic load

- Click on the **OK** button from the dialog box to create the load.

Applying Pressure and Gravity

The procedures to apply pressure and gravity are same as discussed earlier for force. Select the **Pressure** option from the **Type** drop-down to apply pressure and select the **Gravity** option from the **Type** drop-down to apply gravity load. On selecting the **Gravity** option, you need to select desired coordinate system from **Coordinate System** drop-down to be used for defining direction of gravity.

Applying Remote Force

The **Remote Force** option is used to apply effect of distant load at specified point. The procedure to apply remote force is given next.

- Select the **Remote Force** option from the **Type** drop-down. The options in the dialog box will be displayed as shown in Figure-71.
- Select the face on which you want to apply load.
- Click in the selection box of the **Remote Force Location** area and select the point at which remote force is located; refer to Figure-72.

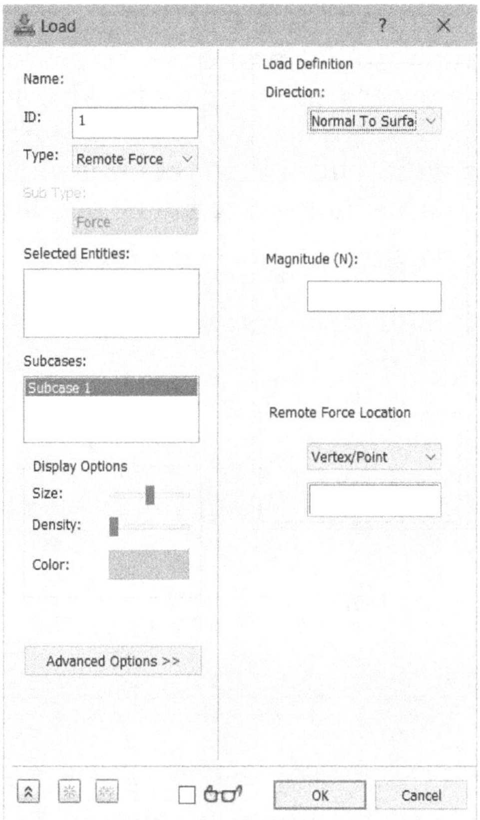

Figure-71. Load dialog box with Remote Force options

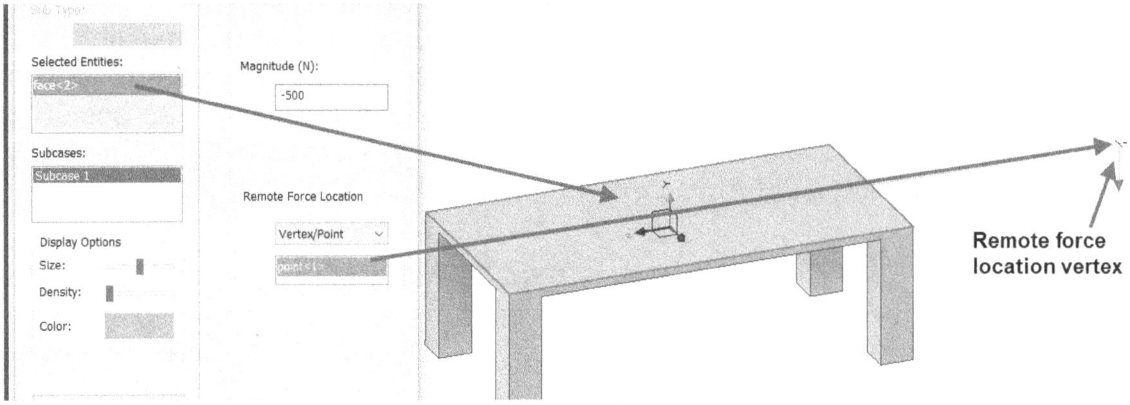

Figure-72. Applying remote force

- Specify desired value of remote force in **Magnitude** edit box.
- The advanced options are same as discussed earlier. Click on the **OK** button from the dialog box to apply load.

Applying Bearing Load

Bearing load is used to apply radial and axial forces on selected round faces to represent bearing load. The procedure to apply bearing load is given next.

- Select the **Bearing Load** option from the **Type** drop-down after activating the **Load** dialog box. The options in this dialog box will be displayed as shown in Figure-73.

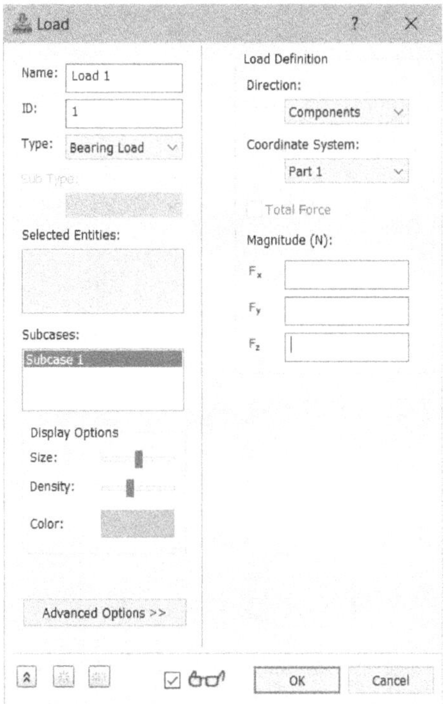

Figure-73. Load dialog box with Bearing Load options

- Select the round face on which bearing load is to be applied.
- Specify various components of bearing load in edit boxes of the **Magnitude** area; refer to Figure-74.

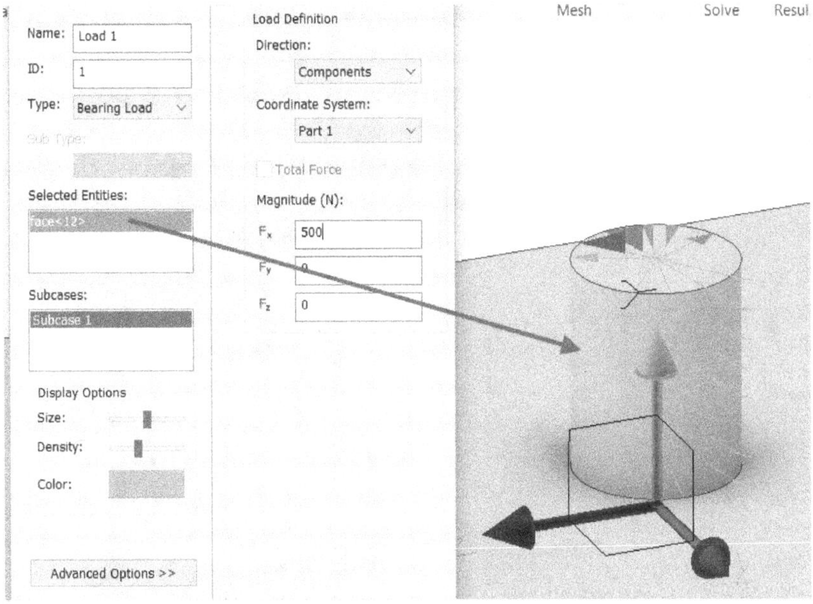

Figure-74. Applying bearing load

- After setting desired parameters, click on the **OK** button to apply bearing load.

Applying Rotational Force

Rotational force is applied to rotate the model at defined velocity and acceleration. The procedure is given next.

- Select the **Rotational Force** option from the **Type** drop-down after activating **Load** dialog box. The options in this dialog box will be displayed as shown in Figure-75.

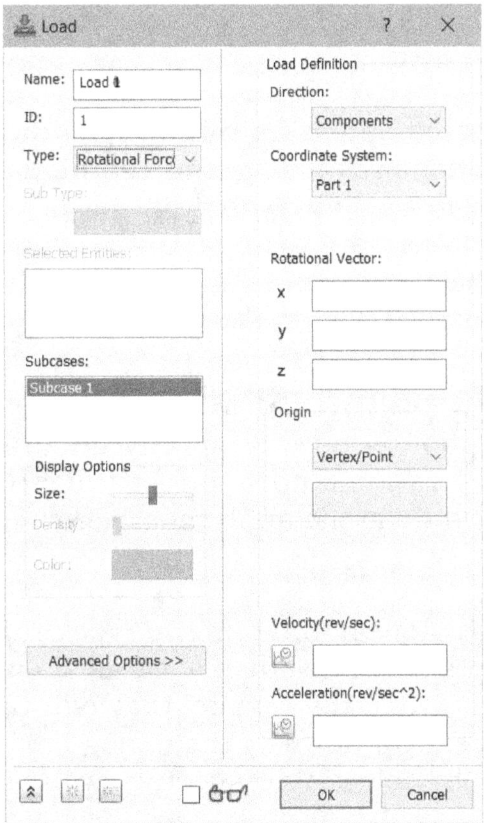

Figure-75. Load dialog box with Rotational Force options

- Click in the **Selected Entities** selection box and select the face of model on which you want to apply rotational force.
- Click in the selection box of **Origin** area and select the point on rotational axis to define origin for rotation; refer to Figure-76.
- Specify desired value of velocity and acceleration in respective edit boxes.

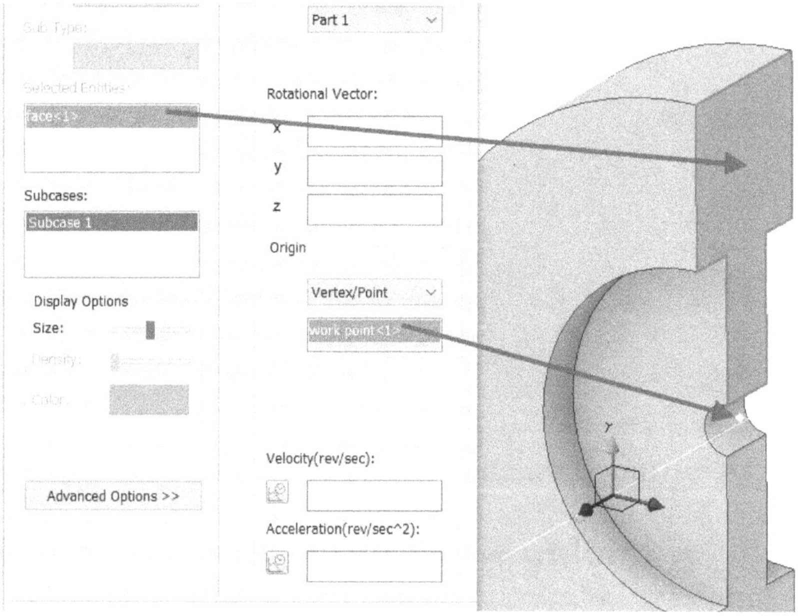

Figure-76. Applying rotational force

- Set desired parameters and click on the **OK** button.

Applying Enforced Motion Load

The **Enforced Motion** option is used to apply specified translation or rotation. The procedure to do so is given next.

- Select the **Enforced Motion** option from the **Type** drop-down after activating the **Load** dialog box. The options related to enforced motion will be displayed.
- Select desired option from the **Sub Type** drop-down.
- Select the face on which you want to apply translation or rotation and specify the related value in **Magnitude** edit box.
- After setting desired values, click on the **OK** button from the dialog box.

Applying Initial Condition

The **Initial Condition** option is used to specify initial conditions of analysis like temperature, velocity, acceleration, and so on for the study. The initial condition is applicable for nonlinear and dynamic analyses. The procedure to use this option is given next.

- Select the **Initial Condition** option from the **Type** drop-down after activating the **Load** dialog box. The options will be displayed as shown in Figure-77.
- Specify desired temperature in the **Temperature** edit box if **Temperature** option is selected in the **Sub Type** drop-down in the dialog box. Similarly, you can specify other initial conditions by selecting respective options from the **Sub Type** drop-down.
- After setting desired values, click on the **OK** button.

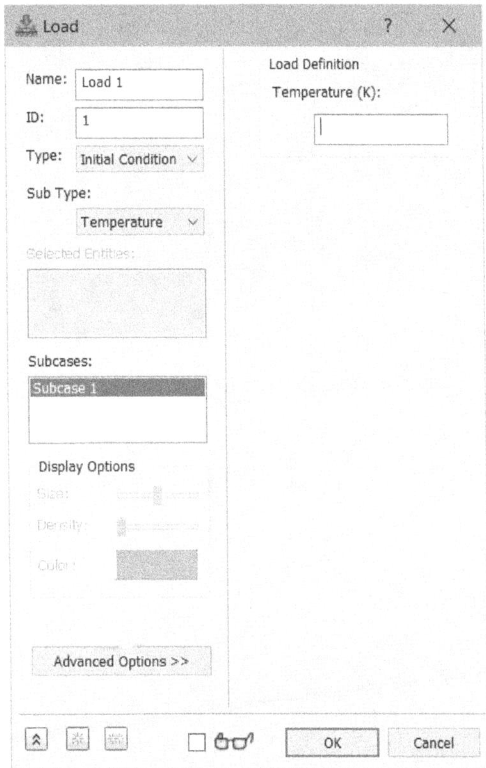

Figure-77. Load dialog box with Initial Condition options

Applying Body Temperature

The **Body Temperature** option is used to set desired temperature for the model. To set body temperature, select the **Body Temperature** option from the **Type** drop-down of **Load** dialog box. The options for body temperature are same as for initial condition of temperature. After setting desired parameters, click on the **OK** button.

Applying Temperature

The **Temperature** option is used to specify desired temperature to selected faces/edges/vertices. The procedure to use this option is given next.

- After activating the **Load** dialog box, select the **Temperature** option from the **Type** drop-down. The options in the dialog box will be displayed as shown in Figure-78.
- Select desired faces/edges/vertices to which you want to apply temperature.
- Specify desired temperature value in the **Temperature** edit box.
- Set other parameters as required and click on the **OK** button.

Figure-78. Load dialog box with Temperature options

Applying Thermal Convection

The **Convection** option is used to apply thermal convection coefficient to selected faces/edges/vertices. The procedure to use this tool is given next.

- Select the **Convection** option from the **Type** drop-down in the **Load** dialog box. The options in the dialog box will be displayed as shown in Figure-79.
- Select the faces/edges/vertices on which you want to specify heat convection source.
- Specify surrounding environment temperature in **Ambient Temperature** edit box.
- Specify the convection coefficient value in the **Convection Coefficient** edit box.
- If you want to make convection rate temperature dependent then select the **Temperature Dependence** check box. The table options below it will become active. Click on the **Define New Table** button to define convection coefficient at different temperatures. The **Table Data** dialog box will be displayed; refer to Figure-80.

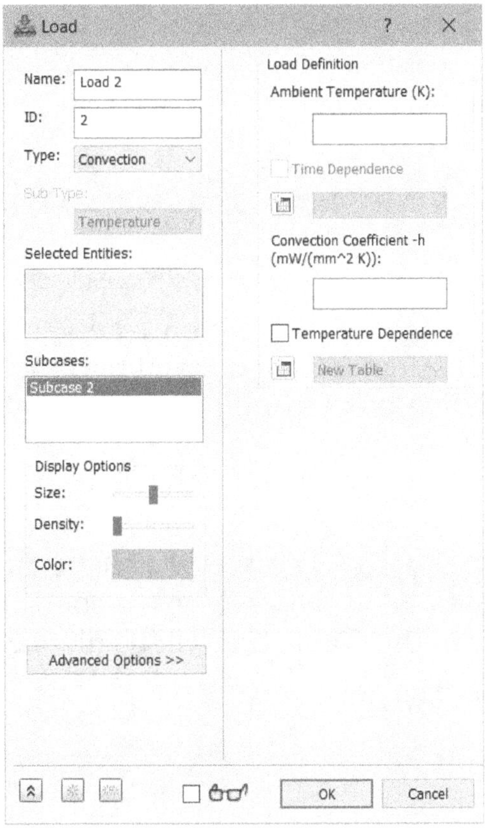

Figure-79. Load dialog box with Convection options

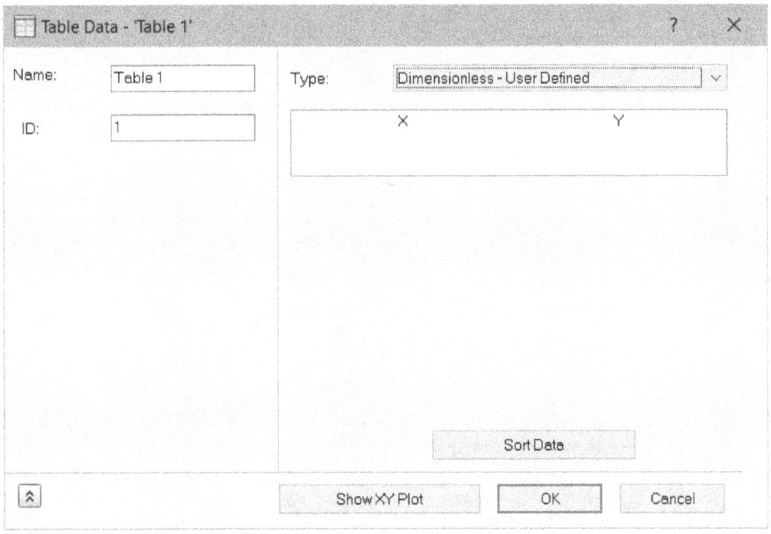

Figure-80. Table Data dialog box

- Select the **Convection Coefficient vs. Temperature** option from the **Type** drop-down to specify convection coefficients at different temperatures.
- Double-click in the fields and specify desired values; refer to Figure-81.

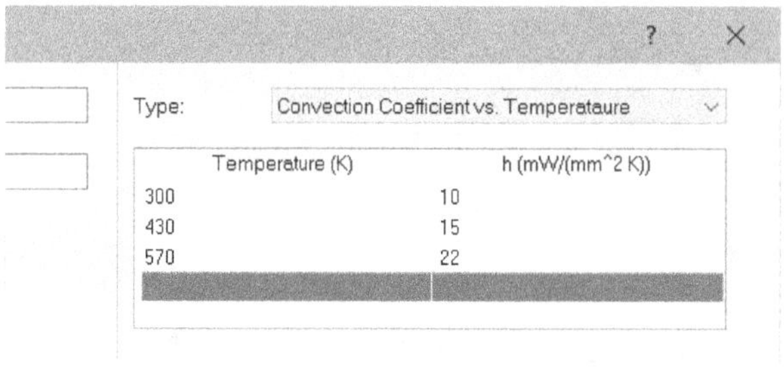

Figure-81. Convection rates specified for temperatures

- If you want to check the plot of convection rate v/s temperature then click on the **Show XY Plot** button. After setting desired parameters, click on the **OK** button from the **Table Data** dialog box to apply convection coefficient. The **Load** dialog box will be displayed again.
- After setting desired parameters, click on the **OK** button from the **Load** dialog box.

Applying Thermal Radiation

- After activating the **Load** dialog box, select the **Radiation** option from the **Type** drop-down. The options in the dialog box will be displayed as shown in Figure-82.

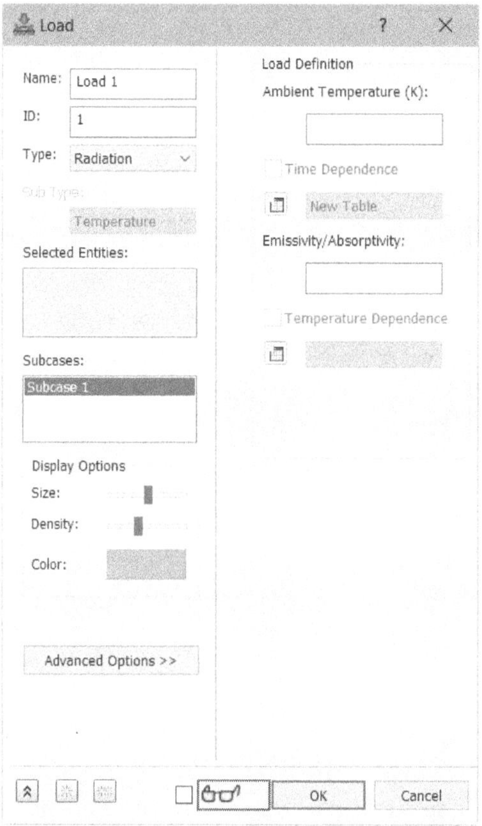

Figure-82. Load dialog box with Radiation options

- Select the faces/edges/vertices on which you want to apply radiation heat.
- Specify desired values for temperature, absorptivity/emissivity, and so on in respective edit boxes of the dialog box.
- After setting desired parameters, click on the **OK** button.

Applying Heat Generation

The **Heat Generation** option is used to apply heat generation at selected faces/edges/vertices. The procedure to use this option is given next.

- Select the **Heat Generation** option from the **Type** drop-down. The options in the dialog box will be displayed as shown in Figure-83.

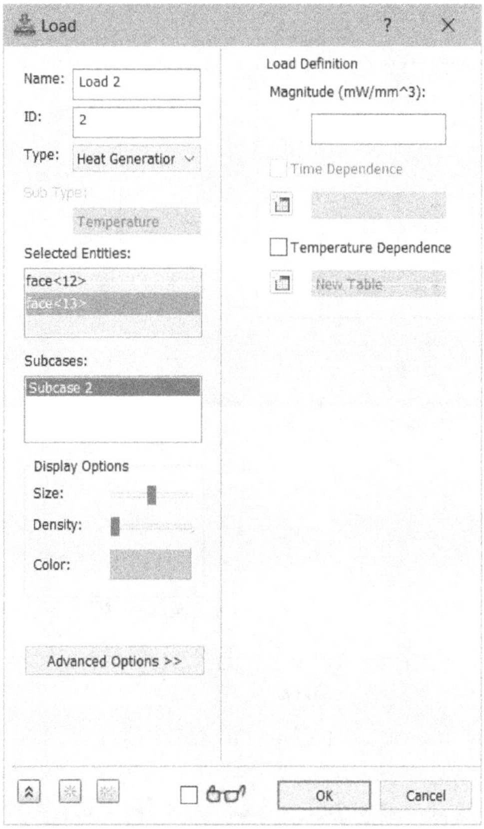

Figure-83. Load dialog box with Heat Generation options

- Select the faces/edges/vertices to which you want to specify heat generation rate.
- Specify desired value of heat generation in the **Magnitude** edit box.
- Set the other options as discussed earlier and click on the **OK** button to apply load.

Applying Heat Flux

Heat Flux is the heat flow rate intensity per unit of area per unit time. The procedure to apply heat flux is given next.

- After activating **Load** dialog box, select the **Heat Flux** option from the **Type** drop-down. The options in the **Load** dialog box will be displayed as shown in Figure-84.

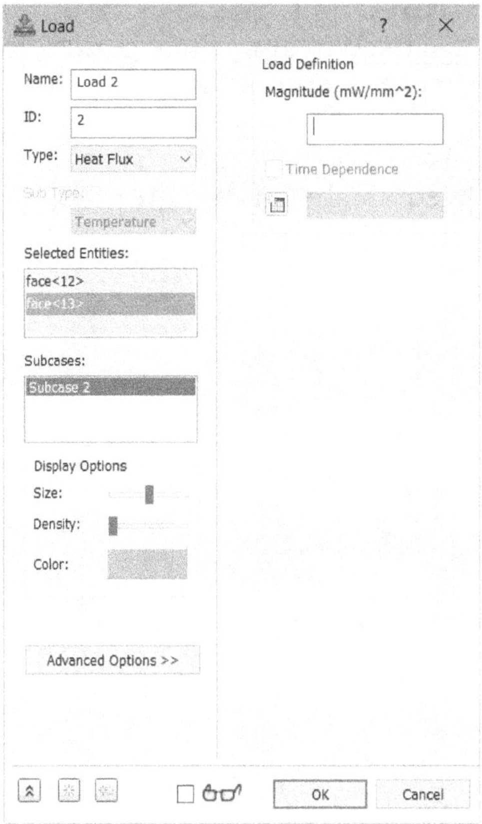

Figure-84. Load dialog box with Heat Flux options

- Select the faces/edges/vertices to which you want to apply heat flux and specify desired heat flux value in **Magnitude** edit box.
- After setting desired values, click on the **OK** button from the dialog box.

Applying Loads based on Analysis Results

- Select the **From Output** option from the **Type** drop-down. The options of **Loads** dialog box will be displayed as shown in Figure-85.
- Click on the **Browse** button next to **Results File** edit box. The **Open** dialog box will be displayed; refer to Figure-86.

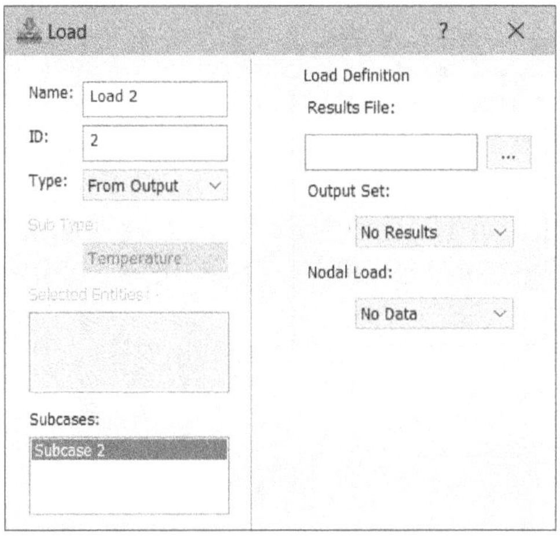

Figure-85. Load dialog box with From Output options

- Select desired result file (.fno or .cfdst) and click on the **Open** button. The nodal load and output set parameters will be displayed in respective drop-downs.

- Set desired parameters and click on the **OK** button to apply loads.

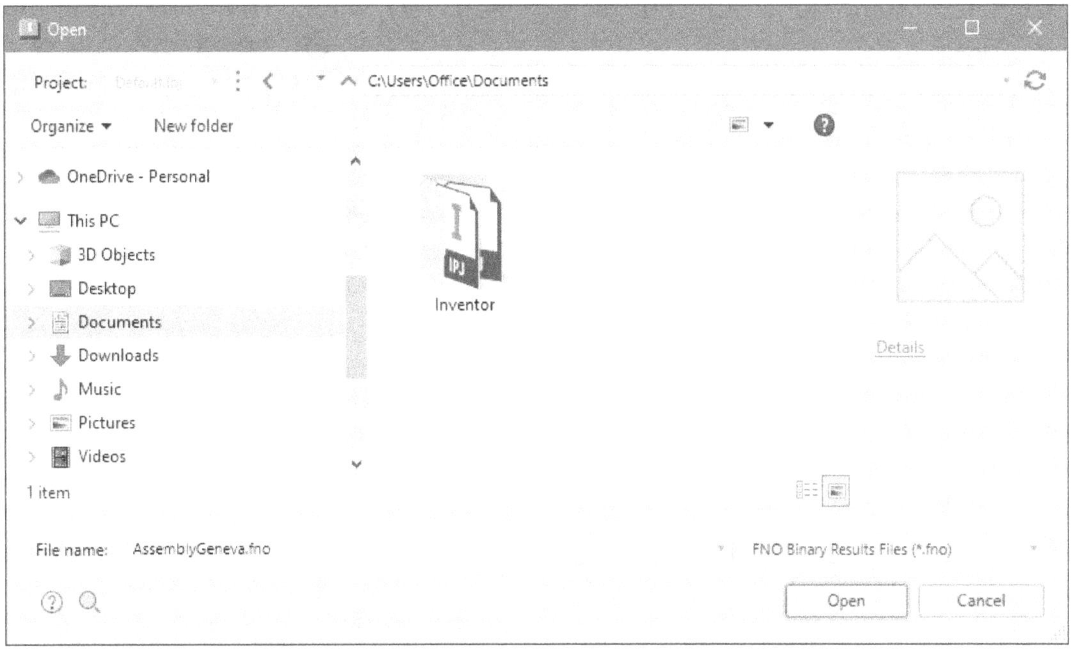

Figure-86. Open dialog box

Applying Rigid Motion (Explicit)

The **Rigid Motion (Explicit)** load is used to enforce time-varying motions on a rigid body. The procedure to apply this load is given next.

- After activating **Load** dialog box, select the **Rigid Motion (Explicit)** option from the **Type** drop-down. The options in the **Load** dialog box will be displayed as shown in Figure-87.

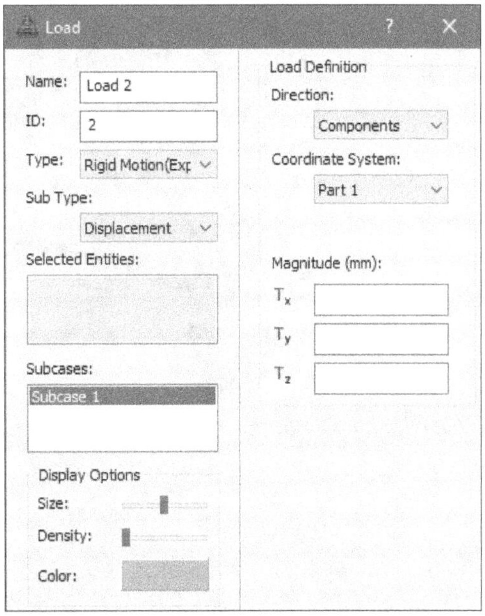

Figure-87. Load dialog box with Rigid Motion options

- Select the Solid body to which you want to apply the Rigid Motion load.
- Specify desired values of rigid motion in the edit boxes of **Magnitude** area.
- After setting desired parameters, click on **OK** button to apply **Rigid Motion** load.

DEFINING CONTACT SETS

There are three tools to define contact sets in Autodesk Inventor Nastran which are **Auto**, **Manual**, and **Solver**. Contacts are used to define how elements of meshes connect with each other at the contact surface for two components of an assembly. The procedures to use these tools are discussed next.

Applying Automatic Contact Sets

The **Auto** tool is used to automatically assign default contacts between various components of the assembly. The procedure to set contacts automatically is given next.

- Click on the **Auto** tool from the **Contacts** panel in the **Autodesk Inventor Nastran** tab of **Ribbon**. The information box will be displayed; refer to Figure-88.

Figure-88. Detecting Automatic Contacts information box

- Once the detection is complete, the contacts will be applied automatically which is generally bonded type; refer to Figure-89. You can change default contact type for your analysis by selecting desired option from the **Contact Type** drop-down in **Options** tab of **Analysis** dialog box; refer to Figure-90. The options of this dialog box have been discussed earlier.

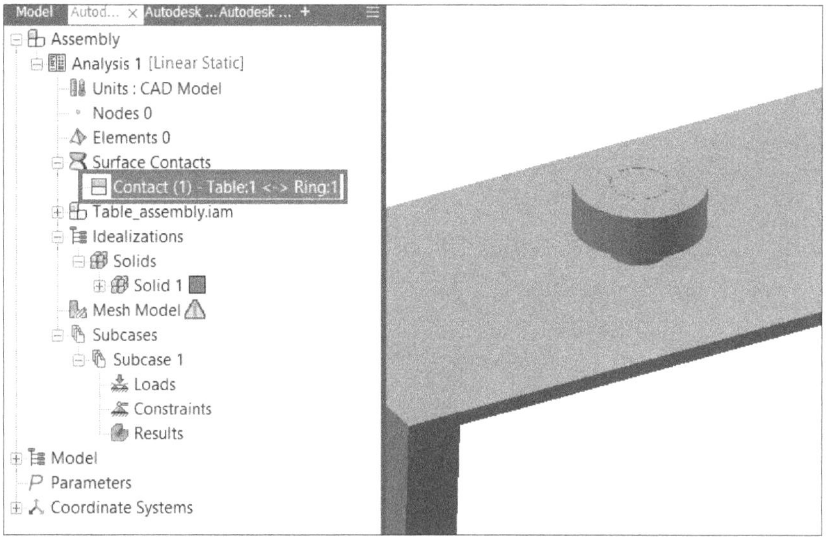

Figure-89. Contact applied automatically

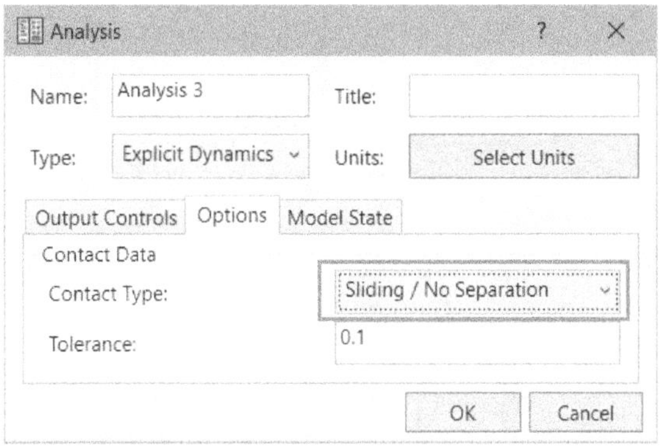

Figure-90. Contact Type drop-down

Applying Manual Contacts

The **Manual** tool in the **Contacts** panel is used to apply different types of contacts manually to assembly components. The procedure to use this tool is given next.

- Click on the **Manual** tool from the **Contacts** panel in the **Autodesk Inventor Nastran** tab of **Ribbon**. The **Surface Contact** dialog box will be displayed; refer to Figure-91.
- Specify desired name and id for contact in **Name** and **ID** edit boxes, respectively.
- Select desired contact type from the **Contact Type** drop-down. The options in this drop-down are **Separation**, **Bonded**, **Sliding/No Separation**, **Separation/No Sliding**, **Offset Bonded**, **Shrink Fit/Sliding**, **Shrink Fit/No Sliding**, and **Disable**. Select the **Separation** option if there is one object placed over another without any bonding. This type of contact allows both sliding and gap between selected faces. Select the **Bonded** option if the selected surfaces are bonded together. In case of metals, you can assume that the two surfaces are welded together. Select the **Sliding/No Separation** option if you want the objects to be bonded at selected surfaces in such a way that they cannot move up or down but they can slide over one another. Note that friction is not applied in case of this contact. Select the **Separation/No Sliding** option if you want components to form gap in case of load application but do not want them to slide over one another. This option is applicable for non-linear analyses only. Select the **Offset Bonded** option if you want the objects to be welded at selected surfaces while maintaining specified gap between them. Select the **Shrink Fit/Sliding** option if you want to apply initial interference between the part and allow sliding. Select the **Shrink Fit/No Sliding** option if you want to apply initial interference between the part and do not allow sliding between parts. Select the **Disable** option from the **Type** drop-down to disable any contact between selected surfaces. Note that for explicit type of analyses, you can apply only bonded and separation contacts. Figure-92 shows output of different contact types for same analysis.

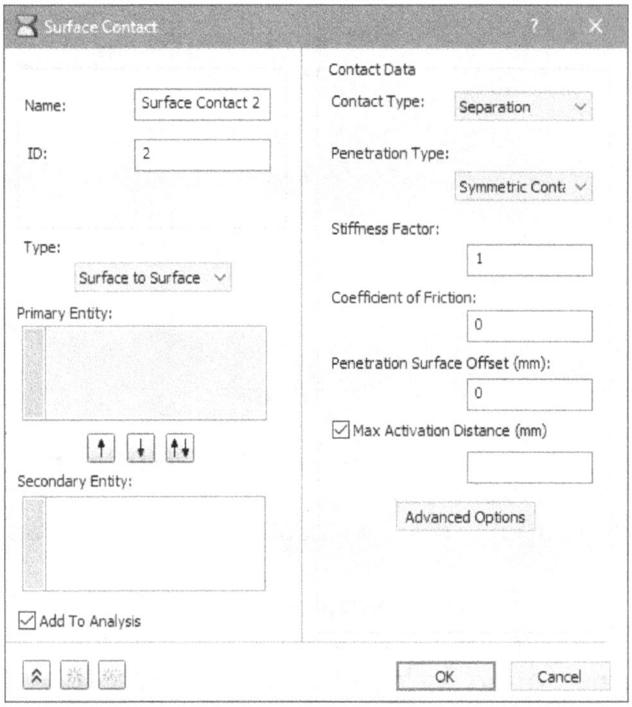

Figure-91. Surface Contact dialog box

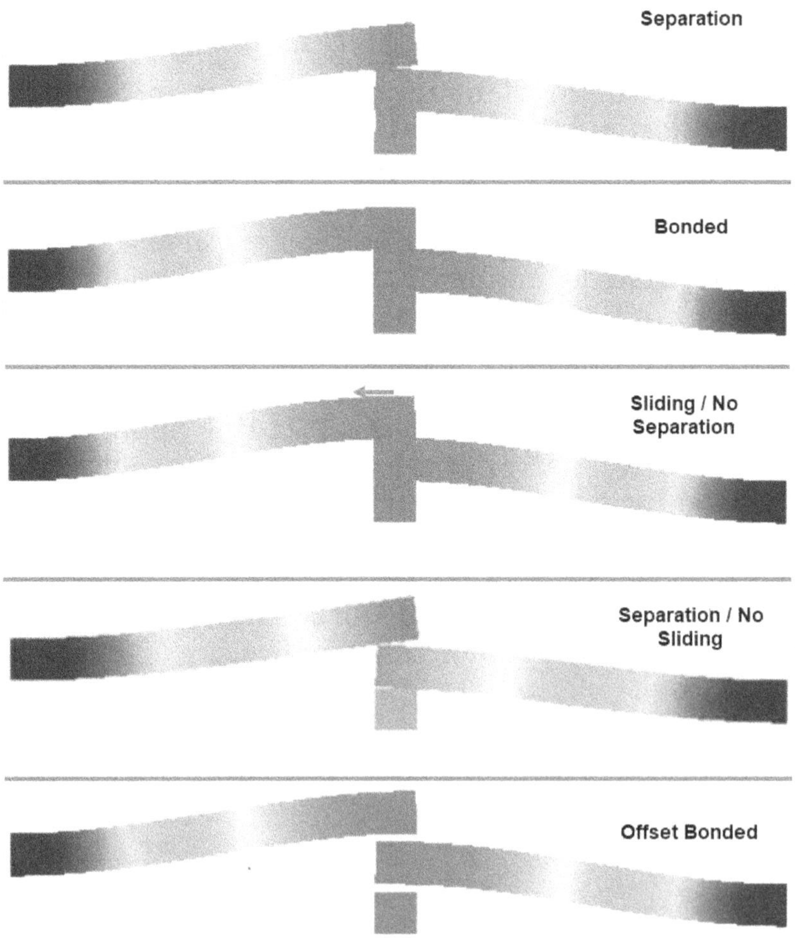

Figure-92. Output for common contact types

- Select desired option from the **Penetration Type** drop-down to define penetration of master slave nodes during analysis. This drop-down is not available if the **Edge to Surface** option is selected in **Type** drop-down or **Offset Bonded**, **Shrink Fit/Sliding**, or **Shrink Fit/No Sliding** option is selected in the **Contact Type** drop-down of the dialog box. There are two options available in **Penetration Type** drop-down viz. **Unsymmetric Contact** and **Symmetric Contact**. Select the **Unsymmetric Contact** option if you want to check the penetration of slave nodes in master node. This option produces fast result at the loss of accuracy. Select the **Symmetric Contact** option if you want to check the penetration of both master and slave nodes. This option uses extra resources to produce result hence increasing the processing time.
- Specify desired value of stiffness factor at contact site in the **Stiffness Factor** edit box.
- Specify desired value of friction coefficient at the contact site in **Coefficient of Friction** edit box.
- Specify desired value in **Penetration Surface Offset (mm)** edit box to define the depth up to which two surfaces will penetrate. Make sure to provide a realistic value otherwise the analysis will not converge.
- Set the parameters in other edit boxes as discussed earlier.
- Click in the **Primary Entity** selection box and select the contacting face of first component.
- Click in the **Secondary Entity** selection box and select the contacting face of second component; refer to Figure-93.

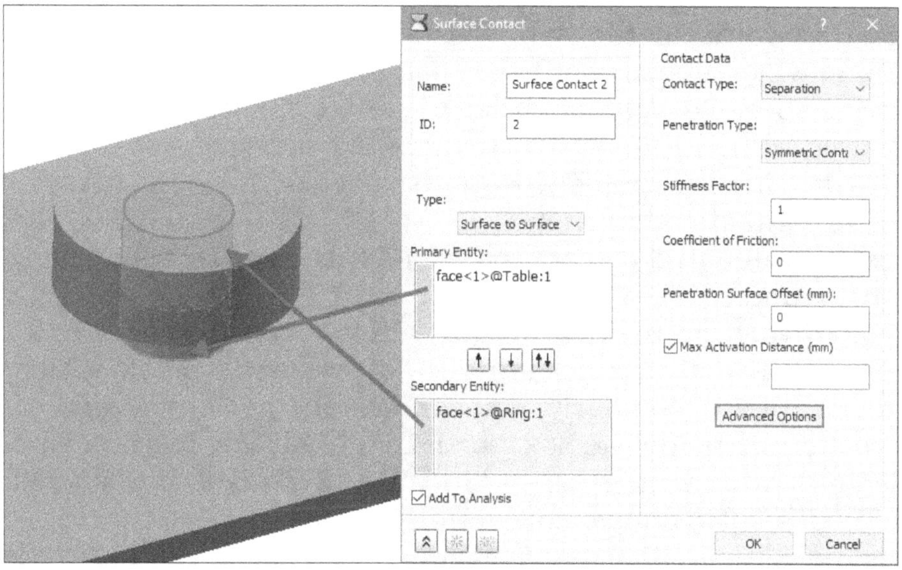

Figure-93. Faces selected for contact

Advanced Contact Options

- Click on the **Advanced Options** button to set advanced parameters for contact. The **Contact Parameters** dialog box will be displayed; refer to Figure-94. The options in this dialog box are divided into two area: **General** and **Weld Damage Model**. If you are trying to simulate a welded joint between two components then options in the **Weld Damage Model** area provide the options for represent that contact. Note that for welding contact type **Offset Bonded** is generally used because in reality there is a gap between the two parts till they have been welded. Various options of the dialog box are given next.

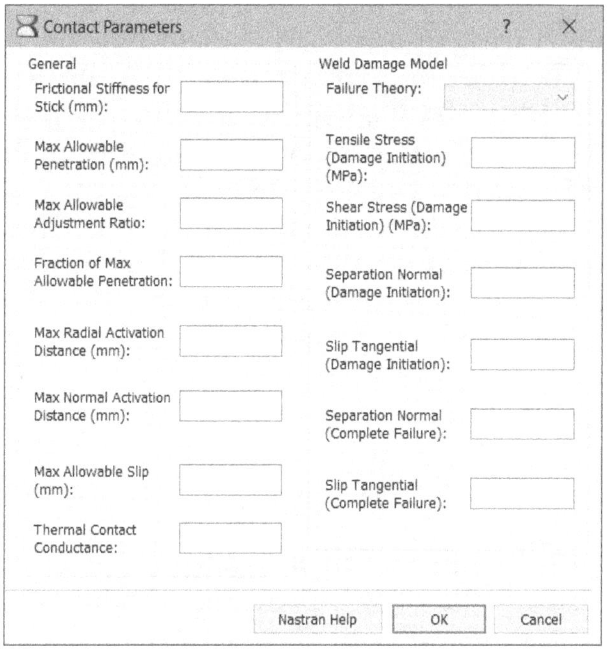

Figure-94. Contact Parameters dialog box

- Specify desired value in **Frictional Stiffness for Stick** edit box to define the sliding distance up to which contacting parts will be held together before slip occurs due to external load. Once the contacting parts have slide over one another up to specified distance, there are free to break the contact or slide like roller skates!! (Read about Stick-slip phenomena on Internet for more information).
- Specify desired value in the **Max Allowable Penetration** edit box to define distance up to which nodes of one part can penetrate into another part. Note that penetration is specified perpendicular to contact plane.
- Specify desired value in the **Max Allowable Adjustment Ratio** edit box to define variation allowed in contact node locations based on previous iterations of analysis for improving contacts adaptively.
- Specify desired value in the **Fraction of Max Allowable Penetration** edit box to define lower bound of allowable penetration.
- Specify desired value in the **Max Radial Activation Distance** edit box to define radial distance between contact surfaces of two parts below which the selected contact will be applied. Similarly, you can specify the activation distance value in normal direction by using the **Max Normal Activation Distance** edit box.
- Specify desired value in the **Max Allowable Slip** edit box to define allowable slipping of nodes between two contacting faces.
- Specify desired value in **Thermal Contact Conductance** edit box to define thermal conductivity of the nodes at contact region. This option is useful if you are using brazing or other joint techniques for joining two parts under analysis and the thermal conductivity of material is different for the joint.

Weld Damage Model Options

- Select desired option from the **Failure Theory** drop-down to define method to be used for analyzing damage of weld joints. There are two options available in this drop-down which are **Weld Failure Model** and **Cohesive Zone Model**. The Weld Failure Model uses two modes for checking failure which are Stress based weld failure and Deformation based weld failure. Select the Stress based Weld Damage Model theory if welded (Bonded) contact is applied in the model. Select the Deformation based Weld Damage Model theory if offset weld (Offset Bonded) contact is applied in the model. The Cohesive Zone Model theory also supports only bonded contact. Cohesive Zone Model theory works on crack propagation at the weld joint due to load and predict the failure of joint.
- Specify the parameters in **Weld Damage Model** area as discussed earlier and click on the **OK** button. The **Surface Contact** dialog box will be displayed again.
- Click on the **OK** button from the dialog box to apply the contact and exit the dialog box.

Defining Solver Settings

The **Solver** tool in the **Contacts** panel is used to specify the region in which contacts will be applied automatically and the parameters like stiffness factor, friction coefficient, and so on which will be applied at runtime of analysis. The procedure to use this tool is given next.

- Click on the **Solver** tool from the **Contacts** panel in the **Autodesk Inventor Nastran** tab of the **Ribbon**. The **Surface Contact** dialog box will be displayed as shown in Figure-95.

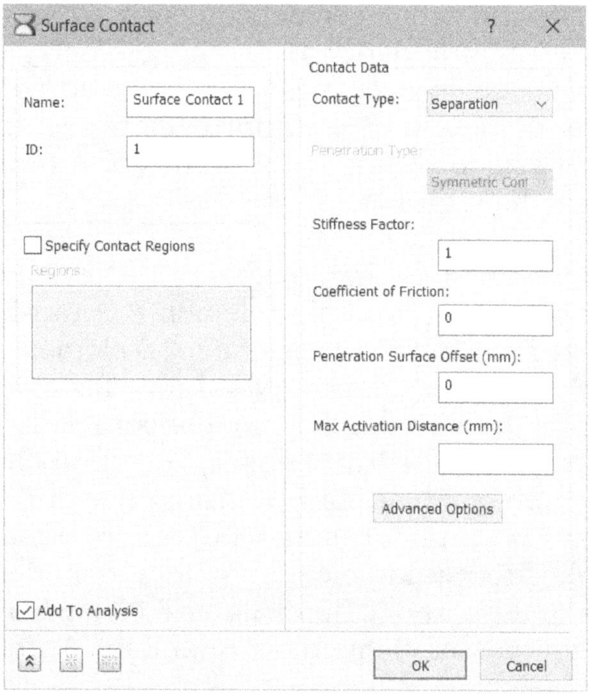

Figure-95. Surface Contact dialog box with Solver options

- Select the contact type which you want to apply from the **Contact Type** drop-down.
- By default, complete model is analyzed to apply contacts. If you want to define a specific region in which contacts will be applied automatically then select the **Specify Contact Regions** check box. The **Regions** selection box will become active.
- Select the edges/faces/solids to define region; refer to Figure-96.

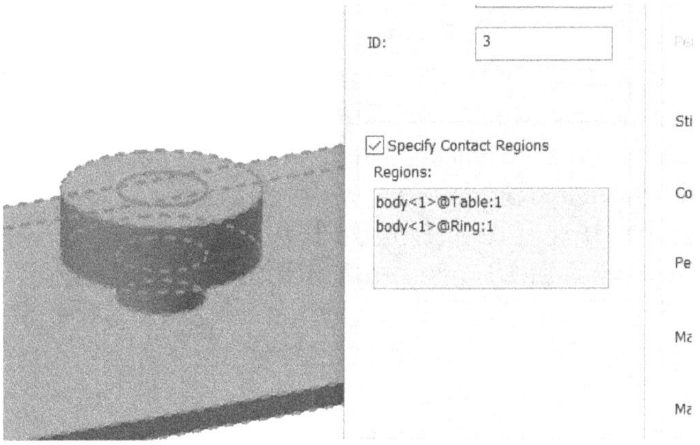

Figure-96. Region selected to define auto contacts

- After setting desired parameters, click on the **OK** button. The contact will be created.

MESHING

Meshing is the base of FEM. Meshing divides the solid/shell models into elements of finite size and shape. These elements are joined at common points called nodes. These nodes define the load transfer from one element to other element. Meshing is a very crucial step in design analysis. The automatic mesher in the software generates a mesh based on specified global element size, tolerance, and local mesh control specifications. Mesh control lets you specify different sizes of elements for components, faces, edges, and vertices.

The software estimates a global element size for the model taking into consideration its volume, surface area, and other geometric details. The size of generated mesh (number of nodes and elements) depends on the geometry and dimensions of the model, element size, mesh tolerance, mesh control, and contact specifications. In the early stages of design analysis where approximate results may suffice, you can specify a larger element size for a faster solution. For a more accurate solution, a smaller element size may be required.

Meshing generates 3D tetrahedral solid elements, 2D quadrilateral and triangular shell elements, and 1D beam, bar, and pipe elements. A mesh consists of one type of elements unless the mixed mesh type is specified. 3D elements are naturally suitable for bulky models. 2D elements are naturally suitable for modeling thin parts (sheet metals), and 1D elements are suitable for modeling structural members. Autodesk Inventor Nastran uses linear tetrahedral (4 nodes) and parabolic tetrahedral (10 nodes) elements for solid objects. For Shell objects, triangular and quadrilateral elements are available with linear (1st) and parabolic(2nd) orders. Linear triangular elements have 3 nodes, parabolic triangular elements have 6 nodes, linear quadrilateral elements have 4 nodes and parabolic quadrilateral elements have 8 nodes. For line objects, there are three types of elements available in Autodesk Inventor Nastran Beam, Bar, and Pipe.

Defining Mesh Settings

The **Mesh Settings** tool in **Mesh** panel is used to define global mesh size, element order, tolerance, and other related parameters. The procedure to apply mesh settings is given next.

- Click on the **Mesh Settings** tool from the **Mesh** panel in **Autodesk Inventor Nastran** tab of **Ribbon**. The **Mesh Settings** dialog box will be displayed; refer to Figure-97.

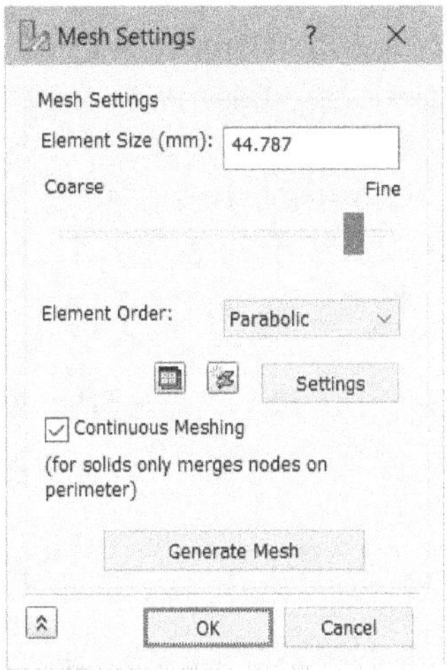

Figure-97. Mesh Settings dialog box

- Specify desired value of element size in the **Element Size** edit box. You can also define mesh size by using the slider. Moving slider towards **Coarse** makes the mesh element size large and moving slider towards **Fine** makes the mesh element size smaller.
- Select the **Parabolic** option from the **Element Order** drop-down to create 2nd order elements. Select the **Linear** option from the **Element Order** drop-down to create 1st order elements. Selecting **Parabolic** option for 3D objects increases the computing process but gives more accurate solutions for irregular shaped objects. Selecting **Linear** option gives faster results due to lesser variables involved in iterations of analysis but can give less accurate results for irregular objects.
- Click on the **Settings** button to define advanced parameters for meshing. The **Advanced Mesh Settings** dialog box will be displayed; refer to Figure-98.

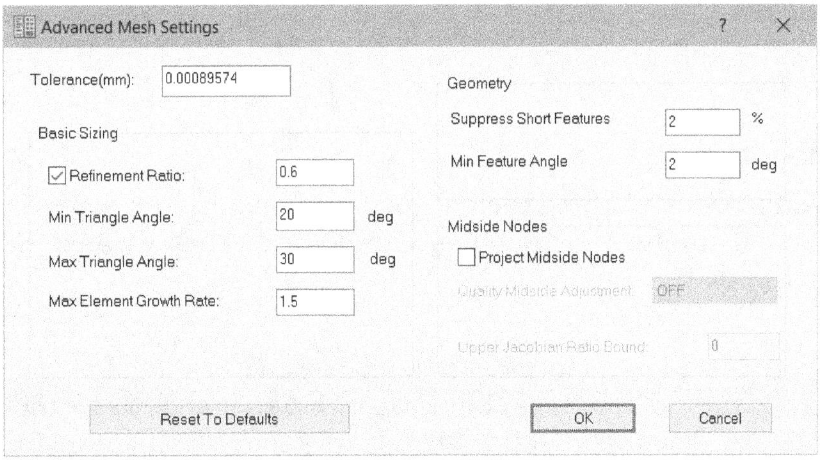

Figure-98. Advanced Mesh Settings dialog box

- Specify minimum tolerance value up to which mesh elements will be created.
- Select the **Refinement Ratio** check box to set mesh size more uniform. The larger the refinement ratio, the larger is the mesh size. Specify desired refinement ratio in the **Refinement Ratio** edit box.
- Specify minimum triangle angle and maximum triangle angle values in **Min Triangle Angle** and **Max Triangle Angle** edit boxes respectively.
- Specify desired element growth rate in **Max Element Growth Rate** edit box.

- Specify desired value in **Suppress Short Features** edit box to define the percentage of small features like holes, bumps etc. to be suppressed for meshing.
- Specify desired value in degree in **Min Feature Angle** edit box to specify the mesh angle around complex features like holes, edges etc. This is the minimum angle value to be considered for meshing below this value, the angle features of faces will be suppressed.
- Select the **Project Midside Nodes** check box to define parameters related to midside nodes. Midside nodes are created on elements along curves and edges of model. On selecting this check box, the options in the **Midside Nodes** area become active.
- Select desired option from the **Quality Midside Adjustment** drop-down. Select **ON** option from the drop-down to automatically adjust mid side nodes for generating positive Jacobian ratio.
- Specify desired value in **Upper Jacobian Ratio Bound** edit box to define the quality of midside nodes.
- After setting parameters, click on the **OK** button. The **Mesh Settings** dialog box will be displayed again.

Mesh Table Parameters

- Click on the **Mesh Table** button from the **Mesh Settings** dialog box to define size of mesh. The **Mesh Table** dialog box will be displayed; refer to Figure-99. You can display the same dialog box by clicking on **Table** button in **Mesh** panel.

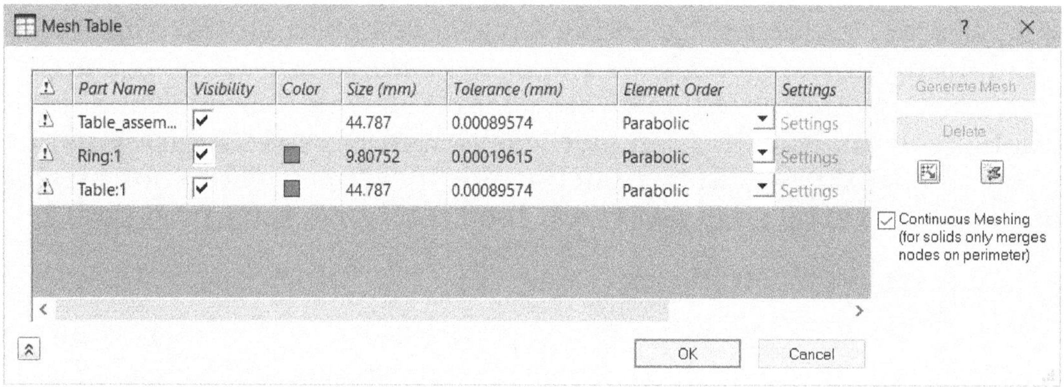

Figure-99. Mesh Table dialog box

- Click in the edit boxes under **Size** column and specify the size of mesh elements. Set the other parameters for each of the components in assembly in the table and click on the **OK** button.

Generating Mesh

- After setting all the parameters, click on the **Generate Mesh** tool from the **Mesh** panel of **Autodesk Inventor Nastran** tab in **Ribbon**. An information box will be displayed and the mesh will be generated; refer to Figure-100.

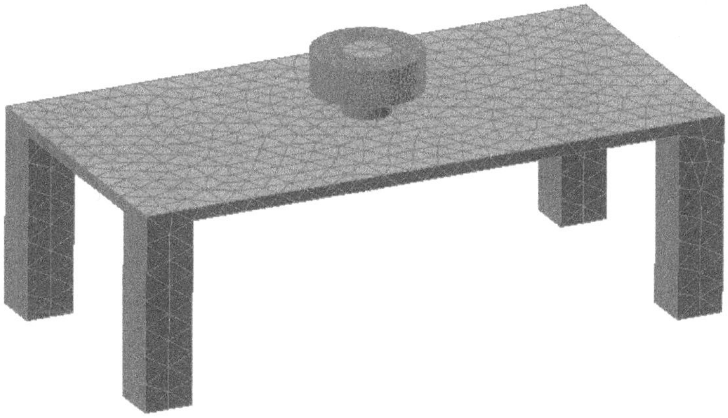

Figure-100. Mesh generated

Setting Mesh Control

The **Mesh Control** tool is used to set fine or coarse mesh at selected locations. The procedure to use this tool is given next.

- Click on the **Mesh Control** tool from the **Mesh** panel in **Autodesk Inventor Nastran** tab of **Ribbon**. The **Mesh Control** dialog box will be displayed; refer to Figure-101.

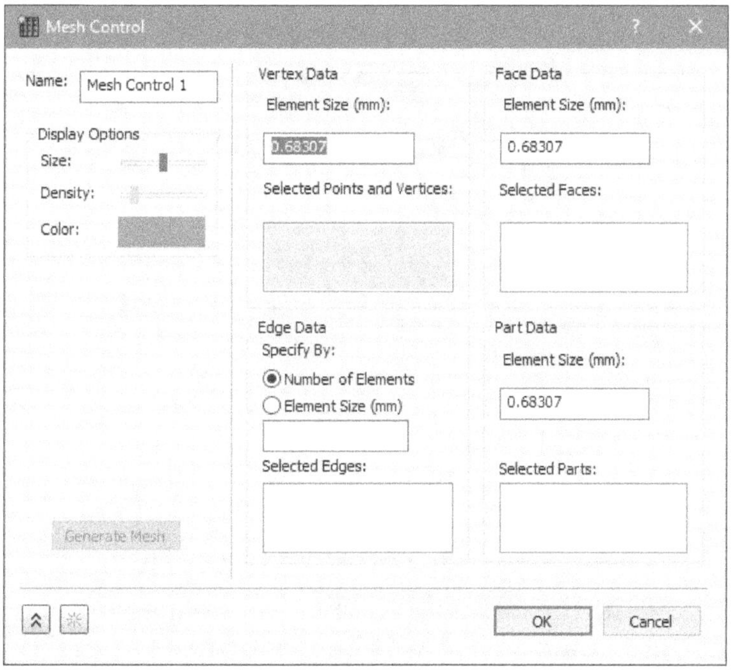

Figure-101. Mesh Control dialog box

- Click in the **Selected Points and Vertices** selection box and select the points/ vertices on which you want to apply mesh control.
- Specify desired element size in the **Element Size** edit box above the selection box to define mesh size.
- Similarly, you can use the other options to define mesh element sizes for faces, edges, or parts. Note that higher the number of elements in mesh, more time it will take to solve the analysis.
- After setting desired parameters, click on the **OK** button.

Adaptive Meshing using Convergence Settings

Adaptive meshing is technique used to modify the size of mesh elements based on geometry of model and accuracy of results generated by iterations running. Note that when using adaptive meshing, the element sizes are updated after each iteration till you get to the parameters specified in **Convergence Settings** dialog box. The procedure to use options of this dialog box are discussed next.

Note: Mesh convergence is available only for Linear static analysis. You can not use it for other types of analyses in Autodesk Inventor Nastran. Also, the convergence is applicable to solid tetrahedral elements. It is not available for shell and line elements in Inventor Nastran.

- Click on the **Convergence Settings** tool from the **Mesh** panel in the **Autodesk Inventor Nastran** tab of the **Ribbon**. The **Convergence Settings** dialog box will be displayed; refer to Figure-102.
- Select the **Global Refinement** radio button from dialog box if you want to apply uniform adaptive meshing refinement to all the elements in the model. In this case, software may generate a very large number of elements which are unnecessary for accuracy of analysis. Select the **Local Refinement** radio button if you want to refine only local regions of model with maximum error as compared to rest of the model.

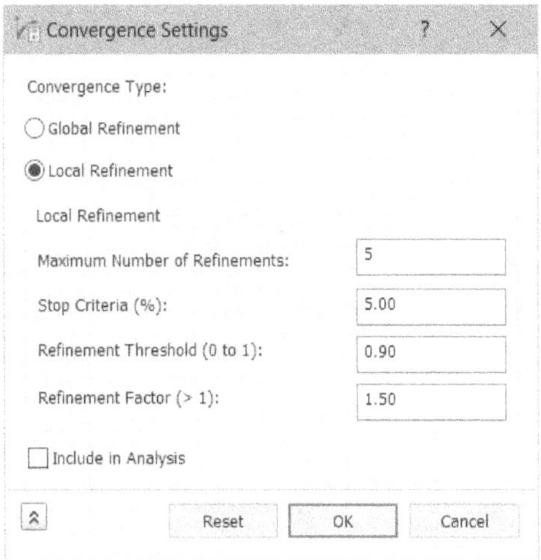

Figure-102. Convergence Settings dialog box

- Specify desired value in the **Maximum Number of Refinements** edit box to define the number of times refinement cycle will be performed on mesh during analysis to increase accuracy of result.
- Specify desired value in the **Stop Criteria** edit box to define element size difference between current element and next refined element at which h-refinement will stop. For example, if current element size is 3 mm and next refined element size is 2.95 then refinement ratio is 100 x (3-2.95)/3 = 1.67%. If you have specified stop criteria value as 5% then refinement will stop but if you have specified 1% then refinement will continue up to specified number of refinements.
- If you are working with **Global Refinement** option then **Error Threshold** edit box will be displayed. Specify desired value in this edit box to define threshold strain energy error at which refinement will be stopped. If the strain energy error is less than or equal to this value then there will be no further refinement in mesh. System calculates this error value by using the formula given next.

$$Error = \sqrt{\frac{Strain\ Enery\ Error}{Total\ Strain\ Energy + Strain\ Energy\ Error}}$$

- If you are working with **Local Refinement** option then **Refinement Threshold** and **Refinement Factor** edit boxes will be displayed in the dialog box. Specify desired value in the **Refinement Threshold** edit box to define percentage of elements with maximum error that will be considered for further refinement. For example if 0.95 is specified in this edit box then only top 5% elements with errors will be considered for next refinement. Specify desired value in the **Refinement Factor** edit box to define growth rate by which number of elements will increase in each refinement. If you have specified the value as 2 then number of elements will double on each refinement. Note that only the elements that fall under specified refinement threshold will be increased not all the elements.
- Select the **Include in Analysis** check box to include mesh convergence in current analysis. If the check box is not selected then no refinement will be performed in analysis.
- After specifying desired parameters, click on the **OK** button to apply mesh convergence criteria and exit the dialog box.

Mesh Troubleshooting

The **Mesh Troubleshooter** tool is used to check for errors in the generated mesh and perform repairs in the model/mesh to get optimum result. The procedure to use this tool is given next.

- Click on the **Mesh Troubleshooter** tool from the **Mesh** group in the **Autodesk Inventor Nastran** tab of the **Ribbon**. The **Mesh Troubleshooter** dialog box will be displayed; refer to Figure-103.

Figure-103. Mesh Troubleshooter dialog box

- If there are errors in the mesh then they will be displayed in the bottom section of dialog box and faces/sections of model causing the error will be displayed in the top section of the dialog box. Use the options to identify problem faces and rectify the issues.

RUNNING ANALYSIS

Once you have set the parameters for analysis, click on the **Run** button from the **Solve** panel of **Autodesk Inventor Nastran** tab in the **Ribbon**. The system will start solving the analysis. Once the analysis is complete, an information box will be displayed; refer to Figure-104. Click on the **OK** button from the information box. The results will be displayed; refer to Figure-105.

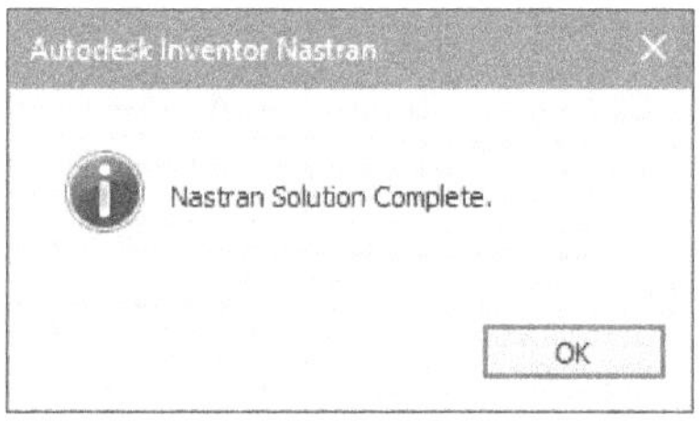

Figure-104. Autodesk Inventor Nastran information box

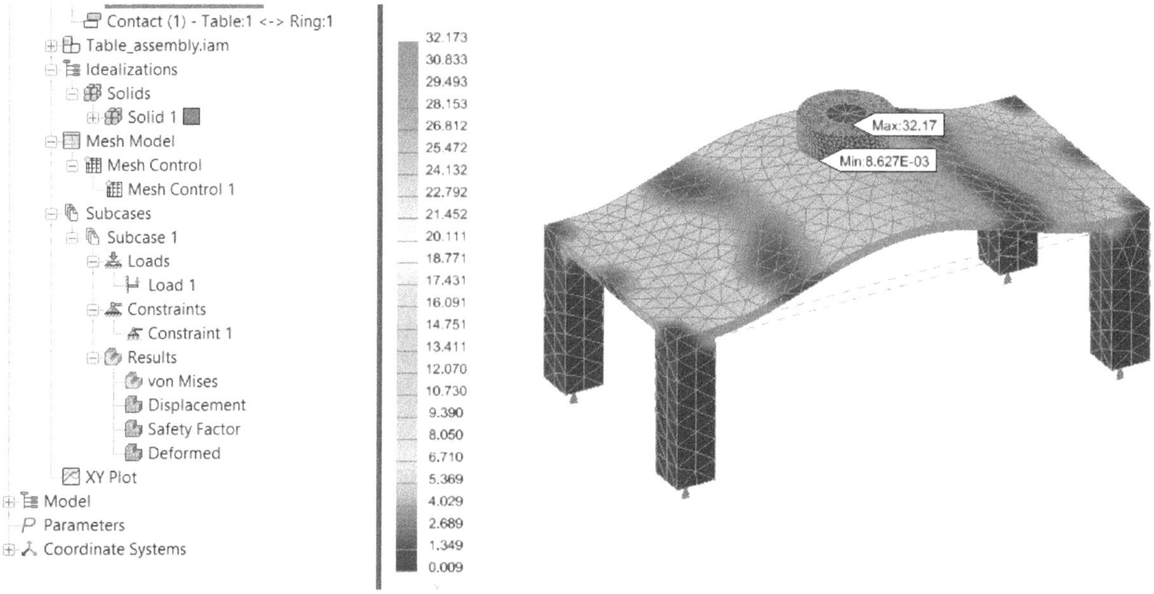

Figure-105. Result generated

To check any result, double-click on it from the **Results** node at the left of application window.

If you have activated convergence settings for the model before running analysis then you will get convergence plot along with results and mesh will be refined after each iteration until specified convergence criteria is met; refer to Figure-106.

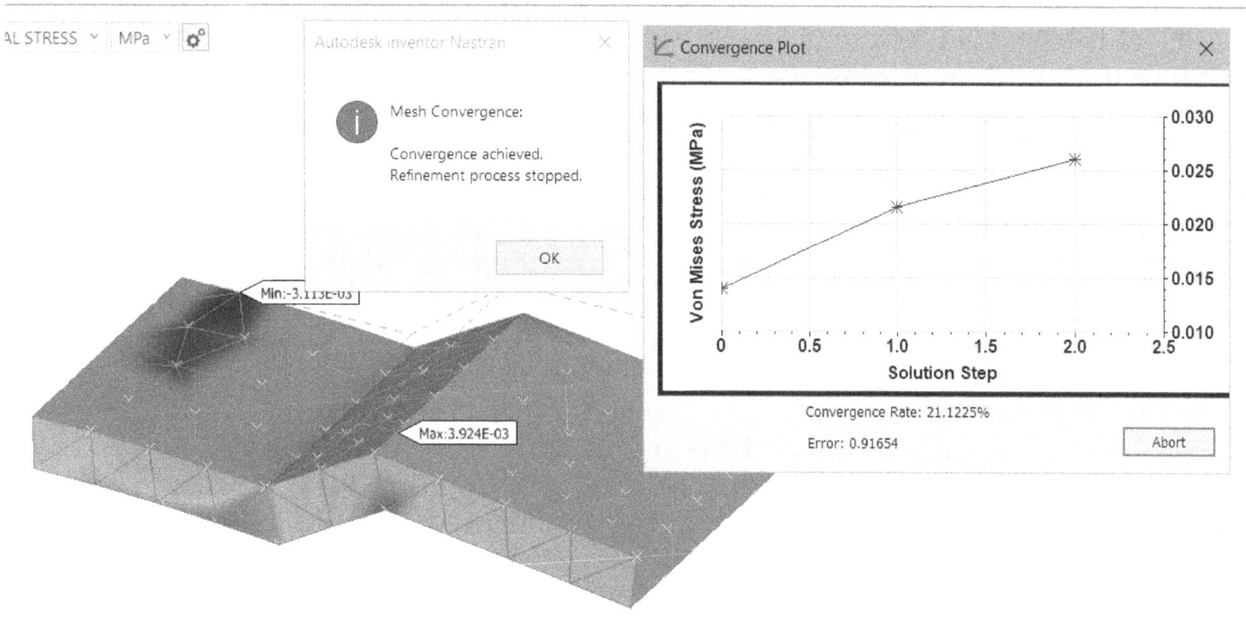

Figure-106. Convergence plot with results

SETTING PLOT OPTIONS

The **Result Options** tool in the **Results** panel is used to set plot options. The procedure to set plot options is given next.

- Select desired sub-case from the **Subcases** drop-down in the **Results** panel of **Autodesk Inventor Nastran** tab. Click on the **Result Options** tool from the **Results** panel of **Autodesk Inventor Nastran** tab in **Ribbon**. The **Plot** dialog box will be displayed; refer to Figure-107.

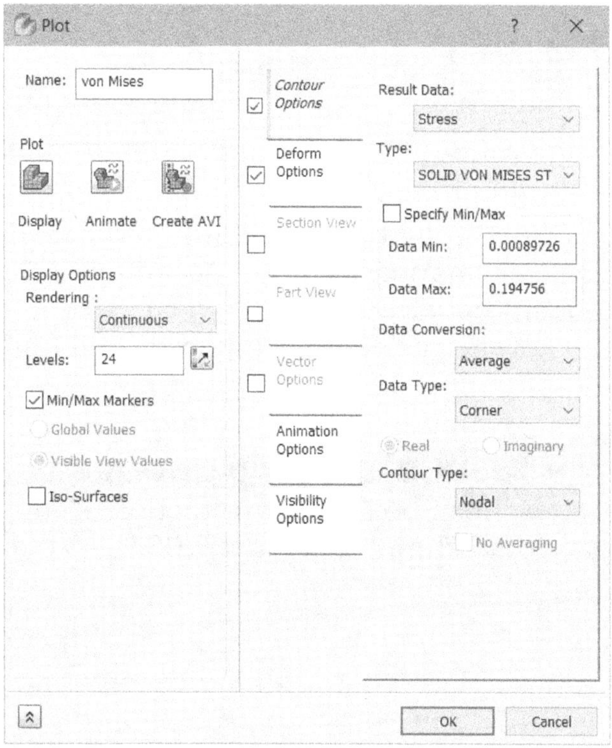

Figure-107. Plot dialog box

Contour Options

- Select the **Contour Options** check box to set contour options. The options related to contour will be displayed.
- Select the **Stress** option from the **Result Data** drop-down to create stress plot. Select the **Displacement** option if you want to create displacement plot. Similarly, use the **Strain**, **Reaction Force**, and **Contact** options to create strain, reaction force, and contact plots.
- If you want to set other plots like mesh convergence error, safety factor, and so on then select the **Other** option from the **Results Data** drop-down and select the respective options from the **Type** drop-down. You can select desired type for stress, strain, and other results from the **Type** drop-down.
- Select the **Specify Min/Max** check box to specify minimum and maximum values of parameter for the plot in **Data Min** and **Data Max** edit boxes.
- Select the **Nodal** option from the **Contour Type** drop-down if you want to generate result node-wise. Select the **Elemental** option if you want to generate results element-wise. If the **Elemental** option is selected then select the **No Averaging** check box to create a discrete plot of result.
- Specify the other parameters as required for contour options.

Deform Options

- Select the **Deform Options** check box to manage deformation of model in result. The options will be displayed as shown in Figure-108.

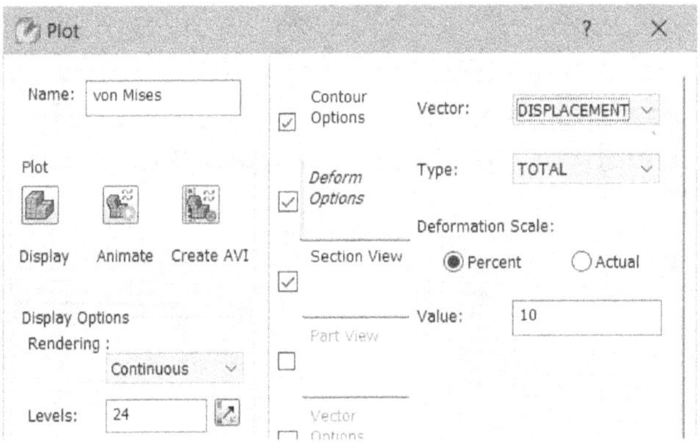

Figure-108. Deform Options

- Select desired option from the **Vector** drop-down to define the parameters to taken into consideration for deformation in plot.
- Select desired component of selected parameter from the **Type** drop-down.
- Select the **Percent** or **Actual** radio button as required and specify desired value for deformation scale.

Section View Options

- Select the **Section View** check box to create section of model in result plots. The options will be displayed as shown in Figure-109.

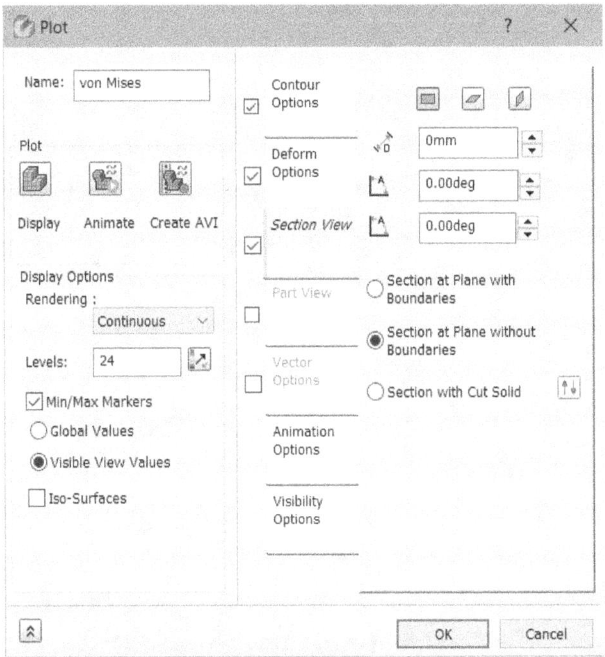

Figure-109. Section View options

- Select desired button to define which plane is to be used for section.
- Specify desired distance and angle for plane to create section view.
- Set the other parameters as required; refer to Figure-110.

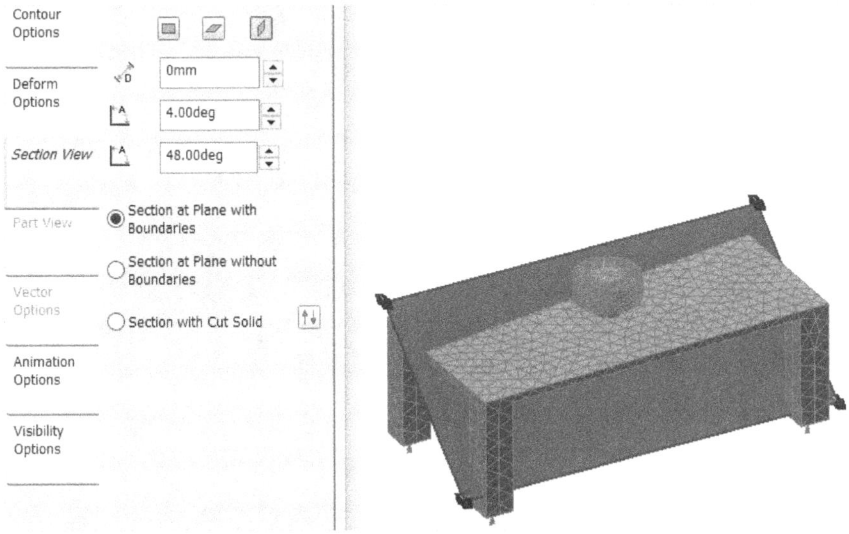

Figure-110. Section view parameters

Setting Part View Options

- Select the **Part View** check box to select the parts to be displayed in the result plots. This check box is active when you are performing analysis on an assembly.
- The **Select Parts** selection box will be activated by default; refer to Figure-111. Select desired parts of assembly to be shown or hidden in results and select the **Show** or **Hide** radio button, respectively.

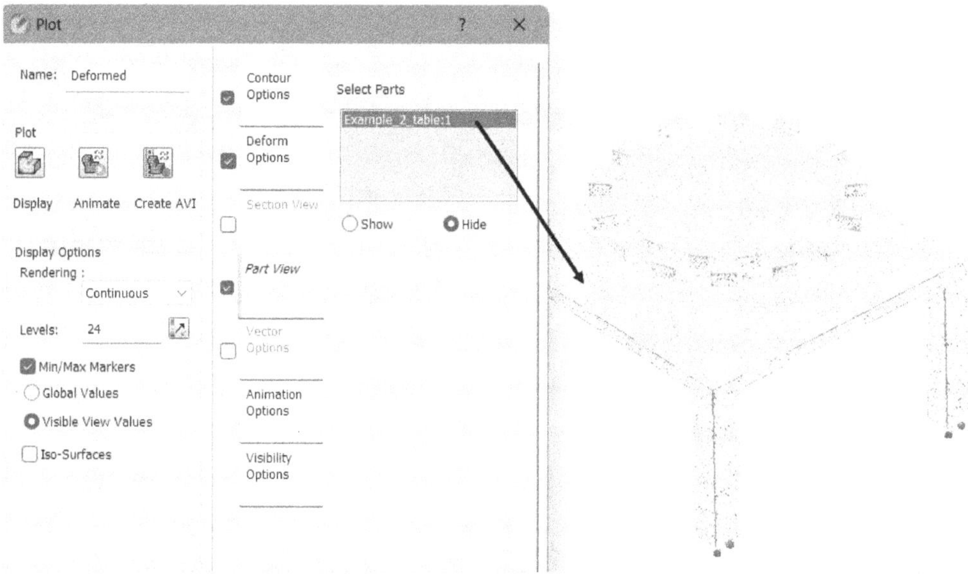

Figure-111. Part View options

Vector Options

The **Vector Options** are used to define the vector to be displayed in the result plot. The procedure is given next.

- Select the **Vector Options** check box from the **Plot** dialog box. The options will be displayed as shown in Figure-112.

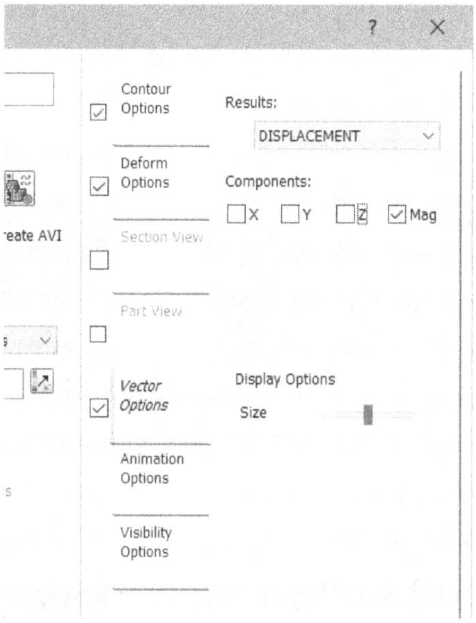

Figure-112. Vector Options

- Select desired options to specify which vector is to be displayed in results.

Animation Options

- Select the **Animation Options** tab from the **Plot** dialog box. The options will be displayed as shown in Figure-113.
- Specify the number of frames in animation, delay between two frames of animation, and modes as required.

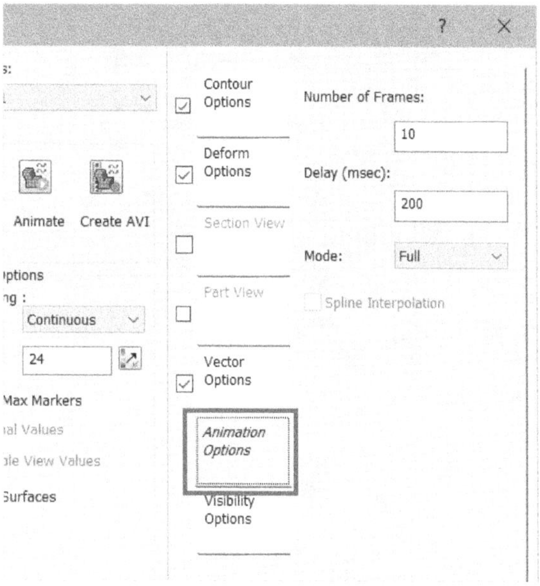

Figure-113. Animation Options

Visibility Options

- Click on the **Visibility Options** tab in the dialog box. The options will be displayed as shown in Figure-114.
- Select desired radio buttons to set entities to be displayed in the result plot.

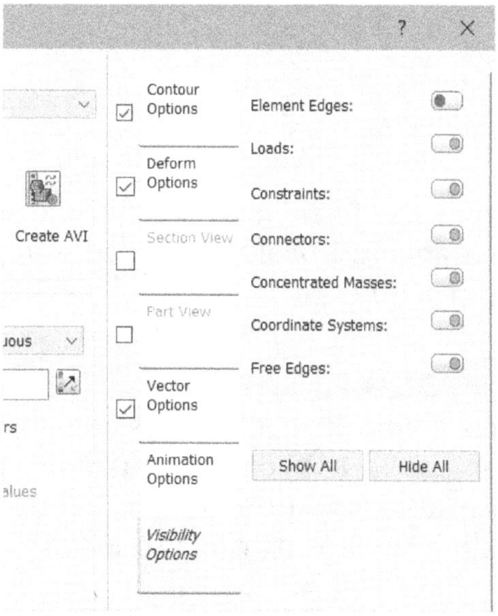

Figure-114. Visibility Options

Now, there are three ways to generate plot viz. **Display**, **Animate**, and **Create AVI** buttons.

Click on the **Display** button to generate 2D image of result plot. Click on the **Animate** button to generate animation of result. The animation of result will run in the viewport. Click on the **Create AVI** button to save the animation. Once the recording is complete, an information box will be displayed; refer to Figure-115. Click on the **OK** button from the information box. The **Save** dialog box will be displayed; refer to Figure-116.

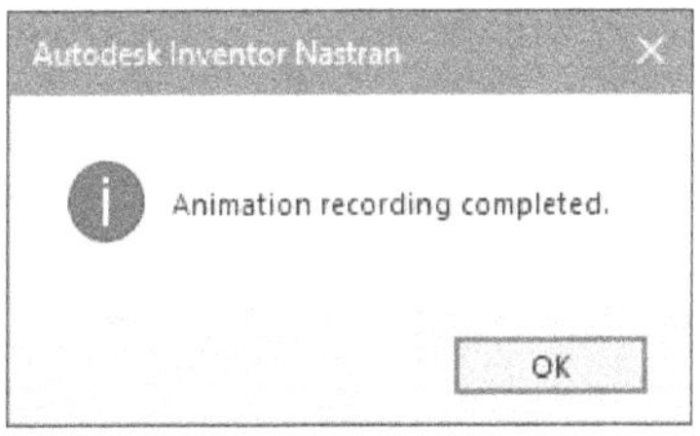

Figure-115. Information box

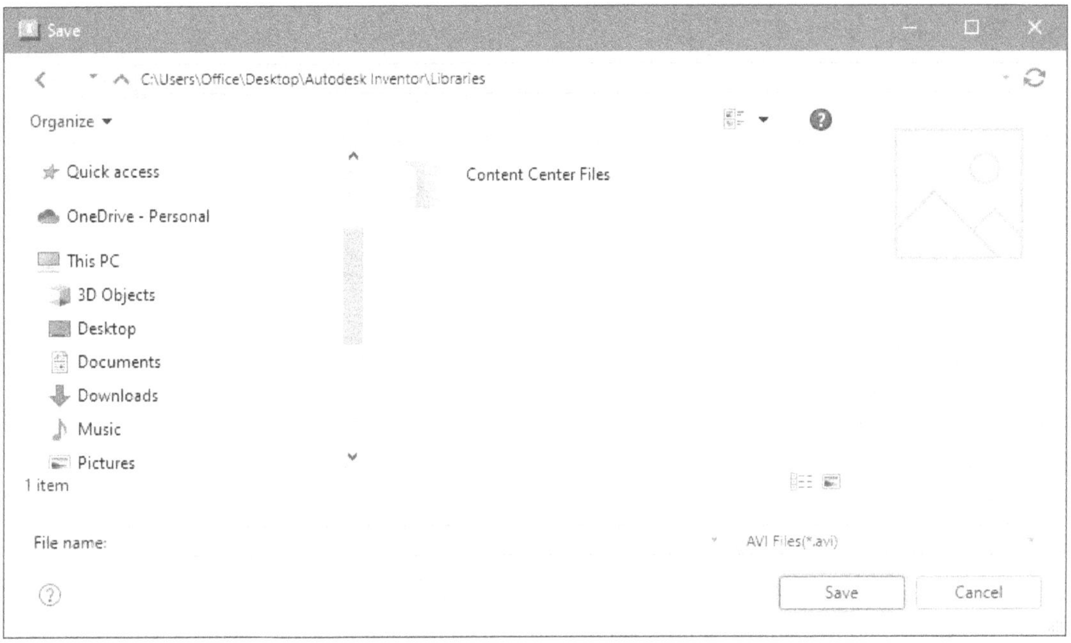

Figure-116. Save dialog box

Specify desired name of file in the **File name** edit box and click on the **Save** button. An information box will be displayed prompting you whether to open the file or not. Click on the **Yes** or **No** button as desired.

Using Probe to Check Node Results

Once the result is displayed, click on the **Probes** toggle button in **Results** panel of **Autodesk Inventor Nastran** tab in **Ribbon**. The cursor will be displayed with a plus sign. Hover the cursor at desired location on result model. The plot result will be displayed on respective node or element; refer to Figure-117.

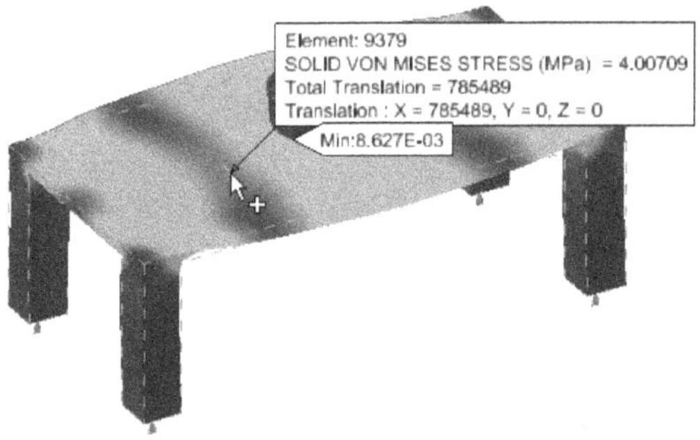

Figure-117. Using probe for result on node

Once the analysis is performed, click on the **Finish Autodesk Inventor Nastran** button from the **Exit** panel to exit analysis.

RESULT OPTIONS

After running analysis, the results of analysis are displayed in graphics area and the options in **Results** panel become active; refer to Figure-118. There are various options in this panel to analyze results like toggling deformed and undeformed shape in results. The options of this panel are discussed next.

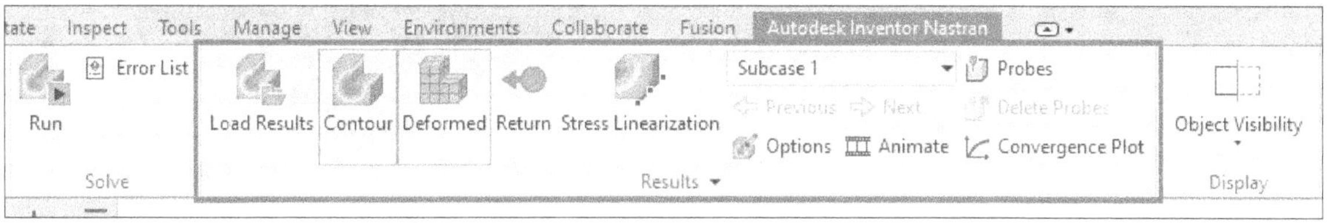

Figure-118. Results panel

Loading Results

The **Load Results** tool in **Results** panel of **Autodesk Inventor Nastran** tab in **Ribbon** is used to load binary result file of analyses performed earlier in Inventor Nastran. On clicking this tool, the **Open** dialog box will be displayed with options to open an FNO binary result file; refer to Figure-119. Select desired result file and click on the **Open** button. The results will be overlaid on the current model. Note that you should select previous result files of current model to check the results. Selecting a result file for different model can cause unexpected displayed of results.

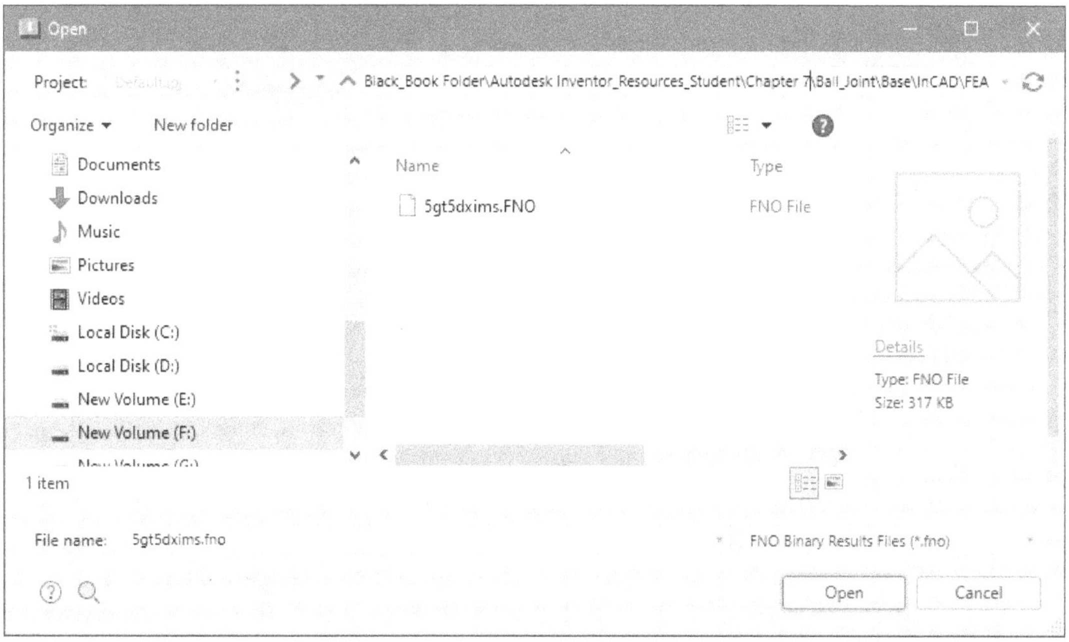

Figure-119. Open dialog box

Toggling Contour Shape

The **Contour** button is the **Results** panel is used to toggle the display of contours on the result model based on selected result parameter; refer to Figure-120.

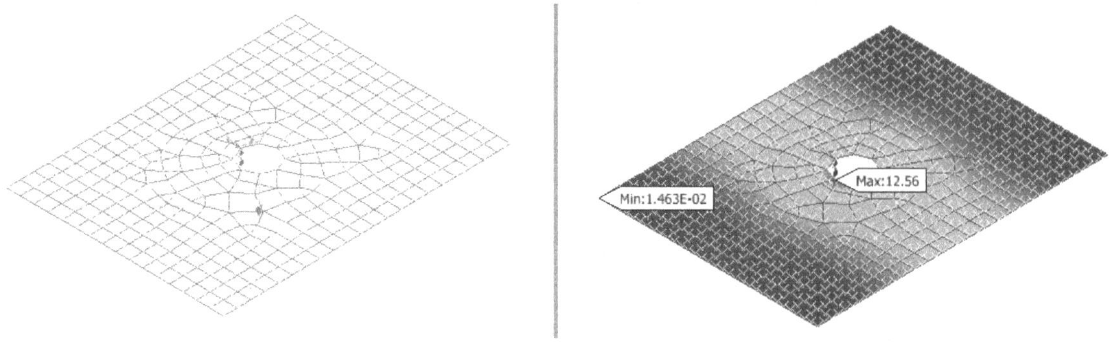

Figure-120. Contour display

Deformed Shape

The **Deformed** button in **Results** panel is used to toggle between deformed and undeformed shapes of the model results; refer to Figure-121.

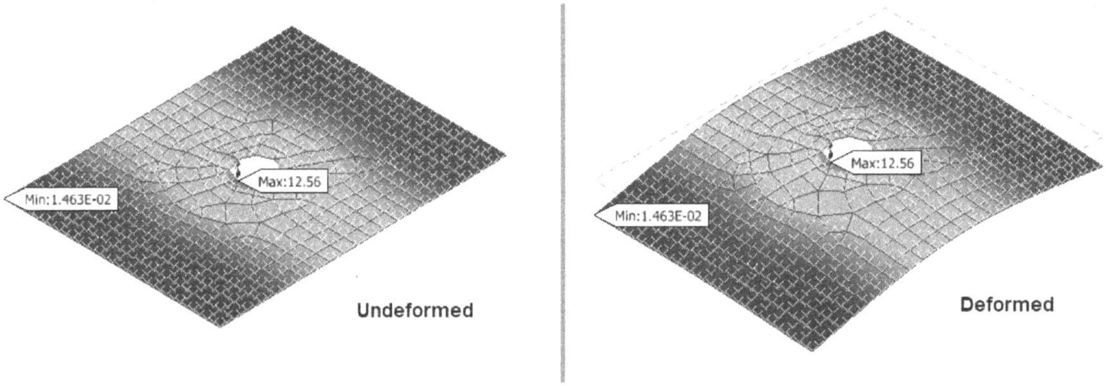

Figure-121. Deformed shape display

Stress Linearization

The Stress Linearization is separation of stresses of a section into constant membrane and linear bending stresses. Generally, this operation is required for designing pressure vessels to find local stress tensors but you can apply the tool to any of your linearization requirements. If you ask why linearization is generally performed for pressure vessels then pressure vessels usually contain structural discontinuity regions where abrupt changes in geometry, material or loading occur. These regions are typically the locations of highest stress in a component. For the evaluation of failure modes of plastic collapse and ratcheting, Stress Classification Lines (SCLs) are typically located at gross structural discontinuities. For the evaluation of local failure and fatigue, SCLs are typically located at local structural discontinuities. Inventor nastran uses both maximum stress and Von-mises stress methods to find bending and membrane stresses of local regions on the model. In simple words, you can use this utility to find bending stresses and membrane stresses along a virtual line created by specifying two points on the model. This virtual line is called Stress Classification Line (SCL). The procedure to use this tool is given next.

- After generating results of analysis, click on the **Stress Linearization** tool from the **Results** panel in the **Autodesk Inventor Nastran** tab of the **Ribbon**. The **Stress Linearization** dialog box will be displayed; refer to Figure-122.

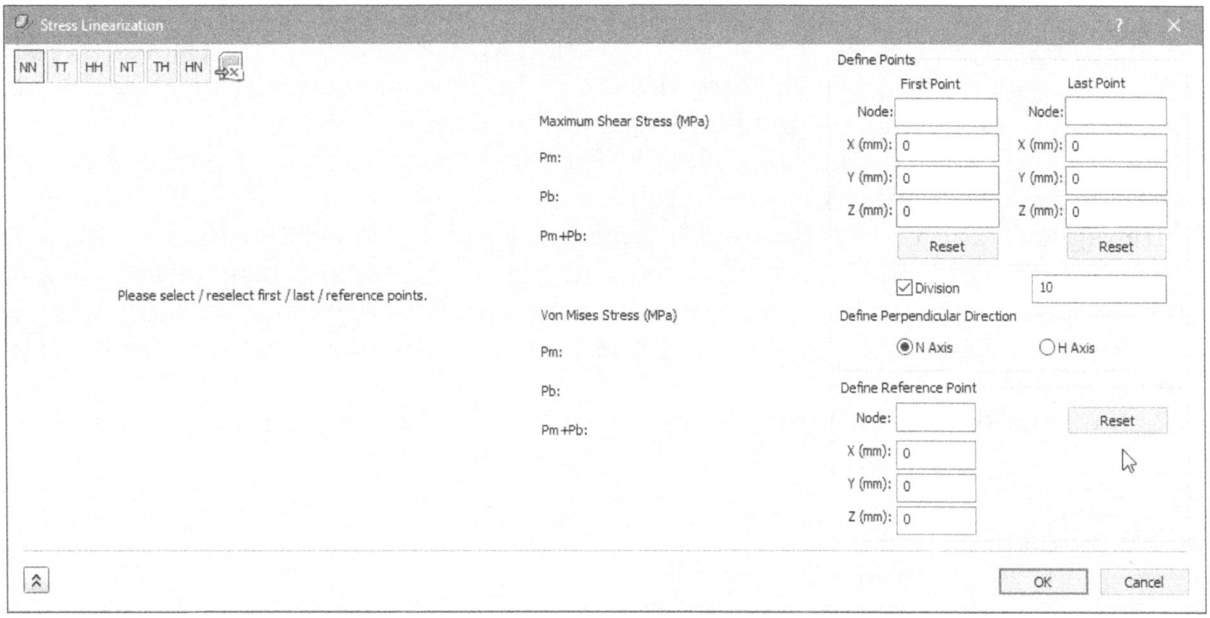

Figure-122. Stress Linearization dialog box

- Select desired button from the left area in the dialog box to define stress tensors to be used as X-Y directions for the plot. H means Hoop tensor, N means Normal tensor and T means Tangential tensor; refer to Figure-123. If you want to check plot of normal stress tensor in normal direction of SCL then select the **NN** button. If you want to check plot of normal stress tensor in tangential direction of SCL then select the **NT** button. Similarly, you can use the other buttons to check respective plots.
- Click in the **Node** edit box for **First Point** column in the **Define Points** area of the dialog box and click on desired node from the model to define it as first point of SCL (Stress Classification Line).
- Similarly, click in the **Node** edit box for **Second Point** column in the **Define Points** area of the dialog box and click on desired node from the model to define it as second point of SCL(Stress Classification Line). Note that the stress values will be plots for the line created by these two end points. You can also specify the coordinates of the end points in **X (mm)**, **Y (mm)**, and **Z (mm)** edit boxes if you do not want to select points from the graphics area.

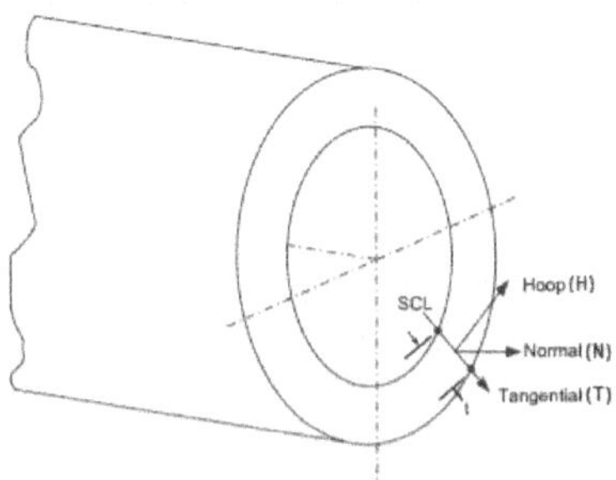

Figure-123. Stress classification line

- Select the **Division** check box to manually specify number of points on the SCL for which stress tensors will be plotted in graph. Clear this check box to let software automatically generate result points for you.

- Select desired radio button from the **Define Perpendicular Direction** area of the dialog box to define the direction for which you are specifying reference point. For example, if you have selected **H Axis** radio button then you can specify hoop direction of stress tensor by defining reference point.
- Click in the **Node** edit box of **Define Reference Point** area of the dialog box and specify desired reference point for direction.
- After specify points and direction reference, click on desired button at the left in the dialog box to check the plot; refer to Figure-124. Note that in the plot, Pm means primary membrane stress and Pb means primary bending stress.
- Click on the **Export** button at the left area in the dialog box to export results in a CSV file.
- Click on the **OK** button from the dialog box to exit the dialog box.

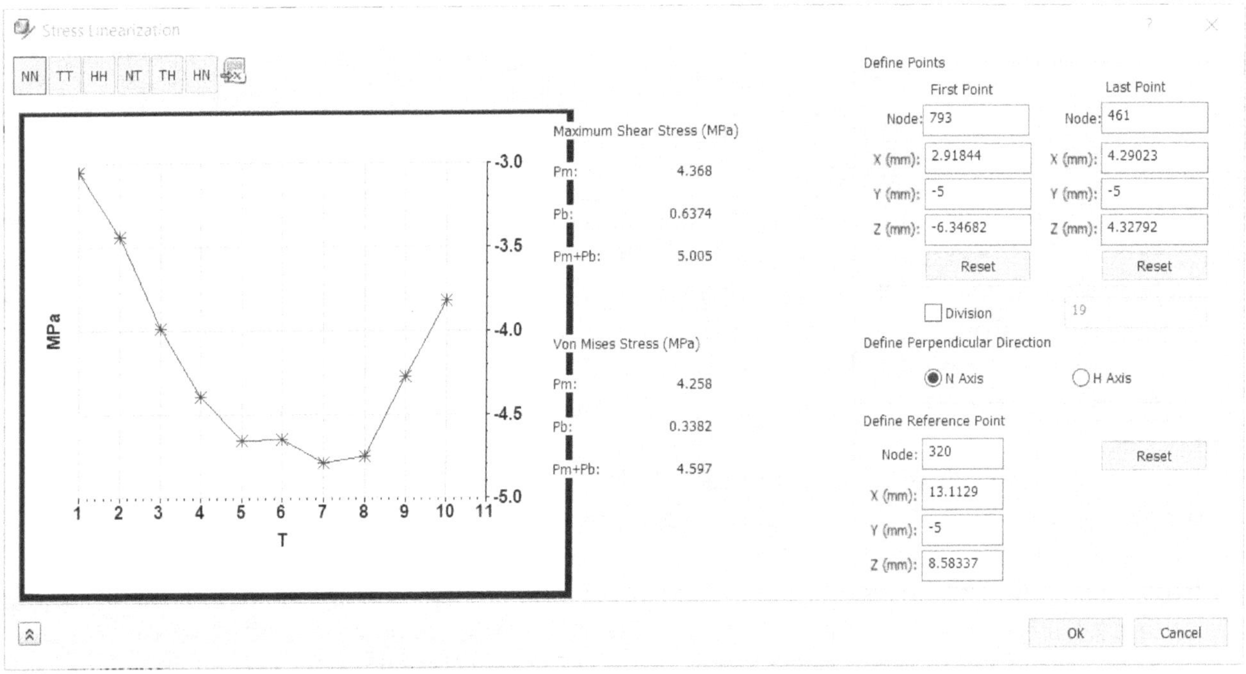

Figure-124. Stress linearization plot

Generating Animation File of Results

The **Animate** tool is used to animate results generated in the graphics area after performing analysis. The procedure to use this tool is given next.

- Click on the **Animate** tool from the **Results** panel in the **Autodesk Inventor Nastran** tab of the **Ribbon** after selecting desired result. The animation of result will be displayed. (To select desired result, double-click on the result name from **Results** node in the **Nastran Model Tree**.)

OBJECT VISIBILITY OPTIONS

The options in the **Object Visibility** drop-down of **Display** panel in **Autodesk Inventor Nastran** tab of **Ribbon** are used to display/hide various objects from the graphics area like CAD bodies, midsurfaces, and constraints; refer to Figure-125. Select check boxes for the objects that you want to display in graphics area.

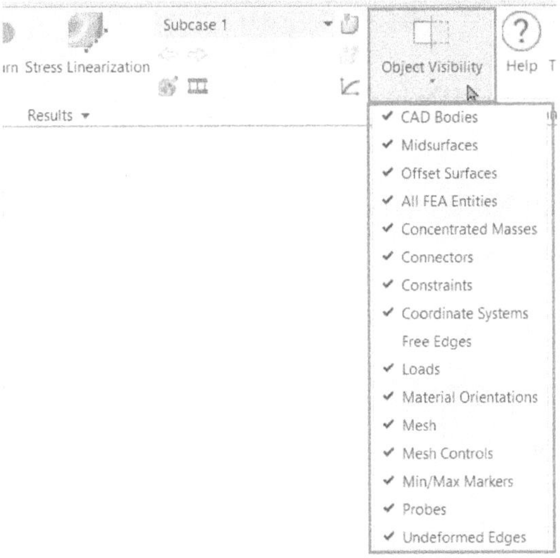

Figure-125. Object Visibility drop-down

SELF ASSESSMENT

Q1. Which tool is used to set display settings in Autodesk Inventor Nastran?

Q2. What do you mean by Meshing? Describe briefly.

Q3. Which of the following options is useful for visualizing vibration mode in **Post Processing** option in **Default Settings** dialog box?

a) Half
b) Full
c) Oscillate
d) None of the Above

Q4. Which of the following connections is applied between assembly components?

a) Rod
b) Rigid Body
c) Bolt
d) All of the Above

Q5. Which of the following loads is used to specify initial temperature for the analysis?

a) Thermal Convection
b) Temperature
c) Initial Condition
d) None of the Above

Q6. The .... tool is used to create, edit, and assign materials on objects under analysis.

Q7. The .... tool is used to find sections which have very low thickness as compared to rest of the model.

Q8. The .... tool in the **Contacts** panel is used to specify the region in which contacts will be applied automatically.

Q9. The **Material DB** dialog box is used to select the materials to be apply on the model. (True/False)

Q10. The **Idealization** tool in **Prepare** panel is used to apply restrictions to translation and rotation of selected objects. (True/False)

Q11. What is the purpose of the Default Settings tool in Autodesk Inventor Nastran?

A. To import stress analysis data
B. To perform mesh analysis
C. To set display and basic settings of the dialog box
D. To define boundary conditions

Q12. What does the 'Optimize Graphics for Fast Rendering' option do in Default Settings dialog box?

A. Increases accuracy of results
B. Enhances animation speed
C. Improves rendering performance
D. Improves display of node labels

Q13. What does the 'Oscillate' option in animation mode do in Default Settings dialog box?

A. Repeats animation continuously
B. Mirrors full-cycle of deformed shape for visualization
C. Runs half-cycle of animation
D. Reverses deformation data

Q14. Which file format is generated when the 'Punch' output option is selected in the Analysis dialog box during new study creation?

A. .NAS
B. .PCH
C. .OUT
D. .TXT

Q15. What does the 'Cyclic Symmetry' checkbox do in Options tab of Analysis dialog box?

A. Removes cyclic constraints
B. Enables rotation of components
C. Searches for cyclic constraints and cylindrical coordinate systems
D. Shows cyclic deformation modes

Q16. What is the use of the 'Import from Stress Analysis' tool?

A. To export stress data to .OUT file
B. To import data from static study
C. To import study parameters from Inventor Stress Analysis
D. To perform linear analysis

Q17. What is the primary purpose of the Materials tool in Autodesk Inventor Nastran?

A. To simulate structural loads on a model
B. To create, edit, and assign materials to objects for analysis
C. To animate the physical properties of objects
D. To calculate factor of safety automatically

Q18. In an isotropic material, Young's Modulus is:

A. Variable in X and Y directions
B. Only effective under compression
C. Different in different directions
D. Same in all directions

Q19. The Mullins effect is associated with which type of material?

A. Nitinol
B. Hyperelastic
C. Viscoelastic
D. Brittle

Q20. Which material type is best for modeling objects like rubber?

A. Anisotropic 3D
B. Hyperelastic
C. Orthotropic 2D
D. Brittle

Q21. What property does the Thermal Exp. Coeff. option define in the Material dialog box?

A. Elastic stiffness under heat
B. Strength degradation in heat
C. Change in size due to temperature
D. Expansion rate under pressure

Q22. Which material type should you select to define properties separately for three directions?

A. Orthotropic 2D
B. Hyperelastic
C. Orthotropic 3D
D. Isotropic

Q23. What kind of deformation do brittle materials usually undergo under stress?

A. Bending
B. Torsional
C. Shattering
D. Yielding

Q24. Nitinol materials are applicable for which kind of analysis only?

A. Static
B. Linear
C. Thermal
D. Nonlinear

Q25. What does the damping coefficient define?

A. Ratio of stress to strain
B. Resistance to shear
C. Ratio of actual damping to critical damping
D. Resistance to thermal expansion

Q26. Which type of materials is best for damping vibrations and noise?

A. Viscoelastic
B. Isotropic
C. Crushable Foam
D. Hyperelastic

Q27. What is the primary purpose of using idealization in Autodesk Inventor Nastran?

A. To enhance graphic rendering of the model
B. To convert the model into simple assumptions for analysis
C. To export the model to other software
D. To reduce the number of materials used in the design

Q28. Which type of idealization should be selected to apply 3D solid elements?

A. Shell
B. Line
C. Laminate
D. Solid

Q29. What does the 'Associated Geometry' checkbox do in Shell Idealization?

A. Changes the model units
B. Automatically assigns shell thickness
C. Enables selection of specific geometry for shell elements
D. Connects parts to external references

Q30. What does the Laminate option in Idealizations allow you to do?

A. Change the surface texture of the model
B. Add drilling degrees of freedom
C. Create composite layers of different materials
D. Define a 1D beam structure

Q31. What is the function of the 'Sym' button in the Ply Option area of the Laminate dialog box?

A. To delete all plies
B. To reverse material orientation
C. To create a symmetric copy of the selected ply
D. To change angle of plies to 90 degrees

Q32. What failure theory option is suitable for checking failure in orthotropic materials with unequal tensile and compressive strengths?

A. Max. Strain
B. HOFF
C. Max. Stress
D. NSM

Q33. What does the SME laminate form do?

A. Defines a honeycomb core
B. Smeared ply effects and ignores stacking sequence
C. Adds damping to the shell
D. Enables drilling DOF

Q34. Which type of idealization applies 1D elements to a model?

A. Shell
B. Solid
C. Laminate
D. Line

Q35. What makes a Pipe element distinct from a Beam or Bar element?

A. It resists only axial loads
B. It includes internal and external pressures
C. It cannot be used in the aerospace industry
D. It does not require geometry association

Q36. What can be defined in the Stress Recovery Coefficients area for line elements in the Idealizations dialog box?

A. Material selection
B. Geometry of shell surface
C. Distance of stress points from element center
D. Cross-sectional area

Q37. In the Pipe Line Element End Condition, what does the Internal Pressure (P) edit box define?

A. External thermal load
B. Pressure inside the pipe
C. Laminate ply stress
D. Distance of cross section

Q38. Which function creates a copy of the current idealization for reuse?

A. OK button
B. Create Duplicate button
C. Add button
D. Sym button

Q39. What is the primary benefit of using the Connectors tool in an assembly analysis?

A. Increases visual appeal of the model
B. Reduces processing time and allows result checking on connectors
C. Enhances part manufacturing
D. Replaces the need for simulation entirely

Q40. Which connector type should be used to model compression and tension without bending?

A. Cable
B. Spring
C. Rod
D. Bolt

Q41. What parameter is unique to a Cable connection and not used in Rod connection?

A. Cross-section area
B. Torsion constant
C. Slack
D. Tension coefficient

Q42. In Cable connection settings, what does selecting the "Continuous" preload option imply?

A. Preload is applied only once
B. Preload is applied at fixed intervals
C. Preload is applied throughout the analysis
D. Preload is ignored

Q43. Which edit boxes define stiffness in the X, Y, and Z directions when using advanced options in Spring connection?

A. K1, K2, K3
B. G1, G2, G3
C. A, B, C
D. D1, D2, D3

Q44. Which type of connection is defined as an equation rather than a physical connector?

A. Cable
B. Rigid Body
C. Rod
D. Bolt

Q45. When applying a Rigid Body connection using interpolation, what is the effect?

A. Infinite stiffness is added
B. The spring property is removed
C. Load is distributed without stiffness
D. Only tension is analyzed

Q46. What type of bolt connection does NOT require a nut?

A. Bolt with washer
B. Cap Screw
C. Nut Screw
D. Threaded Bolt

Q47. In a Bolt connection, which parameter must be specified if Cap Screw is selected?

A. Nut washer height
B. Length of threaded rod
C. Useful length of screw
D. Cross-sectional radius

Q48. What feature is not compatible with a Bolt connection due to automatic generation issues?

A. Constraints
B. Symmetry
C. Static Load
D. Meshing

Q49. What does the Concentrated Masses tool do?

A. Removes mass from model
B. Measures model density
C. Replaces a part with a point mass
D. Adds structural rigidity

Q50. In Concentrated Mass, what does selecting the "Automatic" radio button allow you to do?

A. Choose a fixed point manually
B. Manually enter part mass
C. Replace a part with a point mass based on density
D. Apply damping

Q51. What does the Offset Surfaces tool primarily do?

A. Moves the entire part
B. Creates a new 3D body
C. Offsets selected faces to create shell components
D. Adds holes to the surface

Q52. What is the purpose of the Find Thin Bodies tool in Autodesk Inventor Nastran?

A. To create shell elements in solid models
B. To detect bodies with uniform color distribution
C. To find sections with low thickness compared to the rest of the model
D. To modify the thickness of all model components

Q53. According to the criteria for a thin body, what is the maximum thickness-to-length ratio for a plate to be considered thin?

A. 0.10
B. 0.01
C. 0.05
D. 0.50

Q54. What must be true about a body for the Find Thin Bodies tool to consider it?

A. It should be in wireframe mode
B. It must have uniform thickness
C. It must be a cylindrical body
D. It should be manually selected in the browser

Q55. What is the main function of the Midsurfaces tool?

A. To analyze temperature changes in bodies
B. To change the thickness of selected solids
C. To create shell objects at the mid location of selected solid bodies
D. To convert shell bodies into solid forms

Q56. What does the Structural Members tool allow you to do?

A. Remove unwanted frames
B. Convert 2D sketches into 3D bodies
C. Decide whether members are used as solids or 1D beams in analysis
D. Merge multiple frames into one

Q57. Structural members in a model are typically generated using which environment?

A. Assembly
B. Frame Generator
C. Drawing
D. Simulation

Q58. Which type of constraint would you select to apply translation and rotation restrictions in X, Y, and/or Z directions?

A. Thermal
B. Rigid(Explicit)
C. Structural
D. Pin

Q59. Which constraint type is suitable for cylindrical bodies with movement restrictions in radial, axial, and tangential directions?

A. Frictionless
B. Pin
C. Thermal
D. Response Spectrum

Q60. When using the Frictionless constraint, how does the selected face behave?

A. It moves randomly in 3D space
B. It does not move at all
C. It allows movement along its plane only
D. It breaks into mesh elements

Q61. Which constraint type is only applicable in Heat Transfer analysis?

A. Thermal
B. Structural
C. Frictionless
D. Pin

Q62. What happens when Rigid(Explicit) constraint is applied?

A. Rotation only is restricted
B. Translation only is restricted
C. Both rotation and translation are restricted
D. Only points are restricted

Q63. Which constraint types support the use of Symmetry and AntiSymmetry options?

A. Structural and Rigid(Explicit)
B. Pin and Frictionless
C. Thermal and Response Spectrum
D. Only Structural

Q64. Which axis directions are defined by the Tx, Ty, Tz, Rx, Ry, and Rz checkboxes?

A. Model-relative axis
B. Arbitrary axis
C. Selected face normal
D. Coordinate system selected in dialog

Q65. What must be selected to apply force perpendicular to a selected face?

A. Components
B. Geometric Entity
C. Normal to Surface
D. Transient Load

Q66. How many points are required at minimum to define a linear variable load on a face?

A. 2
B. 3
C. 4
D. 5

Q67. Which type of load is used to define a load that varies with time?

A. Transient Force
B. Heat Flux
C. Rotational Force
D. Variable Load

Q68. What does the "Load Scale Factor vs. Time" option help define in transient load analysis?

A. Heat change over time
B. Temperature range
C. Load magnitude change over time
D. Motion path

Q69. Moment load is applied on a part that:

A. Translates in a direction
B. Accelerates linearly
C. Rotates or tends to rotate
D. Remains stationary

Q70. Which load is applied per unit length of the object?

A. Force
B. Moment
C. Distributed Load
D. Hydrostatic Load

Q71. Hydrostatic pressure is calculated as:

A. Force x Distance
B. Depth / Fluid Density
C. Surface Area x Velocity
D. Fluid Density x Depth

Q72. Which load type requires selecting a top point up to which fluid is exerting pressure?

A. Gravity
B. Remote Force
C. Hydrostatic Load
D. Pressure

Q73. Which option must be selected to apply a load using a distant reference point?

A. Bearing Load
B. Rotational Force
C. Remote Force
D. Gravity

Q74. Which load type is used to apply radial and axial forces on round faces?

A. Bearing Load
B. Rotational Force
C. Moment
D. Distributed Load

Q75. Rotational force requires specifying:

A. Temperature and Velocity
B. Acceleration and Angular Velocity
C. Velocity and Acceleration
D. Force and Pressure

Q76. Enforced Motion is used to apply:

A. Force per unit length
B. Pressure distribution
C. Specified translation or rotation
D. Initial heat conditions

Q77. The Initial Condition load is applicable for:

A. Linear static analysis only
B. Dynamic and nonlinear analyses
C. Thermal analysis only
D. Assembly constraints

Q78. The Body Temperature option is similar in behavior to:

A. Heat Flux
B. Convection
C. Initial Condition
D. Rigid Motion

Q79. To apply heat flow rate intensity per unit area, which load is used?

A. Heat Generation
B. Heat Flux
C. Temperature
D. Radiation

Q80. Which load allows you to define temperature-dependent convection coefficient?

A. Thermal Radiation
B. Temperature
C. Convection
D. Heat Generation

Q81. The Radiation option requires input of:

A. Rotational direction
B. Force direction
C. Absorptivity and Emissivity
D. Depth and Pressure

Q82. Which load is best suited to apply internal heat within selected surfaces?

A. Radiation
B. Heat Flux
C. Heat Generation
D. Temperature

Q83. Loads based on analysis results can be applied using which option?

A. From Output
B. Variable Load
C. Remote Force
D. Rigid Motion

Q84. Rigid Motion (Explicit) load is applied to:

A. Fluids in pipes
B. Welded assemblies
C. Flexible parts
D. Rigid bodies

Q85. Which tool in Autodesk Inventor Nastran is used to assign default contacts automatically between components?

A. Manual
B. Solver
C. Auto
D. Mesh

Q86. What is the default contact type applied by the Auto tool?

A. Separation
B. Bonded
C. Shrink Fit
D. Sliding

Q87. Which contact type allows sliding and gap between selected faces?

A. Bonded
B. Separation
C. Sliding/No Separation
D. Offset Bonded

Q88. For a welded joint with a gap between parts, which contact type is generally used?

A. Separation
B. Shrink Fit/No Sliding
C. Offset Bonded
D. Sliding/No Separation

Q89. Which Penetration Type option provides faster results at the cost of accuracy?

A. Symmetric Contact
B. No Contact
C. Shrink Fit
D. Unsymmetric Contact

Q90. What is defined in the Coefficient of Friction edit box?

A. Strength of contact
B. Surface stiffness
C. Friction at contact site
D. Node temperature

Q91. What is the use of the Max Allowable Penetration option?

A. Define stiffness of contact
B. Set depth for thermal conduction
C. Define penetration distance between nodes
D. Adjust mesh size

Q92. Which failure theory works by analyzing crack propagation at the weld joint?

A. Cohesive Zone Model
B. Bonded Model
C. Shrink Fit Model
D. Offset Bonded Model

Q93. Which contact tool allows you to specify the region for contact application during analysis runtime?

A. Manual
B. Solver
C. Auto
D. Mesh Control

Q94. What type of elements are used for bulky solid models in meshing?

A. 1D elements
B. 2D shell elements
C. 3D tetrahedral elements
D. Mixed elements

Q95. What kind of nodes are present in parabolic tetrahedral elements?

A. 6
B. 8
C. 10
D. 3

Q96. Which mesh element type is used for thin sheet metal parts?

A. 1D beam
B. 2D shell elements
C. 3D solid elements
D. Pipe elements

Q97. Which option in Mesh Settings helps suppress small features like holes?

A. Refinement Ratio
B. Suppress Short Features
C. Min Triangle Angle
D. Quality Midside Adjustment

Q98. What is the effect of selecting Parabolic elements for 3D meshing?

A. Slower processing but more accurate results
B. Faster but less accurate
C. Same as linear
D. Only used for pipes

Q99. What does the Mesh Control tool allow the user to do?

A. Automatically apply mesh
B. Define custom mesh at selected locations
C. Troubleshoot mesh errors
D. Add friction

Q100. What is the purpose of adaptive meshing?

A. Generate mesh automatically
B. Refine mesh based on model geometry and analysis results
C. Create shell elements
D. Add mid-side nodes

Q101. What does the Refinement Factor define in adaptive meshing?

A. Number of contacts
B. How many times solver runs
C. Growth rate of elements per refinement
D. Depth of penetration

Q102. Which tool is used to find and repair mesh errors?

A. Mesh Table
B. Mesh Control
C. Mesh Troubleshooter
D. Convergence Settings

Q103. What is the effect of selecting the “Elemental” option from the Contour Type drop-down?

A. Deformation results are generated
B. Animation is created
C. Node-wise result is shown
D. Results are generated element-wise

Q104. What do the Vector Options in the Plot dialog box allow you to do?

A. Display stress plots only
B. Animate the mesh
C. Define the vector to be displayed in the result plot
D. Select result file for comparison

Q105. What is the function of the “Create AVI” button in result plotting?

A. Animate mesh
B. Save result as CSV
C. Save result animation as video file
D. Export result image

Q106. Which tool is used to check node results by hovering over the model with the cursor?

A. Animate
B. Probe
C. Deform
D. Contour

Q107. What is the purpose of the Load Results tool?

A. Display contours
B. Animate model
C. Load binary result file of earlier analyses
D. Export stress values

Q108. In Stress Linearization, what is an SCL?

A. Stress Correction Line
B. Structural Control Line
C. Stress Classification Line
D. Simulation Correction Line

Q109. What does the Stress Linearization tool help to determine?

A. Nodes for result plotting
B. Animation direction
C. Bending and membrane stresses
D. Total deformation

Q110. What file type is generated when exporting stress linearization data?

A. STL
B. AVI
C. CSV
D. FNO

Q111. What is the Animate tool primarily used for in the Results panel?

A. Load model
B. Animate the result
C. Export as CSV
D. Create section view

Q112. What can be shown/hidden using the Object Visibility options?

A. Result plots only
B. Node values
C. CAD bodies, midsurfaces, constraints
D. Analysis settings

FOR STUDENT NOTES

Chapter 3

Static Analyses

Topics Covered

The major topics covered in this chapter are:

- ***Introduction***
- ***Starting Linear Static Analysis***
- ***Applying Materials, Loads, and Constraints***
- ***Applying Idealizations***
- ***Setting Mesh and other parameters***
- ***Running Analysis and Plotting Results***
- ***Performing Linear Static Analysis on Assembly***
- ***Performing Prestress Static Analysis***
- ***Performing Nonlinear Static Analysis***

INTRODUCTION

The Linear Static analysis is performed to check the effect of static loads on the model. The process to create linear static study is given next.

PERFORMING LINEAR STATIC ANALYSIS ON PART

Perform linear static analysis on a steel bar of 22x10x120 mm with 1000 N load applied on its top flat face.

The procedure to perform linear static analysis is given next.

- Open the part on which you want to perform analysis in Autodesk Inventor; refer to Figure-1.

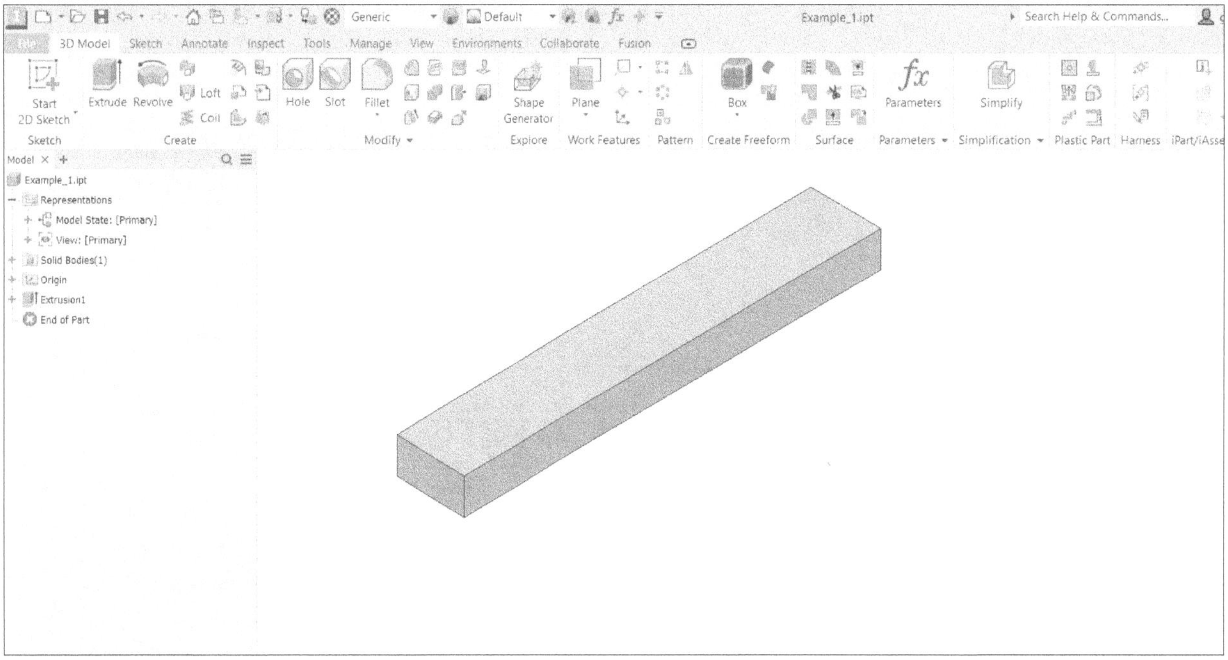

Figure-1. Example 1

- Click on the **Autodesk Inventor Nastran** tool from the **Environments** tab of **Ribbon**. The **Autodesk Inventor Nastran** tab will be added in the **Ribbon** and linear static analysis will start automatically.
- Click on the **Edit** button from the **Analysis** panel in **Autodesk Inventor Nastran** tab of **Ribbon**. The **Analysis** dialog box will be displayed; refer to Figure-2.

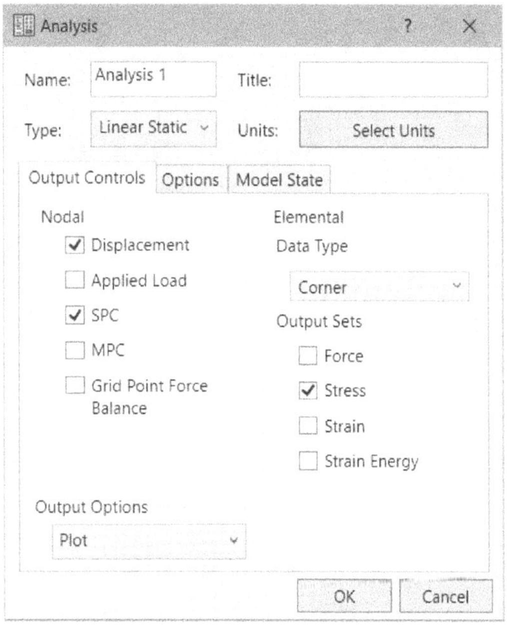

Figure-2. Analysis dialog box for linear static analysis

- Click on the **Select Units** button from the **Analysis** dialog box. The **Units** dialog box will be displayed; refer to Figure-3.

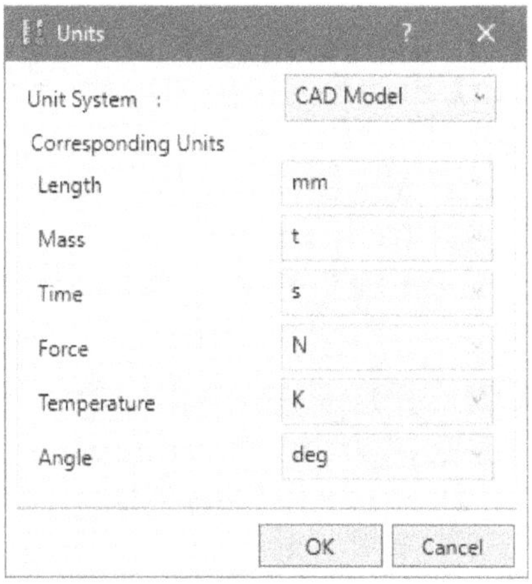

Figure-3. Units dialog box

- Select **SI** option from the **Unit System** drop-down in the dialog box and click on the **OK** button from the **Units** dialog box.
- Click on the **OK** button from the **Analysis** dialog box.

Applying Material

- Click on the **Materials** tool from **Prepare** panel of **Autodesk Inventor Nastran** tab in the **Ribbon**. The **Material** dialog box will be displayed; refer to Figure-4.

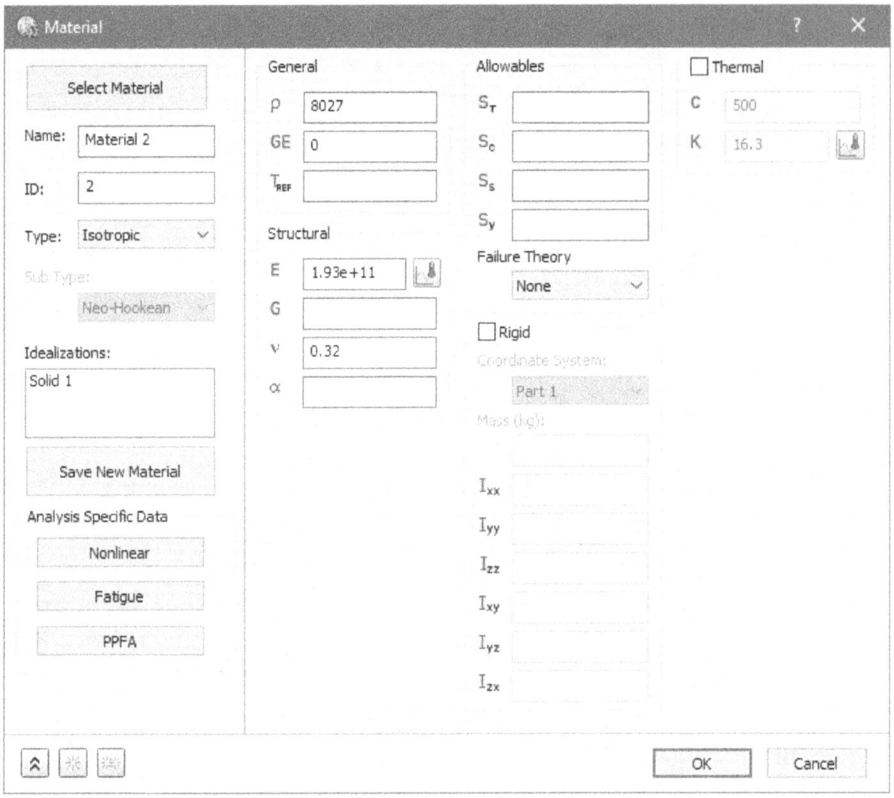

Figure-4. Material dialog box

- Click on the **Select Material** button from the **Material** dialog box. The **Material DB** dialog box will be displayed.
- Select the **Stainless Steel - Austenitic** material from the **Autodesk Material Library** node and click on the **OK** button.
- Click on the **OK** button from the **Material** dialog box to apply material.

Applying Idealizations

- Click on the **Idealizations** tool from the **Prepare** panel in **Autodesk Inventor Nastran** tab of **Ribbon**. The **Idealizations** dialog box will be displayed; refer to Figure-5.

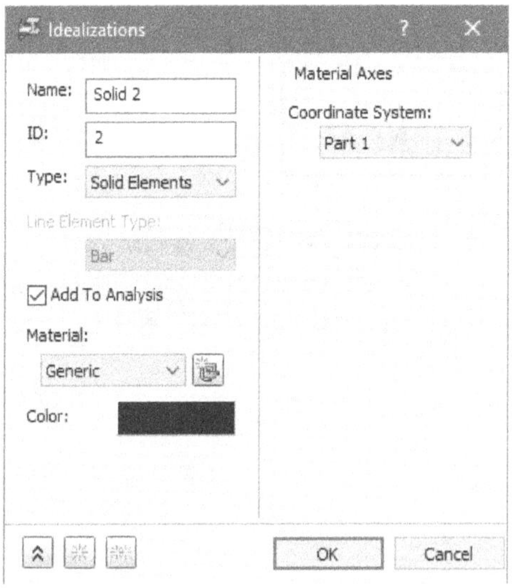

Figure-5. Idealizations dialog box

- Select **Stainless Steel-Austenitic** option from the **Material** drop-down and click on the **OK** button.

Applying Constraints

- Click on the **Constraints** tool from the **Setup** panel in **Autodesk Inventor Nastran** tab of **Ribbon**. The **Constraint** dialog box will be displayed.
- Select the faces as shown in Figure-6.

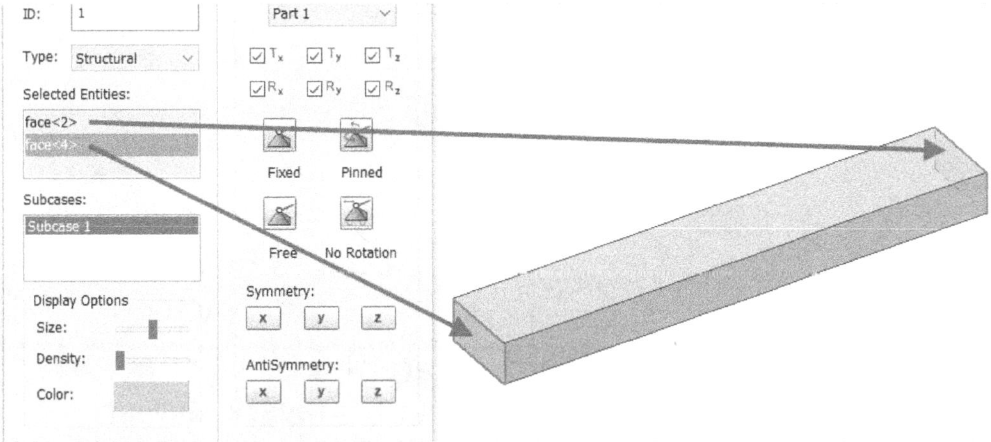

Figure-6. Faces selected for constraints

- Click on the **Fixed** button and then click on the **OK** button from the **Constraint** dialog box. The constraint will be applied.

Applying Force

- Click on the **Loads** button from the **Setup** panel of the **Ribbon**. The **Load** dialog box will be displayed.
- Select the top face of model to apply force; refer to Figure-7.
- Select the **Force** option from the **Type** drop-down and the **Normal To Surface** option from the **Direction** drop-down.
- Specify the value of force as **-1000** in **Magnitude** edit box.
- Click on the **OK** button from the dialog box to apply force.

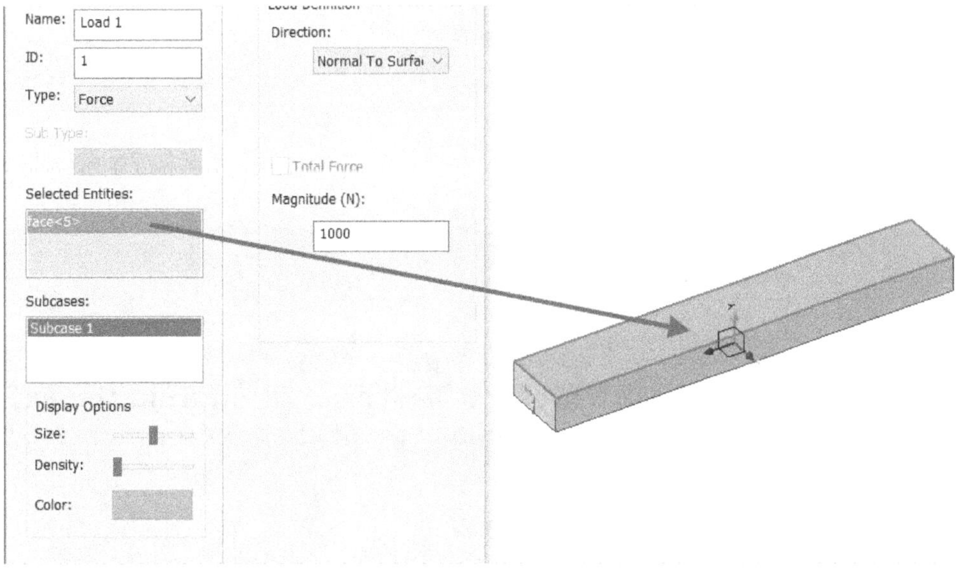

Figure-7. Applying force

Creating Mesh

- Click on the **Mesh Settings** tool from the **Mesh** panel of **Autodesk Inventor Nastran** tab in **Ribbon**. The **Mesh Settings** dialog box will be displayed.
- Specify the element size as **0.01** in **Element Size** edit box and click on the **Generate Mesh** button. The mesh will be created; refer to Figure-8.
- Click on the **OK** button to exit the dialog box.

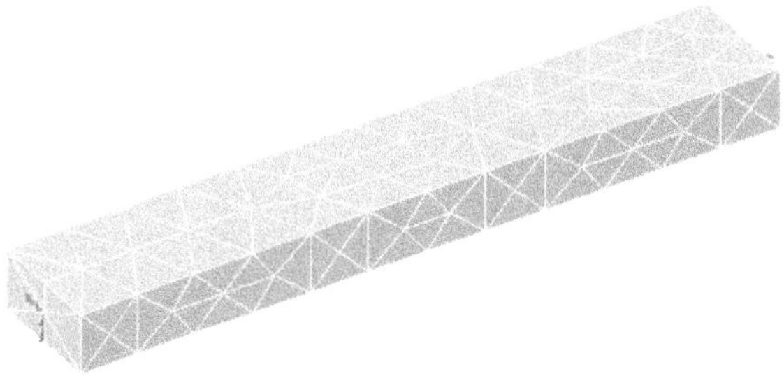

Figure-8. Mesh created

Running Analysis

- Click on the **Run** tool from the **Solve** panel in **Autodesk Inventor Nastran** tab of **Ribbon**. The system will start performing analysis and once complete an information box will be displayed.
- Click on the **OK** button from the information box. The analysis result will be displayed; refer to Figure-9.

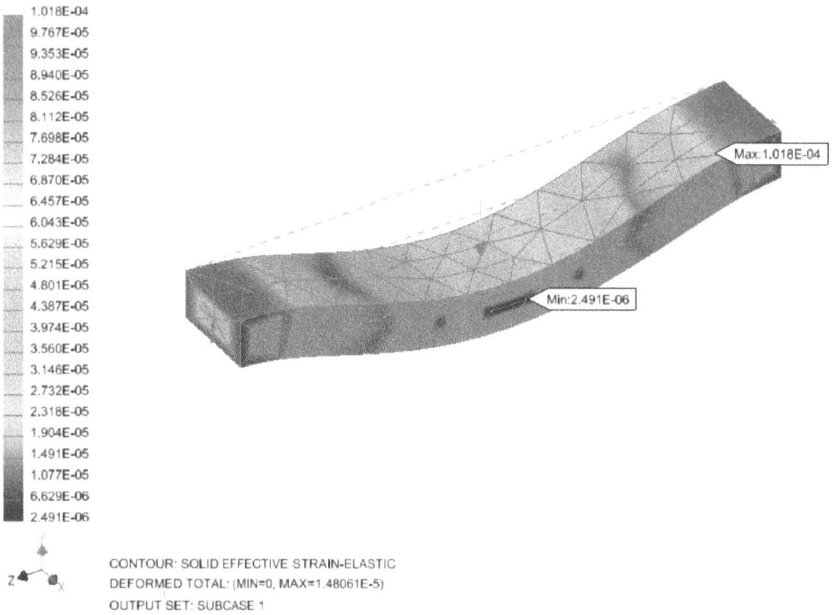

Figure-9. Analysis result created

- Click on the **Finish Autodesk Inventor Nastran** button from the **Exit** panel in **Autodesk Inventor Nastran** tab of **Ribbon** to exit the environment.

PERFORMING LINEAR STATIC ANALYSIS ON AN ASSEMBLY

Perform linear static study on the model shown in Figure-10. Apply bearing load at the connecting surface of table and rotor as per the figure.

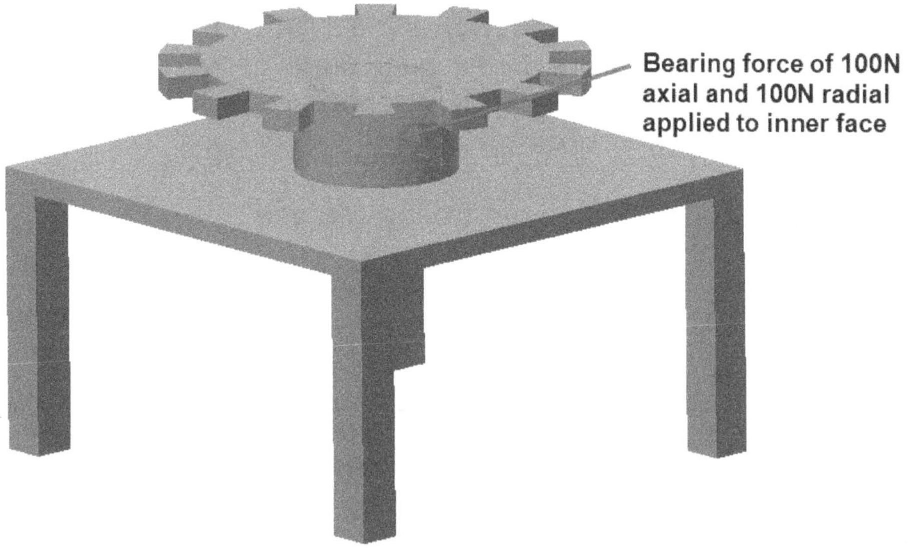

Figure-10. Assembly model for linear static analysis

Starting Linear Static Analysis

- Open the part in Autodesk Inventor and start Autodesk Inventor Nastran; refer to Figure-11.

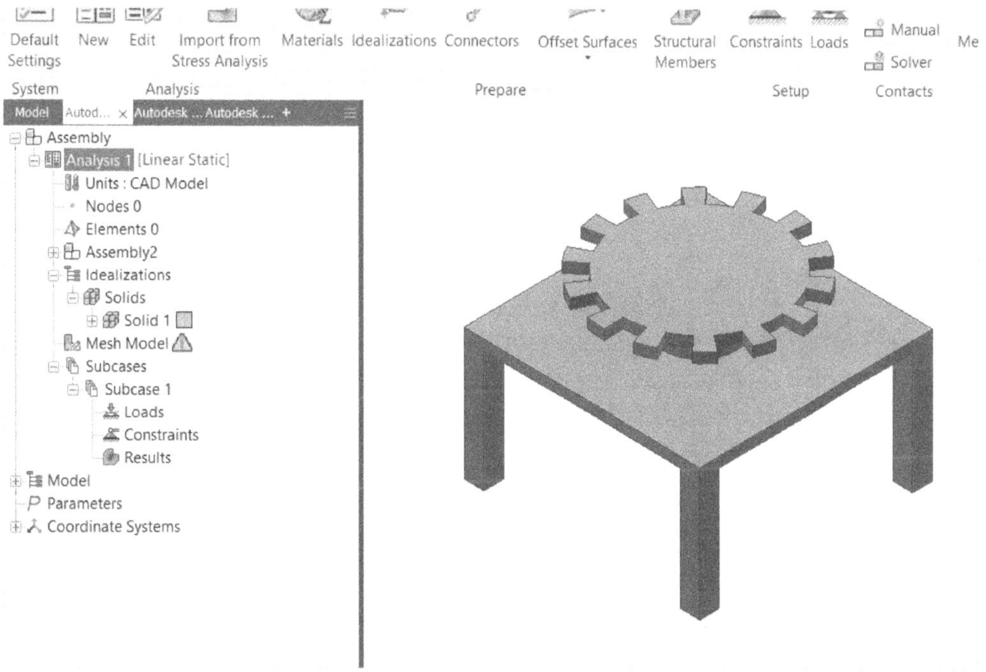

Figure-11. Assembly for linear static analysis

- Click on the **Edit** button from the **Analysis** panel of **Autodesk Inventor Nastran** tab in **Ribbon**. The **Analysis** dialog box will be displayed.

- In this analysis, we want the rotor to rotate under applied torque but do not want it to slide. So, we will use **Separation/No Sliding** as default contact. Click on the **Options** tab and select the **Separation/No Sliding** option from the **Contact Type** drop-down. Select the **SI** units as discussed earlier.
- After setting the parameters, click on the **OK** button.

Applying Material

- Click on the **Materials** tool from the **Prepare** panel of **Autodesk Inventor Nastran** tab in the **Ribbon**. The **Material** dialog box will be displayed.
- Click on the **Select Material** button from the dialog box. The **Material DB** dialog box will be displayed.
- Select the **Steel AISI 1015** material from **Autodesk Material Library** node and click on the **OK** button.
- Click on the **OK** button from the **Material** dialog box to apply material.
- Right-click on **Solid1** option from the **Idealizations** node and select the **Edit** option; refer to Figure-12. The **Idealizations** dialog box will be displayed. Select **Steel AISI 1015** option from the **Material** drop-down and click on the **OK** button.

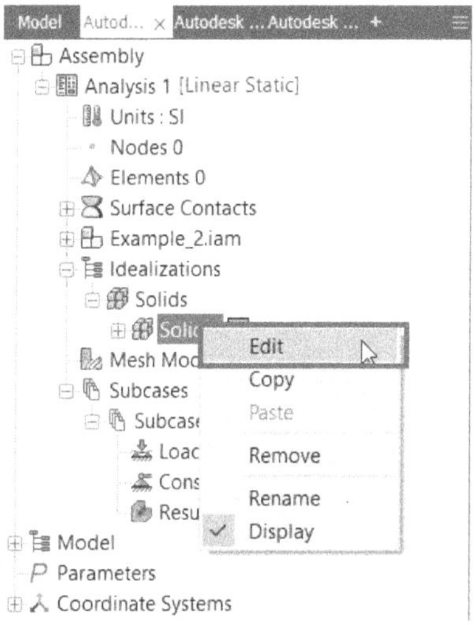

Figure-12. Editing idealization

Applying Contacts

- Click on the **Auto** tool from the **Contacts** panel in the **Ribbon**. The default contacts will be automatically applied in the assembly. Note that we have defined **Separation/No Sliding** as default contact earlier.

Applying Constraint

- Click on **Constraints** tool from the **Setup** panel of **Autodesk Inventor Nastran** tab in the **Ribbon**. The **Constraint** dialog box will be displayed.
- Select the bottom faces of the table to apply fix constraint and click on the **Fixed** button; refer to Figure-13.

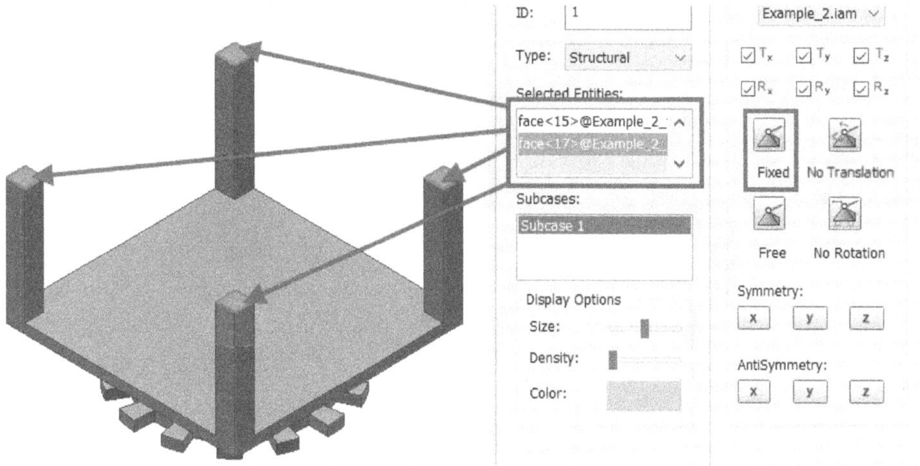

Figure-13. Faces selected for fixing

- Click on the **OK** button from the dialog box after applying constraint.

Applying Loads

- Click on the **Loads** tool from the **Setup** panel of **Autodesk Inventor Nastran** tab in **Ribbon**. The **Load** dialog box will be displayed.
- Select the round face of rotor as shown in Figure-14.

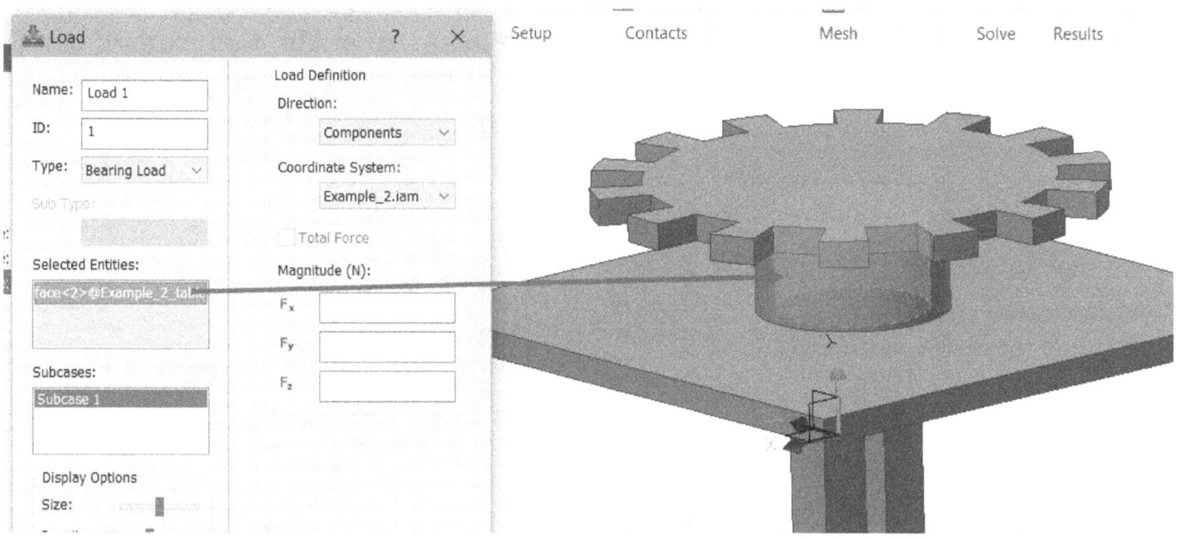

Figure-14. Applying bearing load

- Select **Bearing Load** option from the **Type** drop-down in the dialog box.
- Specify the radial and axial forces of bearing load as **500** in $\mathbf{F_x}$ and $\mathbf{F_y}$ edit boxes.
- Click on the **OK** button from the dialog box to apply load.

Mesh Setting

- Click on the **Mesh Settings** tool from the **Mesh** panel of **Autodesk Inventor Nastran** tab in **Ribbon**. The **Mesh Settings** dialog box will be displayed.
- Specify the element size as **0.01** in the **Element Size** edit box.
- Click on the **Generate Mesh** button from the dialog box. The mesh will be generated with specified mesh element size; refer to Figure-15.

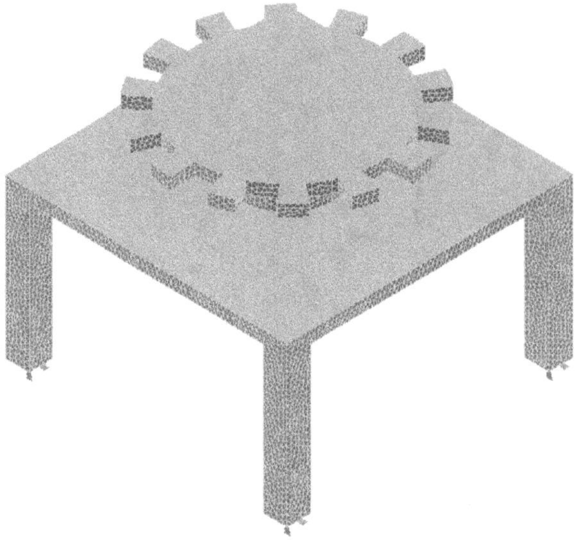

Figure-15. Mesh generated

- Click on the **OK** button from the dialog box.

Running Analysis

- Click on the **Run** button from the **Solve** panel of **Autodesk Inventor Nastran** tab in **Ribbon**. Once the analysis is complete, **Autodesk Inventor Nastran** information box will be displayed. Click on the **OK** button. The analysis results will be displayed; refer to Figure-16.

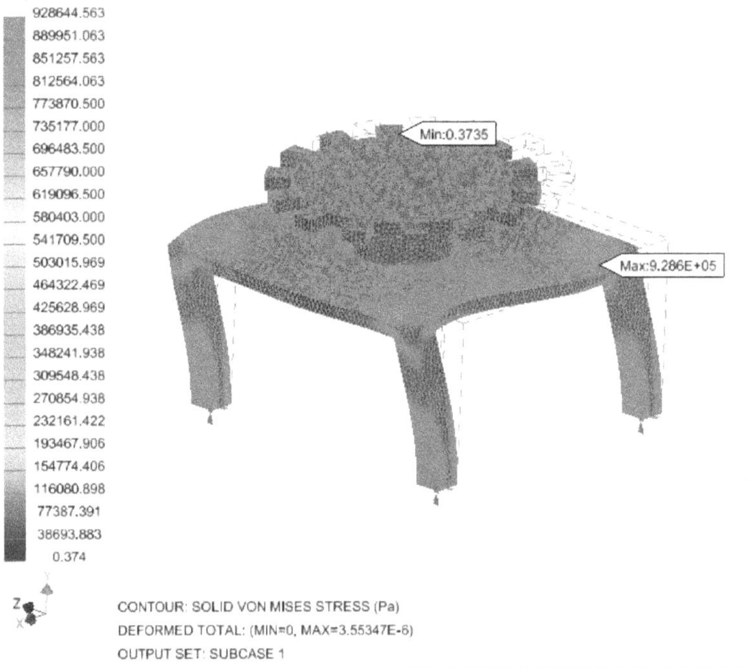

Figure-16. Analysis result of bearing load

- Double-click on desired option from the **Results** node.

PERFORMING ANALYSIS ON FRAME MODEL

When you open a frame model in Autodesk Inventor and start Autodesk Inventor Nastran then model features are automatically identified and beam idealization is applied to them; refer to Figure-17. Hide the CAD body to check 1D beam elements. You can also use sketch points and connectors to perform analysis on line elements. One such example is discussed next.

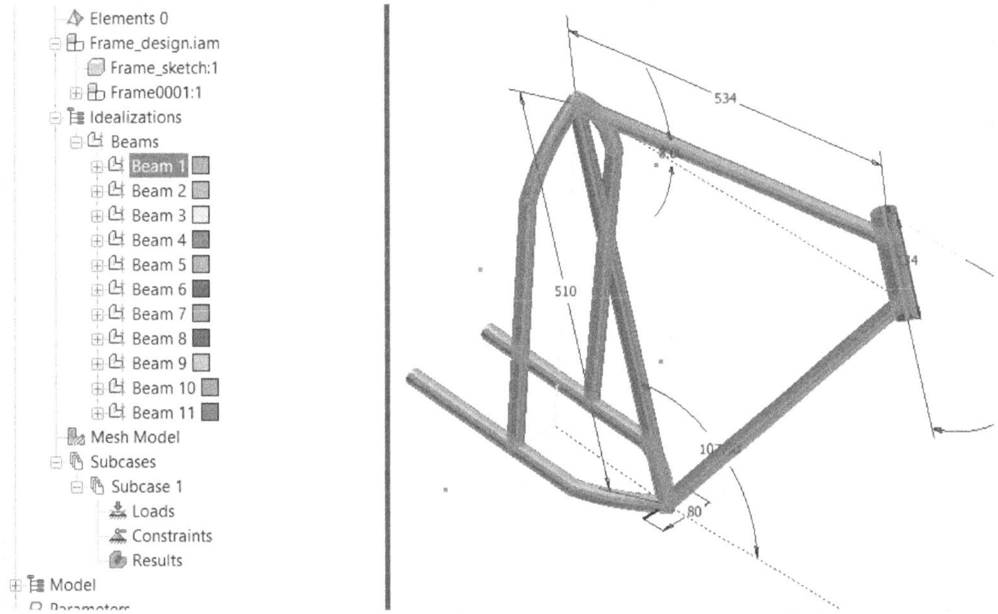

Figure-17. Beam idealization applied automatically

- Create sketch points as shown in Figure-18 on any plane in Autodesk Inventor. Save the part file at desired location.

Figure-18. Points for line element analysis

- Start Autodesk Inventor Nastran as discussed earlier.
- Click on the **Connectors** tool from the **Prepare** panel in the **Autodesk Inventor Nastran** tab of the **Ribbon**. The **Connector** dialog box will be displayed.
- Select the **Rod** option from the **Type** drop-down in the dialog box to define element type.
- Click in the **A** edit box and specify cross-section area of the rod to be created as element.
- Specify the values torsional constant (**J**) and coefficient for torsional stress (**C**) as required in respective edit boxes.
- One by one, select two points to create a connector between them; refer to Figure-19.

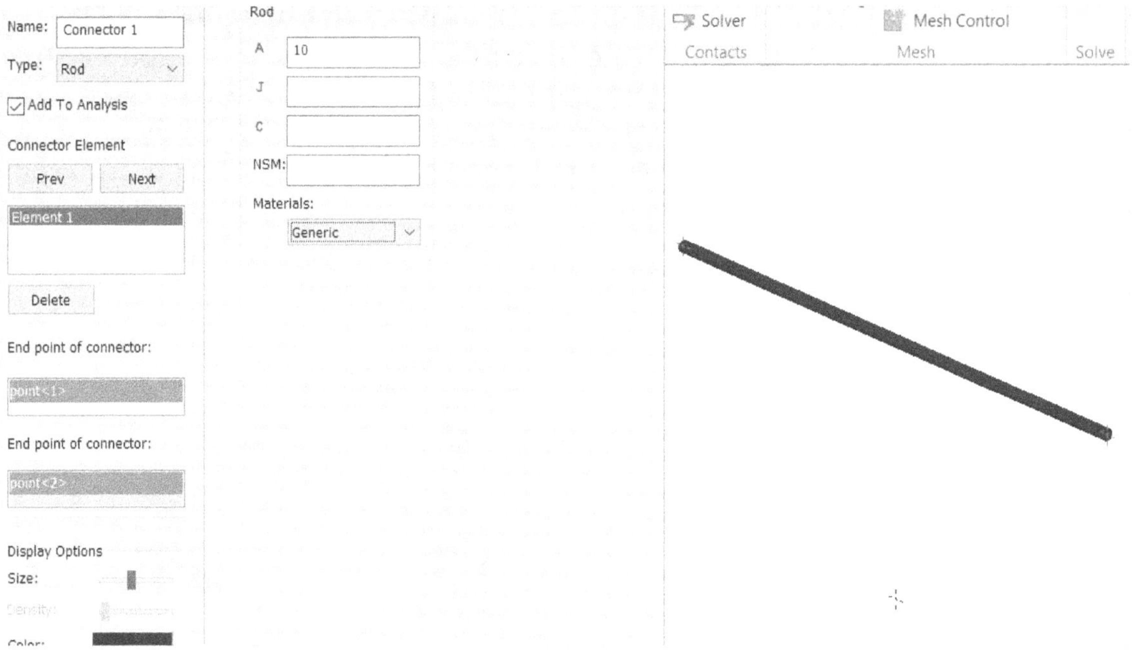

Figure-19. Preview of connector

- Click on the **Next** button from the **Connector Element** area in the dialog box and select points for next connectors; refer to Figure-20.

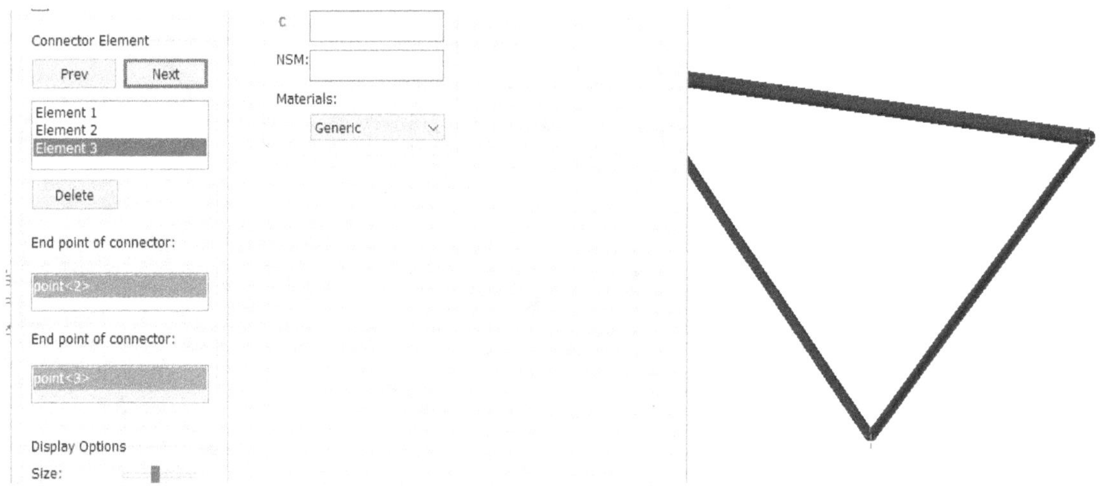

Figure-20. Multiple connectors created

- Click on the **OK** button from the dialog box to create connectors.
- Click on the **Constraints** tool from the **Setup** panel of **Autodesk Inventor Nastran** tab of the **Ribbon**. The **Constraint** dialog box will be displayed.
- Select the sketch points to restrict their movement during analysis; refer to Figure-21 and click on the **OK** button.

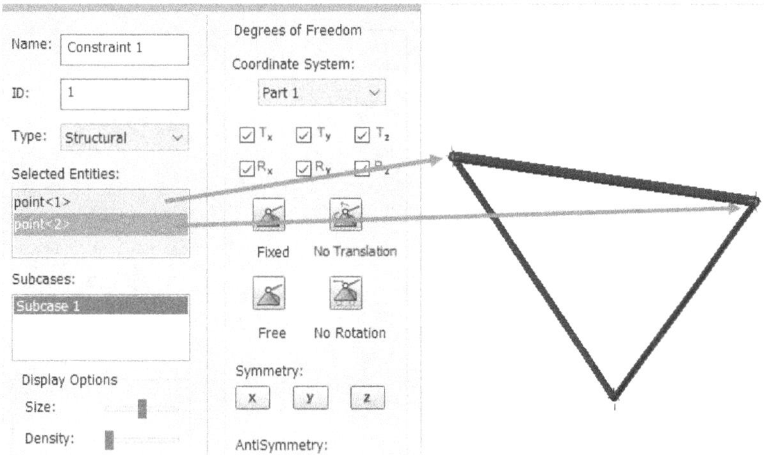

Figure-21. Applying constraints

- Similarly, you can apply load at a point in graphics area.
- Change the material of connectors by double-clicking on the **Generic** option in **Connectors** node in **Nastran Model Tree**; refer to Figure-22. The **Material** dialog box will be displayed which has been discussed earlier.

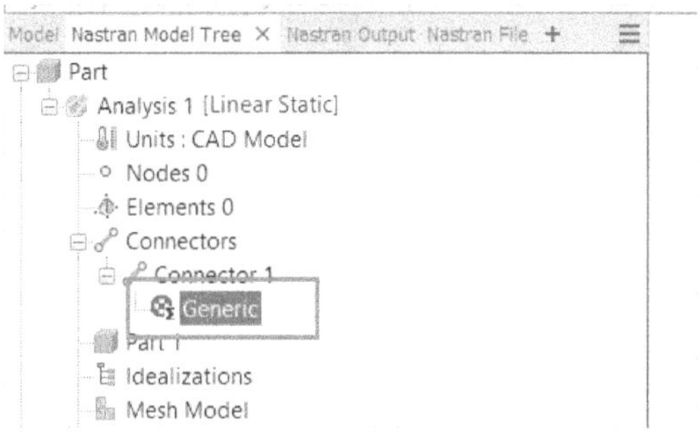

Figure-22. Generic option for material'

- After setting the parameters, click on the **Run** tool from **Solve** panel in the **Ribbon**. The results of analysis will be displayed.

Note that the above described method of analysis is fast and can be used for common engineering problems like checking integrity of body frame of a car.

PERFORMING PRESTRESS STATIC ANALYSIS

Prestress static analysis is used when you are concerned about heavy pre-loading on the model. In case of prestress static analysis, two cases of same load are applied. The first case is used as pre-stressing load and the other is extra loading. The procedure to use this analysis is given next.

- Open desired part and start Autodesk Inventor Nastran. By default, linear static analysis will be created.
- Click on the **Edit** button from the **Analysis** panel of **Autodesk Inventor Nastran** tab in the **Ribbon**. The **Analysis** dialog box will be displayed.
- Select the **Prestress Static** option from the **Analysis** drop-down in the dialog box. Set the other options as required and click on the **OK** button. Parameters for study will be displayed with two load sub-cases automatically created; refer to Figure-23.

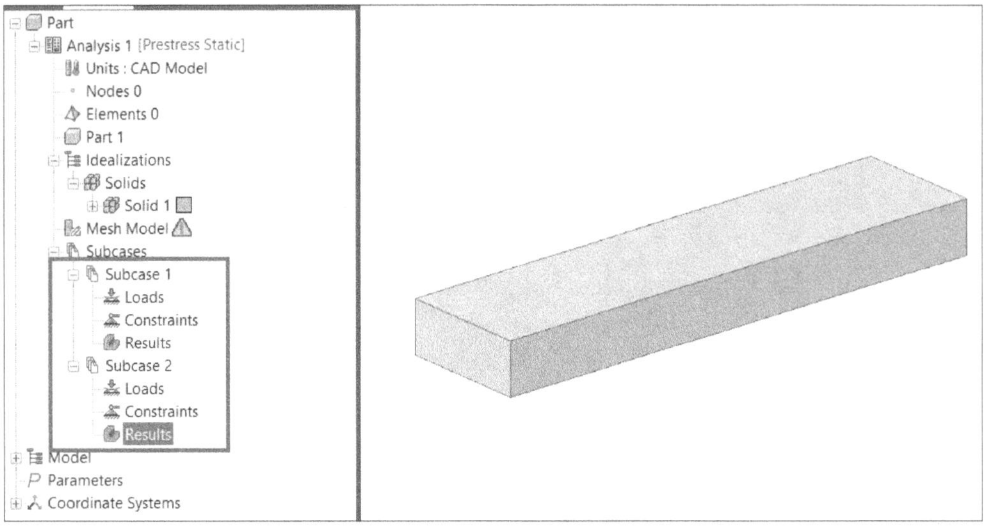

Figure-23. Prestress static analysis parameters

- Right-click on the **Loads** option for **Subcase 1** and select the **New** option from the shortcut menu. The **Load** dialog box will be displayed.
- Select the face on which you want to apply load and specify desired value of load.
- Click on the **OK** button. The specified load will be applied as initial condition.
- Create additional loads as required in Subcase 2.
- Set the other parameters as required and run the analysis.

NON LINEAR STATIC ANALYSIS

All real structures behave nonlinearly in one way or another at some level of loading. In some cases, linear analysis may be adequate. In many other cases, the linear solution can produce erroneous results because the assumptions upon which it is based are violated. Nonlinearity can be caused by the material behavior, large displacements, and contact conditions.

You can use a nonlinear study to solve a linear problem. The results can be slightly different due to different procedures.

In nonlinear finite element analysis, a major source of nonlinearity is due to the effect of large displacements on the overall geometric configuration of structures. Structures undergoing large displacements can have significant changes in their geometry due to load-induced deformations which can cause the structure to respond nonlinearly in a stiffening and/or a softening manner.

For example, cable-like structures generally display a stiffening behavior on increasing the applied loads while arches may first experience softening followed by stiffening, a behavior widely-known as the snap-through buckling.

Another important source of nonlinearity stems from the nonlinear relationship between the stress and strain which has been recognized in several structural behaviors. Several factors can cause the material behavior to be nonlinear. The dependency of the material stress-strain relation on the load history (as in plasticity problems), load duration (as in creep analysis), and temperature (as in thermoplasticity) are some of these factors.

This class of nonlinearity, known as material nonlinearity, can be idealized to simulate such effects which are pertinent to different applications through the use of constitutive relations.

A special class of nonlinear problems is concerned with the changing nature of the boundary conditions of the structures involved in the analysis during motion. This situation is encountered in the analysis of contact problems.

Pounding of structures, gear-tooth contacts, fitting problems, threaded connections, and impact bodies are several examples requiring the evaluation of the contact boundaries. The evaluation of contact boundaries (nodes, lines, or surfaces) can be achieved by using gap (contact) elements between nodes on the adjacent boundaries.

Yielding of beam-column connections during earthquakes is one of the applications in which material nonlinearity are plausible.

THEORY BEHIND NON-LINEAR ANALYSIS

As you have learnt from introduction, there are three factors which cause non-linearity in the body which are elastic behavior of material, large displacement in body, and variation in contact. In terms of equation this can be expressed as

$$[K(D)]\{D\} = \{F\}$$

Here, K(D) is stiffness matrix which is function of displacement.

D is the displacement matrix
and F is the Force applied

So, from the above equation you can easily understand that the stiffness is changing according to the displacement. Note that displacement is vector and it also has a direction. If we compare the linear static analysis and non-linear static analysis curves then we can find out different effects of load in both conditions; refer to Figure-24.

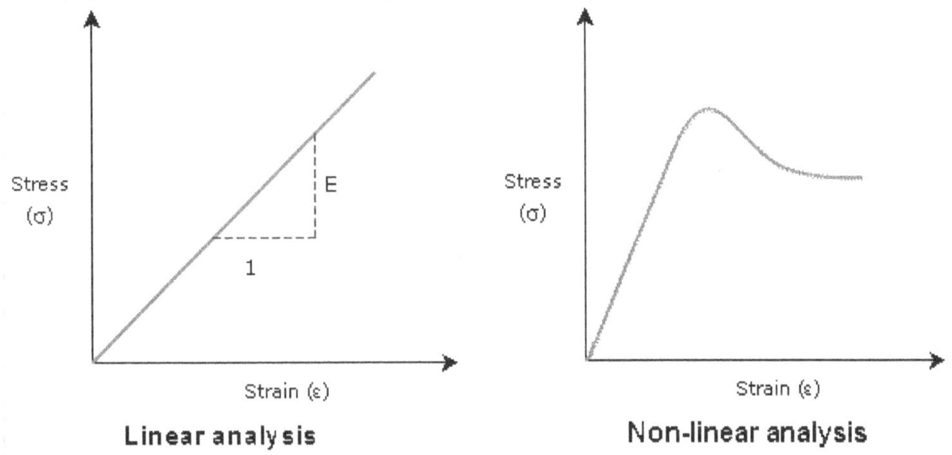

Figure-24. Stress Strain diagrams

In terms of load and displacement, the curve for both analyses can be given by Figure-25.

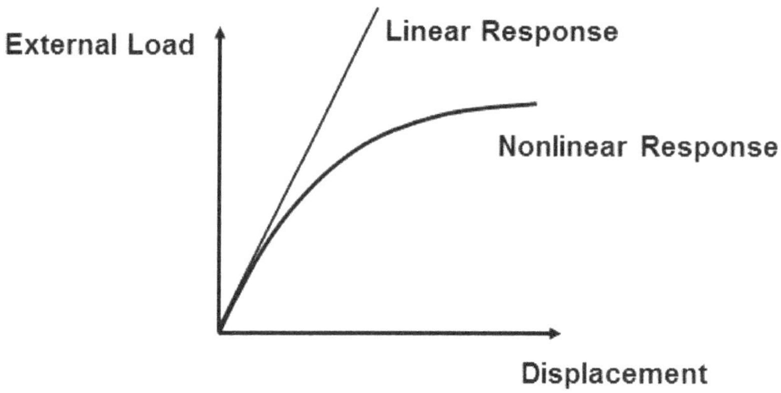

Figure-25. Load displacement curve

The normal incremental iteration does not work good for the non-linear analysis and generate errors as shown in Figure-26. So, Newton-Raphson algorithm is used to solve the non-linear equation.

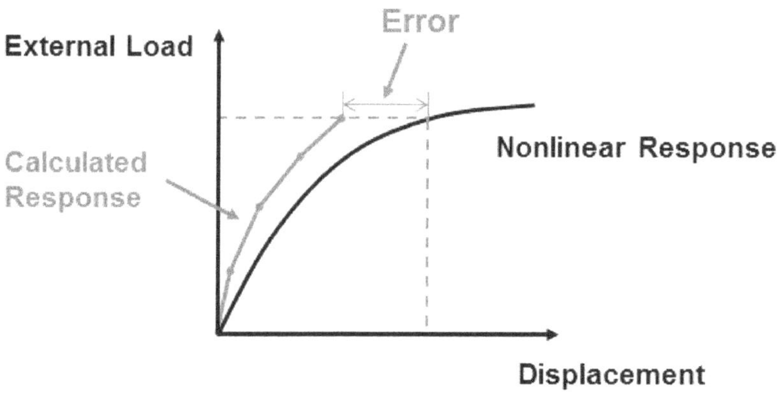

Figure-26. Error in incremental interative method

The equation for Newton-Raphson method is given as:

$$[K_T]\{\Delta u\} = \{F\} - \{F^{nr}\}$$

$[K_T]$ = tangent stiffness matrix
$\{\Delta u\}$ = displacement increment
$\{F\}$ = external load vector
$\{F^{nr}\}$ = internal force vector

The iteration continues till {F} - {Fnr} (difference between external and internal loads) is within a tolerance; refer to Figure-27.

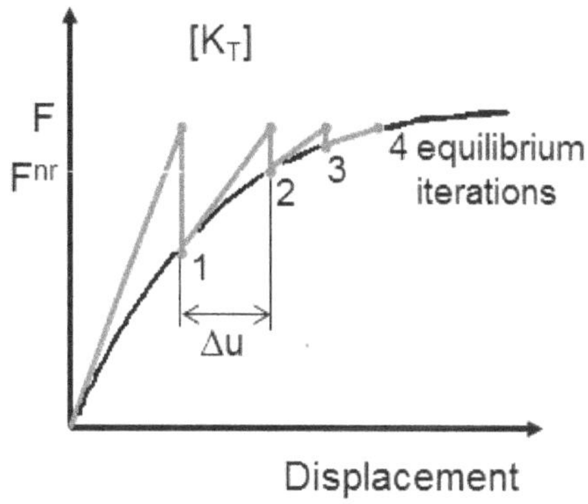

Figure-27. Newton-Raphson method

Thus a nonlinear solution typically involves the following:

- One or more load steps to apply the external loads and boundary conditions.(This is true for linear analyses too.)
- Multiple sub-steps to apply the load gradually. Each sub-step represents one load increment.(A linear analysis needs just one sub-step per load step.)
- Equilibrium iterations to obtain equilibrium (or convergence) at each sub-step. (Does not apply to linear analyses.)

Role of Time in Non-Linear Analysis

Each load step and sub-step is associated with a value of time. Time in most nonlinear static analyses is simply used as a counter and does not mean actual, chronological time. Figure-28 shows a load-time curve.

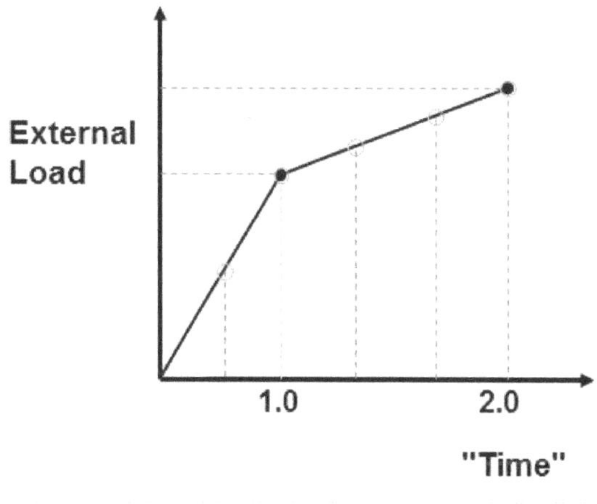

Figure-28. Load time curve

By default, time = 1.0 at the end of load step 1, 2.0 at the end of load step 2, and so on. For rate-independent analyses, you can set it to any desired value for convenience. For example, by setting time equal to the load magnitude, you can easily plot the load-deflection curve.

The "time increment" between each sub-step is the time step Δt. Time step Δt determines the load increment ΔF over a sub-step. The higher the value of Δt, the larger the ΔF, so Δt has a direct effect on the accuracy of the solution.

Now, we are going to start with Non-linear Static Analysis which means there is no damping or resistance to the force. Note that the last example in previous chapter, an assembly of wall bracket, was a problem of Nonlinear static analysis because there was large displacement in the body. Now, we will learn the procedure to perform Nonlinear static analysis.

PERFORMING NON LINEAR STATIC ANALYSIS

Basic steps to perform a nonlinear static analysis are given next.

- Open the part on which you want to perform nonlinear static analysis in Autodesk Inventor.
- Click on the **Autodesk Inventor Nastran** tool from the **Environments** tab in the **Ribbon**. The **Autodesk Inventor Nastran** tab will be added in the **Ribbon** and tools related to analysis will be displayed. Note that linear static analysis starts automatically when you activate the Nastran environment.
- Click on the **Edit** tool from the **Analysis** panel in **Autodesk Inventor Nastran** tab of **Ribbon**. The **Analysis** dialog box will be displayed.
- Select the **Nonlinear Static** option from the **Type** drop-down in the dialog box.
- Set desired options in **Output Controls** tab of the dialog box.
- Click on the **Options** tab in the dialog box and select the **On** option from the **Large Displacements** drop-down if large displacement is expected in analysis; refer to Figure-29.

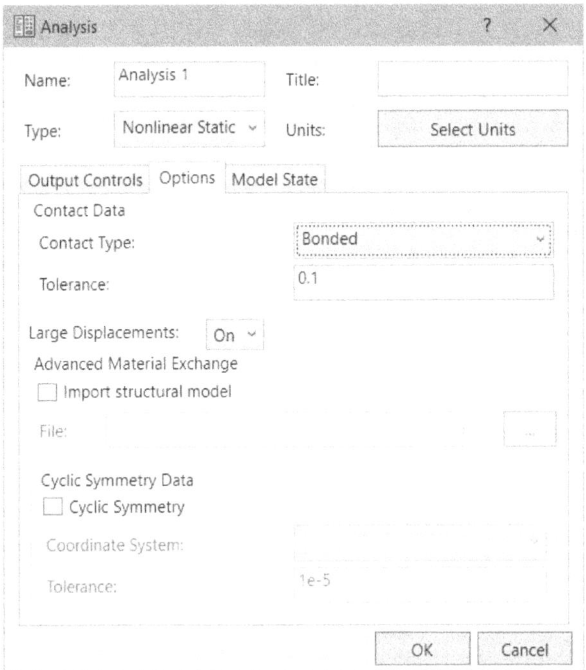

Figure-29. Large Displacements option

- If you want to import structural model from a nastran file earlier created then select the **Import structural model** check box and open desired file using **Browse** button.
- After setting desired parameters, click on the **OK** button from the dialog box. The options in the analysis browser will be displayed as shown in Figure-30.

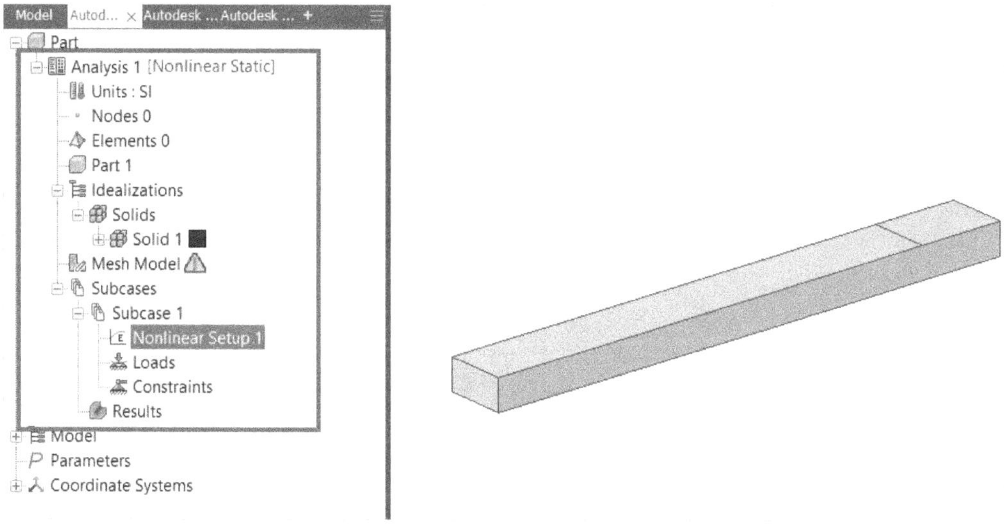

Figure-30. Options for nonlinear analysis

Nonlinear Setup Parameters

- Right-click on **Nonlinear Setup 1** option from the **Subcase 1** node and select the **Edit** option. The **Nonlinear Setup** dialog box will be displayed; refer to Figure-31.

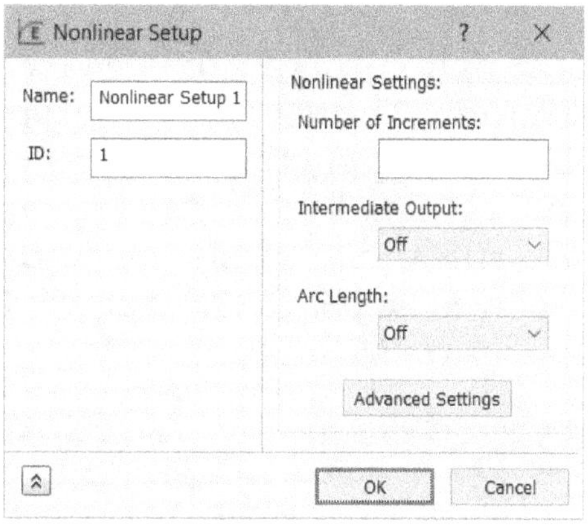

Figure-31. Nonlinear Setup dialog box

- Specify desired number of steps in which load will be increased during the analysis in the **Number of Increments** edit box.
- Select the **Off** option from the **Intermediate Output** drop-down if you do not want to save output at each load increment. Select the **On** option to save output at each load increment. Select the **All** option from the **Intermediate Output** drop-down if you want to save all the outputs of analysis when nonlinear analysis bisects the load increment.
- Select the **On** option from the **Arc Length** drop-down if you are concerned about softening, buckling failure or material failure during the analysis. Note that activating this option takes more computing power for analysis.
- Click on the **Advanced Settings** button to set advanced nonlinear static parameters. The **Nonlinear Static Parameters** dialog box will be displayed; refer to Figure-32.

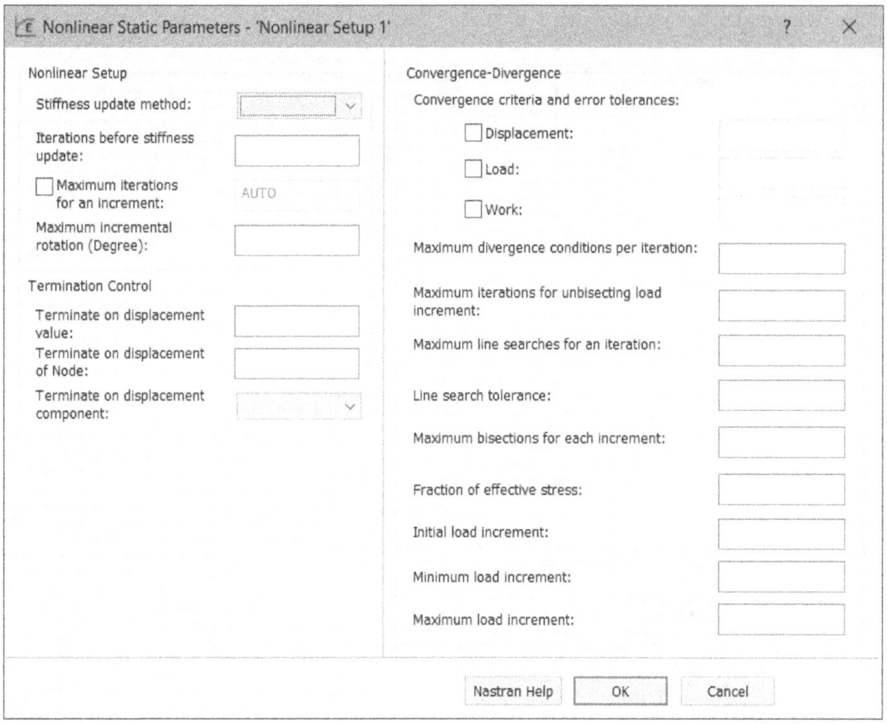

Figure-32. Nonlinear Static Parameters dialog box

- Set desired parameters (The options of this dialog box have been discussed in next topic) and click on the **OK** button. The **Nonlinear Setup** dialog box will be displayed again. Click on the **OK** button to apply the parameters and exit the dialog box.
- Apply material, constraint, and load as discussed earlier.
- Click on the **Run** button to run the analysis. Once the analysis is complete, the stages of result will be displayed as per the **Number of Increments** set in **Nonlinear Setup** dialog box; refer to Figure-33.

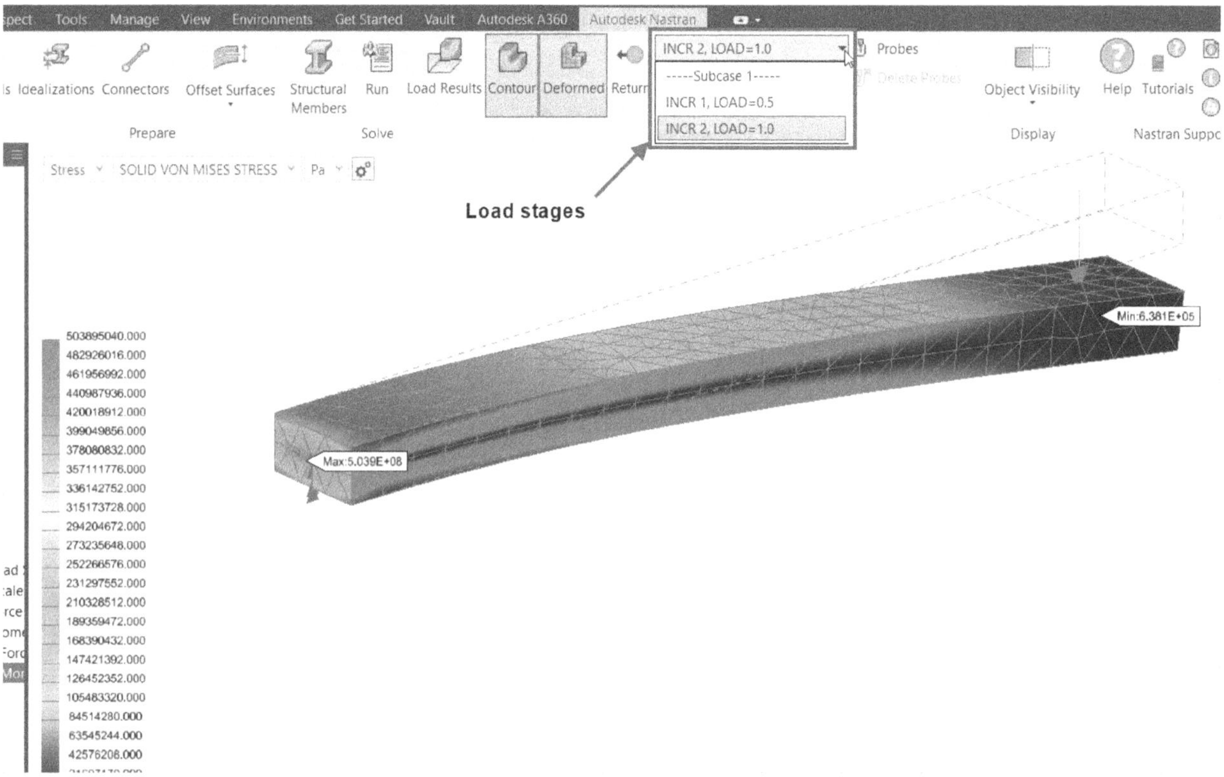

Figure-33. Result of nonlinear static analysis

The other options in **Autodesk Inventor Nastran** tab are same as discussed earlier. After performing the analysis, save the results and click on the **Finish Autodesk Inventor Nastran** tool from the **Exit** panel to exit.

Nonlinear Static Parameters

- Select desired option from the **Stiffness update method** drop-down to define how stiffness matrix is updated during the course of non-linear analysis. Select the **AUTO** option if you want the software to automatically select suitable strategy based on convergence rate of analysis. In this case, stiffness will update automatically if solution of analysis diverges or number of iterations has exceeded the maximum iterations specified for analysis. Select the **SEMI** option if load on model increase with each time step. In this case, software will update stiffness matrix, each time new load is applied. Select the **ITER** option if you want the stiffness matrix to be updated after each iteration till convergence.
- Specify desired value in the **Iterations before stiffness update** edit box to define initial number of iterations up to which analysis should run before stiffness matrix is updated.
- Select the **Maximum iterations for an increment** check box to define number of iterations to be performed before an increase is applied to iterations. After selecting check box, specify desired value in the edit box next to check box. By default, **AUTO** is selected for this option so increment is automatically applied based on convergence rate.
- Specify desired value in the **Maximum incremental rotation (Degree)** edit box to define maximum amount of rotation in stiffness matrix that is tolerant before load bisection occurs.
- Specify desired value in the **Terminate on displacement value** edit box to define displacement achieved by the model at which analysis will terminate.
- Specify desired value in the **Terminate on displacement of Node** edit box to define node location on model matrix which if moved under load then analysis will terminate.
- Select desired option from the **Terminate on displacement component** drop-down to define direction of displacement for node.
- Select desired check box for **Convergence criteria and error tolerances** option to define criteria for convergence of analysis. For example, select the **Displacement** check box and specify desired displacement value which once reached will converge the analysis for current load increment. The main reason to change the convergence tolerance is: analysis failing to converge or converging slowly and you are ready to sacrifice accuracy for a faster run time.
- Specify desired value in the **Maximum divergence conditions per iteration** edit box to define number of divergences to occur for terminating the iteration.
- Specify desired value in the **Maximum iterations for unbisecting load increment** edit box to define maximum iterations to be performed without bisecting load increment. Here, bisecting means reducing the value of load increment.
- Specify desired value in the **Maximum line searches for an iteration** edit box to define number of line searches to be performed for solving an iteration. Line searches are performed to predict the scale for displacement increment and minimize the energy potential if system is not converging by ordinary iterations. Note that you need to specify tolerance range value in the **Line search tolerance** edit box for limiting the scope of this algorithm based on nature of the analysis.

- Specify desired value in the **Maximum bisections for each increment** edit box to define number of bisections of load that can be performed if divergence occurs. If system does not converge after specified number of bisections then FATAL error will be generated and analysis will terminate.
- Specify desired value in the **Fraction of effective stress** edit box to define fraction of total stress acting on the model which will be used to limit increase in size of nonlinear material elements.
- Specify desired values in **Initial load increment**, **Minimum load increment**, and **Maximum load increment** edit boxes to define initial load increment, minimum load increments, and maximum load increments to be added using non-linear loading curve.

Note: You can learn more about the theory behind these values and non-linear analysis by visiting the link: **https://dianafea.com/manuals/d102/Theory/Theorych54.html**

MATERIAL ORIENTATION

The **Material Orientation** option is used to define the direction of material flow in the model. This option is available for 2D Shell bodies only. The procedure to use this tool is given next.

- After generating mesh of 2D shell body, right-click on name of analysis in the **Nastran Model Tree** and select the **Material Orientation** option from **New** cascading menu of the shortcut menu; refer to Figure-34. The **Material Orientation** dialog box will be displayed; refer to Figure-35.

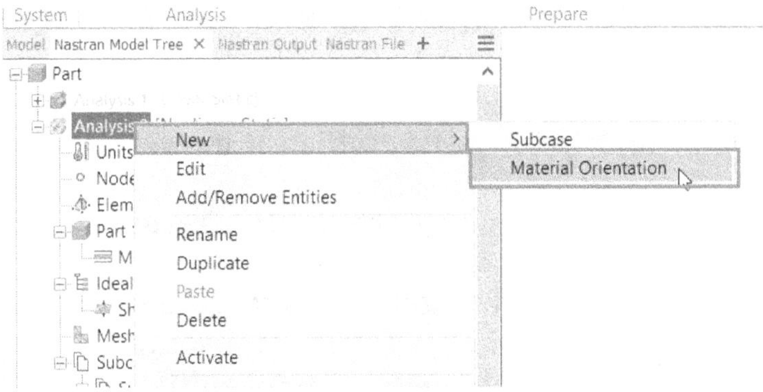

Figure-34. Material Orientation option

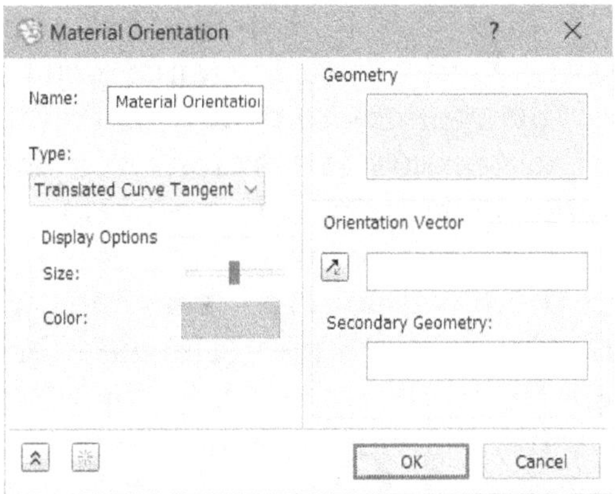

Figure-35. Material Orientation dialog box

- Select desired option from the **Type** drop-down to define direction reference. By default, the **Translated Curve Tangent** option is selected in this drop-down. Select the face of shell whose material orientation is to be modified. Click in the **Orientation Vector** selection box and select reference entities for defining direction of material. Preview of material orientation will be displayed with green arrows; refer to Figure-36.

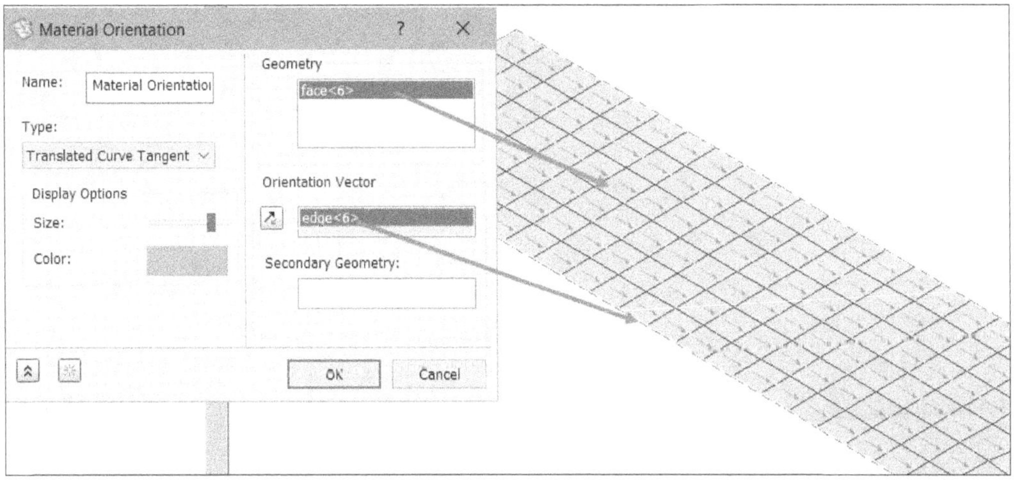

Figure-36. Preview of material orientation

- Select the **Vector Projection** option if you want to specify component of orientation vector for defining direction; refer to Figure-37.

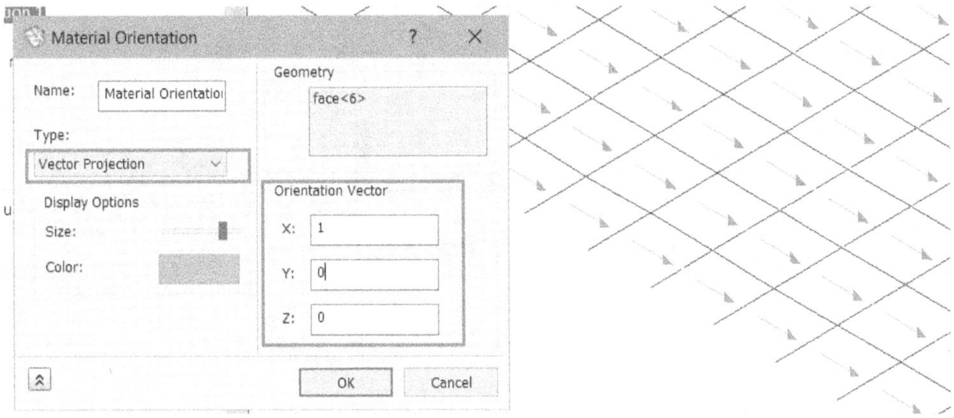

Figure-37. Vector projection option

- Similarly, you can use other options in this dialog box to define material orientation.
- After setting desired parameters, click on the **OK** button to apply orientation.

SUB-CASES

Sub-cases are used to create different load sets. For example, you want to check stresses on the same model under two different loads of 10 N and 100 N then you can create two sub-cases to run the analysis. Using sub-cases is faster than running two analysis on the same model with just load difference because the time consumed for building structure matrix of model is common when running sub-cases. After performing analysis using sub-cases, you will have option to switch between results of the two sub-cases. Note that you can have multiple sub-cases in an analysis it is not by any means limited to just two sub-cases. The procedure to create a new sub-case is given next.

- Right-click on **Analysis** node in the **Nastran Model Tree** for which you want to create sub-cases and select the **Subcase** option from **New** cascading menu of the shortcut menu; refer to Figure-38. The **Subcase** dialog box will be displayed; refer to Figure-39.

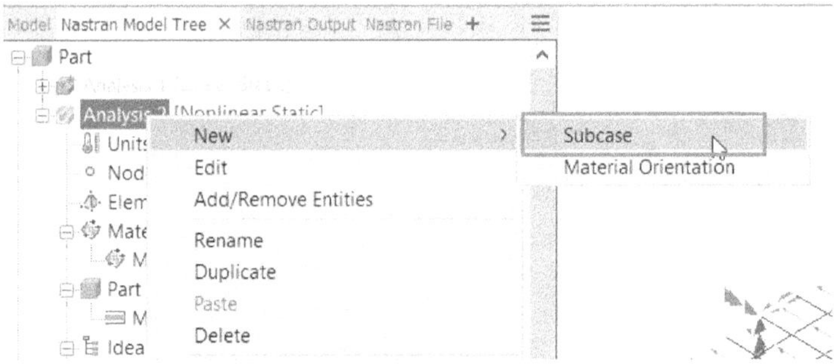

Figure-38. Subcase option

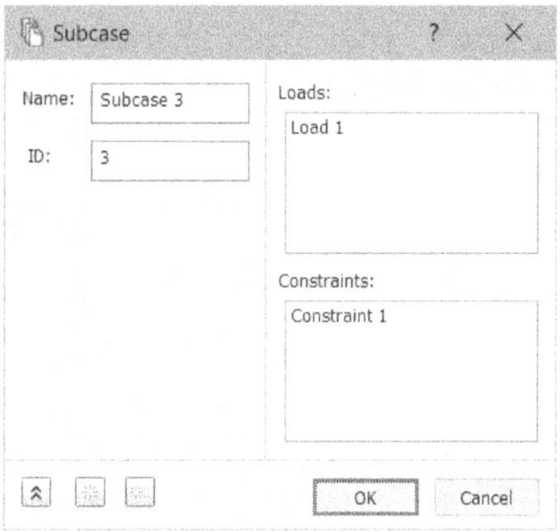

Figure-39. Subcase dialog box

- Select the loads and constraints earlier applied in the model from the **Loads** and **Constraints** areas respectively to include them in current subcase. The new subcase will be added in **Nastran Model Tree**; refer to Figure-40. You can modify the parameters of subcase as discussed earlier.

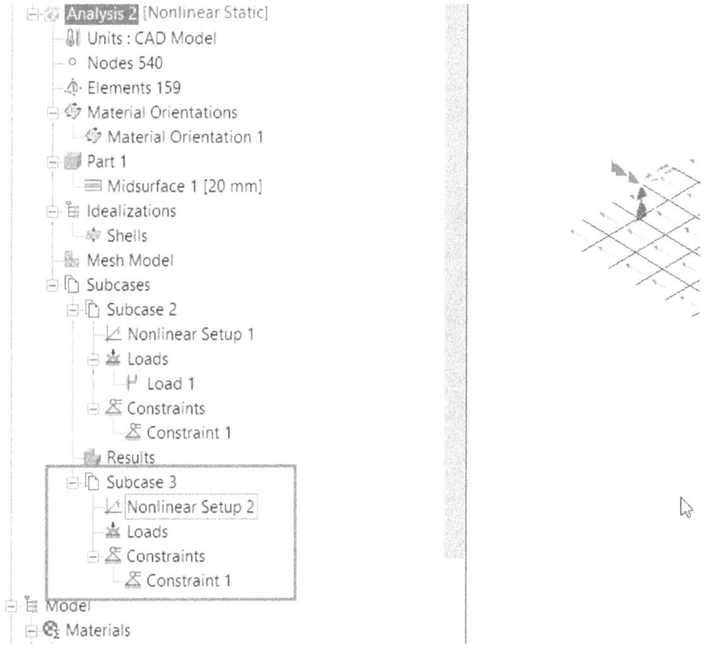

Figure-40. New subcase added

NASTRAN SOLVER PARAMETERS

When you are working on non-linear analyses or some advanced analysis where you get the errors of system not converging or other similar errors. As a designer, you know well that there is no finite solution for current analysis and you want to check some intermediate results. In such cases, there are some override parameters for modifying general behavior of Nastran solver. You can access these parameters by using **Parameters** option at the bottom in **Nastran Model Tree**; refer to Figure-41. The procedure to use this option is given next.

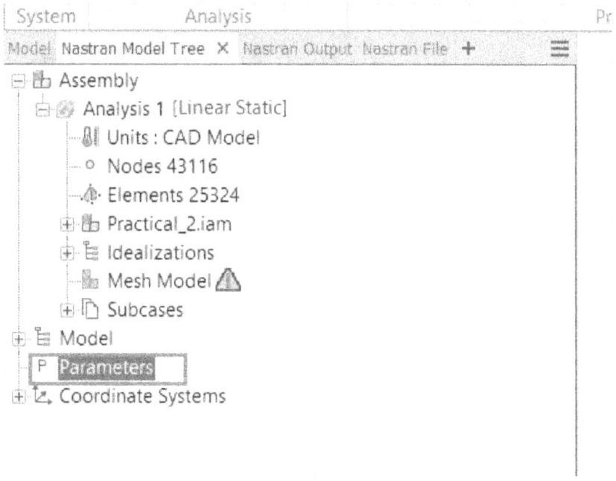

Figure-41. Parameters option

- Double-click on the **Parameters** option from the bottom in **Nastran Model Tree** after starting an analysis. The **Parameters** dialog box will be displayed; refer to Figure-42.
- Select the **Advanced Settings** check box to modify advanced parameters of solver. On selecting this check box, you will find some additional options in the right area of the dialog box.
- Set desired value of parameters in the dialog box. For example, you can set the **SOLUTIONERROR** advanced parameter to **ON** if singularity is detected in the system and you want to replace the singular/negative definite to a positive one.
- You can search the variables by typing keywords in the **Find** edit box.

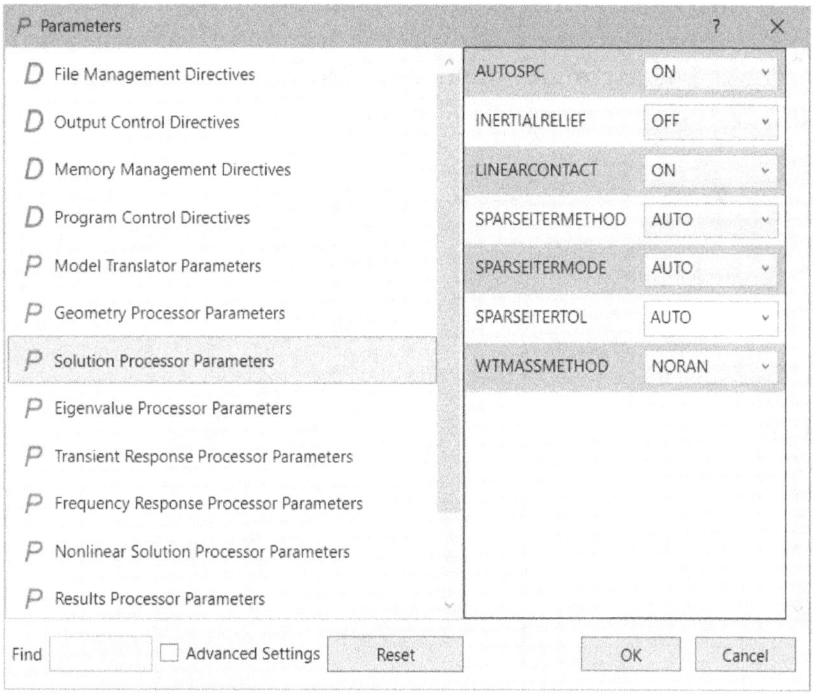

Figure-42. Parameters dialog box

- Click on the **Reset** button to change all the parameters to their default values.
- After setting desired parameters, click on the **OK** button to exit the dialog box.

PRACTICAL 1

Apply the conditions as shown in Figure-43 and perform linear static analysis on the model.

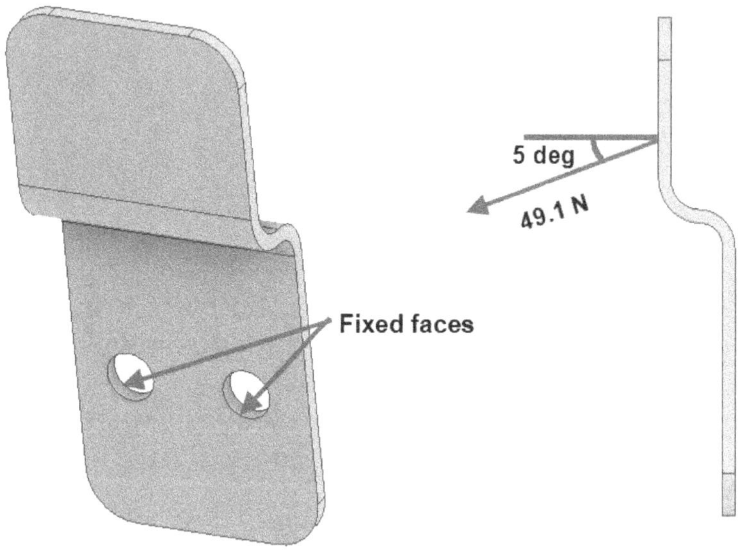

Figure-43. Practical 1

Opening Part and Starting Linear Static Analysis

- Open Practical 1 part file from Chapter 3 folder of Resources of this book and click on **Autodesk Inventor Nastran** tool from **Begin** panel of **Environments** tab in the **Ribbon**. The tools to perform linear static analysis will be displayed; refer to Figure-44.

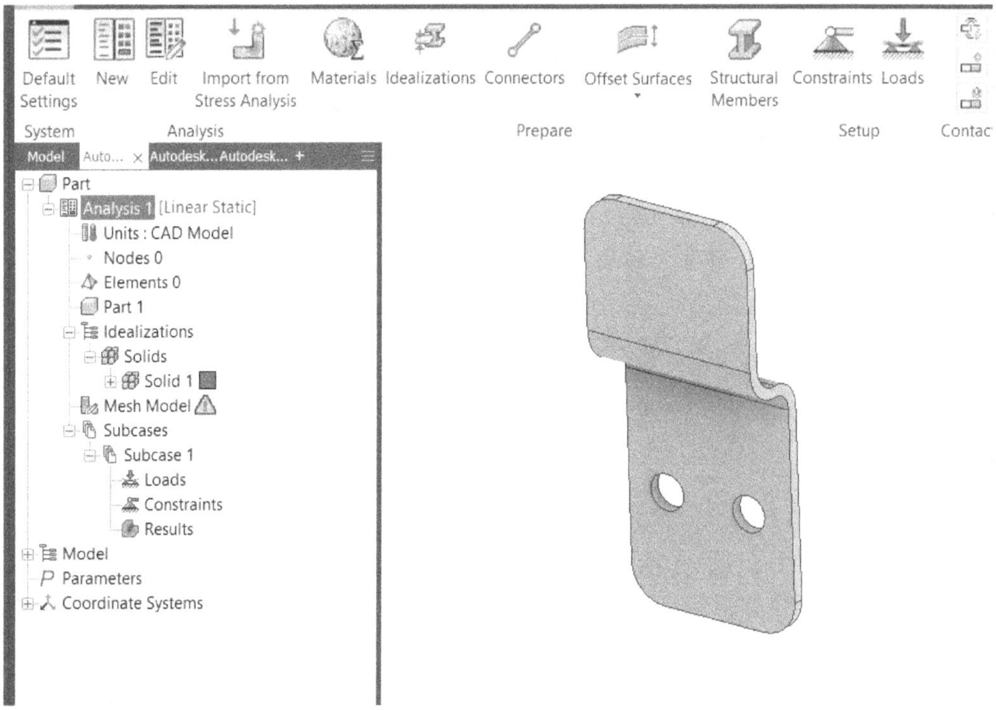

Figure-44. Linear static analysis options

Applying Material and Setting Idealization

- Click on **Materials** tool from the **Prepare** panel of **Autodesk Inventor Nastran** tab in the **Ribbon**. The **Material** dialog box will be displayed.
- Click on the **Select Material** button from the dialog box. The **Material DB** dialog box will be displayed.
- Select **Alloy Steel** material from the **Autodesk Material Library** node in the dialog box and click on the **OK** button.
- Click on the **OK** button from the **Material** dialog box. The material will be applied with solid idealization.
- Click on **Idealizations** tool from the **Prepare** panel in the **Autodesk Inventor Nastran** tab of **Ribbon**. The **Idealizations** dialog box will be displayed; refer to Figure-45.
- Select desired color from the color section of the dialog box.
- Select the **Alloy Steel** option from the **Material** drop-down and click on the **OK** button.

Generating Mesh

- Click on **Mesh Settings** tool from the **Mesh** panel of **Autodesk Inventor Nastran** tab in the **Ribbon**. The **Mesh Settings** dialog box will be displayed.
- Specify element size as **3.5** in **Element Size** edit box.
- Click on **Generate Mesh** tool from the dialog box. The mesh will be generated; refer to Figure-46.

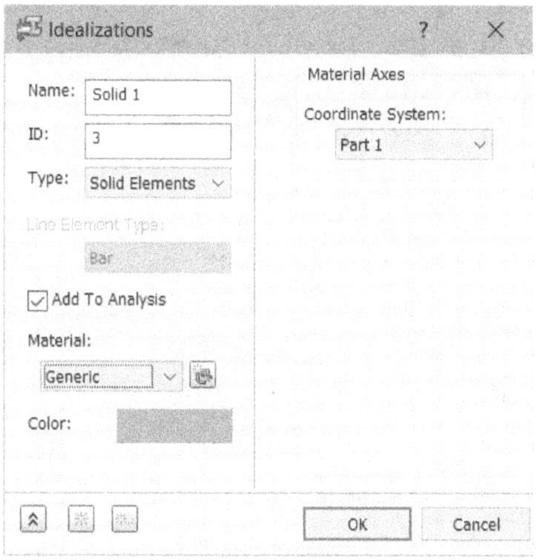

Figure-45. Idealizations dialog box

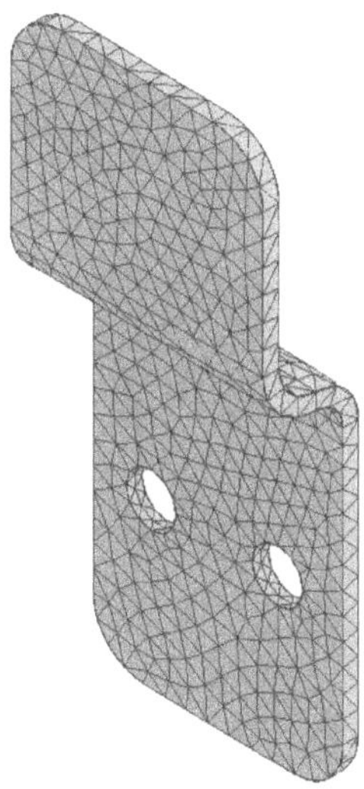

Figure-46. Mesh generated for Practical 1

- Click on the **OK** button from the **Mesh Settings** dialog box.

Applying Constraints

- Click on the **Constraints** tool from the **Setup** panel of **Autodesk Inventor Nastran** tab in the **Ribbon**. The **Constraint** dialog box will be displayed.
- Select the circular faces of holes to be constrained and click on the **Fixed** button; refer to Figure-47.

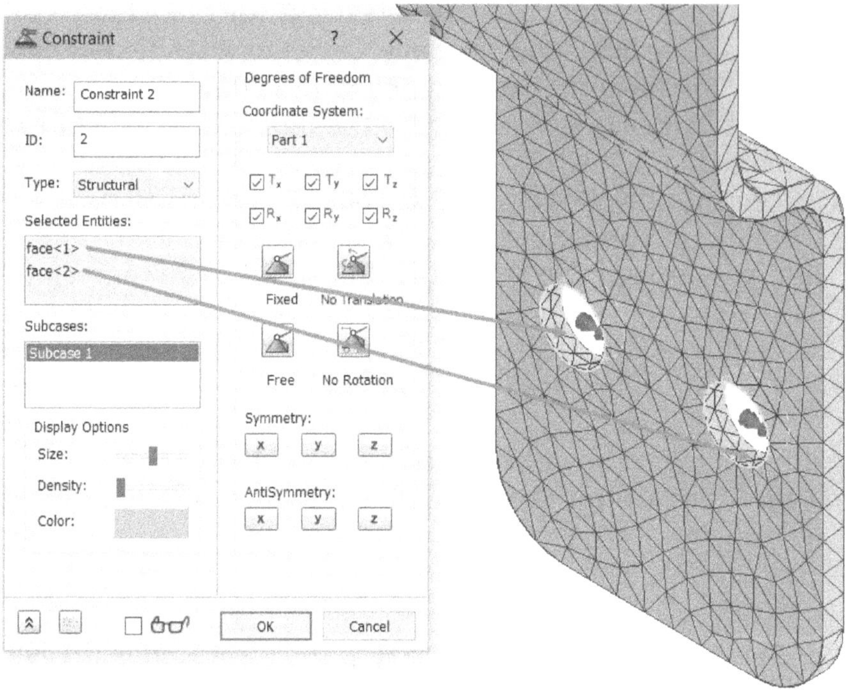

Figure-47. Faces selected for fixing circular faces

- Click on the **OK** button to apply constraint.

Applying Force

- Click on **Start 2D Sketch** tool from the **Sketch** panel of **Sketch** tab in the **Ribbon**. You will be asked to select a face/plane as sketching plane.
- Select the side face of the model; refer to Figure-48. The sketching environment will be displayed.

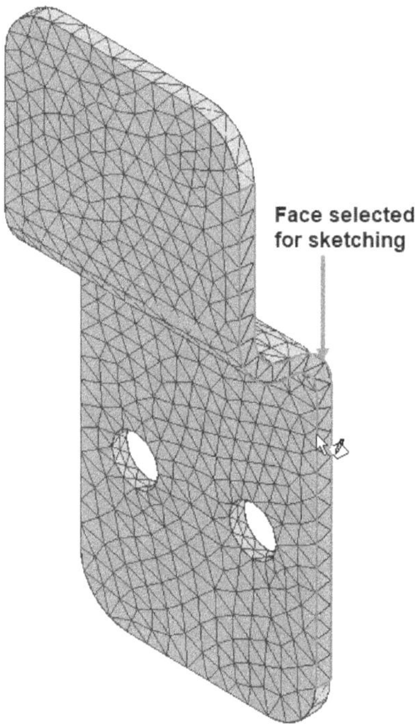

Figure-48. Face selected for sketching

- Click on the **Line** tool from the **Create** panel of **Sketch** tab in **Ribbon**. You will be asked to specify start point of the line.

- Create a line of 5 degree and 50 mm length as shown in Figure-49 and click on the **Finish Sketch** button from **Exit** panel.

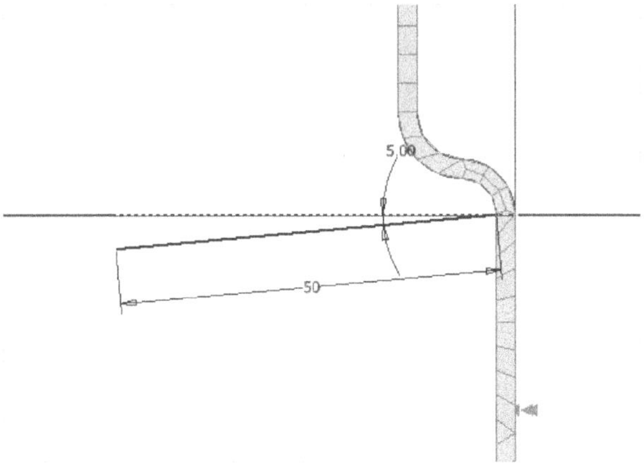

Figure-49. Line created for sketch

- Click on the **Loads** tool from the **Setup** panel of **Autodesk Inventor Nastran** tab in the **Ribbon**. The **Load** dialog box will be displayed.
- Select the **Force** option from the **Type** drop-down and select the upper face of model; refer to Figure-50.

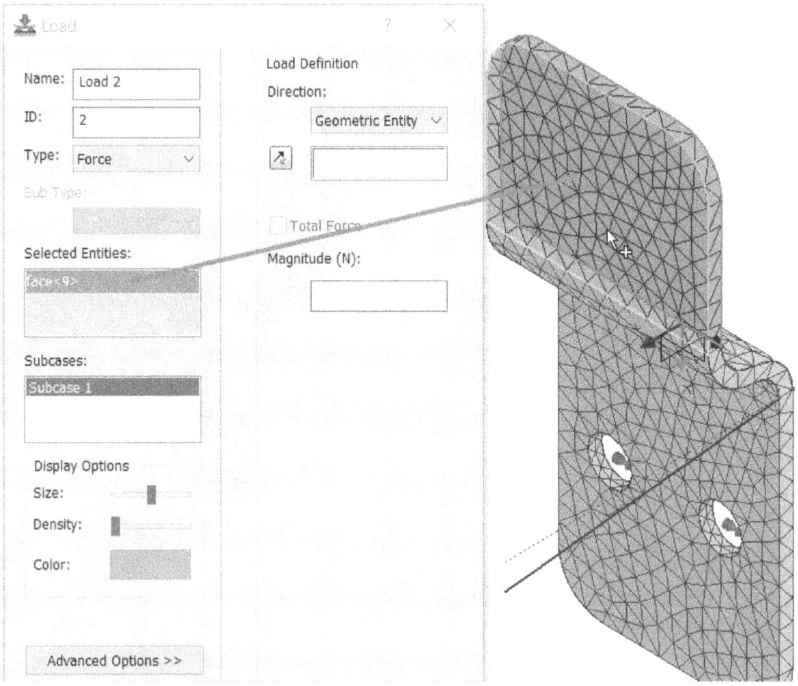

Figure-50. Face selected for force

- Select the **Geometric Entity** option from the **Direction** drop-down. The selection box below it will become active. Select the sketched line earlier created to define direction of force.
- Specify the value of force as **49.1** in the **Magnitude** edit box; refer to Figure-51.
- Click on the **OK** button from the dialog box.

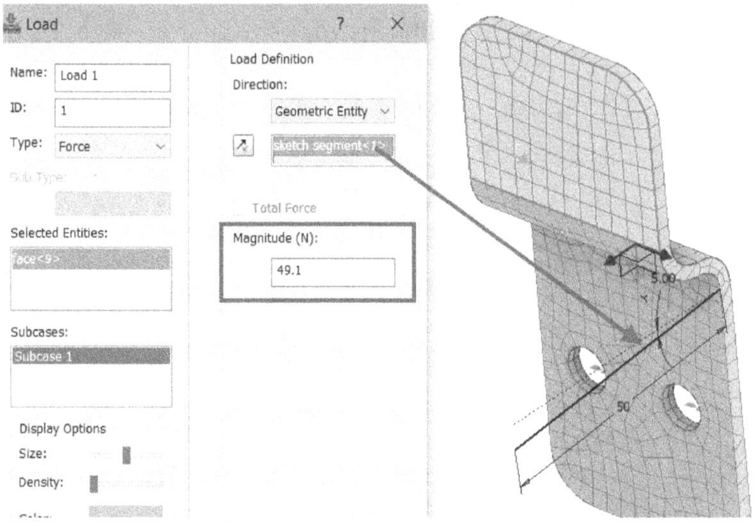

Figure-51. Applying force along selected line

Running Analysis

- Click on the **Run** button from the **Solve** panel of **Autodesk Inventor Nastran** tab in the **Ribbon**. Once the analysis is complete, the **Autodesk Inventor Nastran** information box will be displayed.
- Click on the **OK** button from the information box. The result of analysis will be displayed; refer to Figure-52.

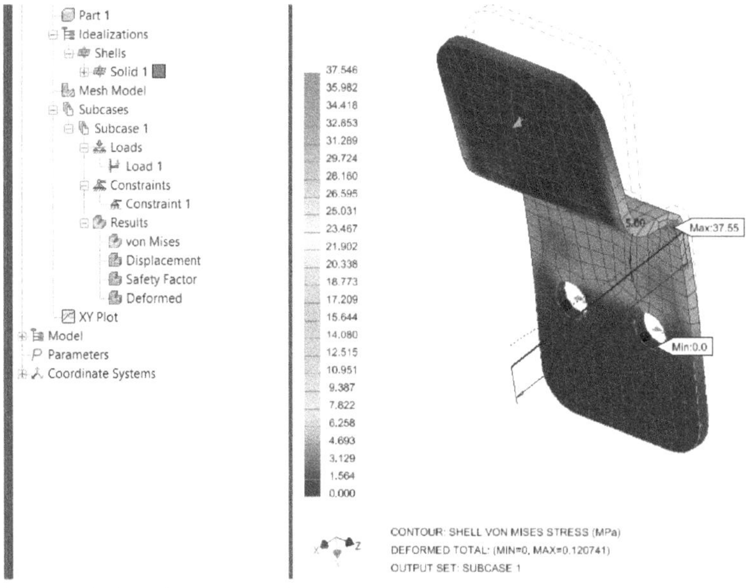

Figure-52. Result of practical 1

- Double-click on **Safety Factor** option under **Results** node to check the factor of safety; refer to Figure-53. Since, factor of safety is over 3 in critical areas of the model so our model is safe for operation. To be sure that the component will function properly, its factor of safety should be at least 3 at each critical location on the model. We can increase the strength of this part is by increasing thickness of part or by adding rib to part.

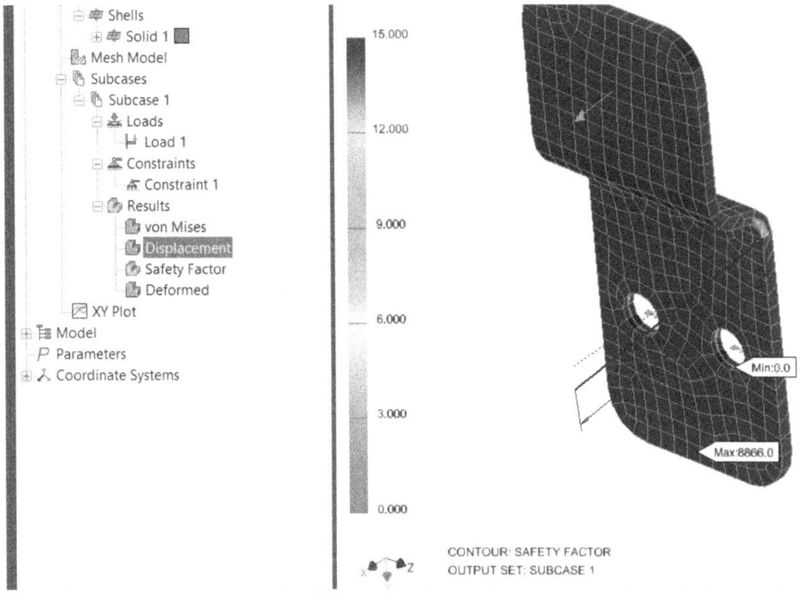

Figure-53. Factor of safety plot for Practical 1

PRACTICAL 2

Perform linear static analysis on the model shown in Figure-54 with specified conditions.

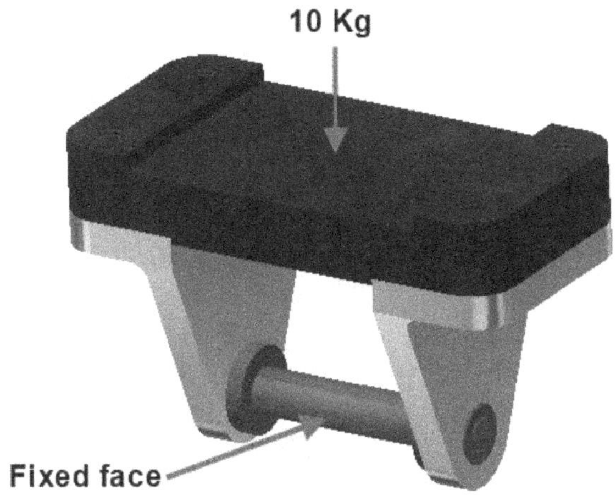

Figure-54. Practical 2

Opening Assembly file and Starting Linear Static Analysis

Open Practical 2 assembly file from Chapter 3 folder of Resources of this book and click on **Autodesk Inventor Nastran** tool from **Begin** panel of **Environments** tab in the **Ribbon**. The tools to perform linear static analysis will be displayed.

Note that solid idealization and materials are already applied to the model.

Applying Constraints

- Click on the **Constraints** tool from the **Setup** panel of **Autodesk Inventor Nastran** tab in the **Ribbon**. The **Constraint** dialog box will be displayed.
- Select the round face of the bolt and click on the **Fixed** button; refer to Figure-55.

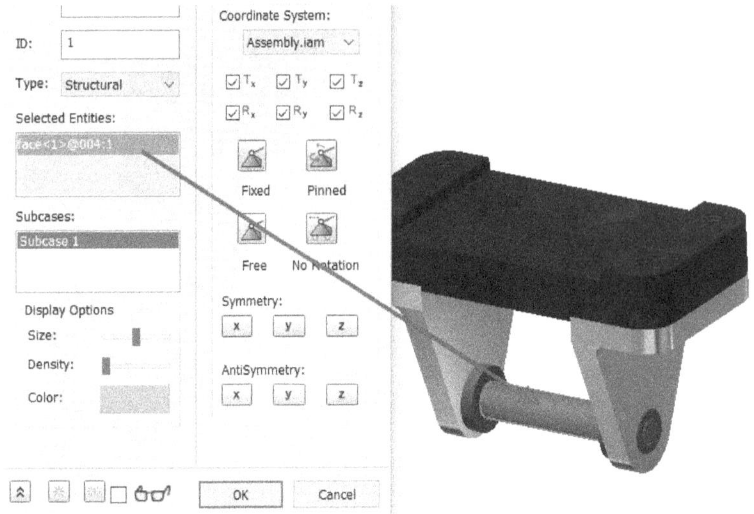

Figure-55. Applying constraint

- After setting desired parameters, click on the **OK** button.

Applying Load

- Click on the **Loads** tool from the **Setup** panel of **Autodesk Inventor Nastran** tab in the **Ribbon**. The **Loads** dialog box will be displayed.
- Select **Force** option from the **Type** drop-down and select the top face of the model.
- Select the **Normal to Surface** option from **Direction** drop-down and specify the force value as **98.1** in the **Magnitude** edit box; refer to Figure-56.

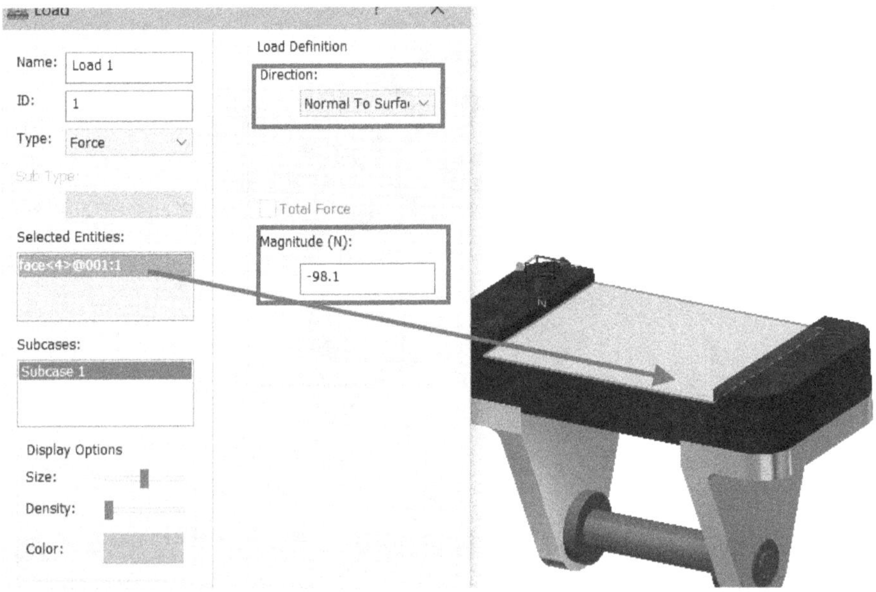

Figure-56. Specifying weight on model

- Click on the **OK** button from the dialog box.

Running the Analysis

- Click on the **Mesh Settings** tool from the **Mesh** panel of the **Ribbon**. The **Mesh Settings** dialog box will be displayed.
- Set the element size as **5** mm in the **Element Size** edit box and click on the **Generate Mesh** button. The mesh will be generated; refer to Figure-57.

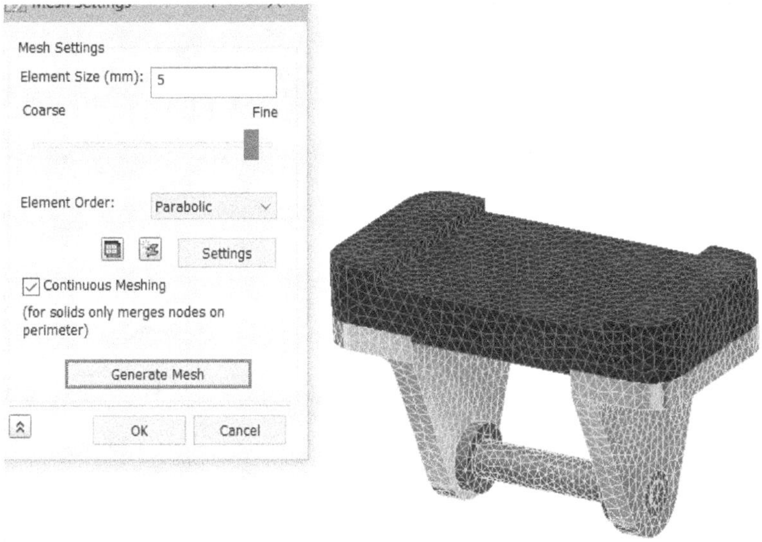

Figure-57. Mesh generated for Practical 2

- Click on the **OK** button from the dialog box.
- Click on the **Run** button from the **Solve** panel of **Ribbon**. Once the analysis is complete, the **Autodesk Inventor Nastran** information box will be displayed.
- Click on the **OK** button from the information box. Results of analysis will be displayed; refer to Figure-58.

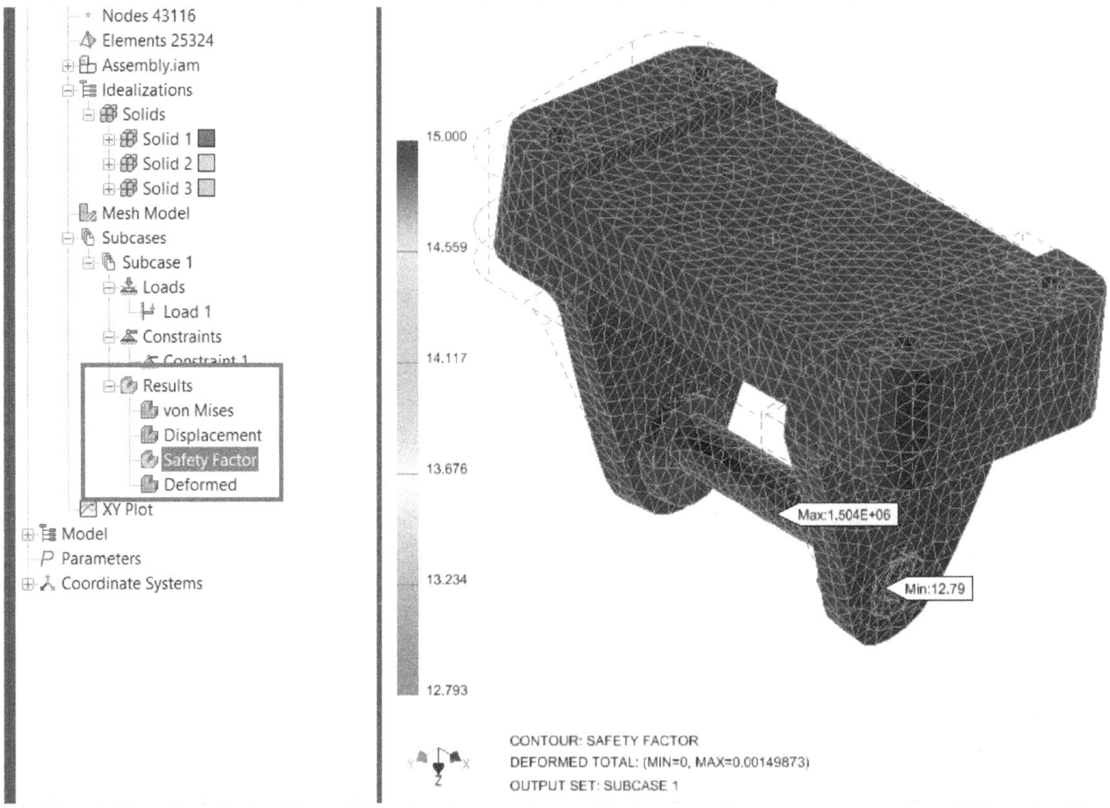

Figure-58. Results of analysis for Practical 2

Check the results and modify the model accordingly.

PRACTICAL 3

In this practical, we will perform non-linear static analysis on an assembly to check the stresses on model at various time steps; refer to Figure-59.

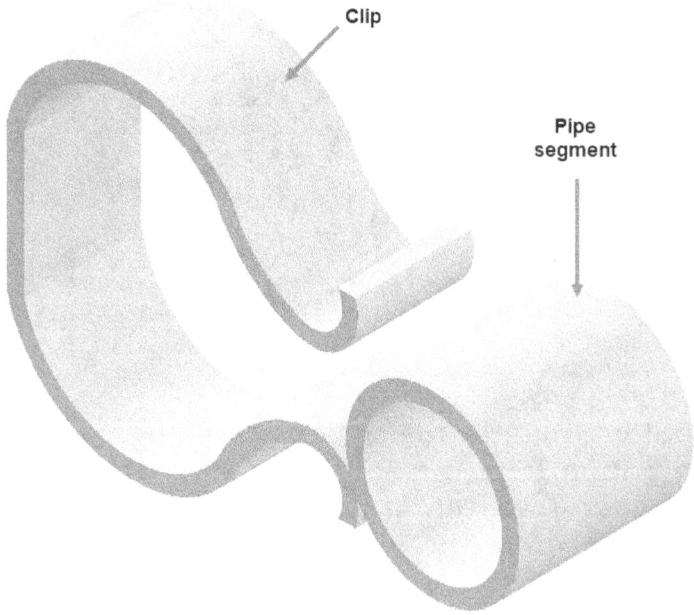

Figure-59. Practical 3 model

Opening Assembly file and Starting Non-linear Static Analysis

- Open Practical 3 assembly file from Chapter 3 folder of Resources of this book and click on **Autodesk Inventor Nastran** tool from **Begin** panel of **Environments** tab in the **Ribbon**. The tools to perform linear static analysis will be displayed.
- Click on the **Edit** button from the **Analysis** panel in **Autodesk Inventor Nastran** tab of the **Ribbon**. The **Analysis** dialog box will be displayed.
- Select **Nonlinear Static** option from the **Type** drop-down to change the analysis type.
- Click on the **Options** tab in the dialog box and select **Separation** option from **Contact Type** drop-down so that two parts can be considered two separate objects in analysis.
- Click on the **Select Units** button and set **Modified SI** option in **Unit System** drop-down. Click on the **OK** button from **Units** dialog box.
- Leave rest of the options in **Analysis** dialog box to default and click on the **OK** button. The options related to Nonlinear analysis will be displayed.

Defining Idealizations and Materials for Parts in Assembly

- Right-click on **Solid1** option from the **Idealizations** node in **Nastran Model Tree** and select the **Edit** option from shortcut menu; refer to Figure-60. The **Idealizations** dialog box will be displayed.
- Click on the **New Material** button next to **Material** drop-down in the dialog box. The **Material** dialog box will be displayed. (We will first apply material to clip.)
- Click on the **Select Material** button from the top in the dialog box. The **Material DB** dialog box will be displayed.
- Select the **Acrylic** option from **Inventor Material Library** node and click on the **OK** button.

- Click on the **Nonlinear** button from **Analysis Specific Data** area in the **Material** dialog box. The **Nonlinear Material Data** dialog box will be displayed.
- Select the **Elasto-Plastic (Bi-Linear)** radio button from dialog box and specify the parameters as shown in Figure-61.

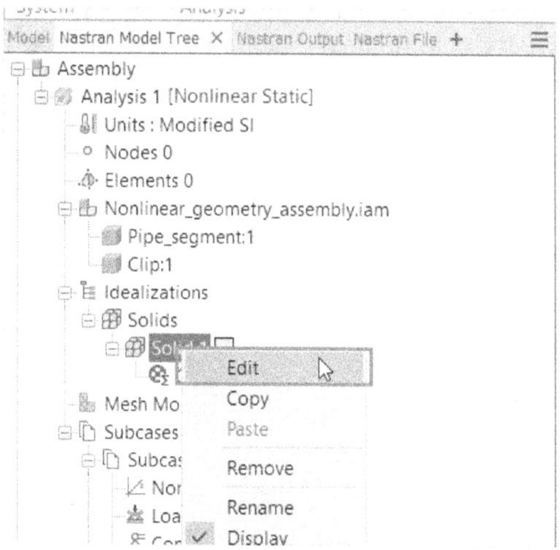

Figure-60. Edit option

- Click on the **OK** button from the dialog box and then click on the **OK** button from the **Material** dialog box. The **Idealizations** dialog box will be displayed again.
- Select the **Associated Geometry** check box from the dialog box and select the Clip part model from graphics area.
- Click on the **OK** button to apply idealization and material.
- Similarly, select **Polyvinyl Chloride - Flexible** material and solid idealization for pipe segment model by using the **Idealizations** tool in the **Prepare** panel of the **Autodesk Inventor Nastran** tab in the **Ribbon**.

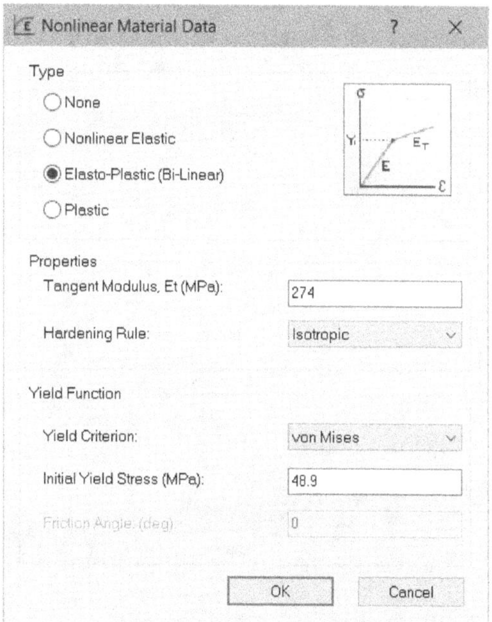

Figure-61. Nonlinear data for acrylic plastic

Applying Contact

To apply contacts to the model, we need to move pipe segment part closer to clip part model in such a way that surfaces of two parts are barely touching each other. You can do so by selecting the pipe segment model and dragging it near the clip; refer to Figure-62. It is important to keep the two parts barely touching before applying contact so that when you define surface contact, the matrix formed for contact is not very large or impractical. The steps to apply no penetration contact are given next.

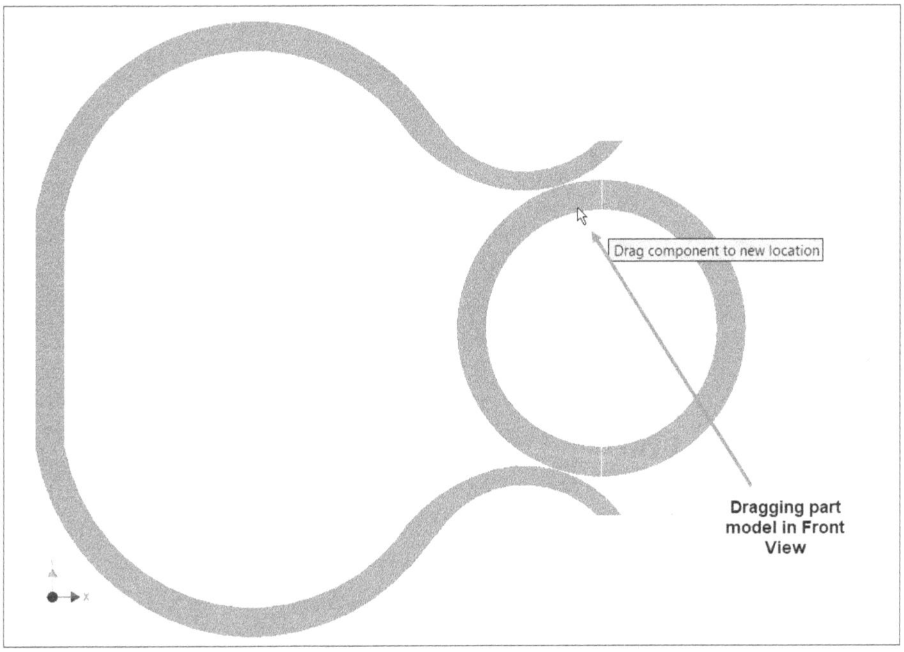

Figure-62. Changing location of part

- Click on the **Manual** tool from the **Contacts** panel in the **Autodesk Inventor Nastran** tab of the **Ribbon**. The **Surface Contact** dialog box will be displayed.
- Select the surfaces as shown in Figure-63 and specify the parameters as in this figure.

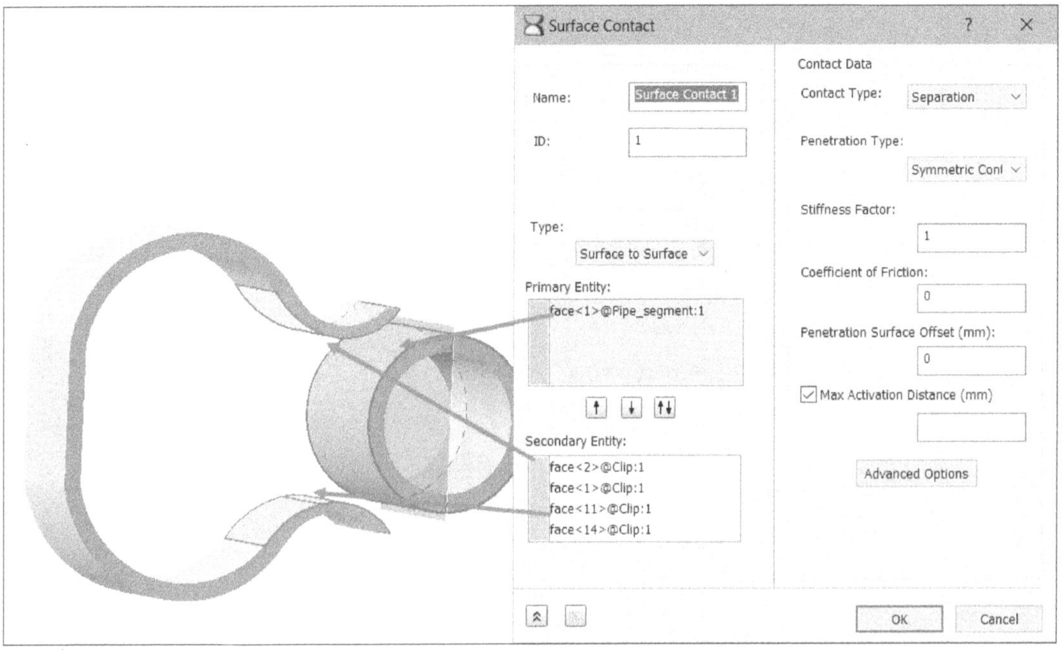

Figure-63. Surfaces selected for contact

- After setting the parameters, click on the **OK** button. The contact will be applied.

Defining Nonlinear Setup Options

- Right-click on **Nonlinear Setup1** option from **Subcases** node and select **Edit** option from the shortcut menu; refer to Figure-64. The **Nonlinear Setup** dialog box will be displayed.
- Specify the parameters as shown in Figure-65. Select the **All** option from **Intermediate Output** drop-down to check the results at various load increment steps. Select the **On** option from **Arc Length** drop-down to check highly non-linear solution.
- Click on the **Advanced Settings** button and select **Displacement** check box to define convergence criteria. Specify the value as **20** in the **Displacement** edit box; refer to Figure-66 and click on the **OK** button.

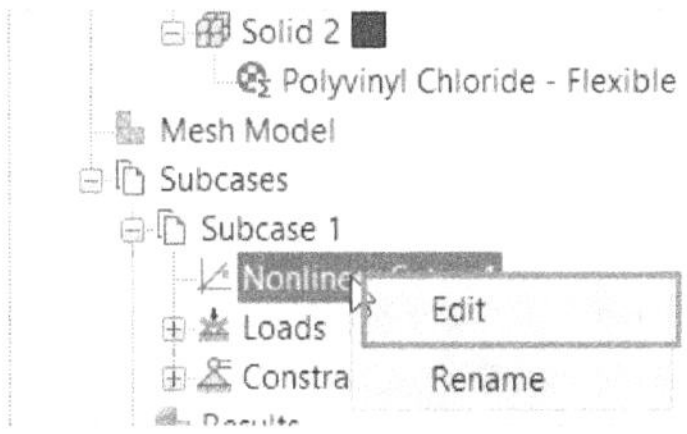

Figure-64. Edit

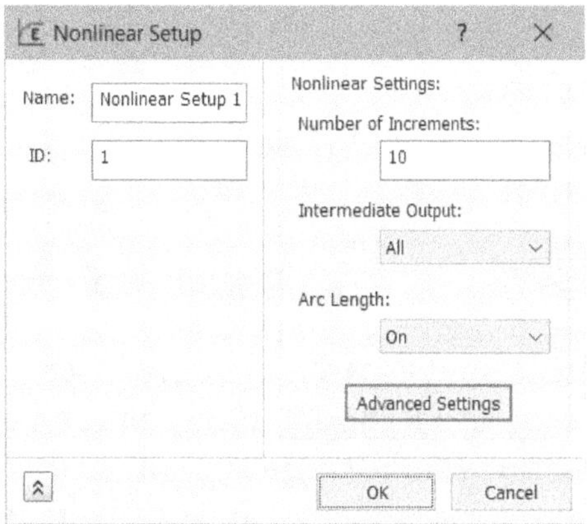

Figure-65. Nonlinear setup options specified

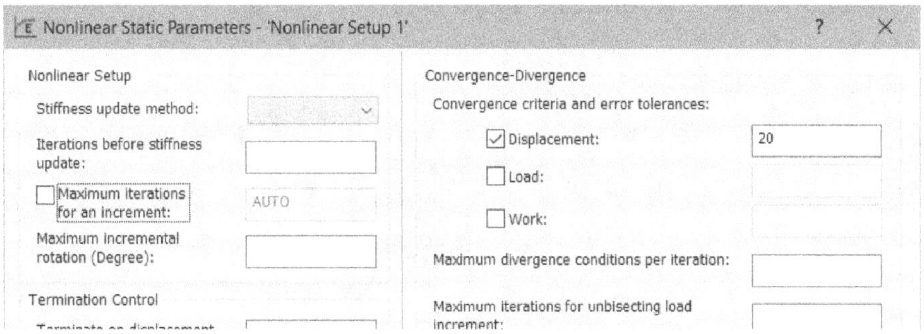

Figure-66. Setting displacement as convergence criteria

- After setting the parameters, click on the **OK** button.

Applying Enforced Motion Load and Constraints

- Click on the **Loads** tool from the **Setup** panel in the **Autodesk Inventor Nastran** tab of the **Ribbon**. The **Loads** dialog box will be displayed.
- Select the inner face of pipe segment model and specify parameters as shown in Figure-67. Note that we have specified motion in negative X direction based on direction shown by the coordinate system at the bottom in graphics area. If your coordinate system is showing different direction (which is highly unlikely) then make sure to specify motion in direction towards the clip.

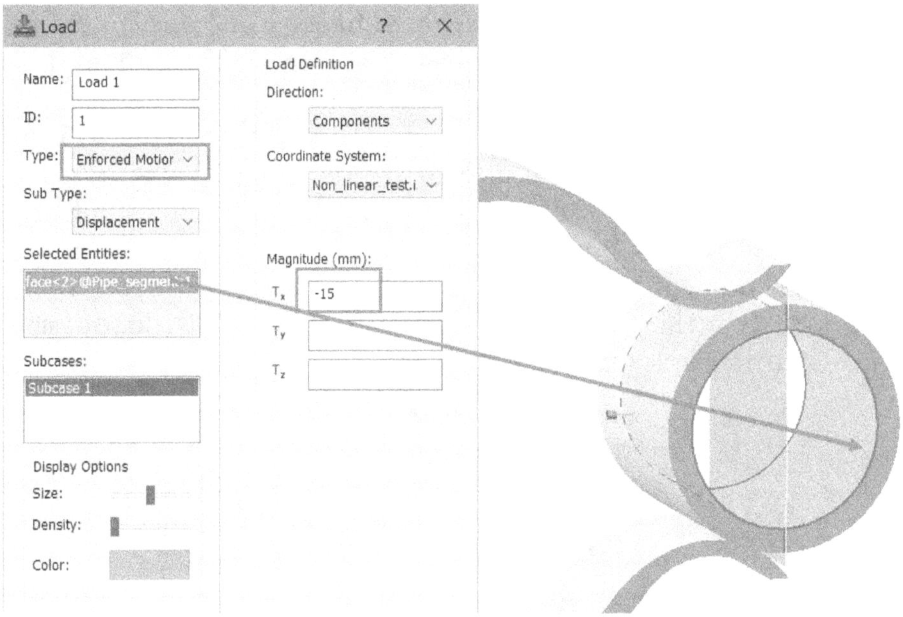

Figure-67. Applying enforced motion

- Click on the **Constraints** tool from the **Setup** panel in the **Autodesk Inventor Nastran** tab of the **Ribbon**. The **Constraint** dialog box will be displayed.
- Select the inner face of pipe segment model which was earlier selected for apply load and restrict the same direction in which load is applied; refer to Figure-68. **Note that without applying this constraint, the enforced motion load will not work in Autodesk Inventor Nastran.**

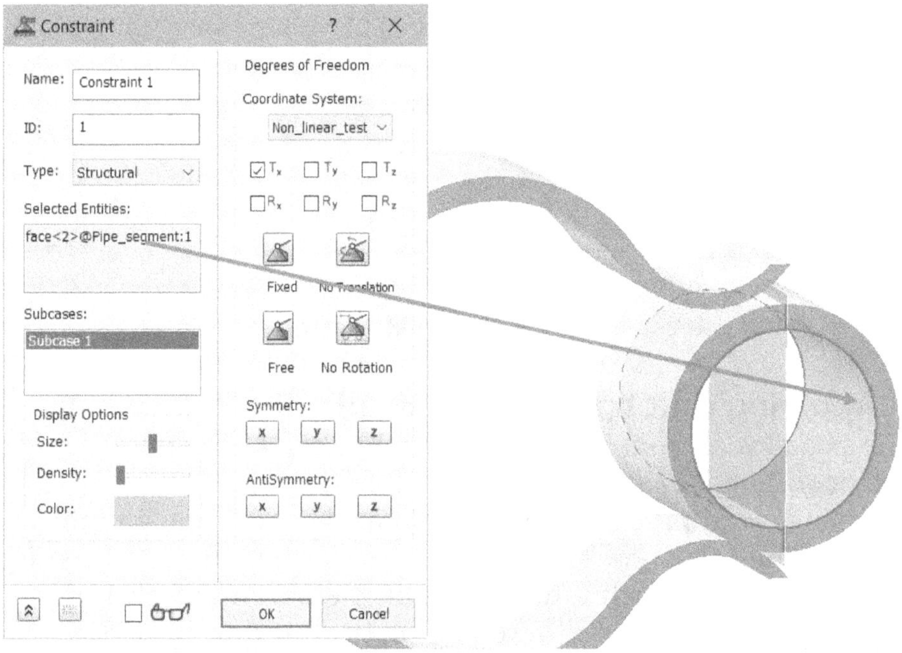

Figure-68. Constraint for enforced motion

- After specifying parameters, click on the **OK** button to exit dialog box.
- Click again on the **Constraints** tool and restrict the motion of pipe segment using outer face as shown in Figure-69.

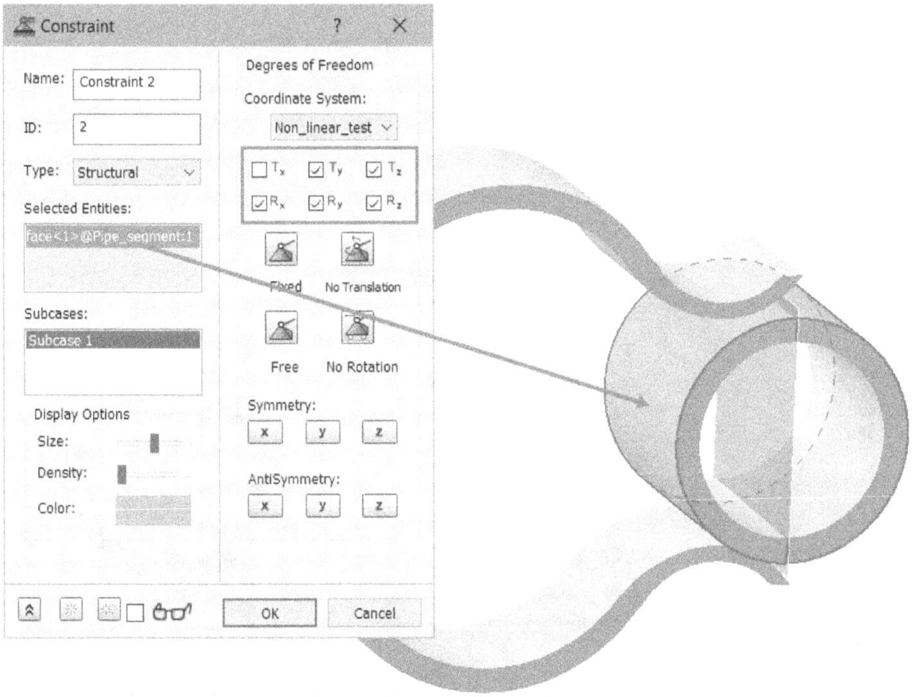

Figure-69. Defining constraint for pipe segment

- Click on the **New** button from the bottom in the dialog box to start a new constraint and select the face as shown in Figure-70.

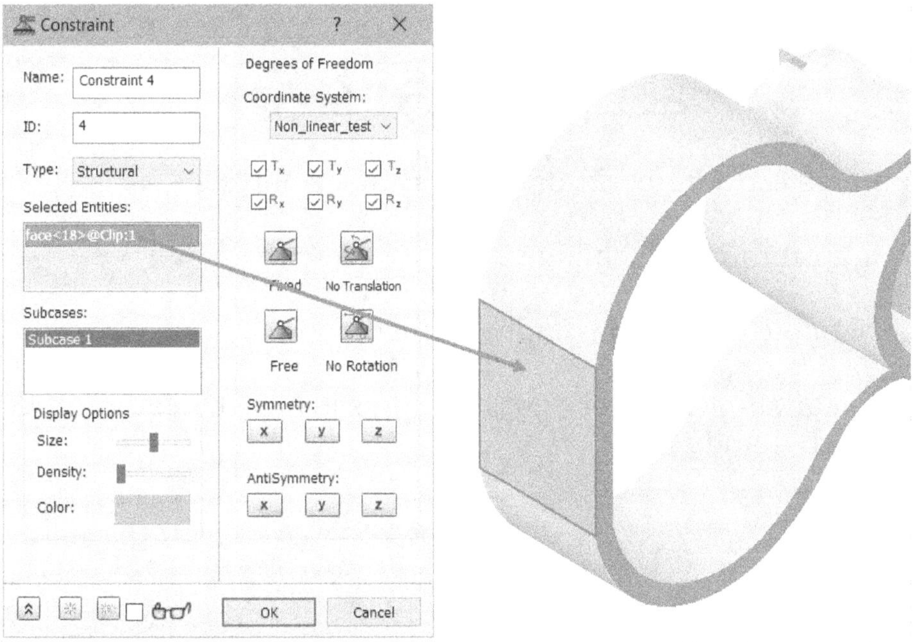

Figure-70. Applying constraint on clip

- Click on the **OK** button from the dialog box to apply constraint.

Solving the Analysis

In this practical, we are not modifying mesh sizes but you can do so by using the **Mesh Settings** tool in **Mesh** panel. Click on the **Run** tool from **Solve** panel in the **Autodesk Inventor Nastran** tab of the **Ribbon**. The results of analysis will be displayed at various load increment steps; refer to Figure-71.

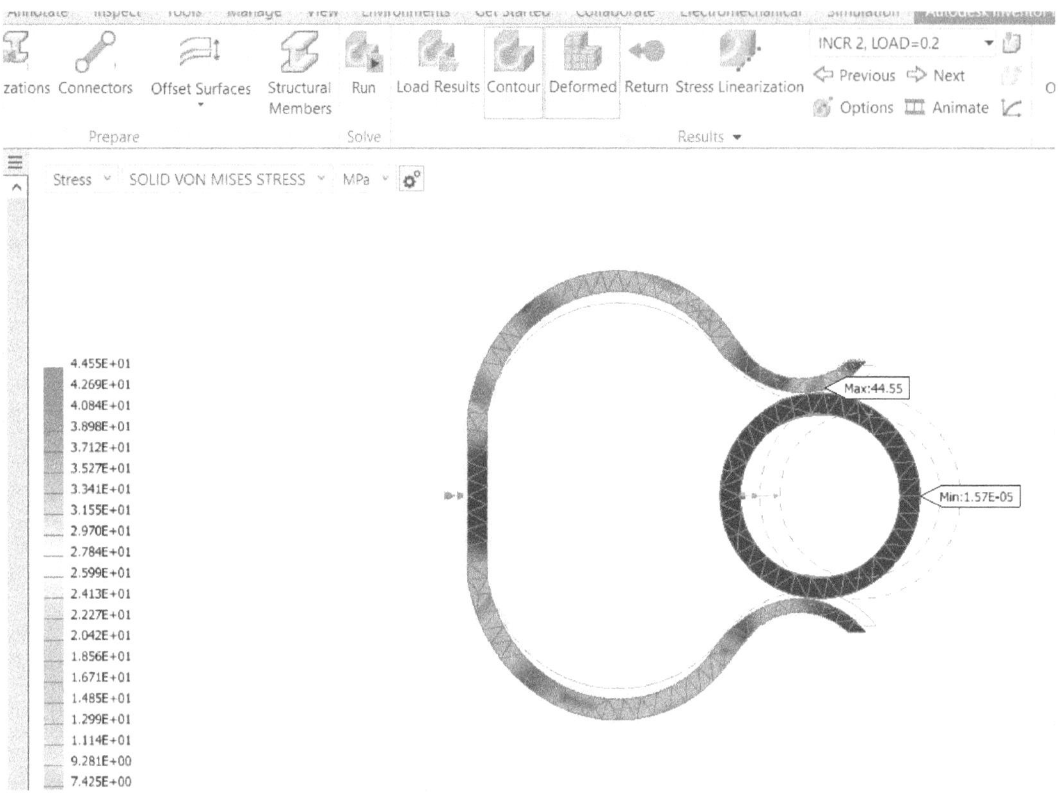

Figure-71. Result of nonlinear analysis

- Save the file by pressing **CTRL+S**.

SELF ASSESSMENT

Q1. What is the objective to perform Linear Static Analysis?

Q2. What is Snap-through Buckling?

Q3. Write a brief note on Newton-Raphson method.

Q4. The Non-linear static analysis can be expressed by the equation [K(D)]{D} = {F}. In this equation, D stands for,

a) Difference occurred
b) Distance applied
c) Displacement Matrix
d) None of the Above

Q5. The equation for Newton-Raphson method is given as: $[K_T]\{\Delta u\} = \{F\} - \{F^{nr}\}$. In this equation, F^{nr} stands for,

a) Internal force vector
b) External load vector
c) Displacement increment
d) None of the Above

Q6. .... analysis is used when you are concerned about heavy pre-loading on the model.

Q7. In Non-linear Static Analysis, Non-linearity can be caused by the .... , ... and ....

Q8. Which contact type should be selected to prevent the rotor from sliding in assembly analysis?

A. Bonded
B. Frictional
C. Separation/No Sliding
D. Free

Q9. Which tool is used to apply mesh settings in the analysis?

A. Mesh Generate
B. Mesh Refinement
C. Mesh Settings
D. Mesh Designer

Q10. What happens when you open a frame model in Autodesk Inventor and start Autodesk Inventor Nastran?

A. Model features are hidden automatically
B. Beam idealization is applied automatically
C. All loads are applied automatically
D. The material is set to steel by default

Q11. What tool is used to create connectors in Autodesk Inventor Nastran?

A. Constraints tool
B. Materials tool
C. Connectors tool
D. Analysis tool

Q12. Which element type should be selected from the Type drop-down to define a rod connector?

A. Beam
B. Shell
C. Solid
D. Rod

Q13. What values must be specified when defining a rod connector?

A. Elastic modulus and Poisson's ratio
B. Displacement and force
C. Cross-section area, torsional constant, and torsional stress coefficient
D. Material density and stiffness

Q14. How do you restrict the movement of sketch points during analysis?

A. By hiding the CAD body
B. By using the Connectors tool
C. By applying constraints
D. By creating loads

Q15. What is the purpose of Prestress Static Analysis?

A. To analyze moving parts
B. To measure thermal stresses
C. To handle heavy pre-loading on the model
D. To calculate damping

Q16. How many load sub-cases are created automatically in Prestress Static Analysis?

A. None
B. One
C. Two
D. Three

Q17. Which of the following is a major source of nonlinearity in finite element analysis?

A. Surface roughness
B. Large displacements
C. Small load increments
D. Mesh size

Q18. What kind of behavior do cable-like structures typically show under increasing loads?

A. Softening
B. Buckling
C. Stiffening
D. Fatigue

Q19. What algorithm is used to solve nonlinear equations in static analysis?

A. Euler method
B. Gaussian elimination
C. Newton-Raphson method
D. Runge-Kutta method

Q20. What does the variable {Fnr} represent in the Newton-Raphson method equation?

A. Tangent stiffness matrix
B. Displacement increment
C. Internal force vector
D. External load vector

Q21. What condition must be met to end the Newton-Raphson iteration?

A. Stiffness becomes zero
B. Displacement exceeds force
C. Difference between external and internal loads is within tolerance
D. Time step reaches zero

Q22. In non-linear static analysis, what does the sub-step represent?

A. Temperature increment
B. A material phase
C. A load increment
D. A node connection

Q23. What does time typically represent in most non-linear static analyses?

A. Actual simulation duration
B. A counter
C. Material aging
D. Load density

Q24. What does the time step Δt determine in non-linear analysis?

A. Material stiffness
B. Heat transfer rate
C. Load increment ΔF
D. Number of mesh elements

Q25. Which of the following is NOT a cause of material nonlinearity?

A. Load history
B. Load duration
C. Load orientation
D. Temperature

Q26. What kind of boundary condition change is addressed in contact problems?

A. Force condition
B. Temperature variation
C. Time-dependent load
D. Motion-based variation

Q27. What element is typically used between nodes in contact boundary analysis?

A. Rod
B. Shell
C. Gap (contact)
D. Solid

Q28. What is used to terminate analysis based on a node's displacement?

A. Material Orientation dialog
B. Terminate on displacement of Node
C. Arc Length option
D. Increment box

Q29. Which option limits the increase in size of nonlinear material elements?

A. Maximum divergence
B. Load bisection count
C. Fraction of effective stress
D. Orientation vector

Q30. What does the Material Orientation tool primarily define?

A. Vector length
B. Material type
C. Flow direction for 2D shells
D. Load cases

Q31. How are different load sets created in a single analysis?

A. Through Solver Parameters
B. By creating sub-cases
C. Using Line Search option
D. Via Material Orientation

Q32. What is the benefit of using sub-cases instead of running separate analyses?

A. Greater mesh accuracy
B. Less solver errors
C. Shared structural matrix computation
D. Improved boundary conditions

Q33. What does setting SOLUTIONERROR parameter to ON do?

A. Pauses simulation
B. Deletes mesh
C. Replaces singular matrices with positive definite ones
D. Disables iteration limit

Q34. Which method updates stiffness matrix after each iteration till convergence?

A. AUTO
B. SEMI
C. ITER
D. TANGENT

Q35. What does selecting the Maximum bisections for each increment control?

A. Load accuracy
B. Energy potential
C. Allowed load bisection attempts
D. Mesh density

FOR STUDENT NOTES

Chapter 4

Normal Modes Analyses

Topics Covered

The major topics covered in this chapter are:

- ***Introduction***
- ***Starting Normal Modes Analysis***
- ***Specifying Modal Setup Parameters***
- ***Applying Materials, Loads, and Constraints***
- ***Applying Idealizations***
- ***Setting Mesh and other parameters***
- ***Running Analysis and Plotting Results***
- ***Performing Prestress Normal Modes Analysis***

INTRODUCTION

Every structure has the tendency to vibrate at certain frequencies, called **natural or resonant frequencies**. Each natural frequency is associated with a certain shape, called **mode shape**, that the model tends to assume when vibrating at that frequency. To check these frequencies, we perform Normal Modes analysis.

When a structure is properly excited by a dynamic load with a frequency that coincides with one of its natural frequencies, the structure undergoes large displacements and stresses. This phenomenon is known as **resonance**. For undamped systems, resonance theoretically causes infinite motion. **Damping**, however, puts a limit on the response of the structures due to resonant loads.

A real model has an infinite number of natural frequencies. However, a finite element model has a finite number of natural frequencies that are equal to the number of degrees of freedom considered in the model. Only the first few modes are needed for most purposes.

If your design is subjected to dynamic environments, static studies cannot be used to evaluate the response. Frequency studies can help you design vibration isolated systems by avoiding resonance in specific frequency band. They also form the basis for evaluating the response of linear dynamic systems where the response of a system to a dynamic environment is assumed to be equal to the summation of the contributions of the modes considered in the analysis.

Note that resonance is desirable in the design of some devices. For example, resonance is required in guitars and violins.

The natural frequencies and corresponding mode shapes depend on the geometry, material properties, and support conditions. The computation of natural frequencies and mode shapes are known as modal analysis, frequency analysis, and normal mode analysis.

When building the geometry of a model, you usually create it based on the original (undeformed) shape of the model. Some loads, like the structure's own weight, are always present and can cause considerable effects on the shape of the structure and its modal properties. In many cases, this effect can be ignored because the induced deflections are small.

Loads affect the modal characteristics of a body. In general, compressive loads decrease resonant frequencies and tensile loads increase them. This fact is easily demonstrated by changing the tension on a violin string. The higher the tension, the higher the frequency (tone). You do not need to define any loads for a frequency study but if you do, their effect will be considered. By having evaluated natural frequencies of a structure's vibrations at the design stage, you can optimize the structure with the goal of meeting the frequency vibro-stability condition. To increase natural frequencies, you would need to add rigidity to the structure and (or) reduce its weight. For example, in the case of a slender object, the rigidity can be increased by reducing the length and increasing the thickness of the object. To reduce a part's natural frequency, you should, on the contrary, increase the weight or reduce the object's rigidity.

In Autodesk Inventor Nastran, you can perform two types of Normal Mode analyses which are Normal Modes analysis and Prestress Normal Modes Analysis.

PERFORMING NORMAL MODES ANALYSIS

The procedure to perform Normal Modes analysis is given next.

- Open the part on which you want to perform normal mode analysis and start Autodesk Inventor Nastran environment.
- Click on the **New** button from the **Analysis** panel of **Autodesk Inventor Nastran** tab in **Ribbon**. The **Analysis** dialog box will be displayed.
- Select the **Normal Modes** option from the **Type** drop-down in **Analysis** dialog box.
- Set the other options as discussed earlier and click on the **OK** button. The options in **Model Tree** will be displayed as shown in Figure-1.

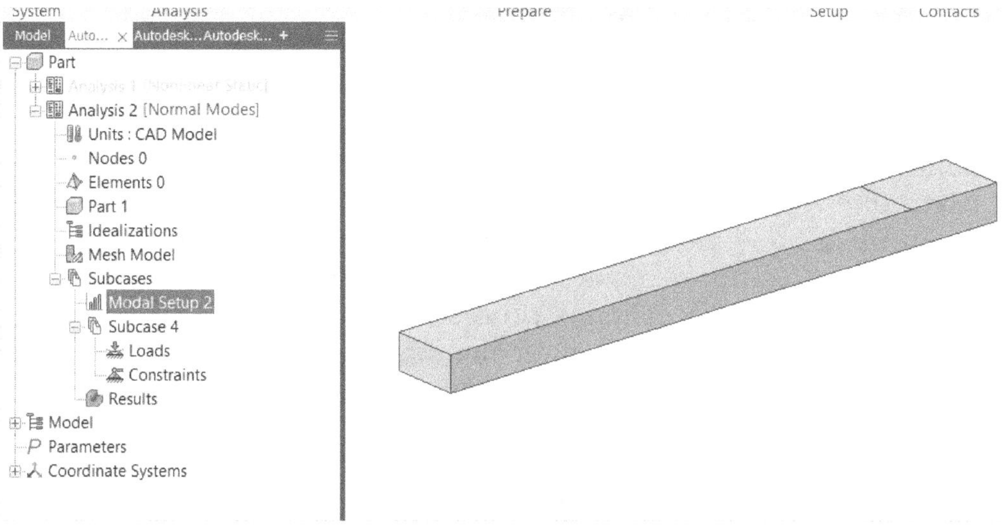

Figure-1. Options for Normal Modes analysis

Modal Setup Options

- Double-click on **Modal Setup** option from **Subcases** node to define parameters related to modal analysis. The **Modal Setup** dialog box will be displayed; refer to Figure-2.

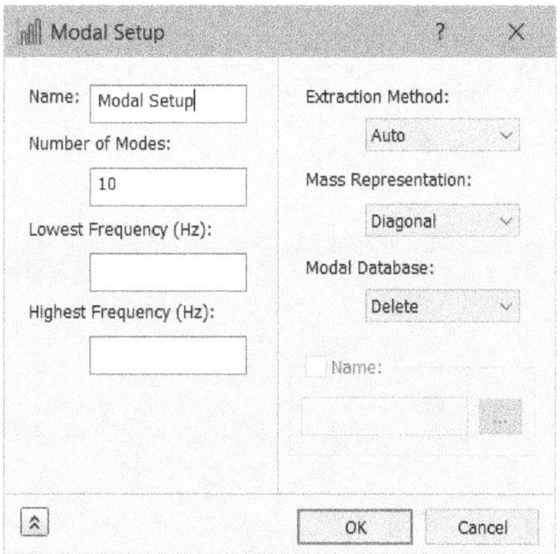

Figure-2. Modal Setup dialog box

- Specify desired name for model setup parameter in the **Name** edit box.

- Specify the number of natural shapes to be found during the analysis in **Number of Modes** edit box.
- Specify desired lower and higher limit of frequencies within which natural modes will be calculated in **Lowest Frequency** and **Highest Frequency** edit boxes, respectively. Note that generally, the values specified here are those frequencies within which your machine will be working. Using this analysis, you want to make sure that the part/assembly to be designed does not have any natural frequency in specified range.
- Select desired option from the **Extraction Method** drop-down to define how natural frequencies will be calculated. Select the **Lanczos Iteration** option for larger problems as it replaces the older values of each equation with new values as they are solved in same iteration which in turn reduces the number of total iterations required for convergence. Select the **Subspace Iteration** option from the drop-down when you need to perform analysis with parallel iterations. Although, the number of iterations required for **Subspace** method is higher but when there is a chance of getting error with Lanczos method then you should use this method.
- Select desired option from the **Mass Representation** drop-down to define how mass matrices will be formed for analysis. Select the **Diagonal** option to create diagonal mass matrix using uncoupled translational components of mass. Use this option when one side of part is heavier than the rest. Select the **Coupled** option to create coupled mass matrix in which translational components are coupled. Use this option for uniform mass distribution of part. Select the **Element Type Default** option to use default mass representation specified for the elements in model. This option is useful with rigid elements in the model.
- Select desired option from the **Modal Database** drop-down to define storage and retrieval of modal data like eigenvalues and eigenvectors. By default, **Delete** option is selected in this drop-down so eigenvalues and eigenvector data is deleted after performing analysis. If you have selected any option other than **Delete** from the **Modal Database** drop-down then options to define location of database will be displayed. Set desired location for database storage. The eigenvalues and eigenvectors will be stored in this database based on option selected.
- After setting desired values, click on the **OK** button.
- Although, the options to apply load are available for Normal Mode analysis, they will not be counted in Normal Mode analysis. There is a special analysis type for such cases called Prestress Normal Mode analysis.
- Apply desired constraint, set idealization, and click on the **Run** button to perform analysis. The results will be displayed with list of mode frequencies; refer to Figure-3.

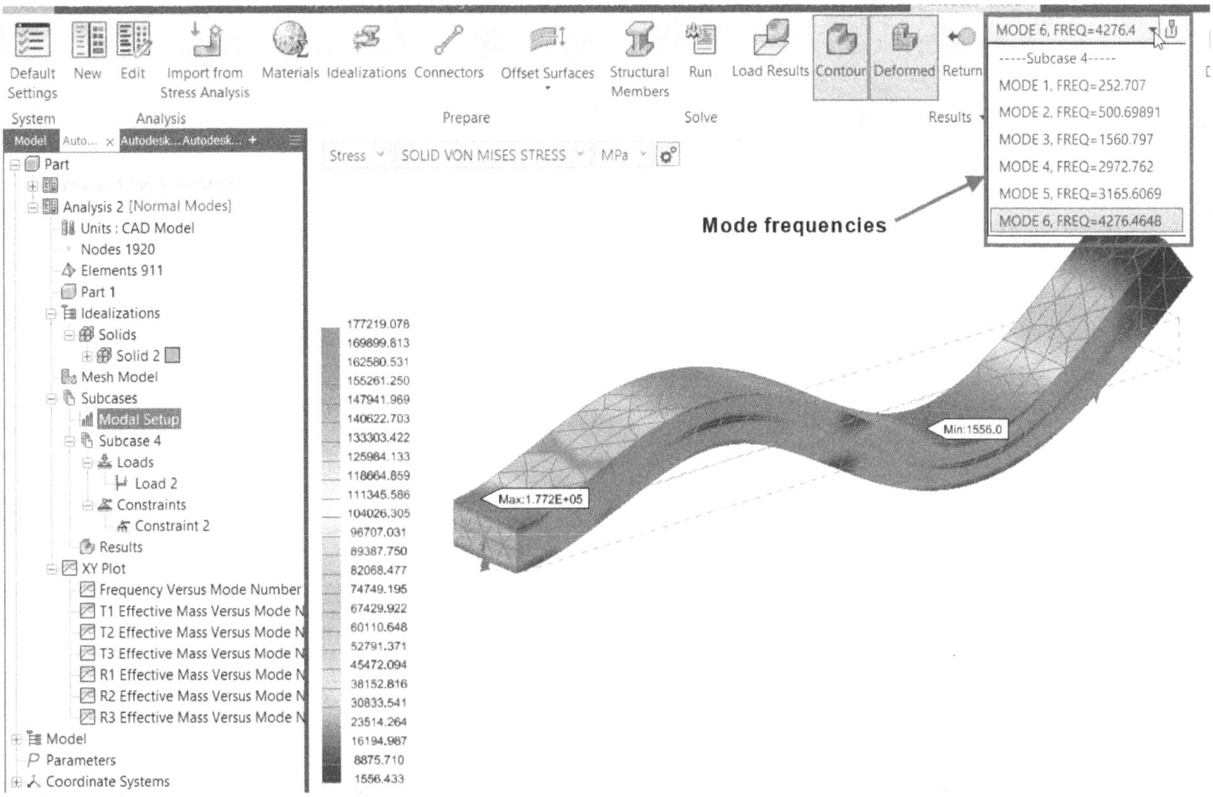

Figure-3. Normal Modes analysis result with mode frequencies

- Double-click on desired result from the **XY Plot** node to check the plots.
- Save the analysis results and exit the **Autodesk Inventor Nastran** environment.

Note: Capturing adequate number of natural frequencies is an important step for using Normal Mode analysis. When we specify number of modes as **10** in the **Modal Setup** dialog box discussed earlier, we define the number of natural frequencies for which we want to check mode shapes of the model. If you know the range of vibrational frequencies within which your designed part will function then you can define the range value. But, how will you decide whether there are 5 natural frequencies or 20 natural frequencies falling in the range? It might be possible that you have missed an important mode shape due to less number of natural frequencies generated by the analysis. In such cases, we generally make sure that at least 85% of **Modal effective mass** is captured by the number of frequencies specified for result in directions of interest. To check percentage of modal effective mass, open the output file of current analysis from the FEA folder in directory where your part file is saved; refer to Figure-4. If you are performing multiple analyses on the current model then you will find various different output files in the folder. To find correct name of your output file, open the **Nastran Output** tab in **Model Tree Browser**; refer to Figure-5. Double-click on this file from directory of your model and open it in Notepad or other word processor application. The parameters of output file will be displayed. Scroll down in the file and look for PERCENT MODAL EFFECTIVE MASS heading; refer to Figure-6. If the percentage is less than 85 in direction of interest then increase the number of frequencies.

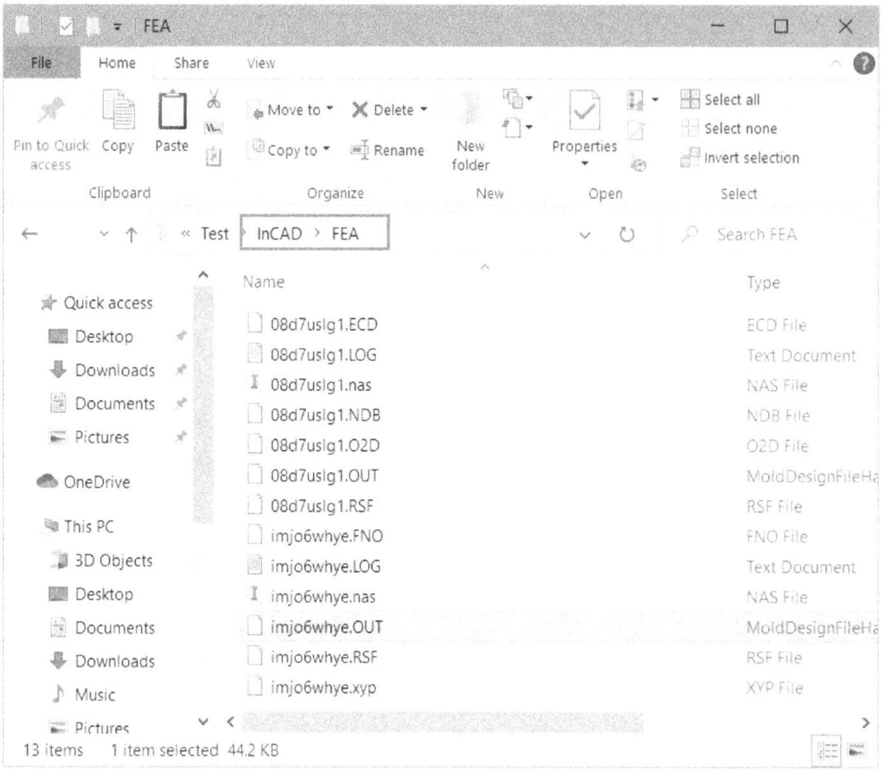

Figure-4. Output file

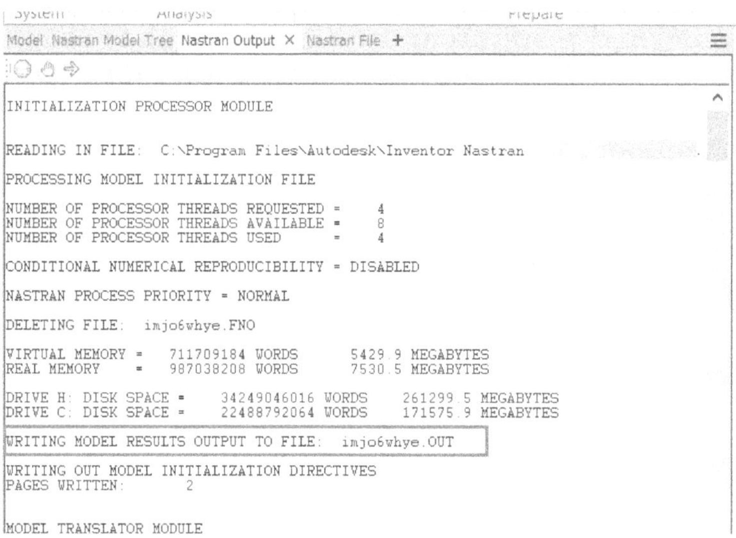

Figure-5. Output file name

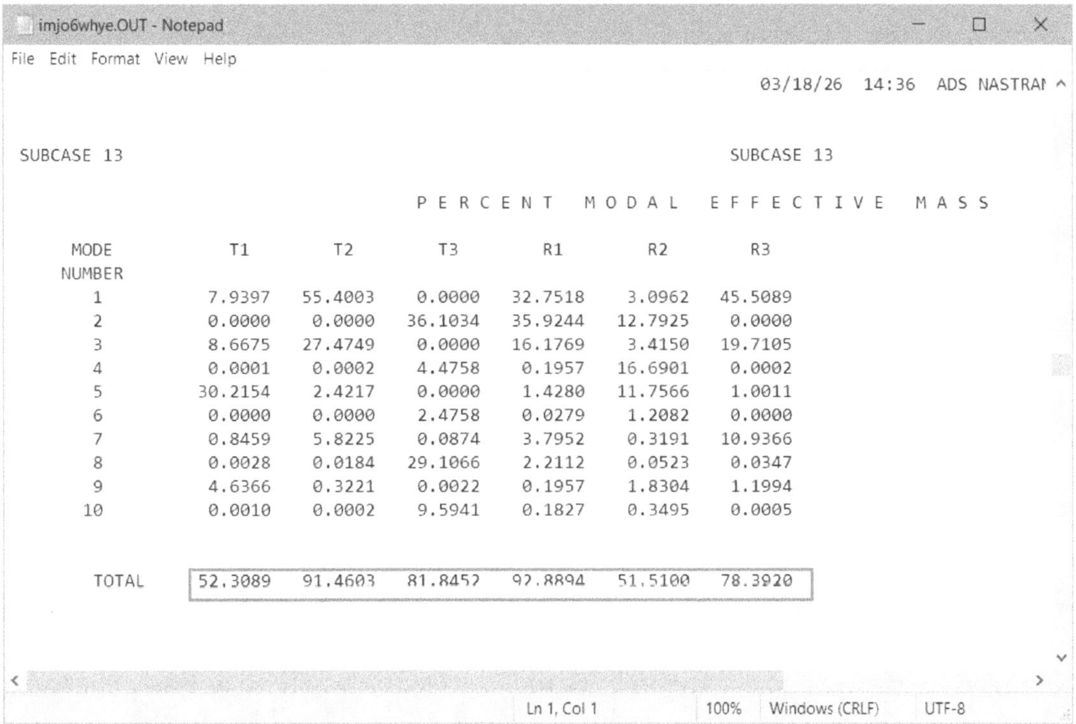

imjo6whye.OUT - Notepad

File Edit Format View Help

03/18/26 14:36 ADS NASTRAN

SUBCASE 13 SUBCASE 13

P E R C E N T M O D A L E F F E C T I V E M A S S

MODE NUMBER	T1	T2	T3	R1	R2	R3
1	7.9397	55.4003	0.0000	32.7518	3.0962	45.5089
2	0.0000	0.0000	36.1034	35.9244	12.7925	0.0000
3	8.6675	27.4749	0.0000	16.1769	3.4150	19.7105
4	0.0001	0.0002	4.4758	0.1957	16.6901	0.0002
5	30.2154	2.4217	0.0000	1.4280	11.7566	1.0011
6	0.0000	0.0000	2.4758	0.0279	1.2082	0.0000
7	0.8459	5.8225	0.0874	3.7952	0.3191	10.9366
8	0.0028	0.0184	29.1066	2.2112	0.0523	0.0347
9	4.6366	0.3221	0.0022	0.1957	1.8304	1.1994
10	0.0010	0.0002	9.5941	0.1827	0.3495	0.0005
TOTAL	52.3089	91.4603	81.8452	92.8894	51.5100	78.3920

Ln 1, Col 1 100% Windows (CRLF) UTF-8

Figure-6. Modal mass results

PERFORMING PRESTRESS NORMAL MODES ANALYSIS

Prestress Normal Modes analysis is performed on models which are already under stress due to continuous load. Prestress can change the stiffness of model so causing changes in the natural frequency of model. The procedure to perform Prestress Normal Modes analysis is given next.

- Open desired model and start **Autodesk Inventor Nastran** environment.
- Click on the **New** button from the **Analysis** panel of **Autodesk Inventor Nastran** tab in the **Ribbon**. The **Analysis** dialog box will be displayed.
- Select the **Prestress Normal Modes** option from the **Type** drop-down and set the other options as discussed earlier.
- Click on the **OK** button from the dialog box. The load sub cases for the analysis will be displayed; refer to Figure-7.

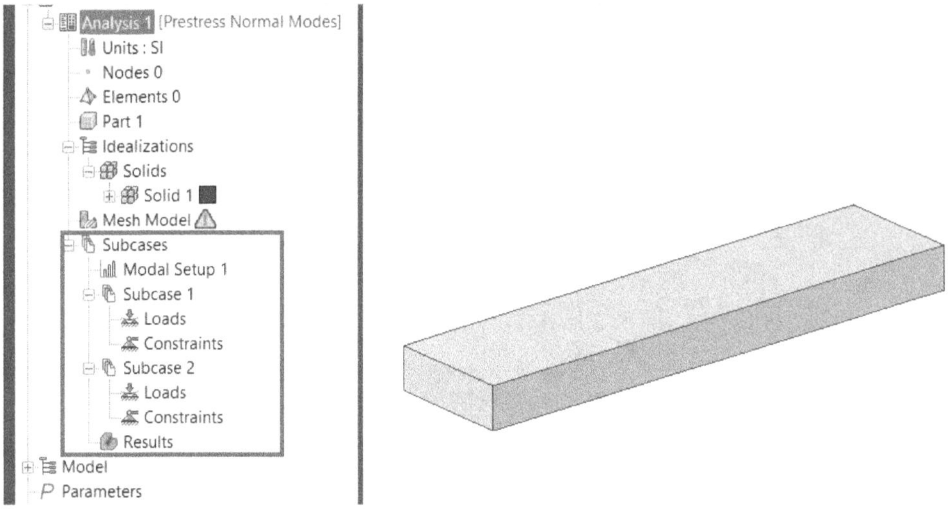

Figure-7. Subcase options for prestress normal modes analysis

- Set desired parameters for normal modes in the **Modal Setup** dialog box as discussed earlier.
- Set desired loads and constraints in Subcase 1 which will be set as prestress loads.
- Set desired loads and constraints in Subcase 2 which will be applied as additional load.
- Apply desired material and set the idealization.
- Click on the **Run** button. The analysis results will be displayed; refer to Figure-8.

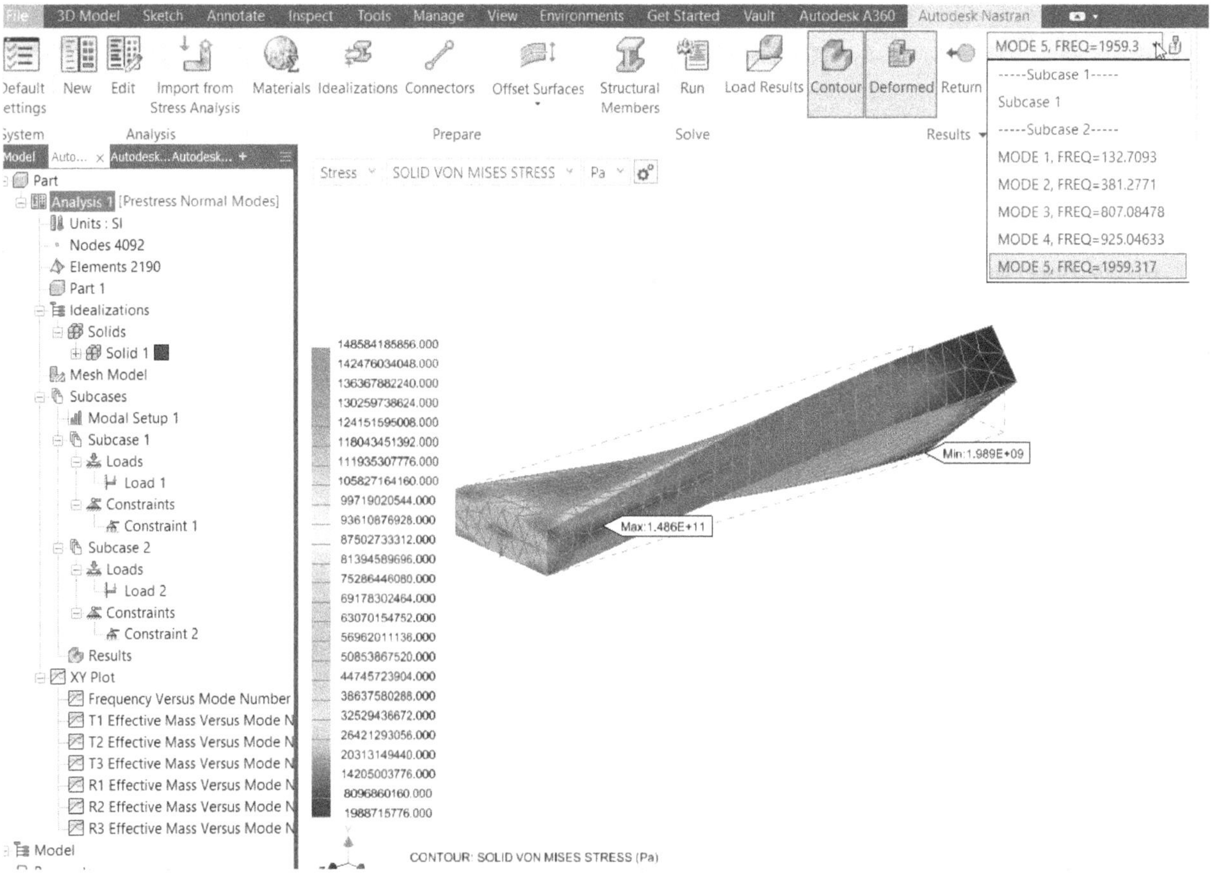

Figure-8. Prestress normal mode analysis result

- Double-click on desired result under **XY Plot** node to check the results.

Tips: To better understand the difference between Normal Mode analysis and Prestress Normal Mode analysis, you can perform both the analysis with same loading on same part and compare the results. You will find that in Prestress Normal Mode analysis, the natural frequency is relatively low because of load applied whereas load is ignored in Normal Model Analysis.

You can also use Normal Mode analysis to find out components in assembly which are causing singularities (flying due to improper constraints and contacts) in static analyses. To do so, convert your current analysis to normal mode analysis by using **Edit** tool in **Analysis** panel and run the analysis. You will find 0 natural frequencies in the result which dictate that there is some loose component flying. Check the displacement results to find out which component is not constrained properly. Note that sometimes very large load on component can cause singularities so you need to consider that as a possibility as well.

After performing Normal Mode analysis, you can decide whether there is a need to run dynamic analysis. If result frequencies match with frequencies of environment where component will function, then you can use dynamic analyses to get more insight of mass distribution of component.

ADDING CONCENTRATED MASS

The Concentrated Masses are used to represent mass objects that have not been modelled in the design. This option is specially useful when working on complex large problems where you are not concerned about stiffness of those objects. To create concentrated mass on particular faces, you need to use rigid links and a point to be used for concentrated mass. The procedure to create concentrated mass is given next.

- Create a sketch point which will be used for defining concentrated mass; refer to Figure-9.

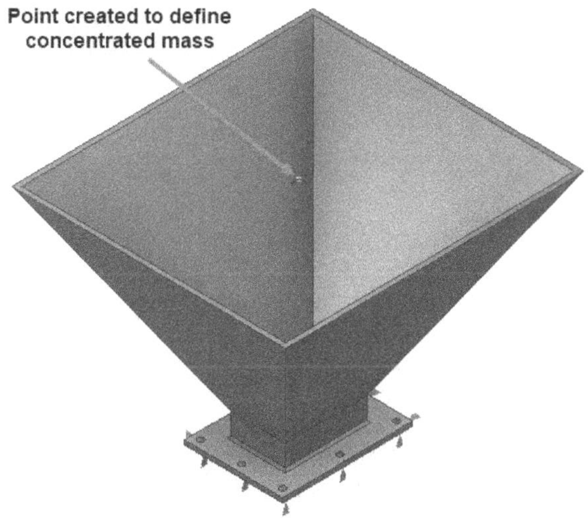

Figure-9. Point for defining concentrated mass

- Click on the **Connectors** tool from the **Prepare** panel in the **Ribbon**. The **Connector** dialog box will be displayed.
- Select the **Rigid Body** option from the **Type** drop-down and select the entities as shown in Figure-10. After specifying the parameters, click on the **OK** button.

- Right-click on the **Concentrated Masses** option from **Idealizations** category in the **Model** node of **Nastran Model Tree**. A shortcut menu will be displayed; refer to Figure-11.

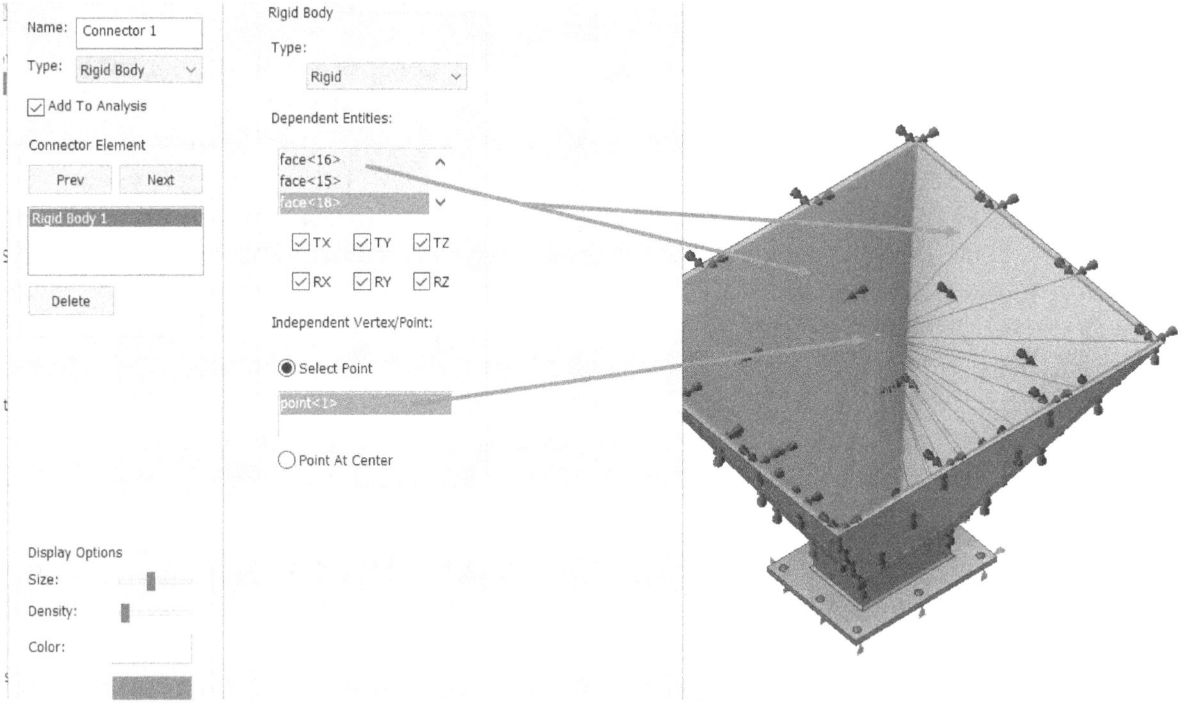

Figure-10. Selection for rigid body

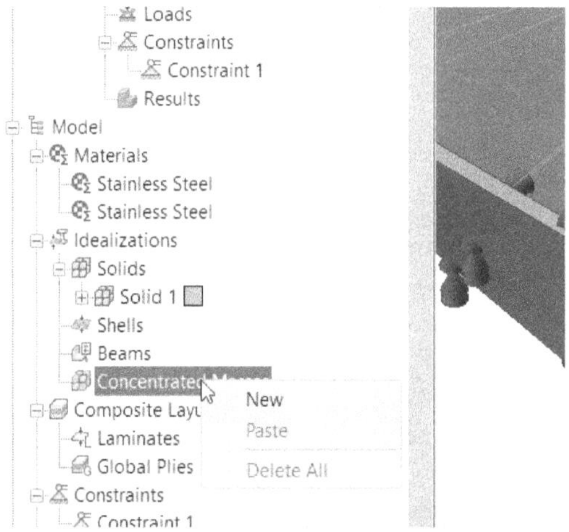

Figure-11. Concentrated Masses shortcut menu

- Select the **New** option from shortcut menu. The **Concentrated Mass** dialog box will be displayed; refer to Figure-12.
- By default, the **Manual** radio button is selected so you need to specify each parameter manually. If you are working on an assembly or multi-body part then you can select the **Automatic** radio button to automatically define mass by specifying density.

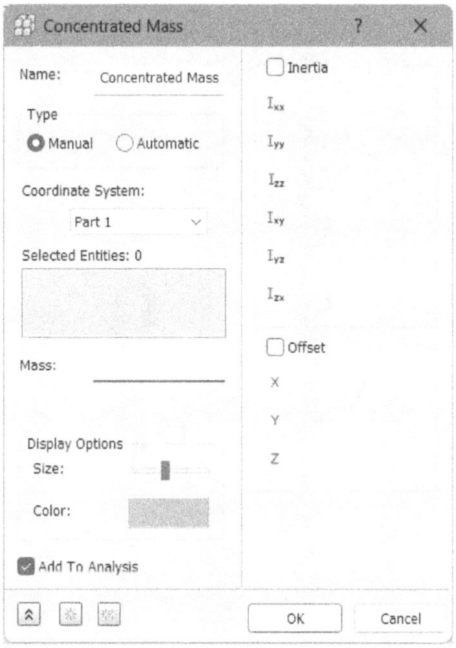

Figure-12. Concentrated Mass dialog box

- Click in the **Selected Entities** selection box and select the sketch point earlier created for defining mass. A box icon will be displayed on selected point denoting that a concentrated mass has been added; refer to Figure-13.

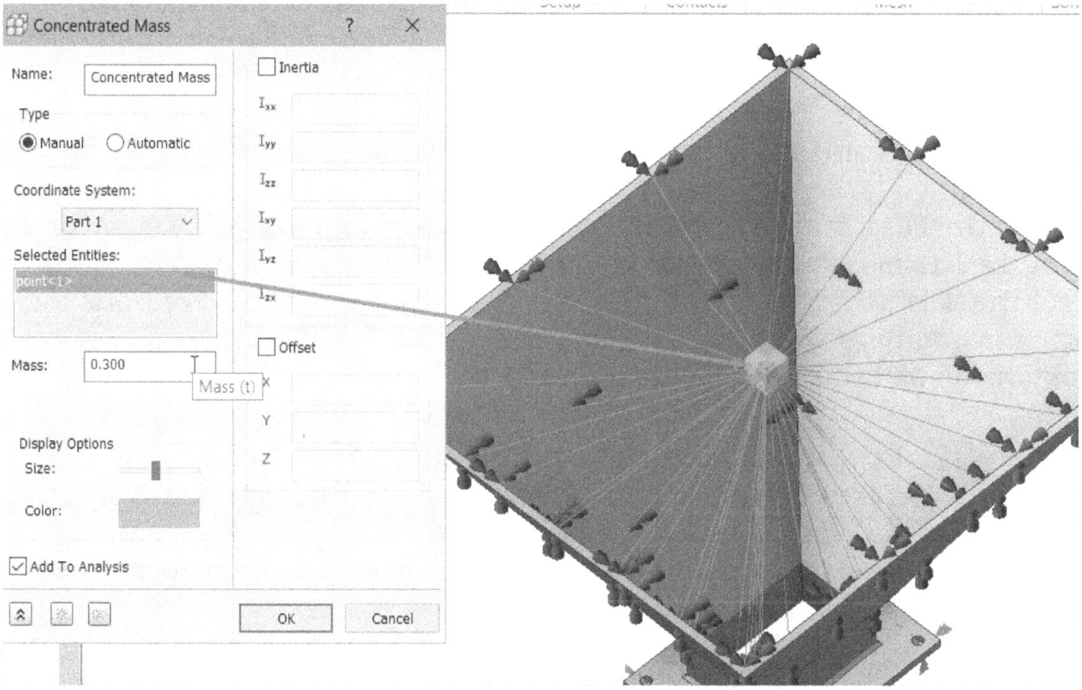

Figure-13. Concentrated mass location

- Specify desired value of mass in the **Mass** edit box. Make sure to check the unit by hovering cursor in the edit box. You can change the units as discussed earlier if you want to.
- Similarly, specify the other parameter like inertia and offsets.
- Click on the **OK** button to create mass and exit the dialog box.

PRACTICAL 1

Find out natural frequencies of tuning fork as shown in Figure-14.

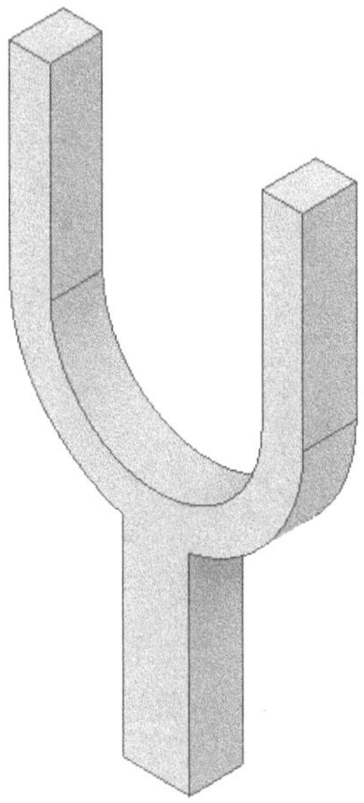

Figure-14. Tuning fork

Opening Part and Starting Autodesk Inventor Nastran

- Open the Tuning Fork part file from Chapter 4 folder of Resource folder for the book.
- Click on **Autodesk Inventor Nastran** tool from the **Begin** panel of **Autodesk Inventor Nastran** tab in the **Ribbon**. Linear static analysis will be activated automatically.
- Click on the **Edit** button from the **Analysis** panel of **Autodesk Inventor Nastran** tab in the **Ribbon**. The **Analysis** dialog box will be displayed.
- Select the **Normal Modes** option from the **Type** drop-down. The options for natural frequency analysis will be displayed.
- Click on the **OK** button from the dialog box.

Applying Material and Setting Idealization

- Click on the **Materials** tool from the **Prepare** panel of **Autodesk Inventor Nastran** tab. The **Material** dialog box will be displayed.
- Click on the **Select Material** button from the **Material** dialog box. The **Material DB** dialog box will be displayed.
- Select the **Stainless Steel** option from the **Inventor Material Library** node of **Material DB** dialog box and click on the **OK** button. The properties of selected material will be displayed in the **Material** dialog box.
- Click on the **OK** button from the **Material** dialog box to apply material.
- Double-click on **Solid 1** option from **Solids** node of **Idealizations** node. The **Idealizations** dialog box will be displayed.
- Select the **Stainless Steel** option from the **Material** drop-down and click on the **OK** button.

Applying Constraints and Generating Mesh

- Click on the **Constraints** tool from the **Setup** panel of **Autodesk Inventor Nastran** tab in the **Ribbon**. The **Constraint** dialog box will be displayed.
- Select the bottom side faces of model as shown in Figure-15 and click on the **Fixed** button from the dialog box.

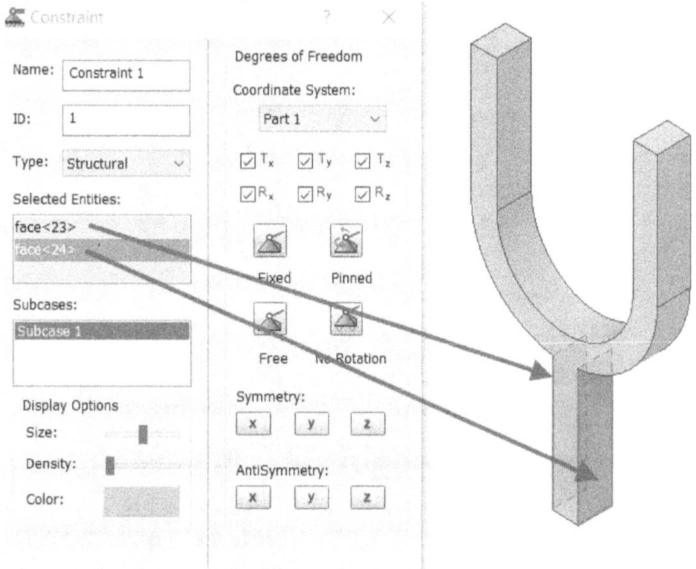

Figure-15. Faces selected for constraining

- Click on the **OK** button from the dialog box.
- Click on the **Mesh Settings** tool from the **Mesh** panel of **Autodesk Inventor Nastran** tab in the **Ribbon**. The **Mesh Settings** dialog box will be displayed.
- Specify the mesh element size as **15** in **Element Size (mm)** edit box.
- Click on the **Generate Mesh** button from the dialog box. The mesh will be generated; refer to Figure-16.

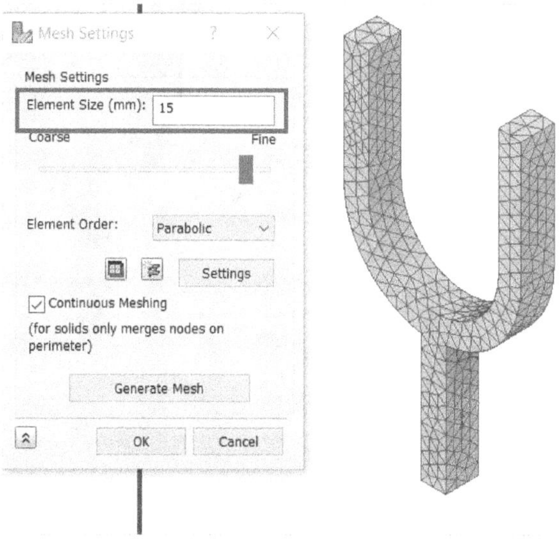

Figure-16. Mesh generated for tuning fork

- Click on the **OK** button from the dialog box.

Applying Modal Setup Parameters

- Double-click on **Modal Setup 1** option from the **Subcases** node in the **Model Tree**. The **Modal Setup** dialog box will be displayed.

- Specify the lowest frequency as **10** Hz and highest frequency as **1500** Hz in respective edit boxes of the dialog box.
- Set the other options as shown in Figure-17 and click on the **OK** button.

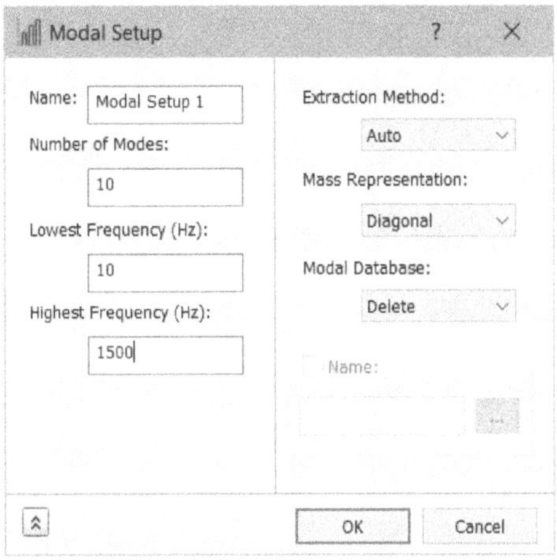

Figure-17. Modal Setup dialog box options to be specified

Running Analysis

- Click on the **Run** tool from the **Solve** panel of **Autodesk Inventor Nastran** tab in the **Ribbon**. Once the analysis is complete, **Autodesk Inventor Nastran** information box will be displayed.
- Click on the **OK** button from the information box. Results of analysis will be displayed; refer to Figure-18. Select the **Displacement** option from the **Stress** drop-down in results to check approximate displacement for various mode shapes; refer to Figure-19.

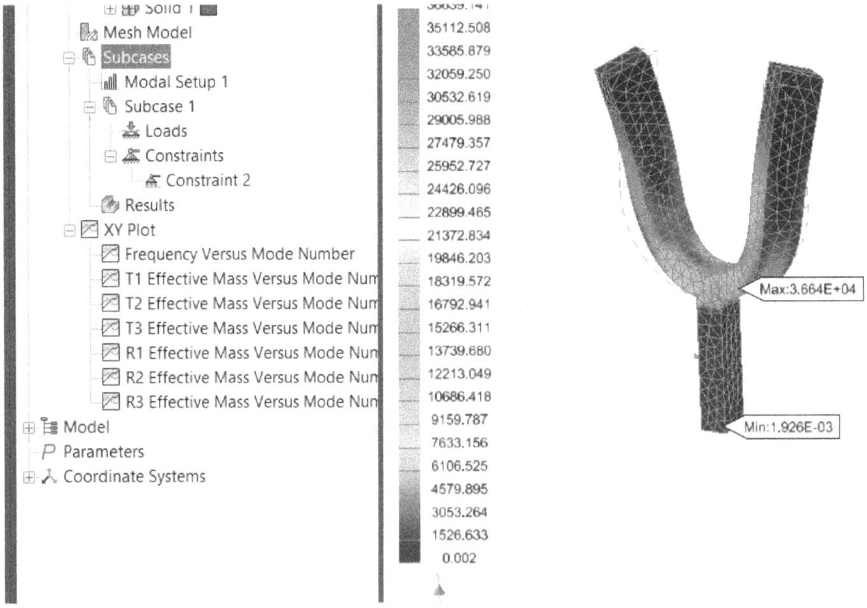

Figure-18. Result of normal analysis

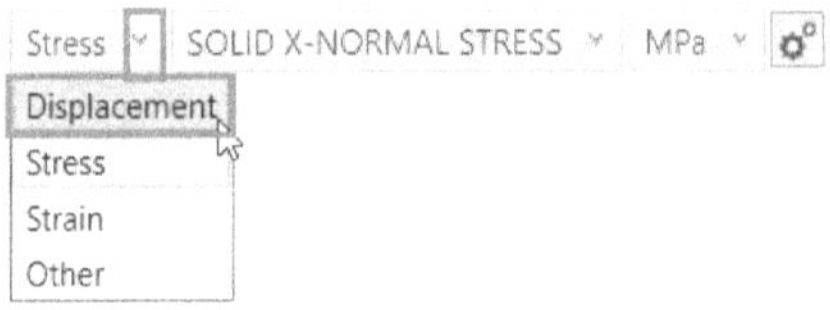

Figure-19. Displacement option

Double-click on **Frequency Versus Mode Number** option from the **XY Plot** node. The **XY Plot** will be displayed with mode numbers and respective natural frequencies; refer to Figure-20.

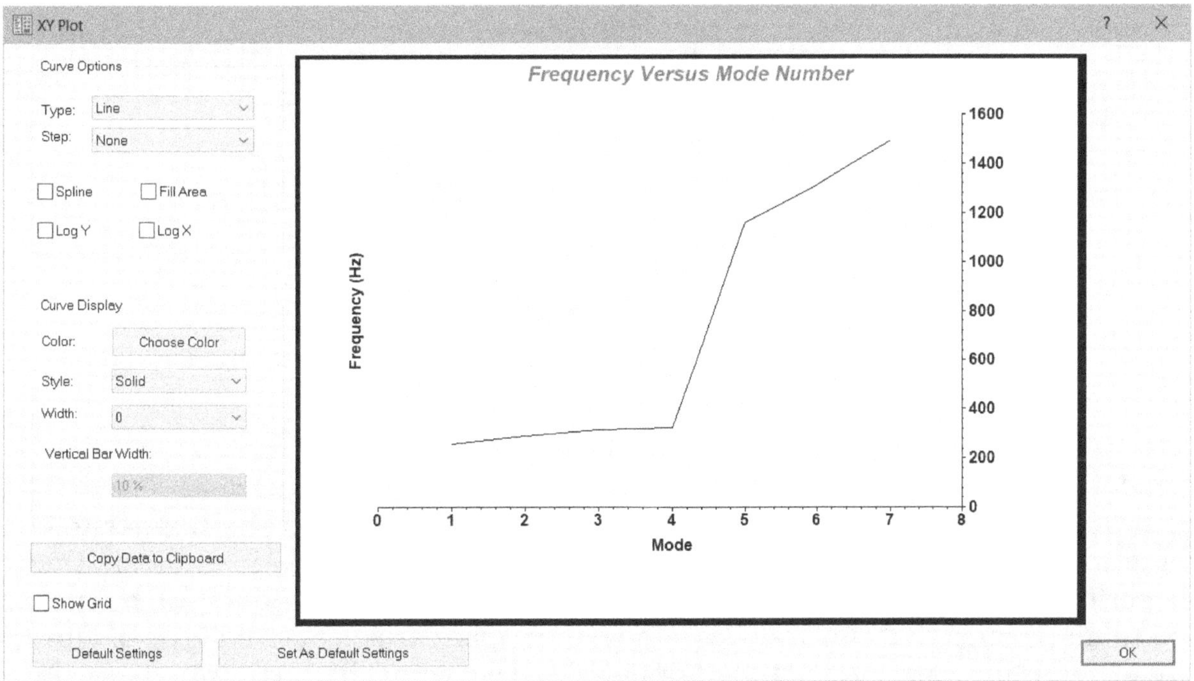

Figure-20. XY Plot for natural frequencies

Check the results and click on the **OK** button. Click on the **Finish Autodesk Inventor Nastran** tool from the **Exit** panel and save the model.

PRACTICAL 2

In this practical, we will check structural integrity of a hopper used for dispensing cement in mixer machine. A sinusoidal force of 30 kgf at a frequency of 85 Hz is applied at the location shown in Figure-21 by using high frequency vibrator. A continuous supply of 300 kg cement will be going through the hopper. We advise you to check the articles related to industrial vibrators for more insight of designing hoppers by scanning the QR codes below.

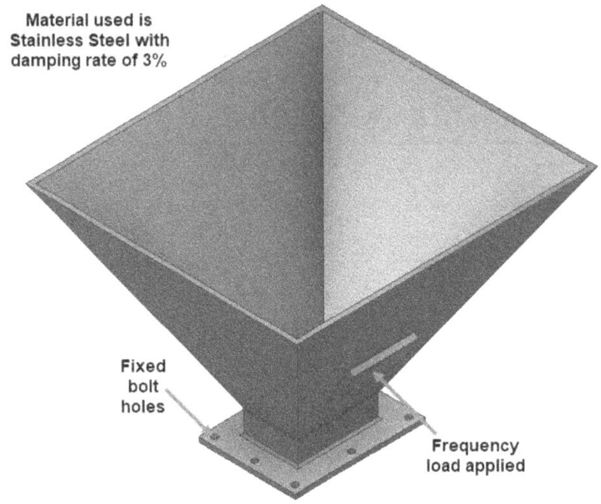

Figure-21. Practical for transient analysis

Steps for Analysis:

Our first concern of design is to check linear static loading on the hopper to check for failure due to static load. If the part succeeds in linear static analysis then we will perform Normal Mode analysis to find out natural frequency of hopper. We need to make sure that natural frequency of hopper causes desired type of vibration displacement in upper body of the hopper since we want the hopper body to vibrate.

Performing Linear Static Analysis

- Open the part file for this practical from resources of the book in Autodesk Inventor and start Autodesk Inventor Nastran as discussed earlier. By default, environment will start with a linear static analysis.
- Click on the **Materials** tool from the **Prepare** panel in **Ribbon**. The **Material** dialog box will be displayed.
- Click on the **Select Material** button in the dialog box and select **Stainless Steel** material from the **Material DB** dialog box. Click on the **OK** button to exit the dialog box.
- Specify the damping coefficient as **0.03** in the **GE** edit box of **Material** dialog box.
- Select the **Solid 1** option from **Idealizations** area in the dialog box to apply material to that idealization and click on the **OK** button to apply material.
- Click on the **Constraints** tool from the **Setup** panel in the **Ribbon**. The **Constraint** dialog box will be displayed.
- Apply fixed constraint to holes in the model as shown in Figure-22 and click on the **OK** button.

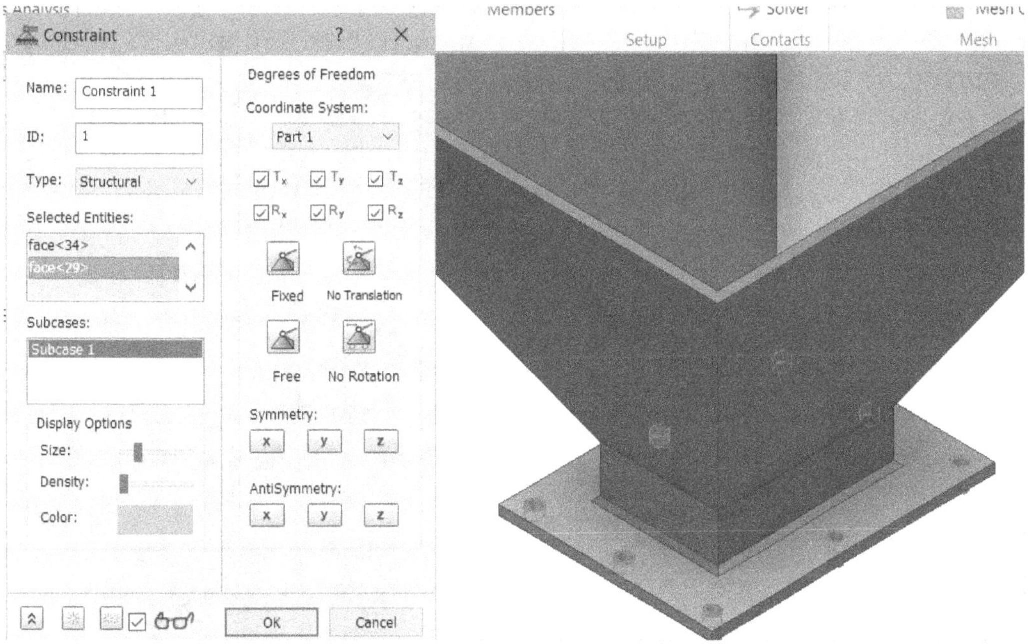

Figure-22. Applying fixed constraint

- Applying concentrated mass of 300 kg as discussed earlier on the inner faces of hopper; refer to Figure-13.
- Apply 30 kgf force at the face where mechanical vibrator will be attached; refer to Figure-23. Note that Nastran does not have kgf unit till writing this book so you need to convert this force value to N, dyn or lbf. We have converted this 30 kgf force to Newton which is approximately 294.2 N. After specifying parameters, click on the **OK** button from the dialog box.

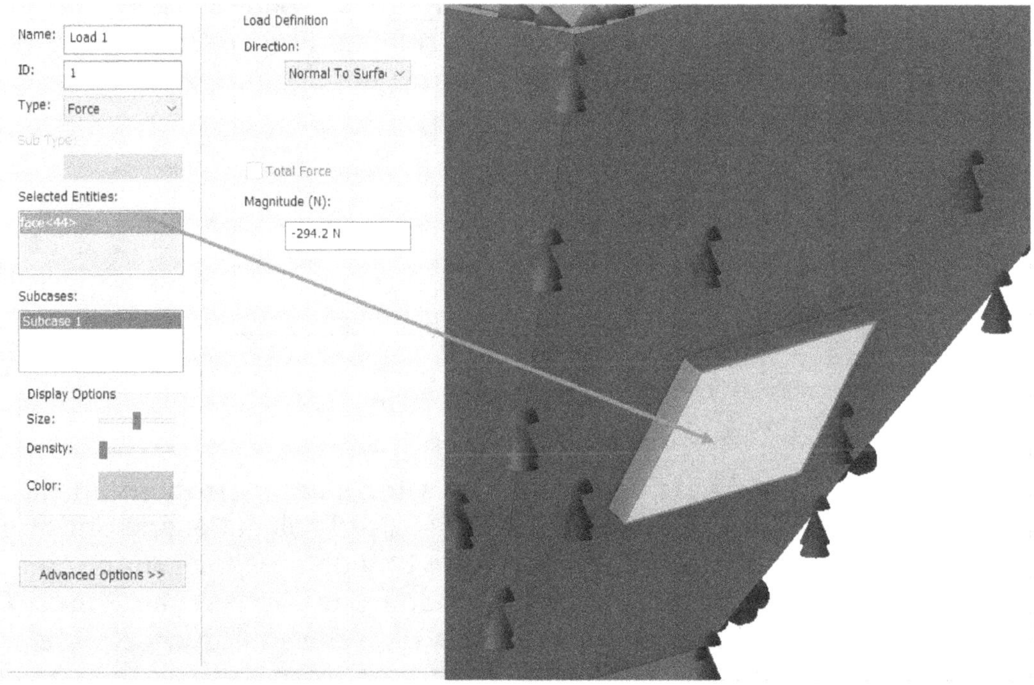

Figure-23. Applying force on hopper

- Click on the **Generate Mesh** button to generate mesh with default specified element sizes.

- Click on the **Run** button from **Solve** panel to solve the analysis. Once the analysis is complete, click on the **OK** button from message box displayed and results will be displayed in the graphics area.
- Double-click on the **Safety Factor** plot option from **Results** node in the **Nastran Model Tree** to check safety factor for the model; refer to Figure-24. Since, the safety factor is 39 much higher than standard requirement of 3 so, our part is safe under static load.

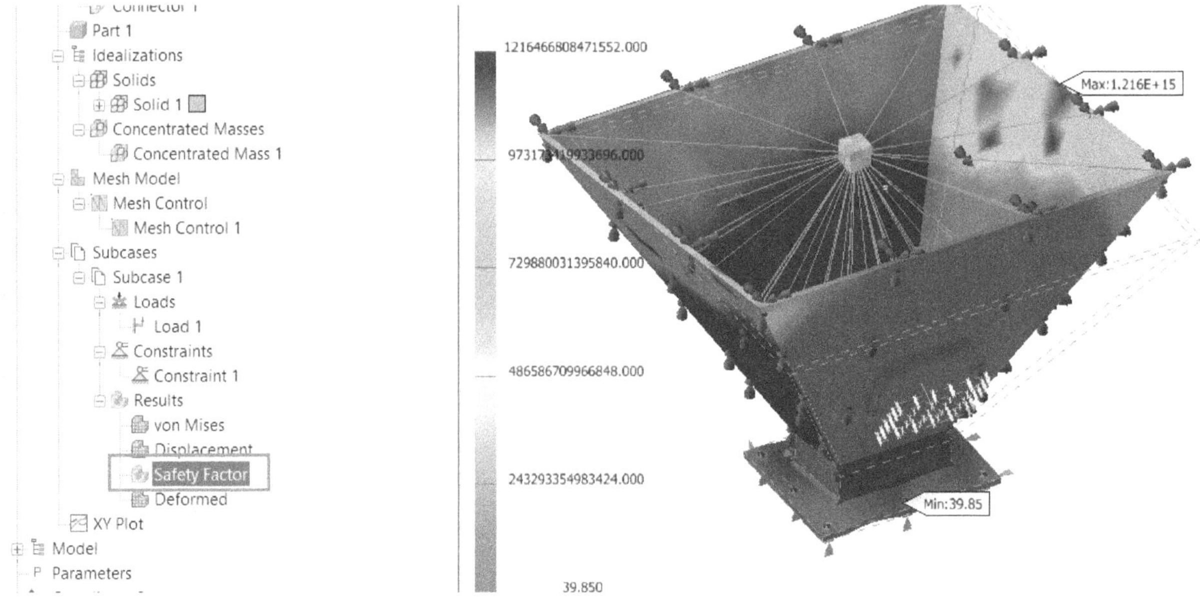

Figure-24. Safety factor plot

Performing Normal Mode Analysis

- Right-click on **Analysis 1** node from the **Nastran Model Tree** and select the **Duplicate** option from the shortcut menu; refer to Figure-25. A copy of current analysis will be created with all the loads and constraints applied and you will be prompted to specify the name of analysis.

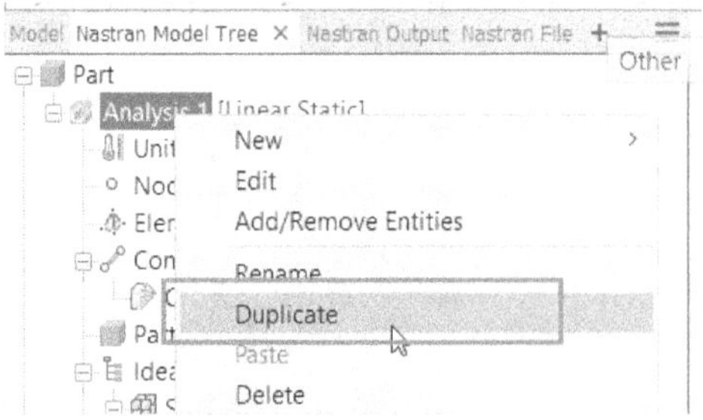

Figure-25. Duplicate option

- Specify the name as **Normal Mode Analysis** for easy identification of analysis. You can right-click on the new copy of analysis and select **Rename** option from the shortcut to rename it if you are not prompted by default for renaming.
- Right-click on the **Normal Mode Analysis** node from the **Nastran Model Tree** and select the **Edit** option to change type of analysis; refer to Figure-26. The **Analysis** dialog box will be displayed.

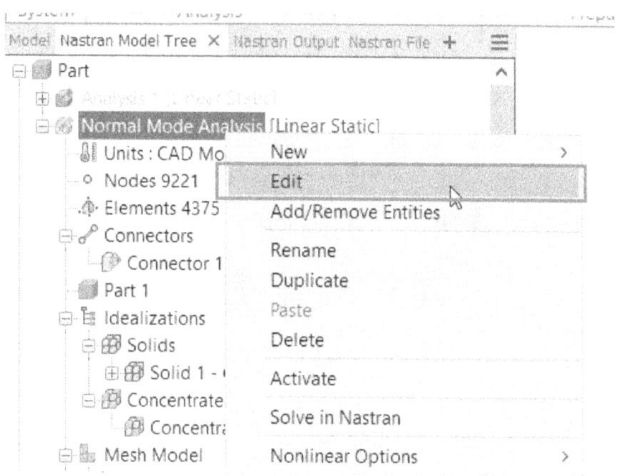

Figure-26. Edit option for analysis

- Select the **Normal Modes** option from the **Type** drop-down to change type of analysis and click on the **OK** button. The type of analysis will change to normal modes.
- Since, all the properties have already been applied to analysis, click on the **Run** tool from **Solve** panel in **Autodesk Inventor Nastran** tab of the **Ribbon**. The results of normal mode analysis will be displayed; refer to Figure-27 for displacement plot at lowest natural frequency.

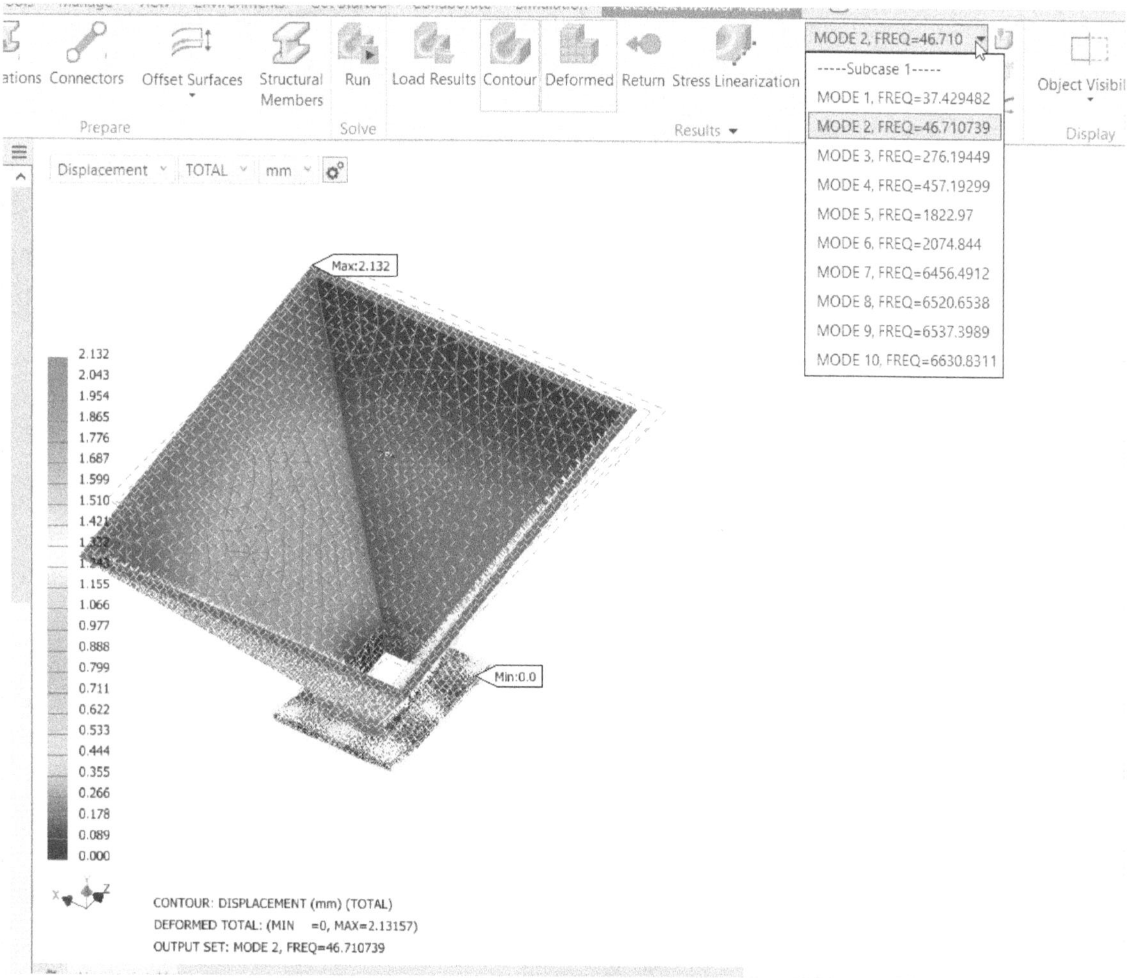

Figure-27. Displacement plot at lowest frequency

- Note that lowest natural frequency which are 37.43 Hz and 46.71 Hz are causing displacements in desired directions and within elastic limit of the model. To check actual deformation with an animation, right-click on the **Results** node from **Nastran Model Tree**. A shortcut menu will be displayed. Select the **Multiset Animation Settings** option from the shortcut menu. The **Multiset Animation Settings** dialog box will be displayed; refer to Figure-28.

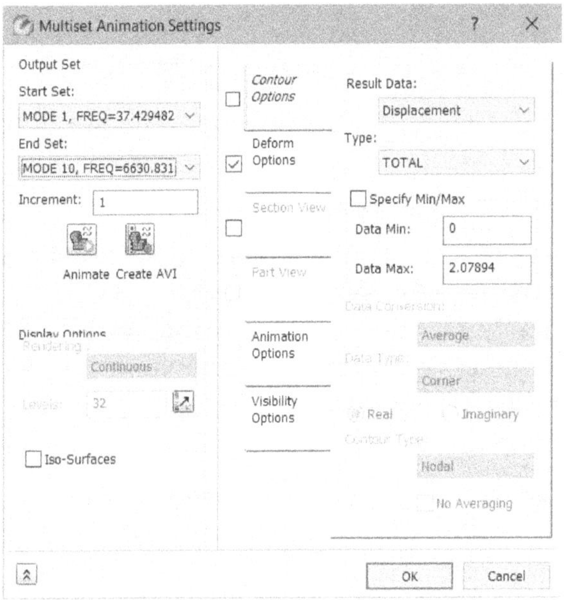

Figure-28. Multiset Animation Settings dialog box

- Set Mode 2 frequency in **End Set** drop-down of the dialog box to play animation from 1st mode frequency to 2nd.
- Select **Deform Options** check box Make sure **Displacement** option is selected in the **Result Data** drop-down and **TOTAL** option is selected in the **Type** drop-down for Deform options.
- Select the **Actual** radio button from **Deformation Scale** section; refer to Figure-29.

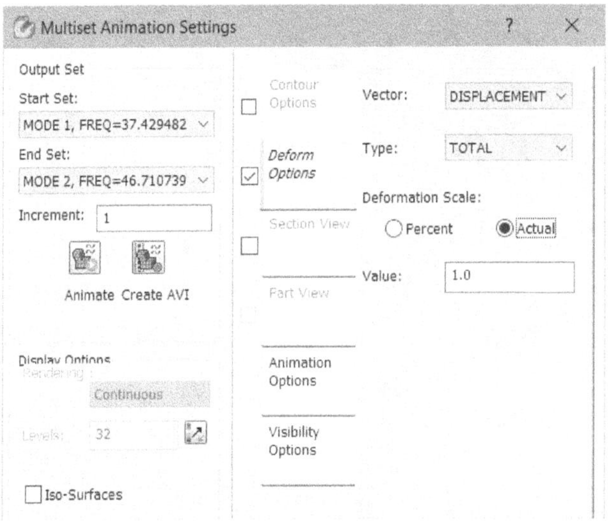

Figure-29. Deform options for multiset

- Click on the **Animate** button to check animation of deformation. You will find the deformation acceptable and necessary. Stop the animation by clicking on the **Animate** button again and click on the **OK** button from the dialog box.

Note that we will work again on this practical so that we can analyze what happens when 30 kgf load with frequency 85 is applied on the hopper.

PRACTICE

Perform Normal mode analysis with prestress on the model as shown in Figure-30. The model used for this practice is same as discussed in Practical above. Compare the two results and discussed the reason of change in natural frequency.

Hint: $\omega = \sqrt{\frac{k}{m}}$

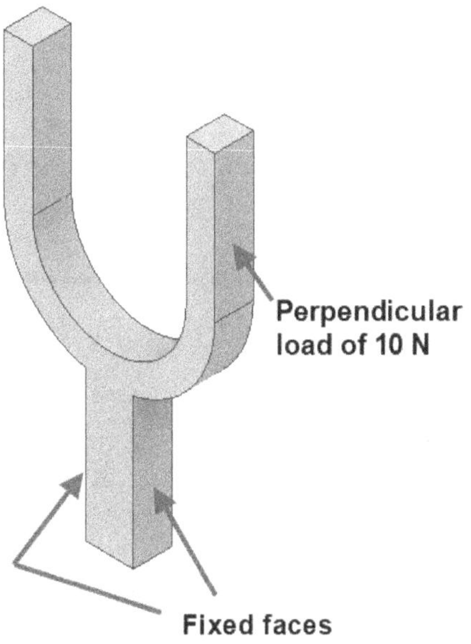

Figure-30. Tuning fork for prestress analysis with normal mode

SELF ASSESSMENT

Q1. What is the objective to perform Normal Modes Analysis?

Q2. What do you mean by Resonance?

Q3. When should you select the Lanczos Iteration option in performing Normal Modes Analysis?

Q4. The computation of natural frequencies and mode shapes are generally performed by .... , ... , and .... analyses.

Q5. .... analysis is performed on models which are already under stress due to continuous load for finding natural frequencies.

Q6. What is the main purpose of performing a Normal Modes analysis?

A. To calculate the static loads acting on a structure
B. To determine the stress concentration in a component
C. To find the natural frequencies and mode shapes of a structure
D. To evaluate thermal response of a model

Q7. What is the result of a structure being excited at its natural frequency?

A. Minimal displacement
B. Reduced stress levels
C. Resonance with large displacements and stresses
D. Static equilibrium

Q8. Which of the following best describes resonance in undamped systems?

A. Causes zero motion
B. Causes small oscillations
C. Causes infinite motion theoretically
D. Has no effect on structural behavior

Q9. How many natural frequencies does a finite element model have?

A. One
B. Infinite
C. Limited by the number of degrees of freedom
D. Depends only on the material

Q10. In vibration design, what is typically not used to evaluate a dynamic system's response?

A. Static studies
B. Frequency studies
C. Modal analysis
D. Normal Modes

Q11. What affects the natural frequencies and mode shapes of a structure?

A. Only material properties
B. Only geometry
C. Geometry, material properties, and support conditions
D. Only support conditions

Q12. What is the effect of tensile load on resonant frequencies?

A. No effect
B. Decreases them
C. Increases them
D. Makes them infinite

Q13. Which Extraction Method is suitable for large problems in modal analysis?

A. Subspace Iteration
B. Diagonal
C. Coupled
D. Lanczos Iteration

Q14. When is the Subspace Iteration method preferred?

A. For faster convergence in large models
B. When parallel iterations are needed
C. When only one natural frequency is needed
D. When using rigid elements

Q15. When should you use the Coupled option for Mass Representation?

A. When part has a heavier side
B. For uncoupled translational components
C. For uniform mass distribution
D. For thermal analysis

Q16. In Modal Setup, what defines the number of natural frequencies to be calculated?

A. Mass matrix
B. Modal Database setting
C. Number of Modes
D. Load magnitude

Q17. What distinguishes Prestress Normal Modes Analysis from Normal Modes Analysis?

A. It considers thermal loads
B. It ignores prestress
C. It includes the effects of pre-existing loads
D. It uses fewer iterations

Q18. What is the purpose of using Concentrated Masses in a design?

A. To increase the stiffness of modeled objects
B. To replace complex geometry with lightweight models
C. To represent mass objects not modeled in the design
D. To automate material assignment

Q19. When working with large complex problems, why might you use concentrated masses?

A. Because they are easier to visualize
B. Because stiffness of the object is not a concern
C. Because they provide better surface finishes
D. Because they help refine the mesh

Q20. Which tool is used to create a rigid body connector?

A. Mass Tool
B. Linker Tool
C. Connectors Tool
D. Structure Tool

Q21. If working on an assembly or multi-body part, how can the mass be defined?

A. By changing the mesh size
B. By using the Automatic radio button and specifying density
C. By selecting a surface feature
D. By importing a STEP file

FOR STUDENT NOTES

Chapter 5

Buckling Analysis

Topics Covered

The major topics covered in this chapter are:

- ***Introduction***
- ***Performing Linear Buckling Analysis***
- ***Performing Nonlinear Buckling Analysis***

INTRODUCTION

Slender structures tend to buckle under axial loading. Buckling is defined as a sudden change in deformation pattern that occurs when the strain energy stored due to axial compression is converted into bending energy, typically without any increase in the applied load. In layman's terms, consider pressing an empty soft drink can with your hand—initially, little happens. However, when the can is placed on the floor and the load is gradually increased by stepping on it, the can suddenly collapses. This abrupt collapse is known as buckling. Mathematically, at the point of buckling, the tangent stiffness matrix becomes singular. The linearized buckling approach used here solves an eigenvalue problem to estimate the critical buckling loads (or load factors) and the associated buckling mode shapes.

A structure can buckle in different shapes depending on the load level. These shapes are called buckling mode shapes, and the corresponding loads are called critical buckling loads. Buckling analysis computes multiple modes as specified in the analysis settings. Designers are typically most interested in the first mode (Mode 1), as it corresponds to the lowest critical load. When buckling governs the design, evaluating multiple modes helps identify potential weak regions. The mode shapes also provide insight into how the geometry or boundary conditions can be modified to delay or prevent buckling.

A more rigorous approach to studying structural behavior at and beyond buckling requires nonlinear analysis methods, which account for geometric and material non-linearities.

In most practical applications, buckling can lead to catastrophic failure. Unlike conventional failure modes governed by material strength, buckling is a stability failure driven by geometry. Once the structure begins to deform significantly, its load-carrying capacity drops sharply, often to a fraction of the original value. A key challenge for engineers is that buckling can occur at stress levels well below the material's yield strength. Therefore, a separate stability check is essential in design.

Slender structures, or structures with slender components subjected to axial loading, can buckle under relatively small loads. Such structures may fail due to instability even when stresses are far below critical material limits. In these cases, the buckling load becomes a governing design criterion. In contrast, stocky structures require significantly higher loads to buckle, and buckling analysis is often unnecessary. In industrial practice, buckling analysis is commonly performed for sheet metal components, as their thickness is small relative to other dimensions.

Buckling is primarily associated with compressive loading. In civil engineering, it must be carefully considered when designing columns, load-bearing walls, and bridge elements. For example, an I-beam may appear safe based on stress analysis alone, yet fail if local buckling occurs in a flange. In mechanical engineering, thin-walled components in structures such as aircraft and automobiles are particularly susceptible. Even when stresses are low, local buckling can trigger progressive instability, leading to rapid structural collapse. The mathematical formula for buckling can be given by Euler buckling equation:

$$F = \frac{\pi^2 EI}{(KL)^2}$$

Here, F is buckling load, E is Young's Modulus, I is Inertia, K is stiffness and L is length of part.

PERFORMING LINEAR BUCKLING ANALYSIS

Slender parts and assemblies with slender components that are loaded in the axial direction buckle under relatively small axial loads. Such structures can fail due to buckling while the stresses are far below critical levels. For such structures, the buckling load becomes a critical design factor. Buckling analysis is usually not required for bulky structures as failure occurs earlier due to high stresses. Linear buckling analysis uses Eigen value solution in Inventor Nastran and if you have lower number of elements in mesh then you might get higher number of eigen values in equation for complex parts. The procedure to use linear buckling analysis in Autodesk Inventor Nastran is given next.

The results generated by this analysis are non-conservative (approximations showing higher values of buckling loads as compared to actual). The reason why we say so is because for software there are no thin sections or material imperfections in the part due to manufacturing defects and material is uniform throughout the part but in real world this is not the case. You should always verify the results with physical buckling test after design phase is over.

- Open the part on which you want to perform buckling analysis and start Autodesk Inventor Nastran environment.
- Click on the **Edit** tool from the **Analysis** panel of **Autodesk Inventor Nastran** tab in **Ribbon**. The **Analysis** dialog box will be displayed.
- Select the **Linear Buckling** option from the **Type** drop-down and set desired parameters in **Output Controls** tab.
- Click on the **Options** tab in the dialog box. The options will be displayed as shown in Figure-1.

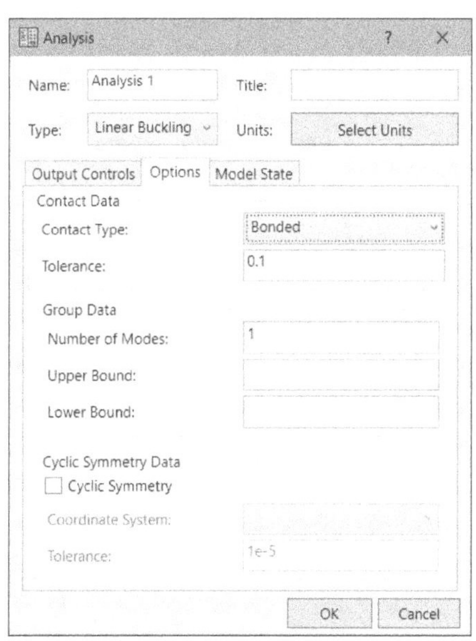

Figure-1. Buckling analysis options

- Set desired number of buckling modes you want to generate in the **Number of Modes** edit box.
- Specify desired load values for upper and lower limits in the **Upper Bound** and **Lower Bound** edit boxes. Note that specifying these values is not mandatory for analysis but if you define the values then analysis will run within specified load boundaries.

Tip: You can specify a positive value of lower bound if you are getting negative buckling load results in the analysis and want to check buckling in specified load direction only. Why you get negative buckling load? A negative buckling load means, buckling is occurring in opposite direction to load vector. This can happen due to reaction forces generated by other components in the assembly.

- Click on the **OK** button from the dialog box. The options related to linear buckling analysis will be displayed.
- Apply desired value of load and set desired constraint.
- Click on the **Run** button from the **Solve** panel. The buckling analysis result will be displayed; refer to Figure-2. (Look at the EIGV value found in this result, its 179.82 which is very high. So, this model is safe from bucking. If you find this value 0.xxx then buckling is going to happen before full load is applied on the model.)

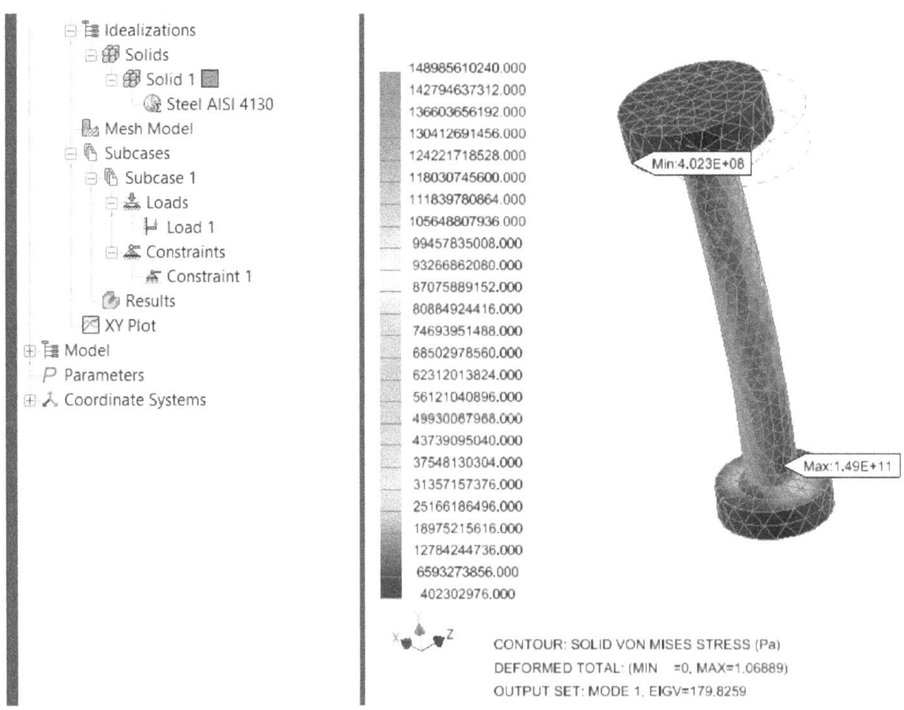

Figure-2. Buckling analysis result

Tip: **Workflow for Performing Buckling Analysis in Industry**
In mechanical industry, we start with a linear static analysis before performing linear buckling analysis because linear static analysis tells about the stresses developing in the model due to actual loading conditions in the assembly. Once we have confirmed that the part is safe for loading then we perform linear buckling analysis to find out eigen value of buckling load factor. Using eigen value, we can find out buckling load of model by multiplying eigen value with load applied on the model. For example if you have earlier applied 1000 N compressive load on the model and eigen value of first buckling mode is 0.8 then buckling will occur on 1000 N x 0.8 = 800 N. Note that in such cases, although part has passed linear static analysis but it can fail due to bucking at 80% of load to be applied. Once you have found that part will fail early due to bucking then it's time to perform non-linear buckling analysis. Non-linear buckling analysis gives better insight of how part is deforming. Now, why we are doing all this? We are doing this to understand what kind of adjustments are needed in the model. Based on displacement vector found in non-linear buckling analysis, we add or modify geometry of model to restrict displacement in that vector direction found by result. (We suggest you to watch the video on buckling using mobile phone QR code scanner given below.)

PERFORMING NON-LINEAR BUCKLING ANALYSIS

The non-linear buckling analysis is used when there is large displacement in model due to buckling and you are concerned about the shape attained by object due to buckling. In other words, if you want the object to buckle under load and want to check its shape attained due to buckling then you should use the non-linear buckling analysis. The procedure to use buckling analysis in Autodesk Inventor Nastran is given next.

- Open the part and start Autodesk Inventor Nastran.
- Click on the **New** button from the **Analysis** panel of **Autodesk Inventor Nastran** tab in **Ribbon**. The **Analysis** dialog box will be displayed.
- Select the **Nonlinear Buckling** option from the **Type** drop-down and set desired parameters in **Output Controls** tab of the dialog box.
- Set desired number of buckling modes, upper bound, and lower bound for the analysis. Make sure to select the **On** option for **Large Displacements** drop-down if there is going to be large deformation.
- Click on the **OK** button from the dialog box after setting desired parameters. The options for nonlinear analysis will be displayed; refer to Figure-3.

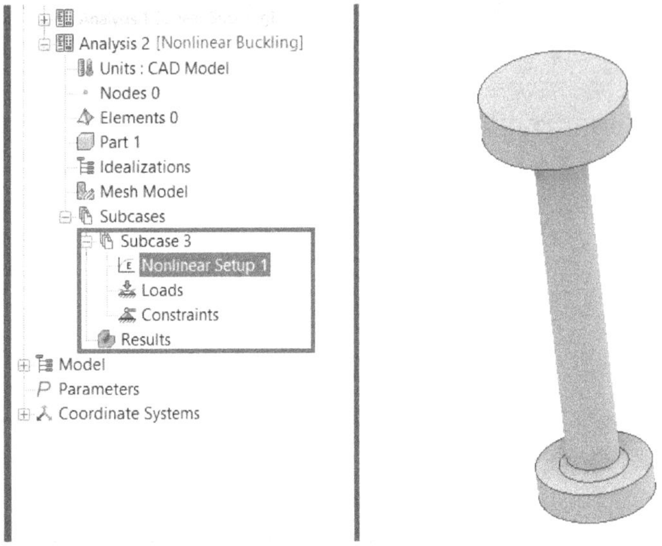

Figure-3. Nonlinear buckling analysis subcase

- Double-click on the **Nonlinear Setup 1** option from the **Subcase** node. The **Nonlinear Setup** dialog box will be displayed. Set the options as discussed earlier and click on the **OK** button.
- The other options are same as discussed for linear buckling analysis. Set desired idealization, load, and constraint.
- After setting desired parameters, click on the **Run** button. Once the analysis is complete, the result of analysis will be displayed; refer to Figure-4. (Note that now Eigen value is 144.74 in the figure which is way less than 179.89 we found in Linear buckling. So, Nonlinear buckling analysis has higher accuracy as compared to linear buckling analysis.)

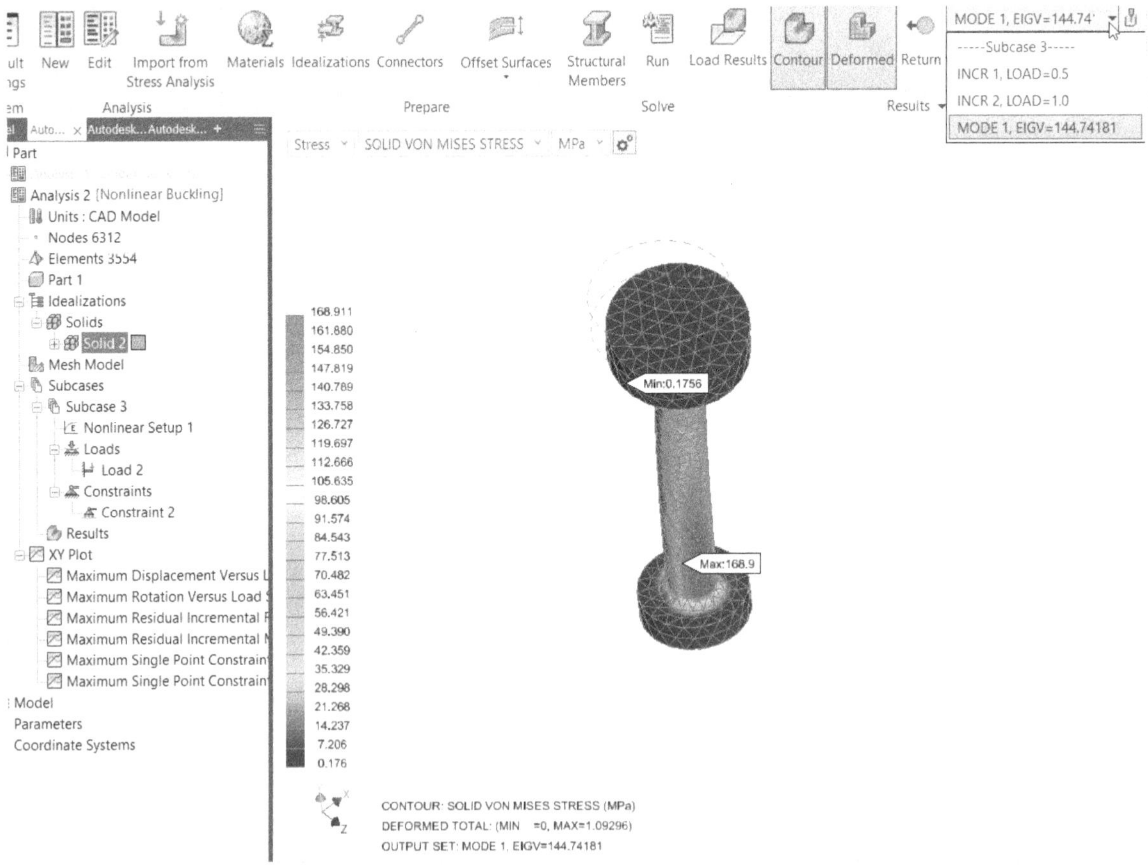

Figure-4. Result of nonlinear buckling analysis

- Double-click on desired result under XY Plot node to results changing with mode shapes and load steps.

PRACTICAL 1

Perform buckling analysis on the model as shown in Figure-5.

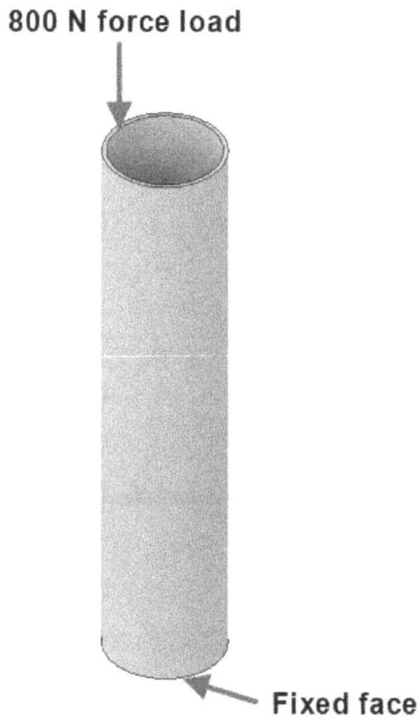

Figure-5. Parameters for buckling analysis

Opening Part and Starting Buckling Analysis

- Open the Practical for buckling analysis part from Chapter 5 folder of Resources for Autodesk Inventor Nastran.
- Click on the **Autodesk Inventor Nastran** tool from the **Begin** panel of **Environments** tab in the **Ribbon**. The linear static analysis will start automatically.
- Click on the **Edit** button from the **Analysis** panel of **Autodesk Inventor Nastran** tab in the **Ribbon**. The **Analysis** dialog box will be displayed.
- Select the **Linear Buckling** option from the **Type** drop-down and click on the **Options** tab. Specify the number of modes as **5** in the **Number of Modes** edit box; refer to Figure-6. (Note that generally we are concerned about 1st or 2nd lowest mode in results.)

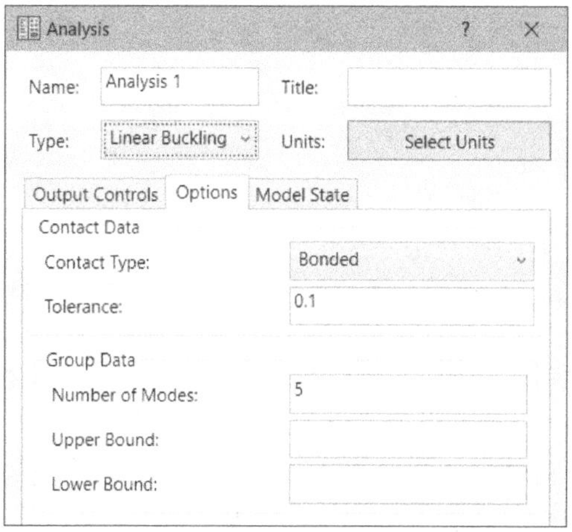

Figure-6. Specifying modes for buckling analysis

- Click on the **OK** button from the dialog box. The options to perform buckling analysis will be displayed.

Applying Material and Setting Idealization

- Click on the **Materials** tool from the **Prepare** panel of **Autodesk Inventor Nastran** tab in the **Ribbon**. The **Material** dialog box will be displayed.
- Click on the **Select Material** button from the **Material** dialog box. The **Material DB** dialog box will be displayed.
- Select the **Stainless Steel** option from the **Inventor Material Library** node of **Material DB** dialog box and click on the **OK** button. The properties of selected material will be displayed in the **Material** dialog box.
- Click on the **OK** button from the **Material** dialog box to apply material.
- Double-click on **Solid 1** option from the **Solids** node of **Idealizations** node in **Model Tree**. The **Idealizations** dialog box will be displayed.
- Select **Stainless Steel** option from the **Material** drop-down and click on the **OK** button.

Applying Constraint and Load

- Click on the **Constraint** tool from the **Setup** panel of **Autodesk Inventor Nastran** tab. The **Constraint** dialog box will be displayed.
- Select the bottom flat face of the model and click on the **Fixed** button; refer to Figure-7.

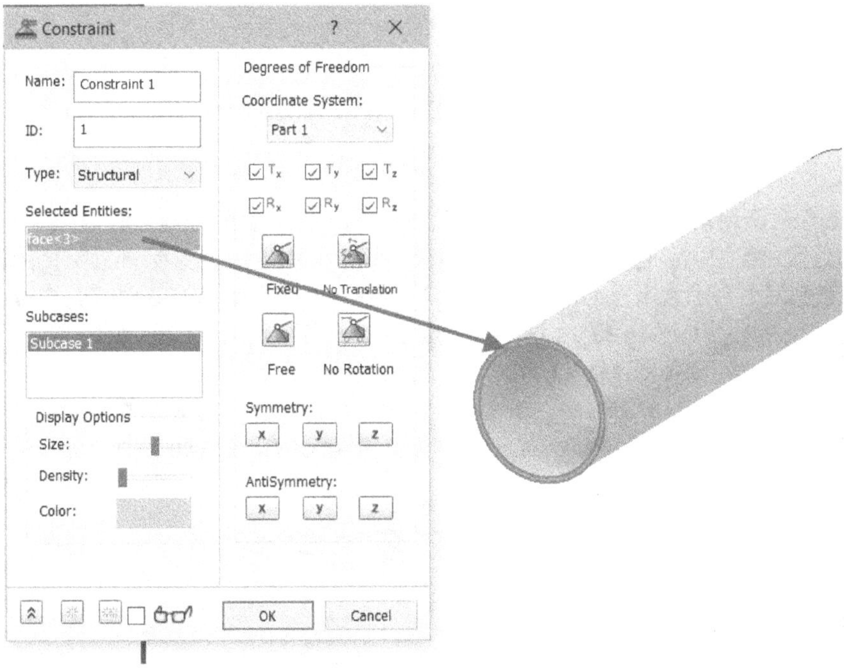

Figure-7. Face selected for fixing

- Click on the **OK** button from the dialog box.
- Click on the **Loads** tool from the **Setup** panel of **Autodesk Inventor Nastran** tab in the **Ribbon**. The **Load** dialog box will be displayed.
- Select the top face of model and select **Normal To Surface** option from the **Direction** drop-down.
- Specify the value of force as **-800** N in the **Magnitude** edit box; refer to Figure-8.
- After setting desired parameters, click on the **OK** button from the dialog box.

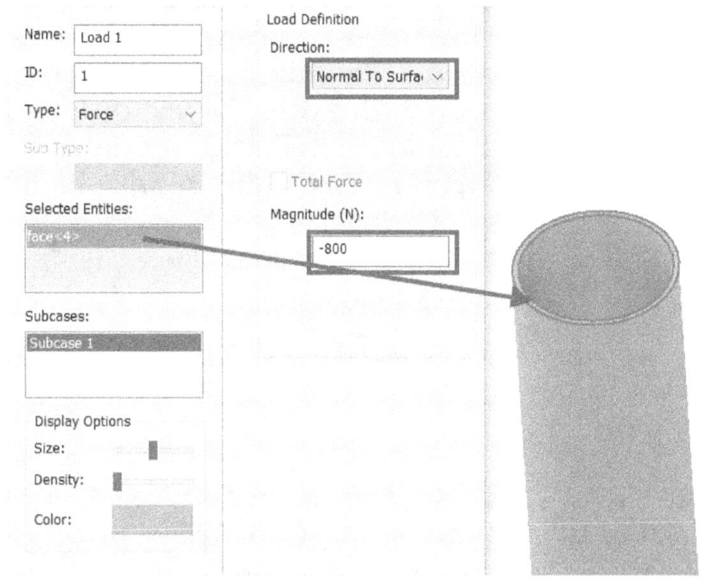

Figure-8. Applying load

Running Analysis

- Click on the **Mesh Settings** tool from the **Mesh** panel of **Autodesk Inventor Nastran** tab in the **Ribbon**. The **Mesh Settings** dialog box will be displayed.
- Specify the size of mesh element as **7** mm in the **Element Size** edit box and click on the **Generate Mesh** button. The mesh will be generated.
- Click on the **OK** button from the dialog box.
- Click on the **Run** tool from the **Solve** panel of **Autodesk Inventor Nastran** tab in the **Ribbon**. Once the analysis is complete, **Autodesk Inventor Nastran** information box will be displayed.
- Click on the **OK** button from the information box. The results of analysis will be displayed; refer to Figure-9. (Generally, tubes are more resistant to buckling as compared to rods/bars.)

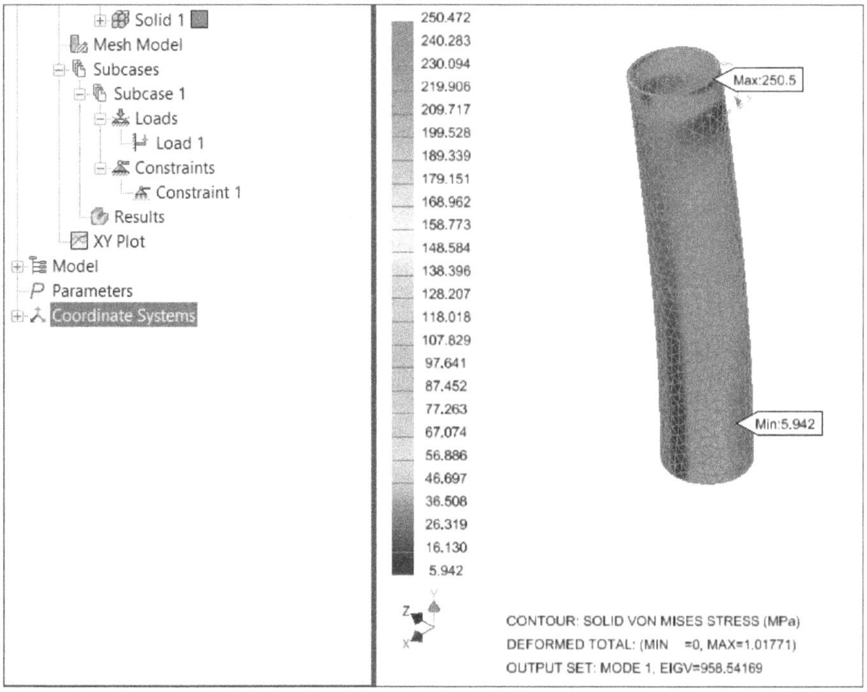

Figure-9. Result of buckling analysis

Note: If you are wondering how eigen value found in buckling analysis define the critical buckling load of model then you need to understand what eigen value and eigen vectors are geometrically. Visit the YouTube link below to get basic understanding of eigen value and vector. Eigen value is the value of vector length which does not change even after slight deformation of model. In Buckling analysis, system calculates last eigen value (Length of stiffness vector in axial direction) which remains constant before buckling.

PRACTICE 1

Perform buckling analysis on the models as shown in Figure-10 and compare the results. The tube is fixed at the bottom and force of **400** N is applied on the top face.

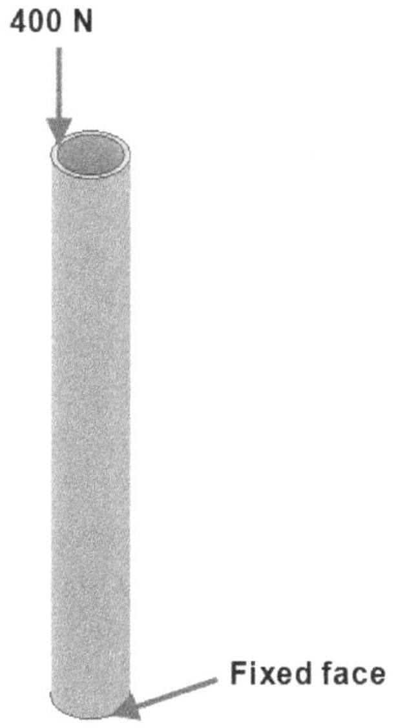

Figure-10. Model for buckling analyses

PRACTICE 2

Perform buckling analysis on 10 mm diameter rod of length 100 mm and compare the results with hand calculation. The value of E is 2.05e+5 MPa for the material (Alloy Steel). The formula for hand calculation of critical buckling load is given by

$$F = \frac{\pi^2 EI}{(KL)^2}$$

SELF ASSESSMENT

Q1. What do you mean by Buckling? Describe briefly.

Q2. Mathematically, when buckling occurs, the .... becomes singular.

Q3. The .... analysis is used when there is large displacement in model due to buckling and you are concerned about the shape attained by object due to buckling.

Q4. .... analysis is usually not required for bulky structures as failure occurs earlier due to high stresses.

Q5. Buckling almost always involves compression. (True/False)

Q6. What is the primary cause of buckling in slender structures?

A. High thermal loads
B. Sudden impact loads
C. Conversion of membrane energy into bending energy
D. Expansion of material under pressure

Q7. What does the buckling mode shape represent?

A. The load at which maximum stress occurs
B. The direction of applied force
C. The shape a model takes while buckling
D. The stiffness of the material

Q8. When is nonlinear buckling analysis preferred over linear buckling analysis?

A. When material is brittle
B. When loading is purely tensile
C. When large deformations are expected
D. When stress distribution is uniform

Q9. What does a negative buckling load indicate in analysis?

A. The model is not likely to buckle
B. Buckling occurs in opposite direction to load vector
C. Load is applied in tangential direction
D. There is no reaction force from components

Q10. What is the formula for calculating buckling load using eigen value from linear analysis?

A. Applied load ÷ Eigen value
B. Applied load x Eigen value
C. Inertia x Length
D. Young's Modulus ÷ Stiffness

Q11. Why is buckling critical even at low stress values?

A. Because it leads to high temperatures
B. Because it causes high vibration
C. Because it results from geometric instability
D. Because material compresses permanently

Q12. In which structures is buckling analysis most often performed in industry?

A. Welded steel beams
B. Cast iron blocks
C. Sheet metal components
D. Solid wooden frames

Q13. Which civil structure is most susceptible to buckling?

A. Water tanks
B. Support columns
C. Elevator shafts
D. Horizontal floors

Q14. How can the designer identify areas prone to buckling?

A. By analyzing stress concentration
B. By studying buckling mode shapes
C. By measuring deflection manually
D. By testing part in a vacuum

Q15. What additional step is recommended after completing software-based buckling analysis?

A. Chemical testing of material
B. Increasing mesh size
C. Physical buckling test
D. Thermal expansion analysis

Q16. What does the option “Large Displacements: On” do in nonlinear buckling setup?

A. Increases stiffness of material
B. Enhances thermal conductivity
C. Allows analysis of large deformations
D. Minimizes reaction force from constraints

Chapter 6

Transient Response Analysis

Topics Covered

The major topics covered in this chapter are:

- ***Introduction***
- ***Performing Direct Transient Response Analysis***
- ***Defining Damping Parameters***
- ***Defining Dynamic Setup Parameters***
- ***Performing Modal Transient Response Analysis***
- ***Performing Nonlinear Transient Response Analysis***

INTRODUCTION

Transient response analysis is a method of computing forced dynamic response. This analysis is used to determine the behavior of a structure subjected to time-varying excitation. During the transient analysis, loads applied to the structure are known at each instant in time. Loads can be in the form of applied forces and enforced motions. The results obtained from a transient response analysis are in the form of displacements, velocities, and accelerations of grid points, or forces and stresses in elements at each output time step.

Transient response analyses fall under the category of dynamic analyses. Static analyses solve the equation F = K.x where as dynamic analyses solve motion equation $R(t) = m.(d^2u/dt^2)+c.(du/dt)+k.u$ where, R(t) is motion response with respect to time, m is mass, c is damping coefficient, and k is stiffness. When there is no damping, c=0 so equation becomes $R(t) = m.(d^2u/dt^2)+k.u$. Note that mass and stiffness both are important factors along with damping coefficient for solving such equation.

Depending upon the structure and the nature of the loading, there are three different transient response analyses:

Direct Transient Response Analysis: This analysis calculates the response of a system to a load over time. The load applied to the system can vary over time or simply be an initial condition that is allowed to evolve over time. This method may be more efficient for models where high-frequency excitation require the extraction of a large number of modes. Also, if structural damping is used, the direct method should be used.

Modal Transient Response Analysis: This analysis is an alternate technique available for dynamics that utilizes the mode shapes of the structure, reduces the solution degrees of freedom, and can significantly impact the run time. This approach replaces the physical degrees of freedom with a reduced number of modal degrees of freedom. Fewer degrees of freedom mean a faster solution. This can be a big time saver for transient models with a large number of time steps. Because modal transient response analysis uses the mode shapes of a structure, this analysis is a natural extension of normal modes analysis.

Nonlinear Transient Response Analysis: This analysis is performed when effect of inertia, damping, and transient loading are significant. Also, if your model is in unstable conditions or can go under buckling deformation then this analysis can give more insight of failure. An important element to having a stable nonlinear transient (NLT) solution is to provide damping in the model. Note that while using damping in a NLT solution for models where the velocity/inertia is the main driver of the analysis such as in an impact solution, damping can have a significant effect on the acceleration/velocity/displacement of the model. This is because the solver cannot make a distinction between rigid body motion/velocity, and flexible motion/velocity, so the damping is applied to any part of the structure that has a velocity. For impact analysis it is recommended to use no damping or a small “stability” damping value.

The procedures to perform these analyses are discussed next.

PERFORMING DIRECT TRANSIENT RESPONSE

The direct transient response analysis is used to test structural objects under high frequency excitation with damping. The procedure to perform direct transient response analysis is given next.

- Open the part on which you want to perform analysis and start Autodesk Inventor Nastran environment. Linear Static analysis will become active automatically.
- Click on the **Edit** tool from the **Analysis** panel of **Autodesk Inventor Nastran** tab in the **Ribbon**. The **Analysis** dialog box will be displayed.
- Select the **Direct Transient Response** option from the **Type** drop-down. Set the other options in the **Analysis** dialog box as discussed earlier and click on the **OK** button. The options in the **Model Tree** will be displayed as shown in Figure-1.

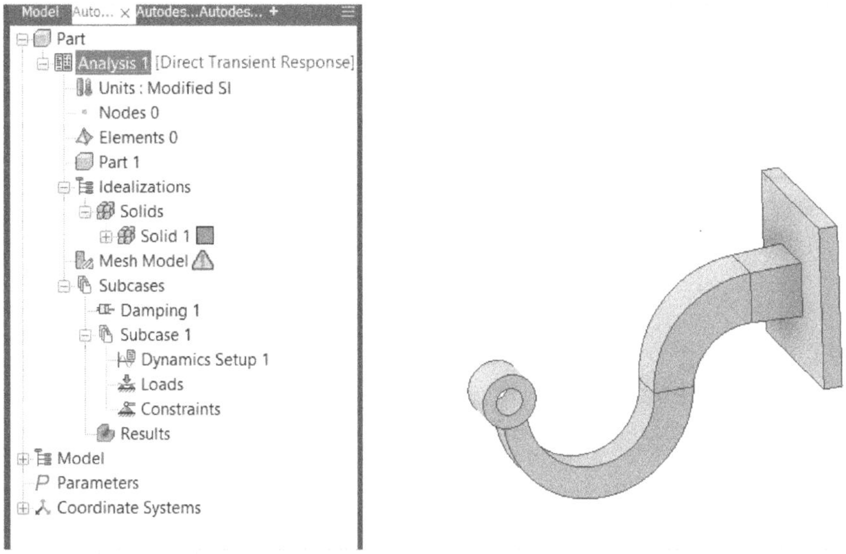

Figure-1. Options for direct transient response analysis

Setting Damping Values

- Double-click on **Damping 1** option from the **Subcases** node. The **Damping** dialog box will be displayed; refer to Figure-2.

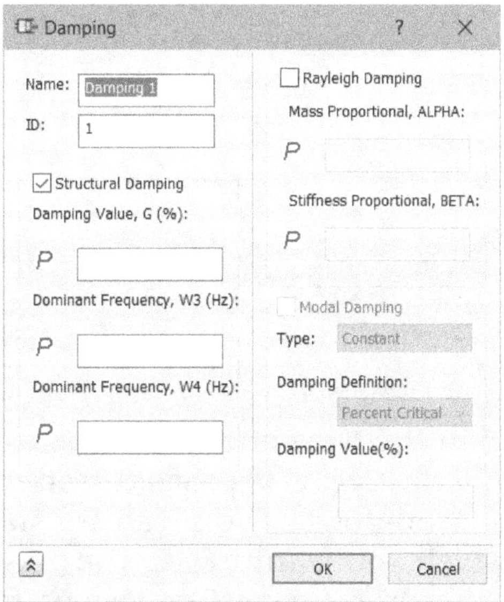

Figure-2. Damping dialog box

- Specify desired name and id for damping in **Name** and **ID** edit boxes.
- By default, **Structural Damping** check box is selected and options to define structural damping are displayed. Structural damping assumes that the damping forces are proportional to the forces caused by stressing of the structure and are opposed to the velocity. This form of damping can be used only if the displacement and velocity are exactly 90° out of phase, which is the case when the excitation is sinusoidal, so structural damping can be used only in steady-state and random response analysis.
- Specify desired value of global damping in the **Damping Value, G(%)** edit box. The value specified here is in percentage.
- Specify desired value of frequency in the **Dominant Frequency, W3(Hz)** edit box at which elemental damping will be converted to equivalent viscous damping. It is a global structural damping setting.
- Specify desired value of frequency in the **Dominant Frequency, W4(Hz)** edit box at which elemental damping will be converted to equivalent viscous damping. It is a material based structural damping setting. So, if you are multiple materials in the model then viscous damping will be different for each element based on frequency specified here.
- Select the **Rayleigh Damping** check box to define mass and stiffness components of rayleigh damping. The edit boxes below the check box will become active.
- Specify desired value of mass proportional and stiffness proportional in respective edit boxes. Rayleigh damping is given by formula: $C^{MN}=\alpha M^{MN}+\beta K^{MN}$
- Note that **Modal Damping** options are available for Modal dynamic analyses so they will not be active in this case.
- Set desired values and click on the **OK** button.

Dynamic Setup Parameters

- Double-click on **Dynamic Setup 1** option from the **Subcase 1** node. The **Dynamics Setup** dialog box will be displayed; refer to Figure-3.

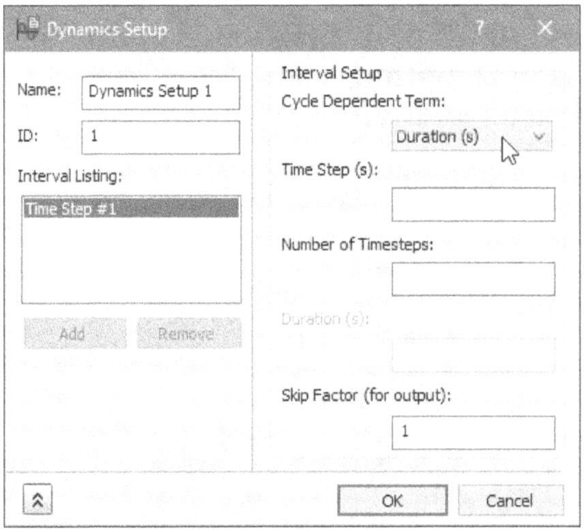

Figure-3. Dynamics Setup dialog box

- Set desired name and id in the **Name** and **ID** edit boxes.
- Select desired option from the **Cycle Dependent Term** drop-down. Select the **Time Step(s)** option from the drop-down if you want to specify number of time steps and total duration for which you want to run the analysis. Select the **Number of Timesteps** option from the drop-down if you want to specify duration of each

time steps and total duration for which you want to run the analysis. Select the **Duration(s)** option from the drop-down if you want to duration of each time step and total number of time steps.

- Specify desired skip factor in the **Skip Factor (for output)** edit box and set the number for time step to be skipped.
- After setting desired parameters, click on the **OK** button.
- Specify desired idealization, load, and constraint for the analysis.
- After setting desired parameters and generating the mesh, click on the **Run** tool from the **Solve** panel.
- Once the analysis is complete, an information box will be displayed. Click on the **OK** button from the information box. The results of analysis will be displayed; refer to Figure-4.

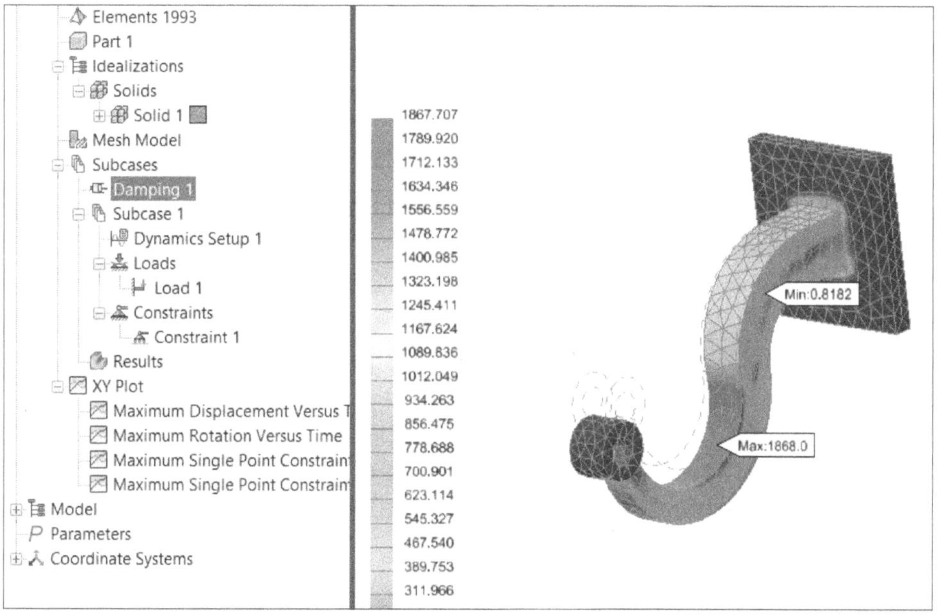

Figure-4. Result of direct transient analysis

- Double-click on desired result in **XY Plot** node to check plots.

PERFORMING MODAL TRANSIENT RESPONSE ANALYSIS

The modal transient response analysis is performed when you want to use modal degrees of freedom in place of physical degrees of freedom for solving the analysis. The procedure to perform analysis is given next.

- Open the model on which you want to perform modal transient response analysis and start **Autodesk Inventor Nastran** environment. The linear static analysis will start automatically.
- Click on the **Edit** tool from the **Analysis** panel of **Autodesk Inventor Nastran** tab in the **Ribbon**. The **Analysis** dialog box will be displayed.
- Select the **Modal Transient Response** option from the **Type** drop-down and set desired parameters as discussed earlier.
- Click on the **OK** button from the dialog box. The options will be displayed as shown in Figure-5.

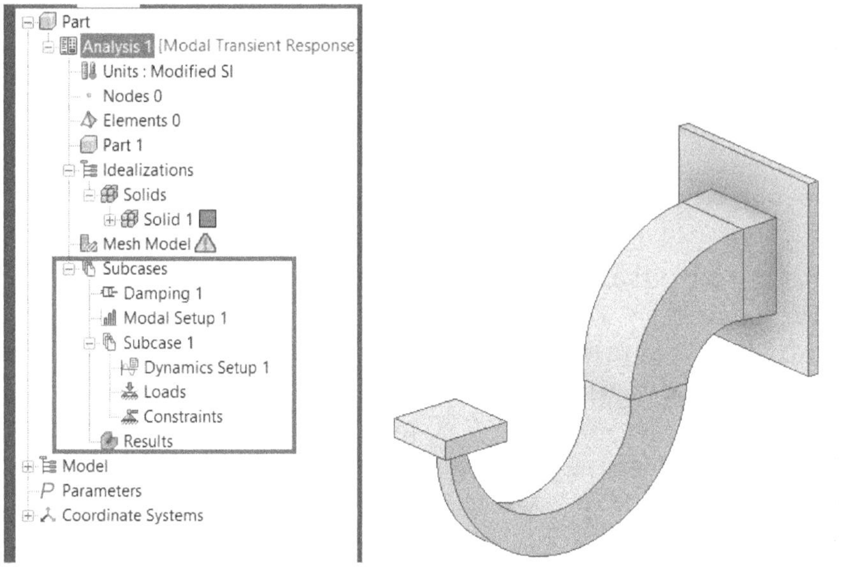

Figure-5. Options for modal transient response analysis

- Apart from direct transient response analysis options, modal setup options will also be displayed. Double-click on **Modal Setup 1** option from the **Subcases** node. The **Modal Setup** dialog box will be displayed. The options in this dialog box are similar to Normal Mode Analysis.
- Set desired parameters as discussed earlier and click on the **OK** button.
- Similarly, set the modal damping parameters in the **Modal Damping** area of **Damping** dialog box.
- Apply material, idealization, load, and constraint as desired and click on the **Run** button. Once the analysis is complete, click on the **OK** button from the **Autodesk Inventor Nastran** information box. The analysis results will be displayed; refer to Figure-6.

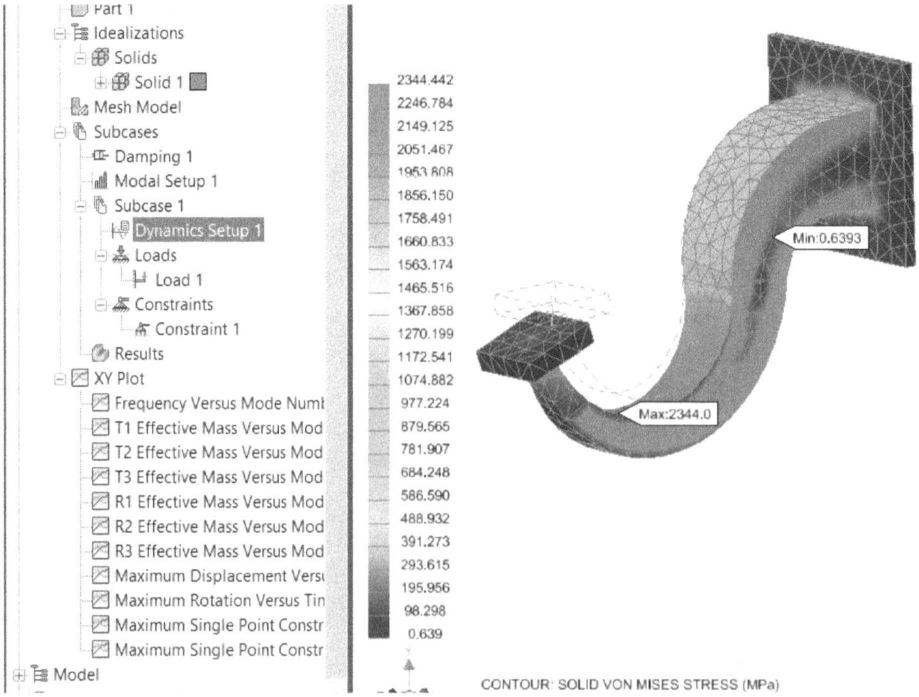

Figure-6. Modal transient response analysis results

- Double-click on desired plot to check the results.

PERFORMING NONLINEAR TRANSIENT RESPONSE ANALYSIS

The nonlinear transient response analysis is performed when damping, vibrational excitation, and large deformation is involved in the analysis study. In this analysis, we want to check changes in shape of model with time due to dynamic loads. The procedure to perform the analysis is given next.

- Open the part on which you want to perform nonlinear transient response analysis and start **Autodesk Inventor Nastran** environment.
- Click on the **New** tool from the **Analysis** panel of **Autodesk Inventor Nastran** tab in the **Ribbon**. The **Analysis** dialog box will be displayed.
- Select the **Nonlinear Transient Response** option from the **Type** drop-down of the dialog box.
- Click on the **Options** tab in the dialog box and select the **On** option from the **Large Displacements** drop-down if you are expecting large deformation.
- Click on the **OK** button from the dialog box. The options to set parameters for nonlinear transient analysis will be displayed in the **Model Tree**; refer to Figure-7.

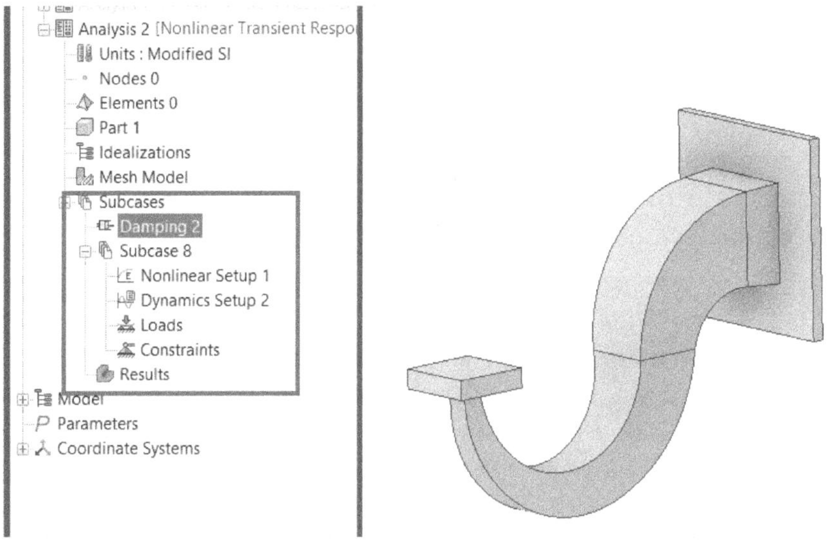

Figure-7. Options for nonlinear transient response analysis

- Set desired parameters for damping, nonlinear setup, and dynamic setup as discussed earlier.
- Specify the loads and constraints as required.
- Specify material and set the idealization.
- Click on the **Run** button from the **Solve** panel of **Autodesk Inventor Nastran** tab in the **Ribbon**. Once the analysis is complete, click on the **OK** button from the **Autodesk Inventor Nastran** information box. The analysis results will be displayed; refer to Figure-8.

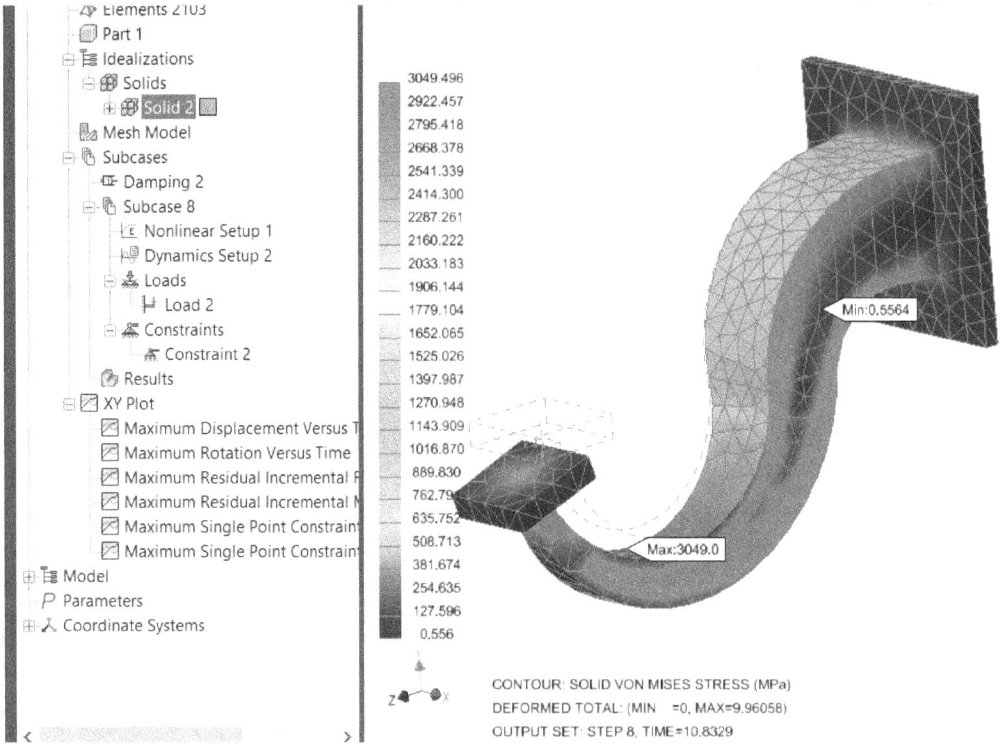

Figure-8. Result of nonlinear transient response analysis

You can also check results at different time steps. Save the results and exit the environment. Note that nonlinear transient response analysis is also used to perform impact analysis which you will learn in next chapter.

PRACTICAL

In this practical, we have applied a time dependent force to revolving ring in opposite direction of revolution and we want to check stresses developing in model with respect to time; refer to Figure-9. The analysis will be performed for 4 seconds as the load will be for 4 seconds only. The variation of load with respect to time is given by graph shown in Figure-10. The value of force applied to face is 17000 N.

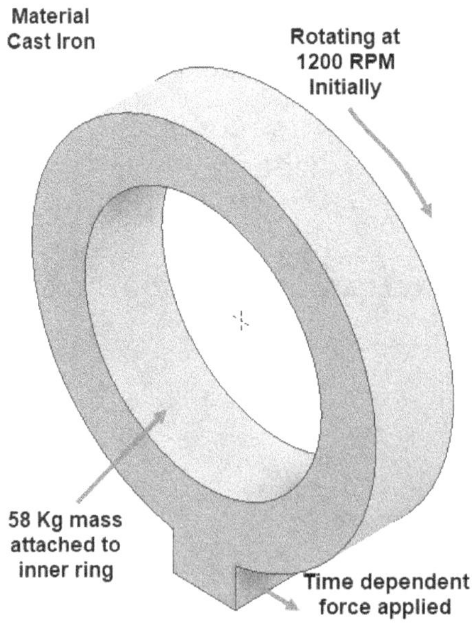

Figure-9. Practical direct transient

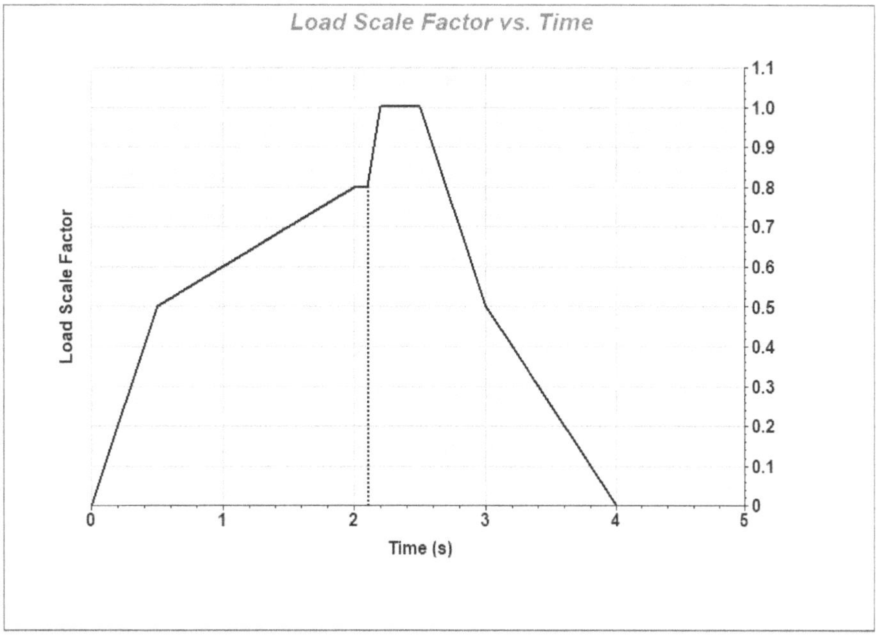

Figure-10. Load scale factor graph

Steps:
In this practical, we need to first apply initial condition of 1200 RPM to the ring using Cylindrical coordinate system and then we will apply force on the face to slow down the ring. We will also attach a mass of 58 Kg to inner face of ring and then we will perform direct transient response analysis. The procedure is given next.

Starting Direct Transient Response Analysis

- Open the Practical part from Chapter 6 folder of Resources for Autodesk Inventor Nastran.
- Click on the **Autodesk Inventor Nastran** tool from the **Begin** panel of **Environments** tab in the **Ribbon**. The linear static analysis will start automatically.
- Click on the **Edit** button from the **Analysis** panel of **Autodesk Inventor Nastran** tab in the **Ribbon**. The **Analysis** dialog box will be displayed.
- Select the **Direct Transient Response** option from the **Type** drop-down in the dialog box. Select the **Velocity** and **Acceleration** check boxes to generate nodal data of respective parameters as well.
- Click on the **Select Units** button and set the unit system as **SI**. Click on the **OK** button from the dialog box after specifying the parameters. The analysis type will change to direct transient response analysis.

Applying Initial Velocity Condition

- Applying initial velocity condition to rotate a part needs rigid connection between center point and faces rotating about that point. So, we will create a rigid connection. But, before that we will need a cylindrical coordinate system to reference rotating loads and constraints. To create a new coordinate system, right-click on **Coordinate Systems** option under **Model** node from the bottom in the **Nastran Model Tree**; refer to Figure-11. A shortcut menu will be displayed.
- Select the **New** option from the shortcut menu. The **Coordinate System** dialog box will be displayed; refer to Figure-12.

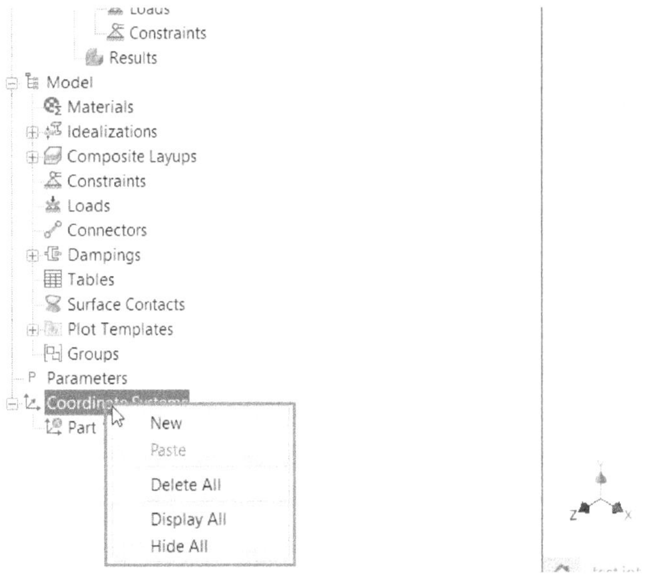

Figure-11. Coordinate Systems shortcut menu

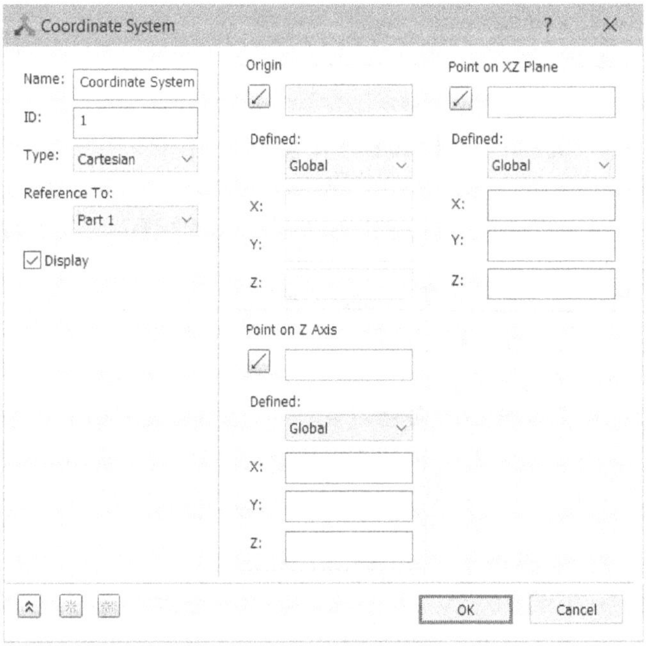

Figure-12. Coordinate System dialog box

- Select the **Cylindrical** option from the **Type** drop-down to create cylindrical coordinate system. Note that you can also create spherical coordinate system if needed by selecting the **Spherical** option from the dialog box.
- Click in the **Origin** selection box from the dialog box and select the point created at the center of the model.
- Click on the button in **Point on XZ Plane** area of the dialog box and select the point to be used to define X direction for coordinate system. Similarly, select point to define Z direction of coordinate system. Preview of coordinate system will be displayed; refer to Figure-13. Note that points have been created by using the sketch point tool.
- After setting parameters, click on the **OK** button. The coordinate system will be created.

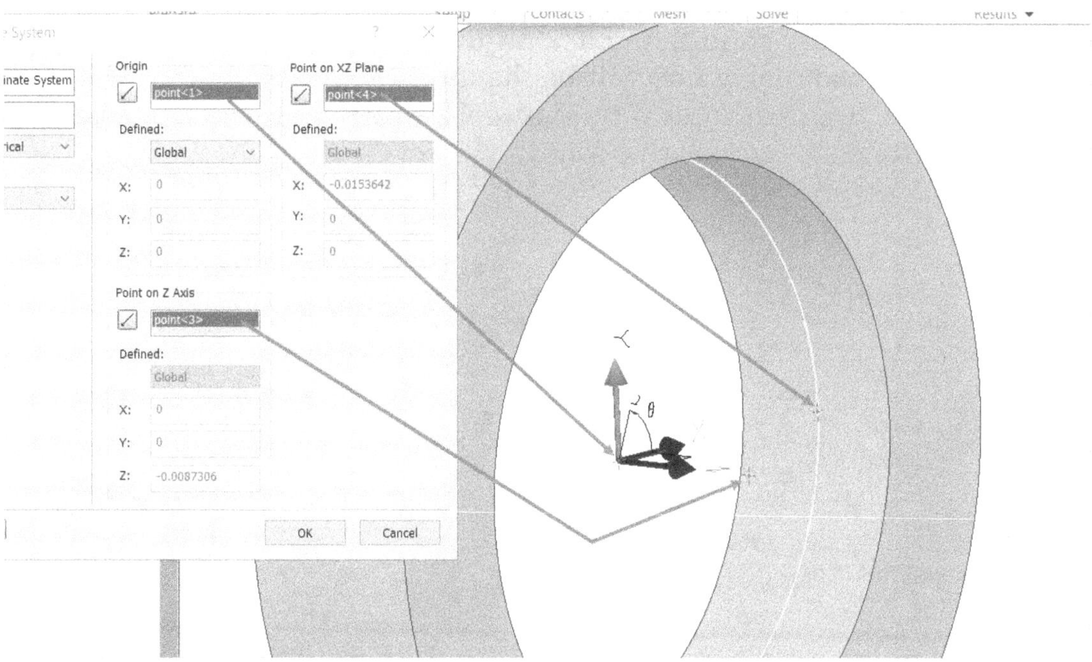

Figure-13. Preview of cylindrical coordinate system

Now, we will create rigid link for applying initial velocity.

- Click on the **Connectors** tool from the **Prepare** panel in the **Autodesk Inventor Nastran** tab of the **Ribbon**. The **Connector** dialog box will be displayed.
- Select the **Rigid Body** option from the **Type** drop-down and **Interpolation** option from the **Type** drop-down in **Rigid Body** area of the **Connector** dialog box.
- Select the faces, point, and other parameters as shown in Figure-14.

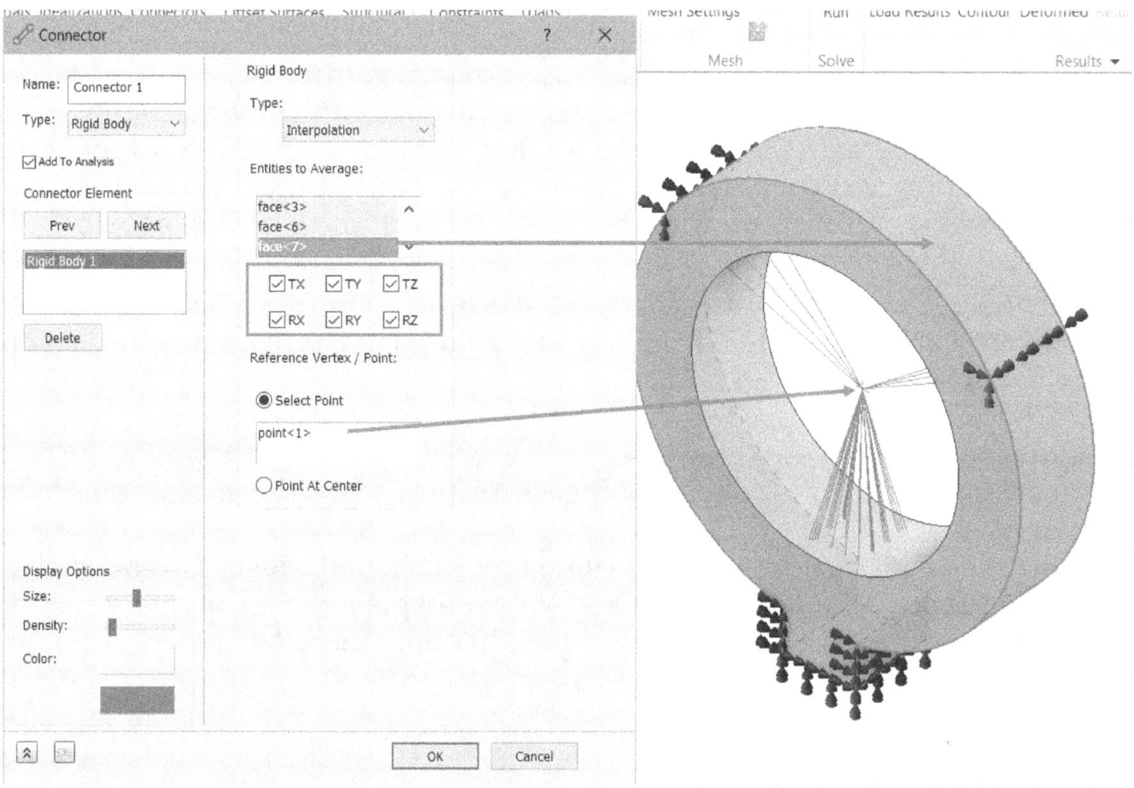

Figure-14. Entities selected for connector

- After specifying parameters, click on the **OK** button to create connector.
- To apply initial velocity condition, click on the **Loads** tool from the **Setup** panel in the **Ribbon**. The **Load** dialog box will be displayed.
- Specify the parameters as shown in Figure-15. Note that we have selected newly created coordinate system for this load.

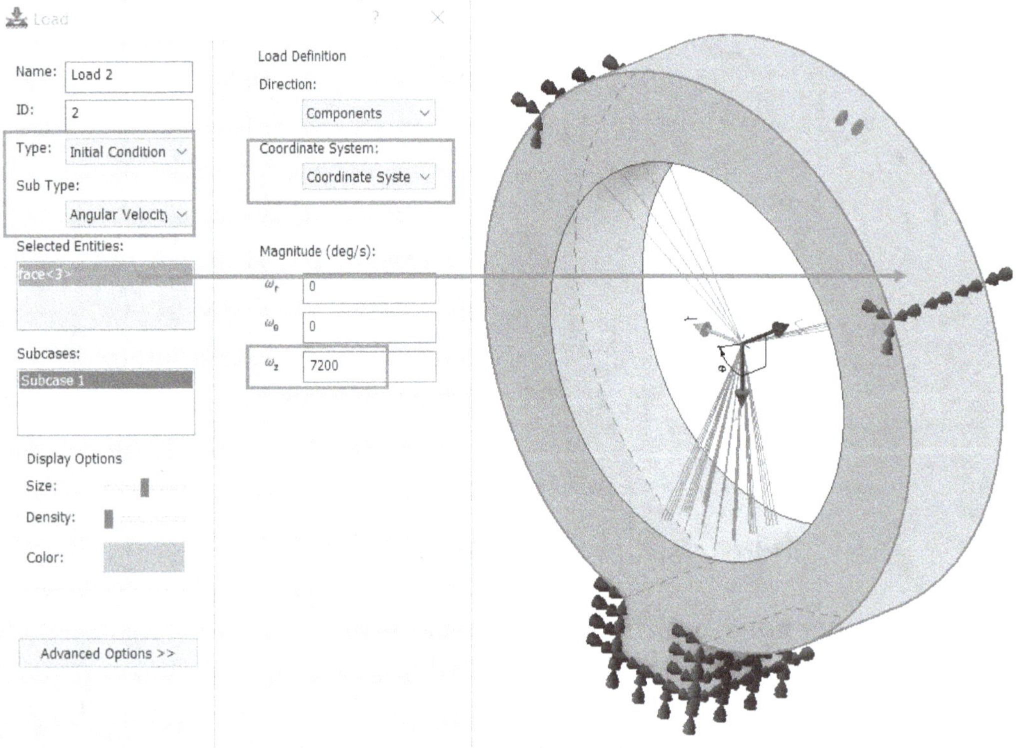

Figure-15. Parameters specified for initial condition

- After specifying the parameters, click on the **OK** button to create initial velocity.

Note that the Pin constraint provided in Autodesk Inventor Nastran works as pin constraint of assembly but for solid elements, it does not provide the flexibility of revolution about any axis. So, we have applied a rigid connection attached to the center of revolution and then applied the initial velocity. Since, this center point is still free to move around, so we will now apply constraint to center point.

Applying Constraints and Loads

- Click on the **Constraints** tool from the **Setup** panel in the **Ribbon**. The **Constraint** dialog box will be displayed.
- Select the center point used for rigid body and specify the parameters as shown in Figure-16.
- After setting parameters, click on the **OK** button from the dialog box to apply constraint.
- Click on the **Loads** tool from the **Setup** panel in the **Autodesk Inventor Nastran** tab of the **Ribbon**. The **Load** dialog box will be displayed.
- Specify the parameters and select the face to apply force as shown in Figure-17.

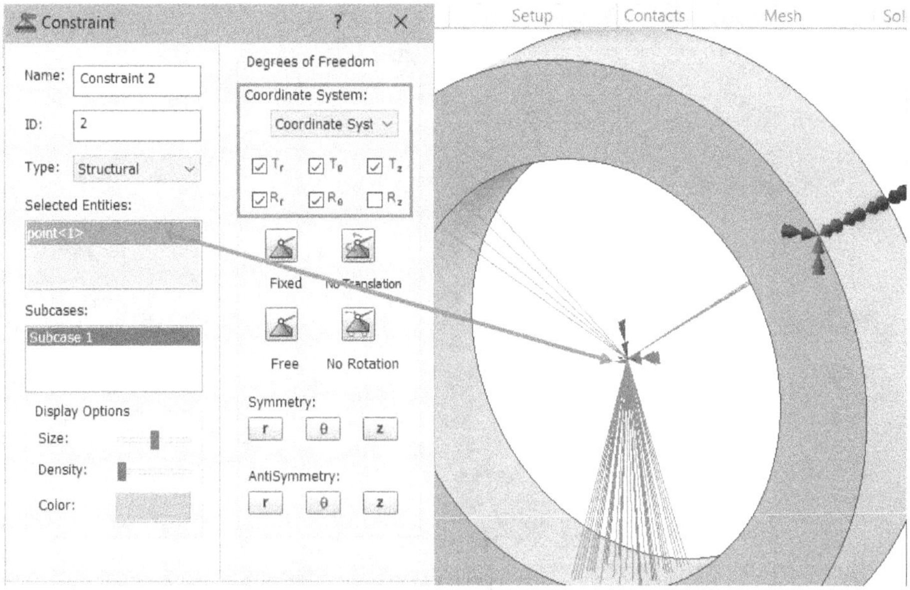

Figure-16. Specifying constraint

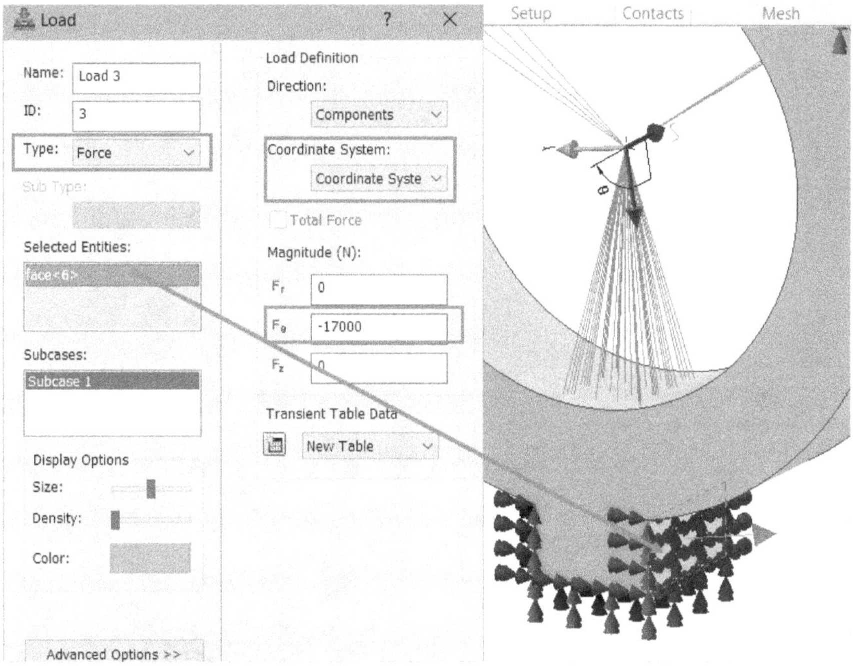

Figure-17. Force applied on the face of ring

- Click on the **Define New Table** button from the **Transient Table Data** area of the dialog box. The **Table Data** dialog box will be displayed.
- Specify the parameters as shown in Figure-18 and click on the **OK** button. The **Load** dialog box will be displayed again.
- After setting the parameters, click on the **OK** button from the dialog box.

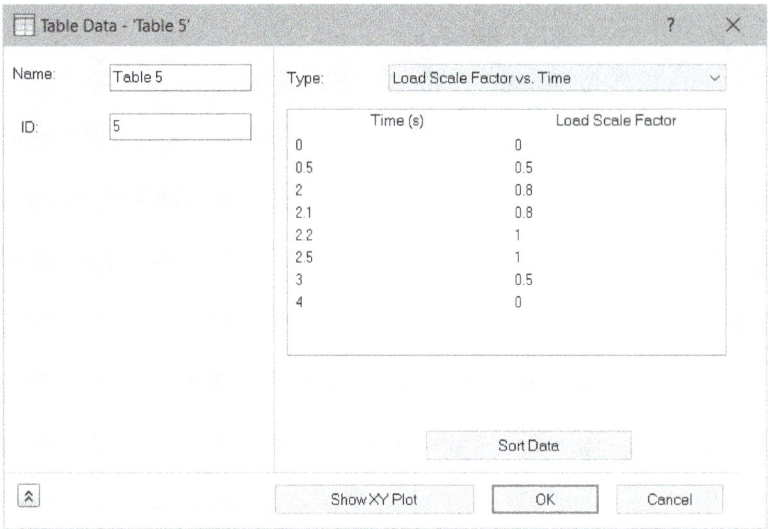

Figure-18. Table Data for force

Adding Concentrated Mass

- Right-click on the **Concentrated Masses** option from the **Idealizations** node in **Model** node of **Nastran Model Tree** and select the **New** option. The **Concentrated Mass** dialog box will be displayed.
- Specify the parameters as shown in Figure-19. Note that we have specified values of inertia so that its effect can be included in rotation of ring. The procedure to easily find inertia of a model is discussed later in this chapter.

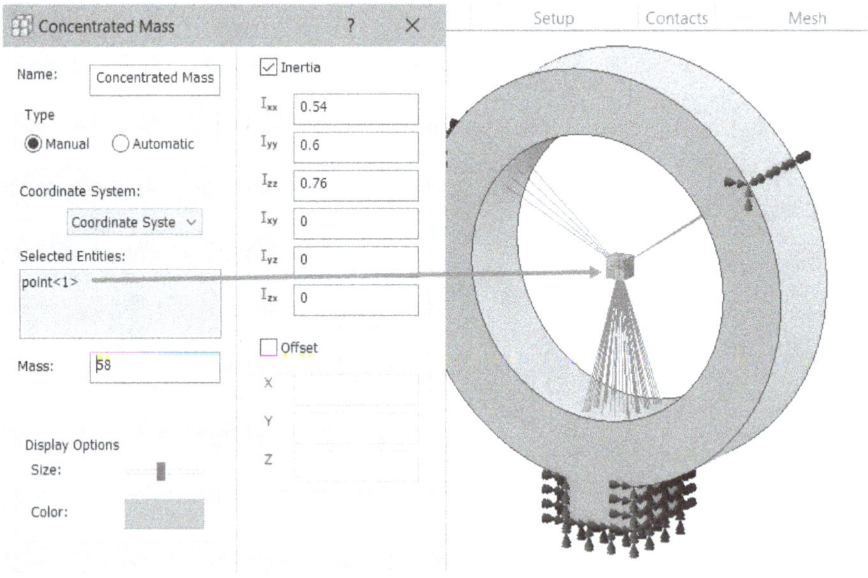

Figure-19. Parameters specified for concentrated mass

- After specifying parameters, click on the **OK** button to create the mass.

Specifying Material, Damping, and Dynamic Setup

- Click on the **Materials** tool from the **Prepare** panel in the **Ribbon**. The **Material** dialog box will be displayed.
- Click on the **Select Material** button and double-click on the Iron-Cast material to select it.
- After selecting material, click on the **OK** button from the dialog box.

- Double-click on the **Damping 1** option from the **Subcases** in the **Nastran Model Tree** and clear the **Structural Damping** option as in this case we are not concerned with damping of the model; refer to Figure-20. After clearing all types of damping, click on the **OK** button from the dialog box.

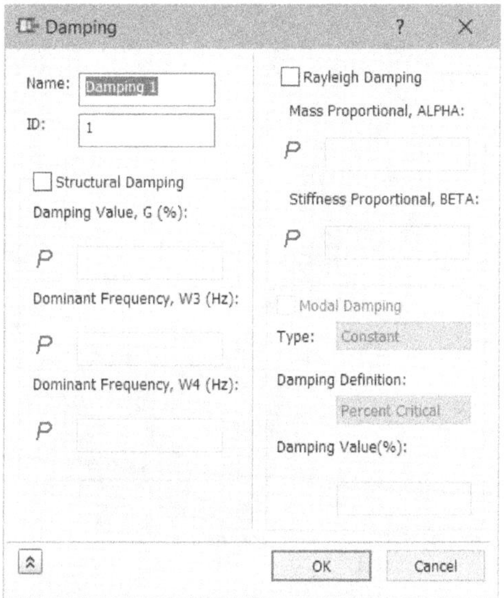

Figure-20. Damping parameters specified

- Double-click on **Dynamics Setup 1** option from the **Nastran Model Tree**. The **Dynamics Setup** dialog box will be displayed.
- Specify the parameters as shown in Figure-21 and click on the **OK** button.

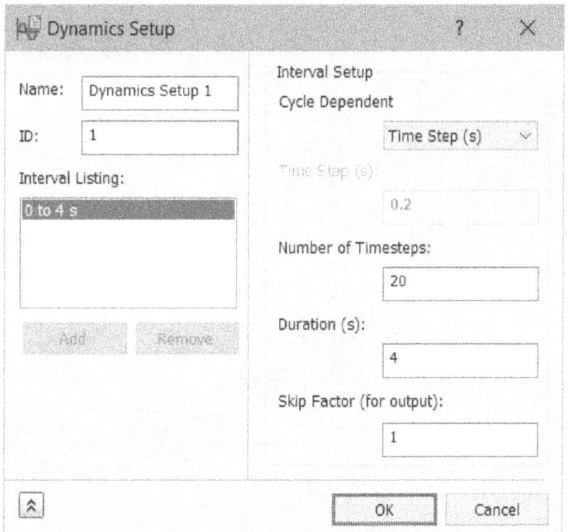

Figure-21. Dynamics Setup parameters for practical

Running Analysis and Analyzing Results

- All the required parameters have been specified so, click on the **Run** button from the **Solve** panel in the **Autodesk Inventor Nastran** tab of **Ribbon**. Once, the processing is complete, results of stress will be displayed in the graphics area; refer to Figure-22. Note the stress at last step is a lot lesser than what occurs when force starts to act opposite to motion direction. So, switch to the time step at which load starts to acting and analyze the results.

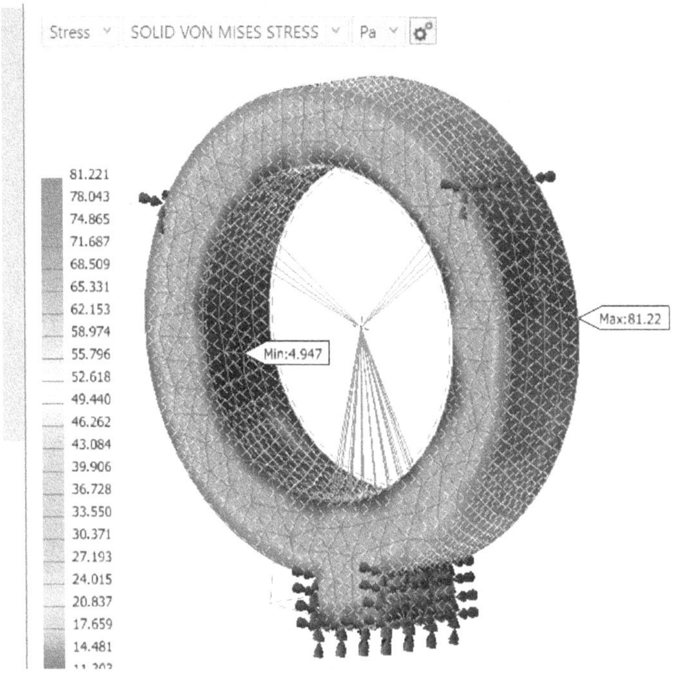

Figure-22. Result of Practical

PRACTICE

Perform nonlinear transient response analysis on the leaf spring as shown in Figure-23.

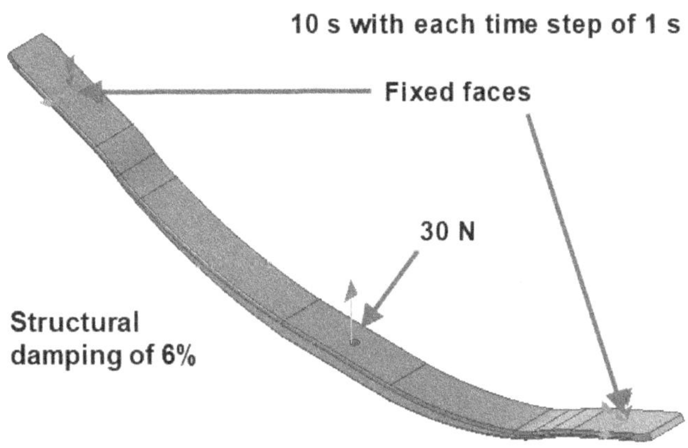

Figure-23. Model for nonlinear transient response analysis

SELF ASSESSMENT

Q1. What is Transient Response Analysis? Describe briefly.

Q2. What are the types of Transient Response Analysis? Describe them briefly.

Q3. The .... analysis is used for structural objects under high frequency excitation.

Q4. Select the .... check box to define mass and stiffness components of rayleigh damping.

Q5. The modal transient response analysis is performed when you want to use modal degrees of freedom in place of physical degrees of freedom for solving the analysis. (True/False)

Q6. The nonlinear transient response analysis is performed when damping, vibrational excitation, and large deformation is not involved in the analysis study. (True/False)

Q7. What is the main purpose of transient response analysis?

A. To evaluate static loads on a structure
B. To determine the natural frequencies of a structure
C. To compute the forced dynamic response of a structure under time-varying excitation
D. To analyze heat flow through a structure

Q8. Which equation represents dynamic analysis including damping?

A. $F = K.x$
B. $R(t) = m.(d^2u/dt^2) + k.u$
C. $R(t) = m.(d^2u/dt^2) + c.(du/dt) + k.u$
D. $R(t) = F - K.x$

Q9. When is Direct Transient Response Analysis preferred over other types?

A. When the model has low-frequency excitation
B. When the displacement is linear
C. When high-frequency excitation is present or structural damping is used
D. When normal modes are known

Q10. What is Modal Transient Response Analysis mainly used for?

A. To account for nonlinear deformations
B. To reduce degrees of freedom using mode shapes
C. To apply thermal loads
D. To eliminate damping from the equation

Q11. What is a key recommendation for damping in Nonlinear Transient Response Analysis for impact solutions?

A. Use high damping for more accuracy
B. Do not use damping at all
C. Use zero damping or minimal "stability" damping
D. Use structural damping exclusively

Q12. In Direct Transient Response Analysis, what condition must be met for structural damping to be valid?

A. The material must be isotropic
B. The load must be static
C. Displacement and velocity must be exactly 90° out of phase
D. Acceleration must be zero

Q13. What is the role of Rayleigh damping in Direct Transient Response?

A. It is used for eliminating displacement
B. It defines proportional mass and stiffness damping
C. It replaces velocity damping
D. It only applies to thermal expansion

Q14. In Nonlinear Transient Response Analysis, which setting should be activated if large deformation is expected?

A. Material damping
B. Frequency analysis
C. Large Displacements
D. Dynamic Constraints

Chapter 7

Impact Analysis

Topics Covered

The major topics covered in this chapter are:

- ***Introduction***
- ***Performing Impact Analysis***
- ***Creating Sketch line for Impact direction***
- ***Defining Impact Parameter***

INTRODUCTION

The Impact analysis is performed for drop-test and projectile impact studies. The input parameters used in this analysis are direction of travel, initial velocity, and acceleration of part. You can also use this analysis to perform crash tests on various automobile components.

PERFORMING IMPACT ANALYSIS

The Impact analysis in Autodesk Inventor Nastran needs at least two parts in an assembly to perform the analysis. The projectile must be a single part whereas the target can be multi-part sub-assembly. Impact analysis is a nonlinear transient response analysis with time steps automatically calculated using Modal analysis. But, you can define the time steps manually as well. The procedure to perform impact analysis is given next.

- Open the model on which you want to perform analysis and start **Autodesk Inventor Nastran** environment; refer to Figure-1.

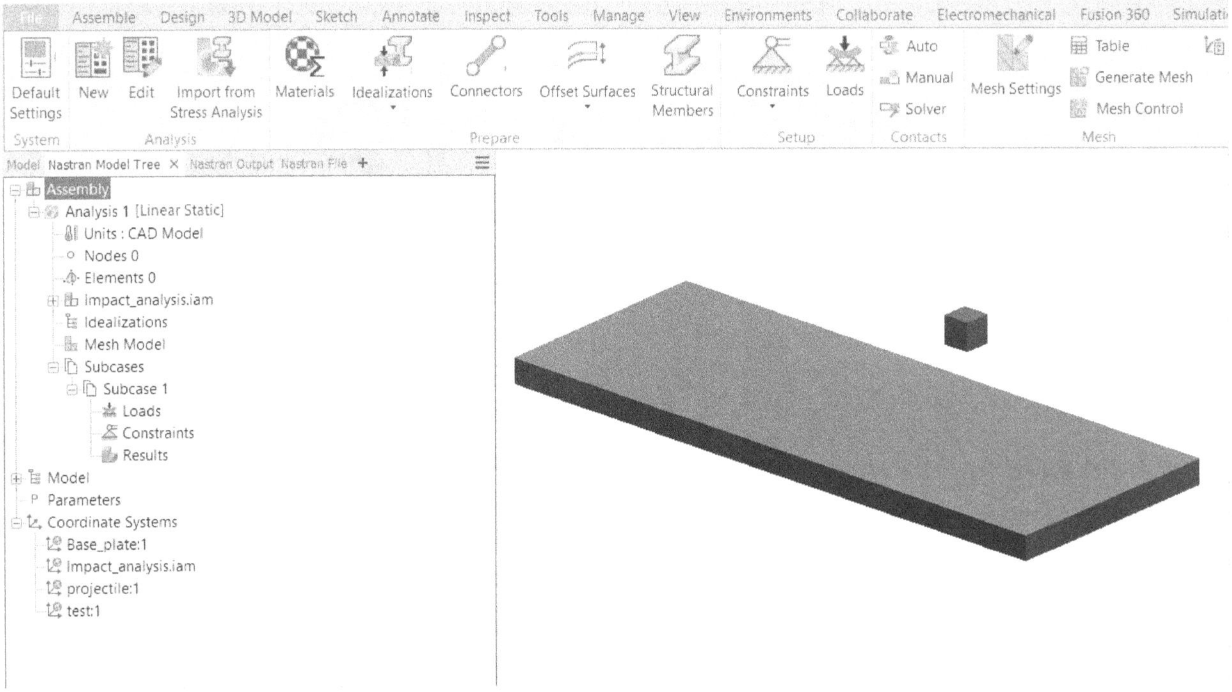

Figure-1. Assembly model for impact analysis

- Click on the **Start 2D Sketch** tool from the **Sketch** panel of **Sketch** tab in the **Ribbon**. You will be asked to select sketching plane.
- Click on the **Model** tab in the **Model Tree** and select XY plane as shown in Figure-2. The sketching tools will be displayed.
- Create the line with end points coincident to model; refer to Figure-3.

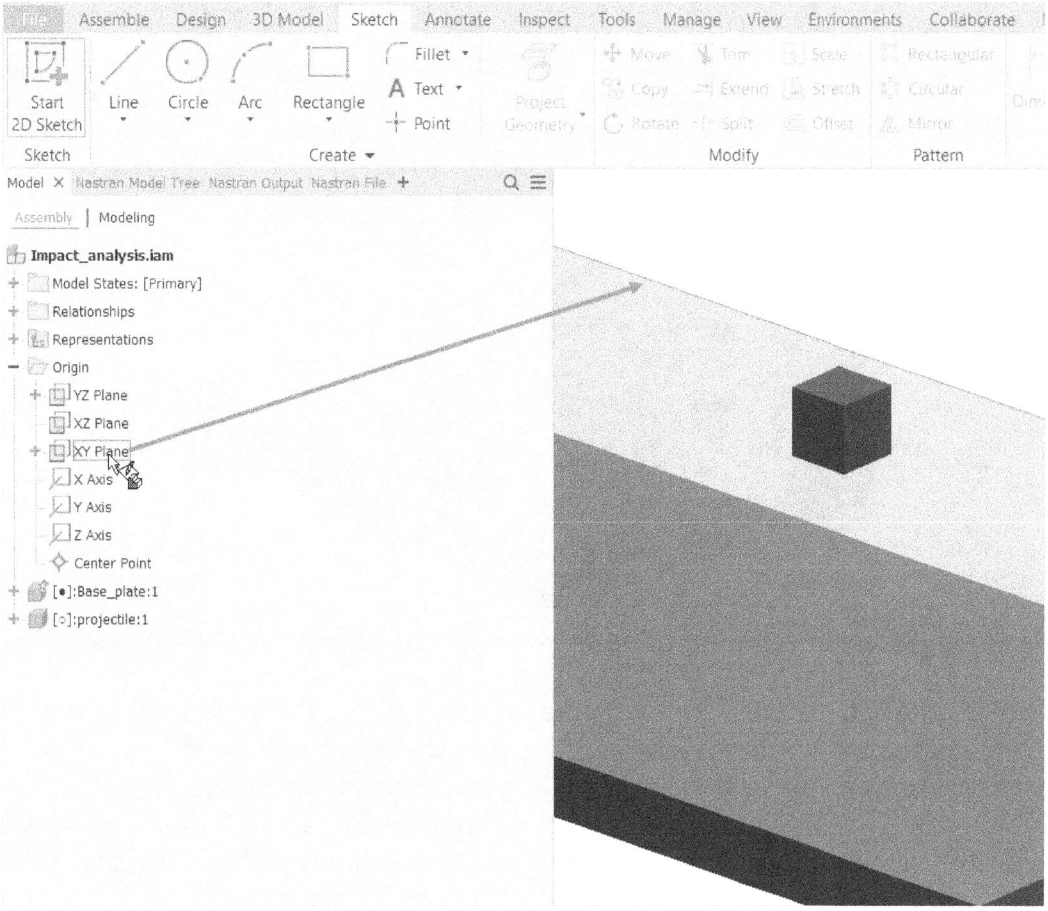

Figure-2. Selecting plane for sketch

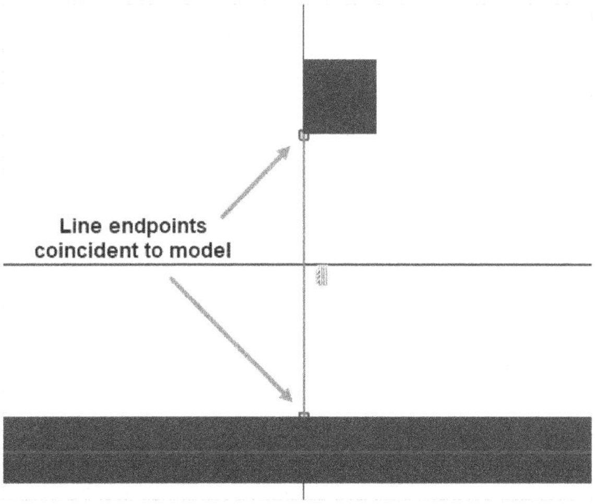

Figure-3. Creating line

- Click on the **Finish Sketch** tool from the **Exit** panel of **Sketch** tab in the **Ribbon**. The model will be displayed as shown in Figure-4.

Note that when you are using automatic impact method which is discussed here, the software automatically moves the projectile part near target and then begins the analysis. Because the path travelled before impact does not generate any stresses and as a designer we are also not concerned about that. You can perform nonlinear transient response analysis to manually perform all the steps involved in impact analysis. We will discuss this method later in this chapter.

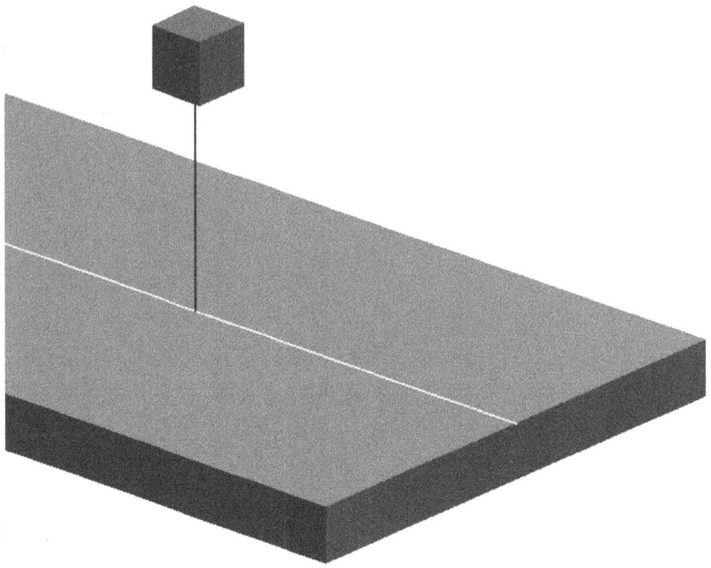

Figure-4. Model with sketch

- Click on the **Edit** button from the **Analysis** panel of **Autodesk Inventor Nastran** tab in the **Ribbon**. The **Analysis** dialog box will be displayed.
- Select the **Impact Analysis** option from the **Type** drop-down.
- Select the **On** option from the **Large Displacements** drop-down and select the **Separation** option from the **Contact Type** drop-down in the **Options** tab.
- Set the other options as required and click on the **OK** button.

Defining Impact Parameters

- Select the **Nastran Model Tree** tab in the left panel and double-click on **Impact Setup** option from the **Subcases** node. The **Impact Analysis** dialog box will be displayed; refer to Figure-5.

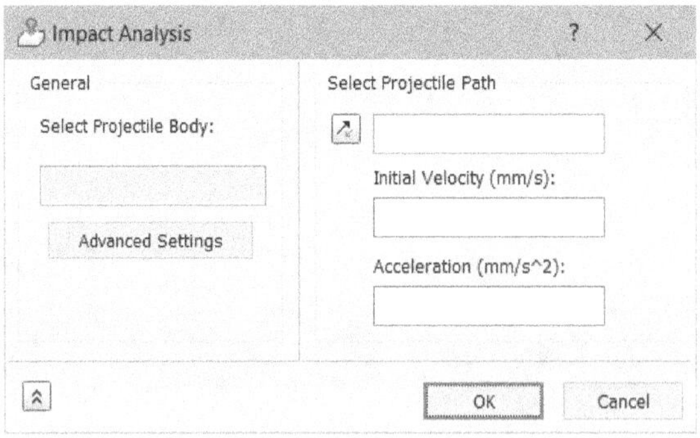

Figure-5. Impact Analysis dialog box

- By default, the **Select Projectile Body** selection box is active and you are asked to select part to be used as projectile. Select the part that you want as projectile in impact analysis.
- Click in the **Projectile Translation Vector** selection box of the **Select Projectile Path** area in dialog box and select the sketch line earlier created to define direction in which projectile part will move. Click on the **Reverse Direction** button to check whether direction of motion is downward if not then click it again.

- Specify desired value for initial velocity and acceleration in respective edit boxes of the dialog box; refer to Figure-6. Make sure the unit is correct otherwise a different kind of magic may happen which was not expected!!

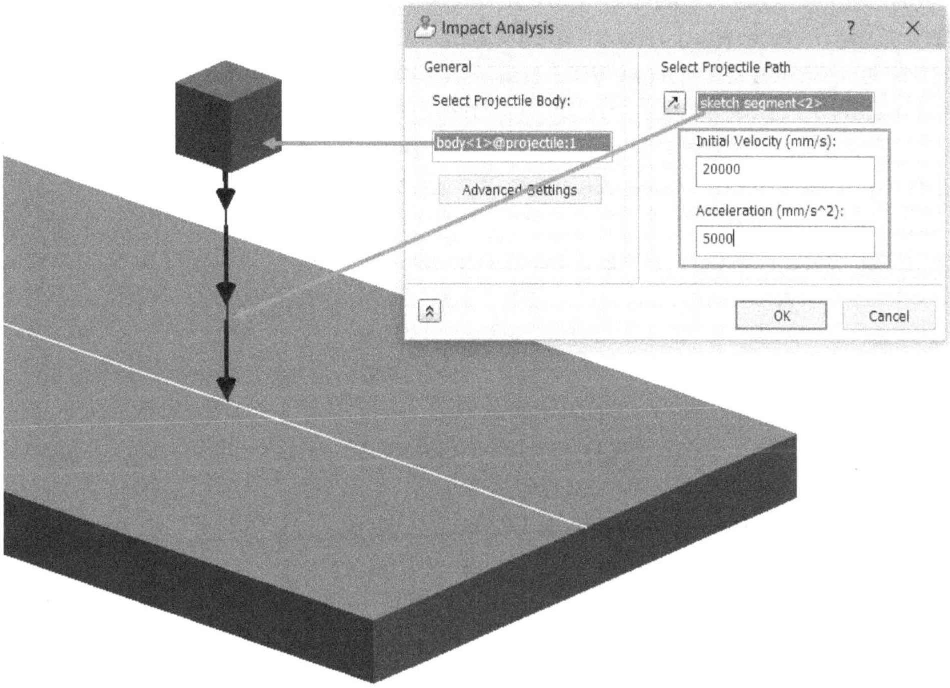

Figure-6. Setting parameters for impact analysis

- Click on **Advanced Settings** button from the dialog box. The **Impact Event Parameters** dialog box will be displayed; refer to Figure-7.

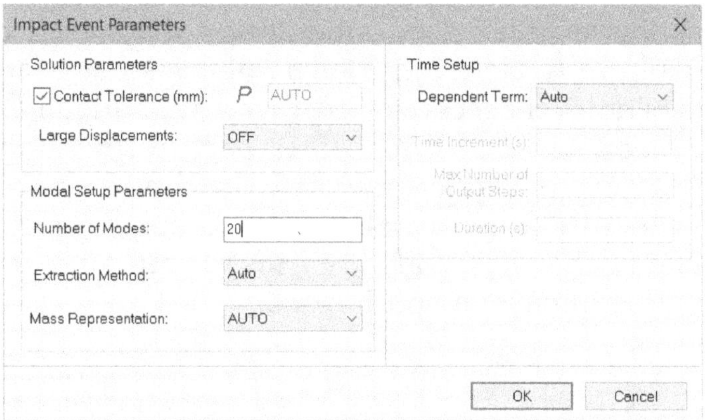

Figure-7. Impact Event Parameters dialog box

- By default, the **Contact Tolerance (mm)** check box is selected so contact activation distance is automatically decided by formula (model reference dimension) x 0.0004 here model reference dimension is the gap between projectile body face and target body face if there is large gap between them. Clear this check box to manually specify activation distance for contact between two bodies in edit box next to the check box.

Note that the contact matrix is not generated at the original locations of bodies. It is generated when two bodies are a distance equal to activation distance. In this way, computational power of system is preserved for main event which in this case is collision.

- By default, **ON** option is selected in the **Large Displacements** drop-down because we are performing a nonlinear type analysis and we expect relatively high value of displacement in the bodies due to impact.
- Specify desired value of number of modes (natural frequencies) to be generated for finding time steps and duration of analysis precisely in the **Number of Modes** edit box. In previous chapter, you have learned about Modal transient response analysis that how modes of analysis are used to define degrees of freedom for performing transient analysis. In case of Impact analysis, these modes are used to define time steps which precisely capture the peaks in stress, strain, and other result data due to impact.
- Select desired option from the **Extraction Method** drop-down are discussed earlier to define eigensolver used for finding natural frequencies. It is better to leave it to default **Auto** option.
- By default, **AUTO** option is selected in the **Mass Representation** drop-down so coupled mass formulation is applied if rigid elements are specified in the model. If you select the **ON** option then couple mass formula is used for forming mass matrix for all elements in the model. If you select the **OFF** option then diagonal mass matrix will be formed. If you want to use lumped mass assumption then select the **OFF** option as it will be computationally more efficient as compared to coupled mass matrix. But, coupled mass matrix also called consistent mass matrix is more accurate at the cost of computational power of system. If you want to dig deeper into mass matrix the scan the QR code below.

- Select desired option from the **Dependent Term** drop-down of **Time Setup** area and define the values of related parameters as discussed earlier for transient analyses; refer to Figure-8. Generally, **Auto** option is used for defining time steps and total duration of analysis because software automatically finds suitable values based on modes. If you are expecting soft impact in the analysis due to material properties then you need to explicitly specify the time steps and duration as auto calculations will generate large number of time steps for a long duration. This happens because in such cases, software tries to equilibrium of motion equations which takes long time in case of soft impact.

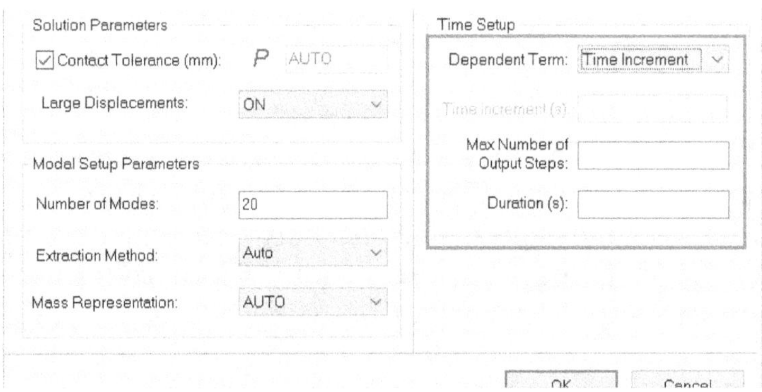

Figure-8. Setting parameters

- After setting desired values, click on the **OK** button.
- Click on the **Materials** tool from the **Prepare** panel of **Autodesk Inventor Nastran** tab in the **Ribbon**. The **Material** dialog box will be displayed.

- Click on the **Select Material** button from the dialog box and select **Alloy Steel** material in **Inventor Material Library** node of the **Material DB** dialog box.
- Click on the **OK** button from the **Material DB** dialog box and then click on the **OK** button from the **Material** dialog box.
- Double-click on **Solid 1** option from the **Idealizations** node. The **Idealizations** dialog box will be displayed.
- Select **Alloy Steel** option from **Material** drop-down and click on the **OK** button.
- After setting desired parameters, generate mesh and click on the **Run** tool from the **Solve** panel of **Autodesk Inventor Nastran** tab in the **Ribbon**. The result of analysis will be displayed at different time steps; refer to Figure-9.

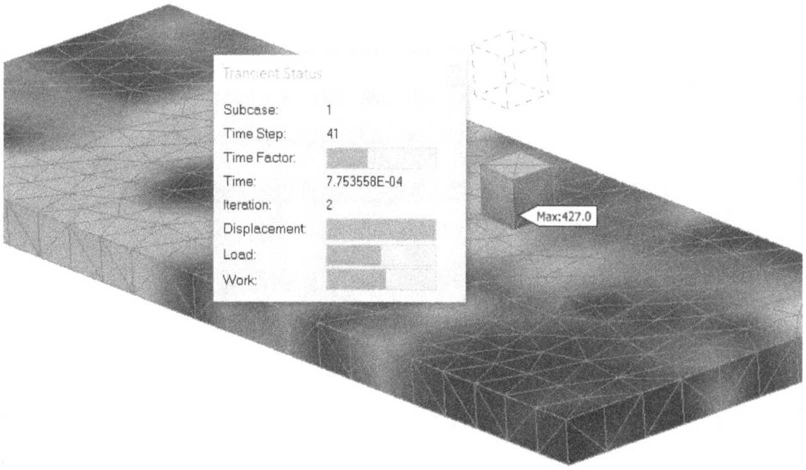

Figure-9. Result of impact analysis

Till now you have learned about the automatic method for impact analysis. The manual method of impact analysis is given next.

MANUAL IMPACT ANALYSIS

In this method, we will be using the same model earlier used for automatic impact analysis. The steps to perform analysis are given next.

- Create a duplicate of **Impact Analysis** earlier created and name it **Nonlinear Transient Impact**. Right-click on name of analysis from the **Nastran Model Tree** and select **Edit** option from the shortcut menu. The **Analysis** dialog box will be displayed.
- Select the **Nonlinear Transient Response** option from the **Type** drop-down and click on the **OK** button to set the analysis.
- Since, transient analysis needs a value of damping for material to reduce vibrations, double-click on the **Damping 1** option from **Subcases** node in the **Nastran Model Tree**. The **Damping** dialog box will be displayed. We have specified Rayleigh Damping values for our materials as shown in Figure-10.

There is a thumb rule for rayleigh damping: If alpha value is less than 1 then it is very little damping, if value is greater than 1 and less than 5 then it is noticeable damping, if value is 5 to 10 then it is significantly damped, and if value is above 10 then expect very little vibrations in the model. Same can be applied to stiffness proportional coefficient beta.

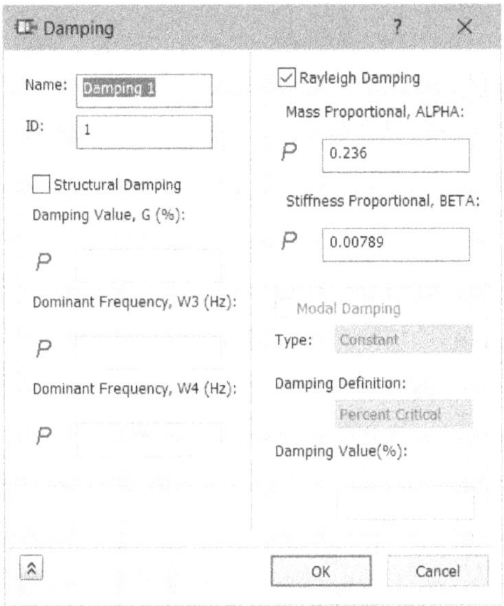

Figure-10. Damping parameters for analysis

- After specifying rayleigh damping parameters, clear the **Structural Damping** check box if it is selected and then click on the **OK** button.
- Double-click on the **Nonlinear Setup 1** option from the **Subcase 1** node in the **Nastran Model Tree**. The **Nonlinear Transient Parameters** dialog box will be displayed.
- Select the **AUTO** option from the **Stiffness update method** drop-down to automatically update stiffness of model during impact. Select the **Displacement** and **Work** check boxes from the **Convergence criteria and error tolerances** area to use these two parameters for convergence of analysis. Note that for complex nonlinear analysis, load convergence can take high amount of time and iterations. On specifying these parameters, the dialog box should look as Figure-11. Note that there is no need to specify tolerance for convergence of selected parameters and you can leave it blank to use default criteria of convergence for the analysis.

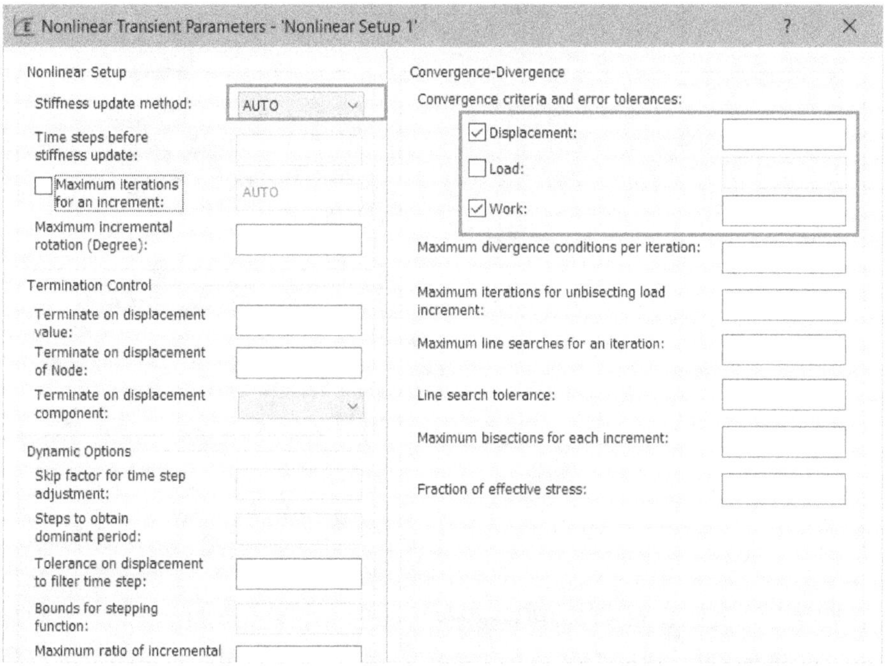

Figure-11. Convergence criteria specified for analysis

- After specifying the parameters, click on the **OK** button to apply parameters.
- Double-click on **Dynamics Setup 1** option from the **Subcase 1** node in the **Nastran Model Tree**. The **Dynamics Setup** dialog box will be displayed.
- Specify the parameters as shown in Figure-12 and click on the **OK** button.

Tip: Finding time steps and duration for running impact analysis manually is a difficult thing if you do not know the trick in Inventor Nastran. The automatic Impact Analysis is very good in finding the time steps and duration for the analysis. So, first perform Impact analysis on the model and check the time at which impact occurs and what is duration of time steps. Once you have this information, you can tweak the values in Nonlinear transient response analysis to get desired output.

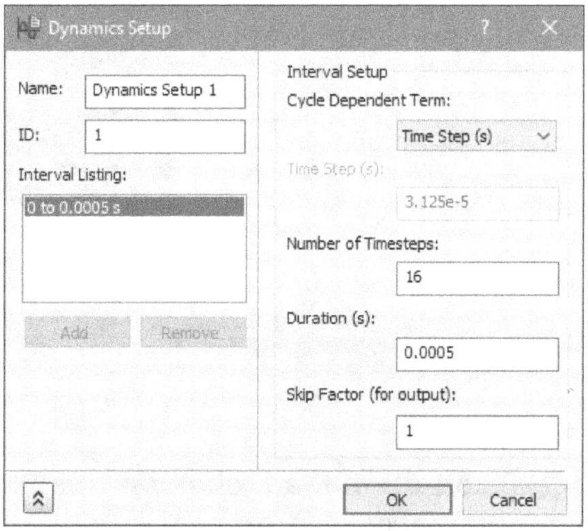

Figure-12. Dynamics Setup parameters for impact analysis

- Click on the **Loads** tool from the **Setup** panel in **Ribbon** and create an initial velocity load as shown in Figure-13. Note that we have applied initial velocity to body not the faces.

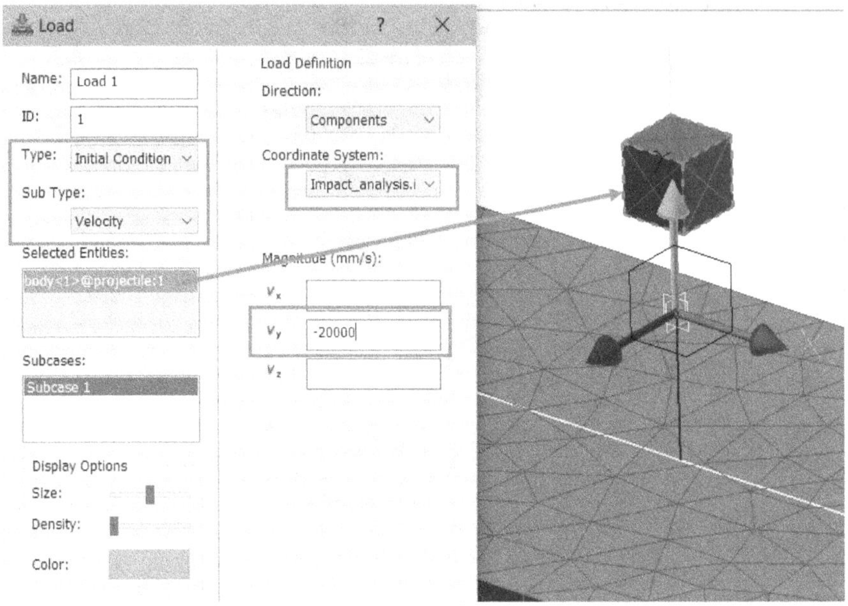

Figure-13. Applying initial velocity to body

Tip: The loads like initial condition, thermal loads, and Rigid Motion (Explicit) can be applied to faces, edges, bodies, vertices. By default, if you click on the model then a face gets selected. To select body, click twice on the same face with a brief pause. It will cause to select face as well as body. Select the face from **Selected Entities** selection box, right-click on it, and select the **Delete** option to remove it from selection; refer to Figure-14. You can also click on the face while holding the **SHIFT** key to remove it from selection. There is another way of selecting bodies in the model. Right-click on the face of body you want to select and click on the **Select Other** option from shortcut menu. A selection box will be displayed on the face; refer to Figure-15. Click on the down arrow of selection box and select the body you want to use.

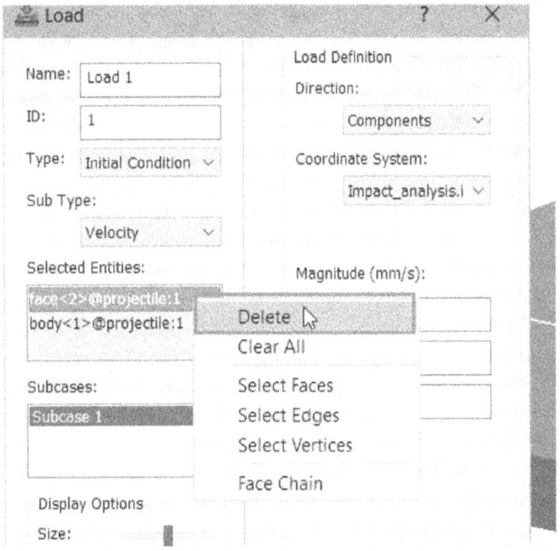

Figure-14. Delete option

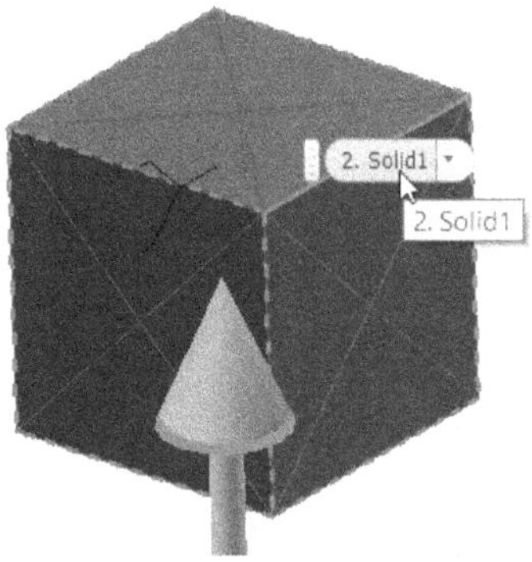

Figure-15. Object selection box

- After specifying the initial condition load, click on the **OK** button to exit the dialog box. Similarly, you can apply acceleration to the body as initial condition.
- Apply the constraints to the target body if they are not copied.
- Now, we need to apply contact between projectile body and target. You have learned the standard way of apply contacts so now we will use a trick for contacts. Move the projectile part by dragging closer to the face of target body; refer to Figure-16.

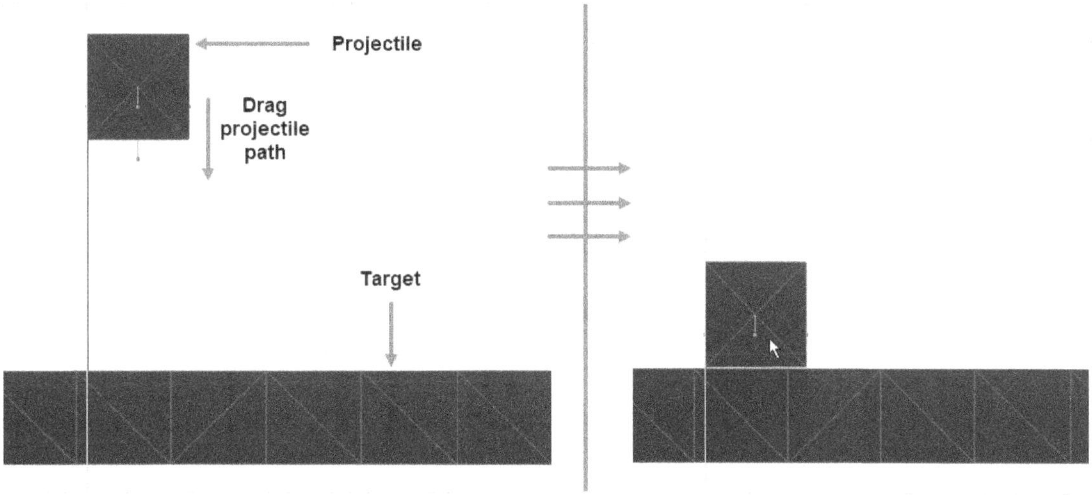

Figure-16. Dragging projectile part

- Once the faces of two bodies are close, click on the **Auto** tool from **Contacts** panel in **Ribbon** to automatically create contacts between the bodies. If the two faces are barely touching each other then a contact will be created and added automatically in the **Nastran Model Tree**; refer to Figure-17.

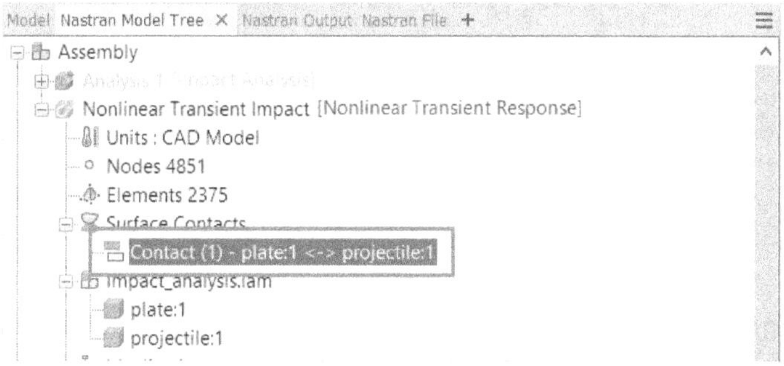

Figure-17. Contact automatically created

- Double-click on this new contact to check whether it is separation or not. If it is other than separation then select the **Separation** option from **Contact Type** drop-down and click on the **OK** button to save changes.
- After applying contacts, you move back the projectile part to its original position by dragging as discussed earlier.
- Change the mesh settings if needed and then click on the **Run** tool from the Solve panel to solve the analysis. You can analyze the results as discussed earlier.

PRACTICE

Perform impact analysis on the model shown in Figure-18.

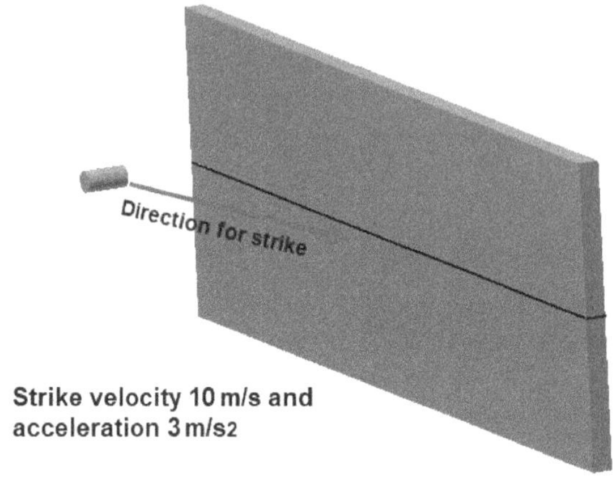

Figure-18. Model for Practice

SELF ASSESSMENT

Q1. What is the objective of performing Impact Analysis?

Q2. Click in the .... selection box of **Select Projectile Path** area in the **Impact Analysis** dialog box to define direction in which projectile part will move.

Q3. On clicking **Advanced Settings** button in the **Impact Analysis** dialog box, the .... dialog box will be displayed.

Q4. In the **Impact Event Parameters** dialog box, the number of modes is to be specify for each time step. (True/False)

Q5. What are the required input parameters for performing Impact Analysis?

A. Material strength, mesh size, and velocity
B. Direction of travel, initial velocity, and acceleration
C. Pressure, velocity, and displacement
D. Temperature, damping, and constraints

Q6. What type of analysis is used in the automatic impact method of Autodesk Inventor Nastran?

A. Static Linear Analysis
B. Modal Analysis
C. Nonlinear Transient Response Analysis
D. Steady-State Heat Transfer Analysis

Q7. What happens if the unit for initial velocity or acceleration is incorrect in the Impact Setup dialog box?

A. Nothing happens
B. The software will automatically correct it
C. A different kind of unexpected behavior might occur
D. The simulation will stop

Q8. What does the "Contact Tolerance" check box control in the Impact Event Parameters dialog box?

A. Color scheme of simulation
B. Initial mesh density
C. Contact activation distance
D. Material selection

Q9. In mass representation, which option gives the most accurate results but uses more computational power?

A. AUTO
B. ON
C. OFF
D. Lumped Mass

Q10. What is the default behavior when the AUTO option is selected in the Dependent Term of Time Setup?

A. No time steps are generated
B. Manual input of time duration is required
C. Software auto-calculates suitable time steps and duration
D. Simulation doesn't run

Q11. What is the rule of thumb for Rayleigh damping alpha or beta values above 10?

A. Causes high vibrations
B. Expect very little vibrations
C. Medium level damping
D. No damping at all

Q12. How can you apply initial velocity to a body instead of a face in Autodesk Inventor Nastran?

A. Use the Material tool
B. Select the body from the Model Tree
C. Double-click on the face to convert it to body selection
D. Click twice with a brief pause or use Select Other

Q13. What must be done after moving the projectile closer to the target face in manual impact analysis?

A. Add mesh constraints
B. Apply loads again
C. Use Auto tool to create contact
D. Change material type

FOR STUDENT NOTES

Chapter 8

Frequency Response Analysis

Topics Covered

The major topics covered in this chapter are:

- ***Introduction***
- ***Performing Direct Frequency Response Analysis***
- ***Performing Modal Frequency Response Analysis***
- ***Defining Damping, Modal Setup, and Dynamic Setup Parameters***

INTRODUCTION

The frequency response analysis is used to compute structural response of model under steady state oscillation. These oscillations might be coupled with some load to represent cyclic loads. For example, a vibrator is attached to hopper body applying 300 N load on hopper face at 80 Hz frequency then you can run frequency response analysis to check the stresses and other result data for the model. There are two types of frequency response analyses available in the Autodesk Inventor Nastran; Direct Frequency Response and Modal Frequency Response.

Direct Frequency Response analysis is performed when structural response is to be found at discrete frequencies. This analysis is useful when large number of modes are to be extracted at high frequency excitation.

Modal Frequency Response analysis is performed when large size model is to be checked under specified mode excitations. This analysis uses the mode shapes of the structure to uncouple the equations of motion (when no damping or only modal damping is used) and, depending on the number of modes computed and retained, the problem size is reduced. Both of these factors tend to make modal frequency response analysis computationally more efficient than direct frequency response analysis.

The procedures to perform these analyses are given next.

PERFORMING DIRECT FREQUENCY RESPONSE ANALYSIS

The procedure to perform direct frequency response analysis is given next.

- Open the part on which you want to perform direct frequency response analysis and start Autodesk Inventor Nastran environment.
- Click on the **Edit** button from the **Analysis** panel of **Autodesk Inventor Nastran** tab in the **Ribbon**. The **Analysis** dialog box will be displayed.
- Select the **Direct Frequency Response** option from the **Type** drop-down. The options in the dialog box will be displayed as shown in Figure-1.

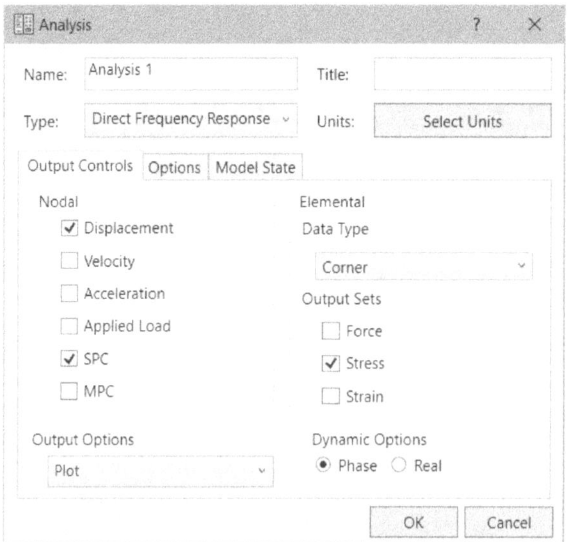

Figure-1. Analysis dialog box for direct frequency response analysis

- Select the **Phase** radio button from the **Dynamic Options** area at the bottom in the dialog box to use magnitude and phase value for output. Select the **Real** radio button to get in-phase and out-of-phase result outputs.

Note on dynamic analysis result types

Frequency response analyses use sinusoidal curves for applying frequency loads and displacement also follows the same. So mathematically, we can say F= load x sine(angle) and graphically it can be represented as Figure-2. If there is no damping applied then maximum displacement will also occur at the same time. But this is not the case in real world. In real world, there is always some amount of damping no matter how minute. Due to damping, the maximum displacement time shifts by phase angle φ. Hence, the mathematical form of displacement becomes D = amplitude x sine(angle+ φ) and graphically represented as Figure-3. So, if you select the **Phase** radio button in **Analysis** dialog box then you will get these outputs. Note that you will get only maximum values of these parameters and not the complete time-history of how load and displacements are changing.

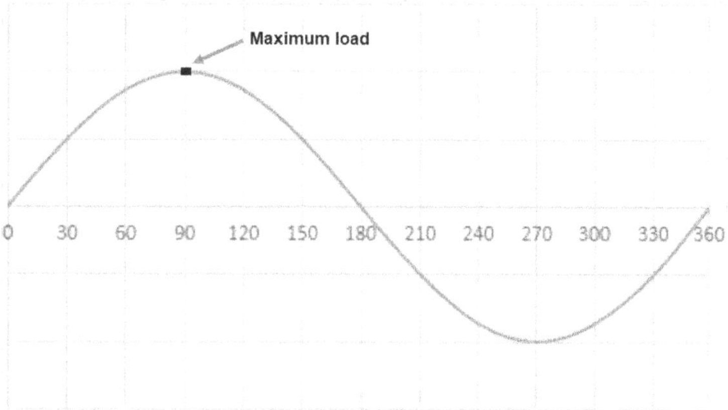

Figure-2. Sinusoidal load

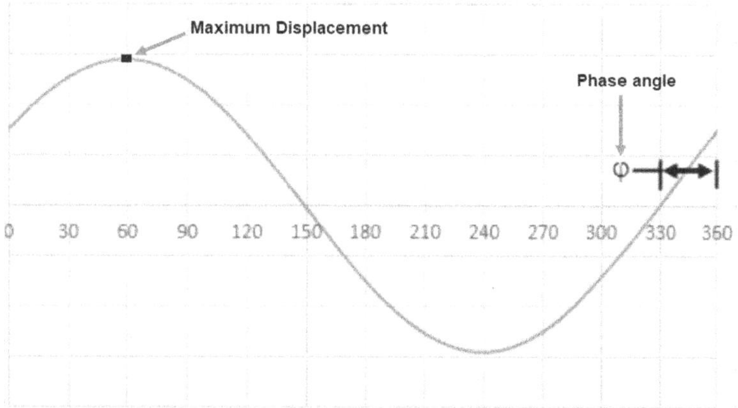

Figure-3. Displacement

Now, consider the second case where displacement curve is represented by sum of two curves as shown in Figure-4. Here, curve 1 is the component of displacement which is in-phase with load and curve 2 is the component of displacement which is out-of-phase with load. Now, if you combine these two curves to find out maximum displacement then it is certain that it does not happen at 90 degree where load is maximum. But, a maximum value can be found at 60 degree by combining two curves using formula D = amplitude1 x sine (angle) + amplitude2 x cosine (angle). This method to find displacement is used when you select the **Real** radio button in **Analysis** dialog box and it gives the same results as discussed for previous method.

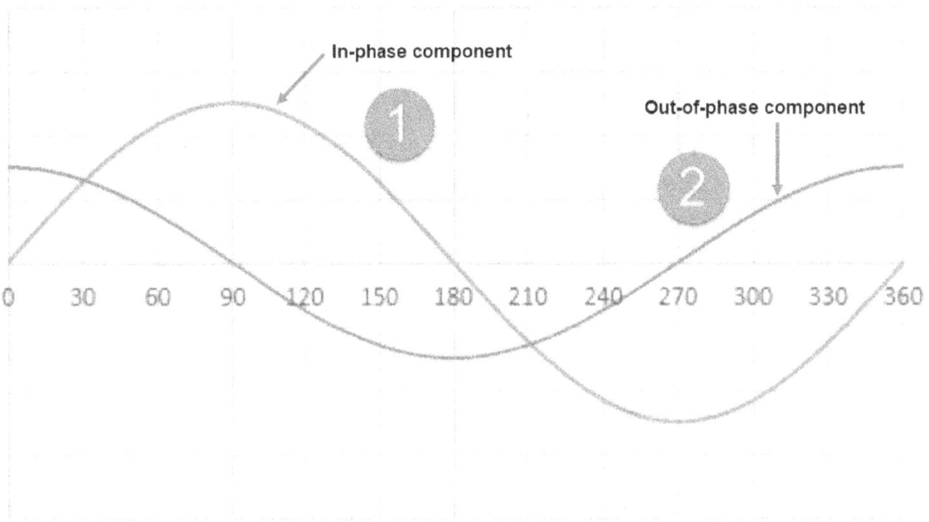

Figure-4. In-phase and out-of-phase components of displacement

- Specify the other parameters as discussed earlier in the dialog box and click on the **OK** button from the dialog box. The options will be displayed as shown in Figure-5.
- Double-click on **Damping** option in **Subcases** node of **Nastran Model Tree** and set the damping parameters as discussed earlier.

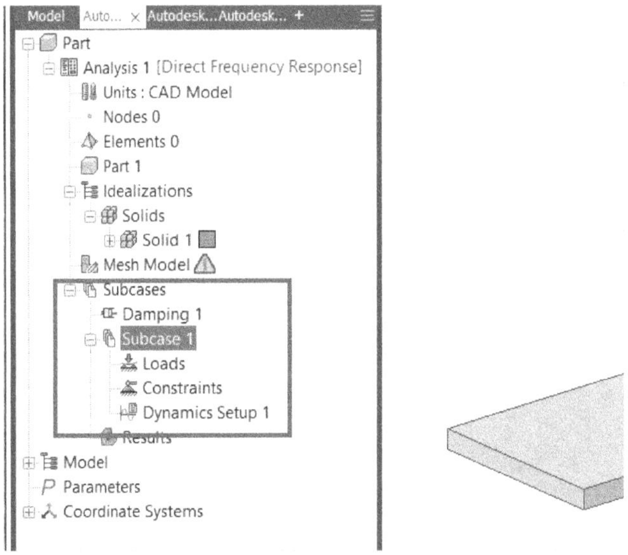

Figure-5. Subcase options for direct frequency response

- Double-click on **Dynamics Setup 1** option from the **Subcase 1** node. The **Dynamics Setup** dialog box will be displayed; refer to Figure-6.

- Set desired upper and lower limits of frequency range in the respective edit boxes at the left in the dialog box. Software will use the frequencies within specified range for performing analysis.

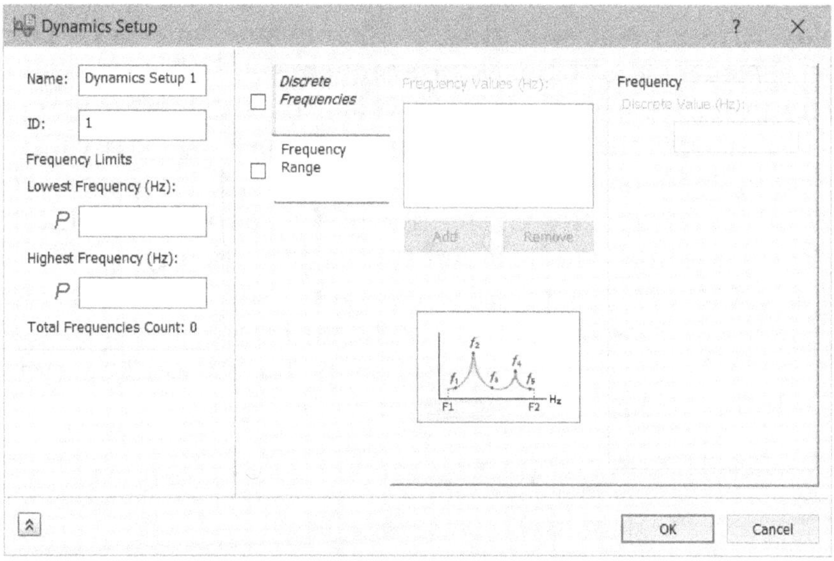

Figure-6. Dynamics Setup dialog box

- Select the **Discrete Frequencies** check box if you want to define specific values of frequencies for excitation of model; refer to Figure-7. **Note that only the specified frequencies will be used when applying load and the analysis will be solved repeatedly for each specified frequency**. Specify desired value of frequency to be included in analysis in the **Discrete Value (Hz)** edit box and click on the **Add** button. Specified frequency will be added to the list of frequencies. If you want to remove any frequency from the list then select it from the list and click on the **Remove** button.

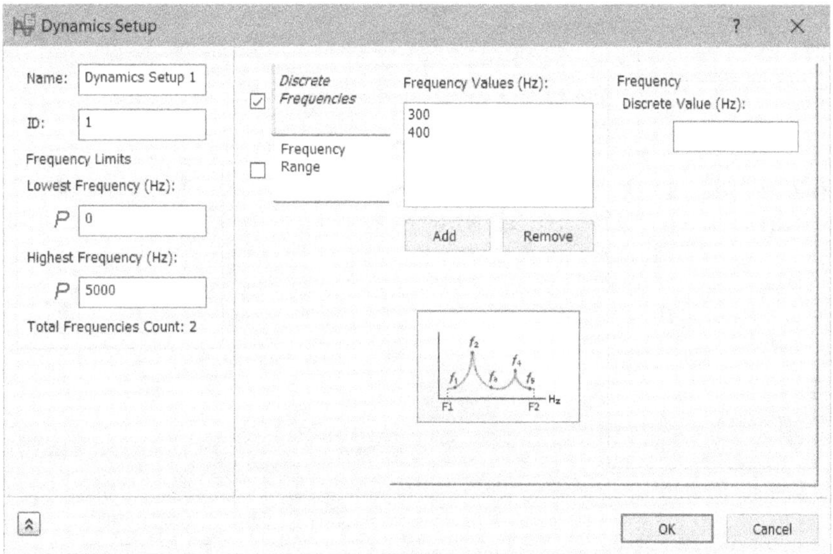

Figure-7. Discrete Frequencies options

- Select the **Frequency Range** check box to define range of frequencies to be used for excitation of system. This option is used when you do not know the frequencies at which model will be vibrating during operation but you know the range in which vibrations will occur. On selecting this check box, options in the dialog box will be displayed as shown in Figure-8. Specify the values in Lowest Frequency and **Highest Frequency** edit boxes of **Frequency Limits** area to define range of frequencies for performing dynamic analysis. Specify the number of frequencies to be generated in the specified range using the **Number of Points in the Range** edit box. The value in **Frequency Increment** edit box will be generated automatically alternatively you can specify the value of frequency increment and value of number of points in range will be generated automatically. Select the **Linear** radio button from the **Increment** section to increase the values of frequencies linearly by specified increment value. Select the **Logarithmic** radio button to increment frequency value by logarithmic factor. This radio button is generally used when the range for finding frequencies is large.

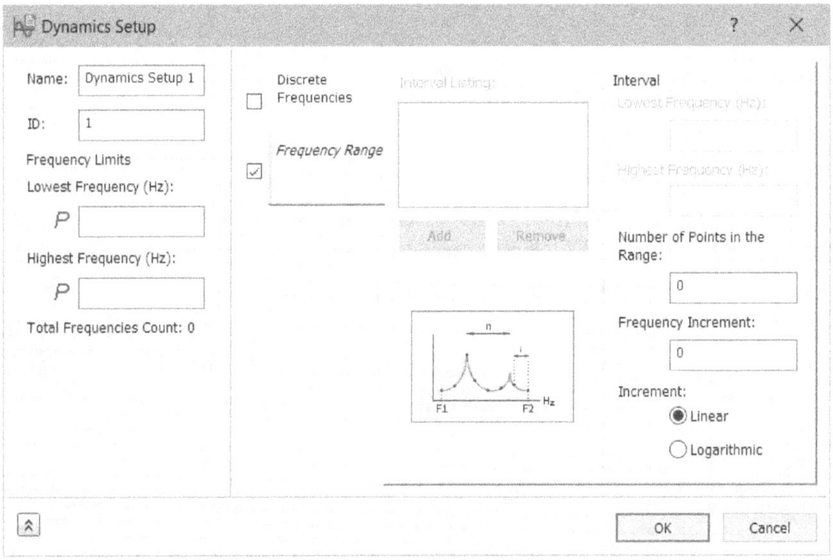

Figure-8. Frequency Range option for Dynamics Setup

- After setting desired values, click on the **OK** button.
- Set the idealization, constraint, and load parameters as discussed earlier and click on the **Run** button. The analysis result will be displayed; refer to Figure-9.

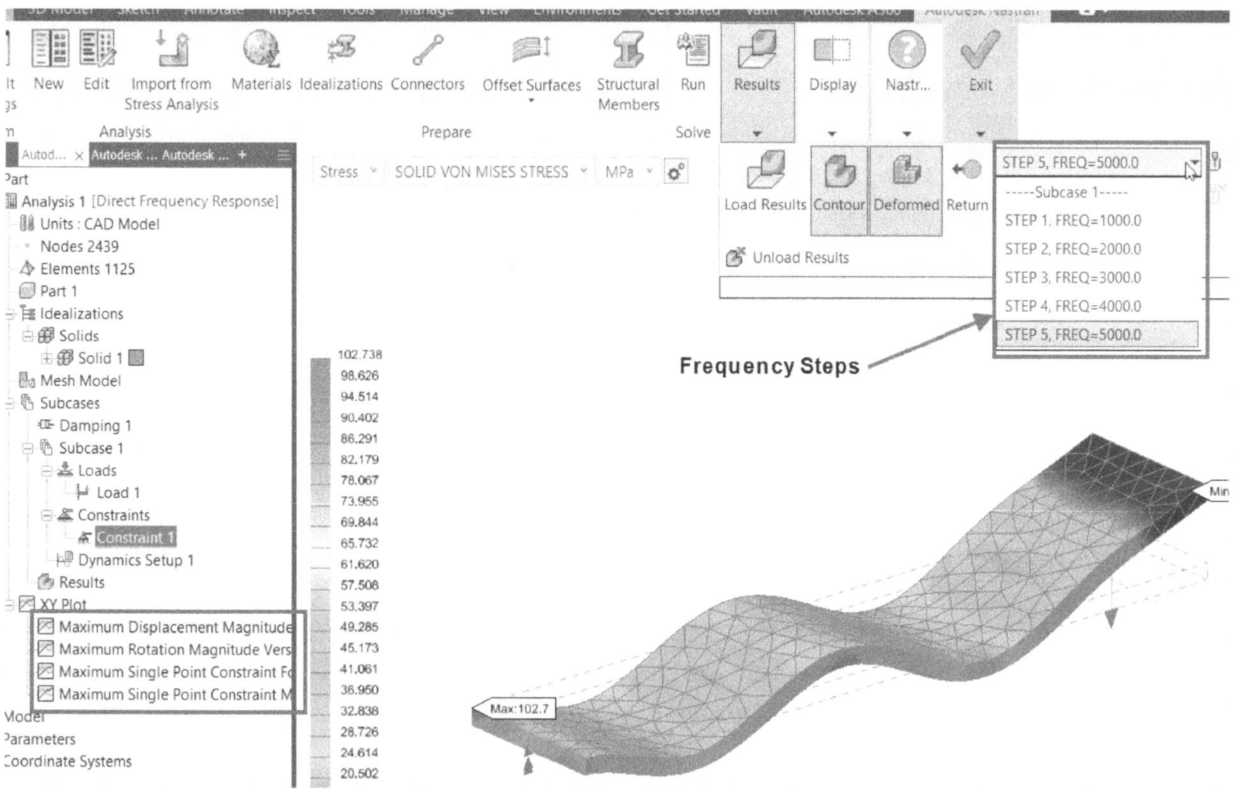

Figure-9. Result of direct frequency analysis

- Select desired frequency step and double-click on result nodes to check the results.

PERFORMING MODAL FREQUENCY RESPONSE ANALYSIS

The Modal frequency response analysis is performed when load is applied on large model with large number of frequencies to be analyzed. The procedure to perform modal frequency response analysis is given next.

- Open the part on which you want to perform modal frequency response analysis and start **Autodesk Inventor Nastran** environment.
- Click on the **New** button from the **Analysis** panel of **Autodesk Inventor Nastran** tab in the **Ribbon**. The **Analysis** dialog box will be displayed.
- Select the **Modal Frequency Response** option from the **Type** drop-down and set the other options as discussed earlier.
- Click on the **OK** button from the dialog box. The options related to modal frequency response analysis will be displayed; refer to Figure-10.

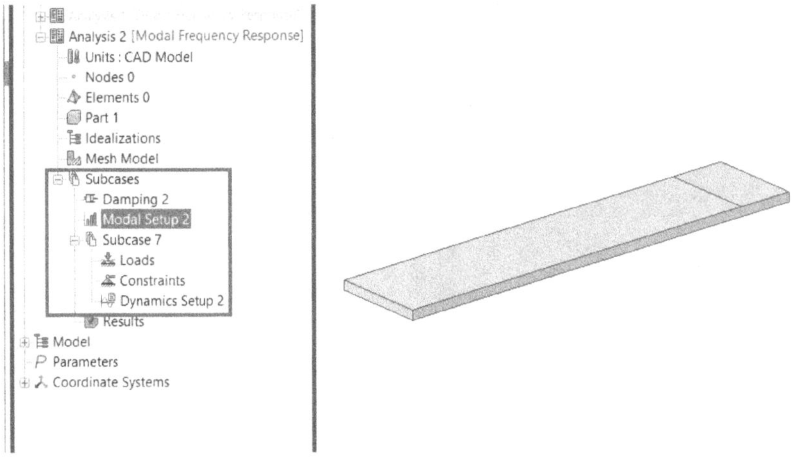

Figure-10. Subcase options for modal frequency response

- Double-click on **Damping** option from the **Subcases** node and set desired structural, modal, and/or rayleigh damping parameters.
- Double-click on **Modal Setup** option in **Subcases** node and set desired parameters to define natural frequencies to be found for defining degrees of freedom for the model; refer to Figure-11. The options of this dialog box have been discussed earlier.

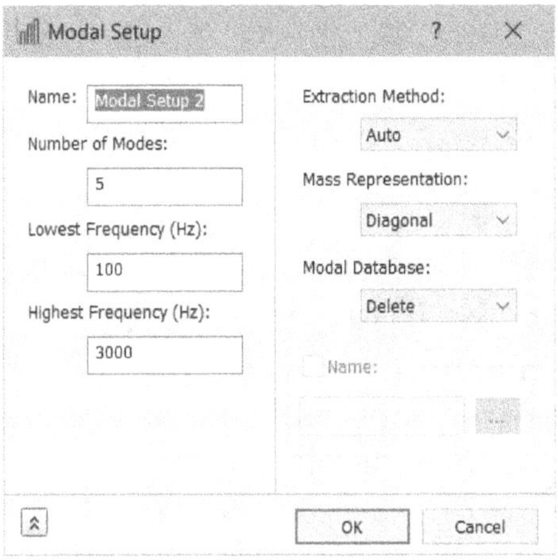

Figure-11. Modal setup options

- Double-click on **Dynamics Setup** option from the **Subcases** node. The **Dynamics Setup** dialog box will be displayed as shown in Figure-12.

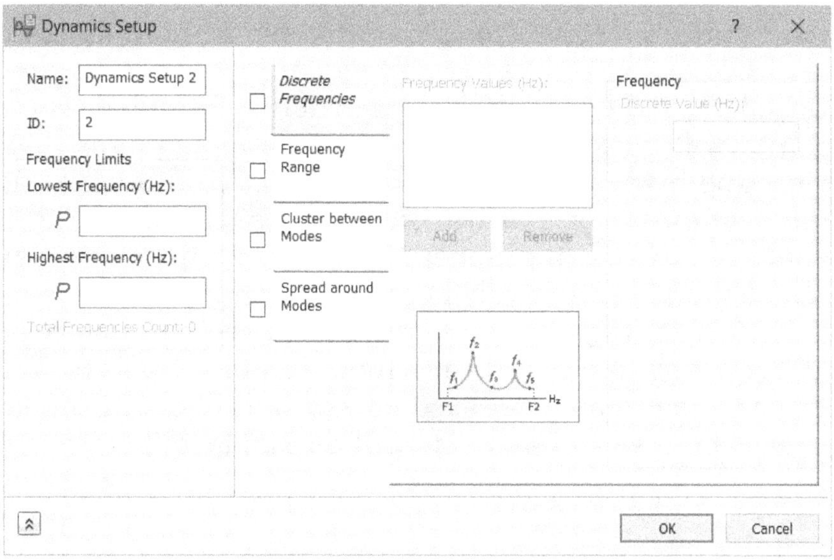

Figure-12. Dynamics Setup dialog box

- Set desired discrete frequencies and frequency range in the dialog box using **Discrete Frequencies** and **Frequency Range** check boxes as discussed earlier. Note that you can define multiple intervals of frequency range in case of Modal frequency response analysis as compared to direct frequency response analysis.
- Select the **Cluster between Modes** check box to define different frequency range clusters and set desired parameters; refer to Figure-13. Note that in this case, you can define bias factor for selecting frequencies in specified range. Specify the value of bias factor as 1 in the edit box if you want to evenly distribute frequency points in the range. For example, if frequency range is 20 to 100 Hz for 5 points and you have specified bias factor as 1 then software will find 5 frequencies near 20, 40, 60, 80, and 100. If you specify the bias factor less than 1 then most of the frequencies will be found near starting value which is 20 Hz in our case. If you specify the value higher than 1 then more frequencies will be found near end value of frequency range which is 100 in our case. Using this factor becomes important when you know the range of frequency and the frequency point near which you get more vibrations due to load.

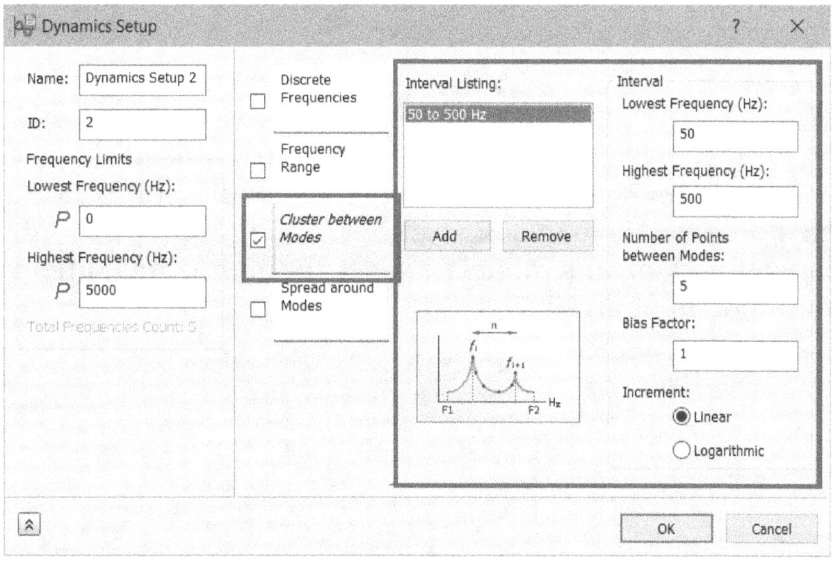

Figure-13. Cluster between Modes parameters

Note that when the **Cluster between Modes** check box is selected then frequencies are found between natural frequencies generated by Normal Mode analysis.

- Select the **Spread around Modes** check box to define frequency range within which frequency points will be found near natural frequency points. Specify desired values of lowest and highest frequencies in respective edit boxes of **Interval** area to define range within which natural frequencies will be found. Specify desired value in the **Number of Points Spread per Mode** edit box to define number of frequencies to be found for analysis near each natural frequency (mode). Specify desired value in **Percentage Spread** edit box to define spread percentage near each natural frequency (mode) within which frequency points will be generated.
- Set the other parameters as discussed earlier and click on the **Run** button from the **Solve** panel. The result of analysis will be displayed; refer to Figure-14.

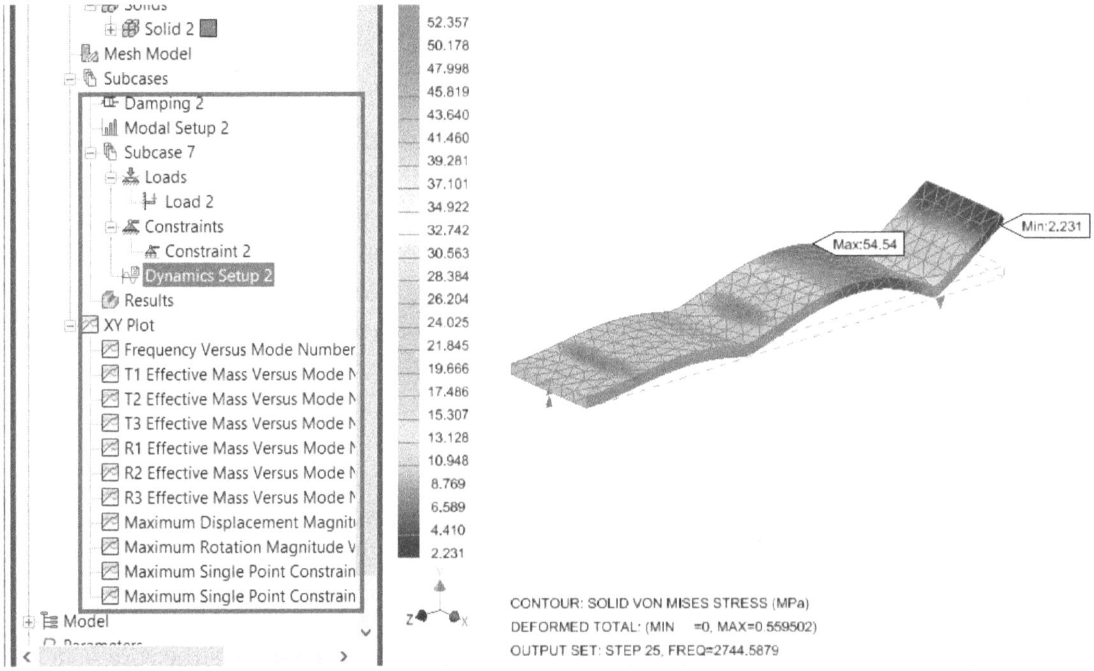

Figure-14. Result of modal frequency analysis

Select desired frequency and double-click on desired result node to check the results of analysis.

PRACTICAL

In this practical, we will use cement hopper model earlier used for performing Normal Modes analysis in Chapter 4; refer to Figure-15. We will apply a harmonic load of 30 kgf at frequencies near 85 Hz to check stresses in the model. Most of the parameters have earlier been defined for this model as we earlier performed linear static analysis as well as normal modes analysis.

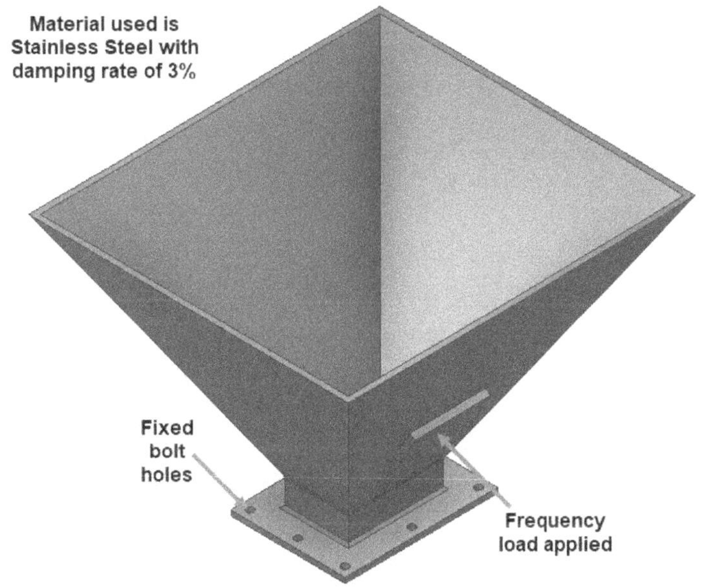

Figure-15. Practical for transient analysis

Steps for Analysis:
In this practical, we will open the final model earlier used in Chapter 4 and create a duplicate study. We will modify this duplicate study to create modal frequency response analysis. In this analysis, we will apply harmonic load of 30 Kgf at frequencies near 85 Hz. We will also like to know the effect of load near lower natural frequencies of the model which were approximately 37.43 Hz and 46.71 Hz.

Starting Model Frequency Response Analysis

- Open the model file for this practical from the Resources folder of this book and start **Autodesk Inventer Nastran**.
- Activate the Linear Static analysis node from the **Nastran Model Tree** if not active and right-click on it. A shortcut menu will be displayed.
- Select the **Duplicate** option from the shortcut menu. A duplicate copy of analysis will be created. Rename it as Modal Response.
- Click on the **Edit** button from the **Analysis** panel in the **Ribbon**. The **Analysis** dialog box will be displayed.
- Select the **Modal Frequency Response** option from **Type** drop-down and set the parameters as discussed earlier.
- Click on the **OK** button to change the analysis type.

Changing Damping, Modal Setup and Dynamic Setup

- Double-click on **Damping** option from **Subcases** node in the **Nastran Model Tree**. The **Damping** dialog box will be displayed.
- Specify the value of structural damping as **3**(%) and clear the **Modal Damping** check box from the dialog box; refer to Figure-16. Click on the **OK** button to apply the changes.

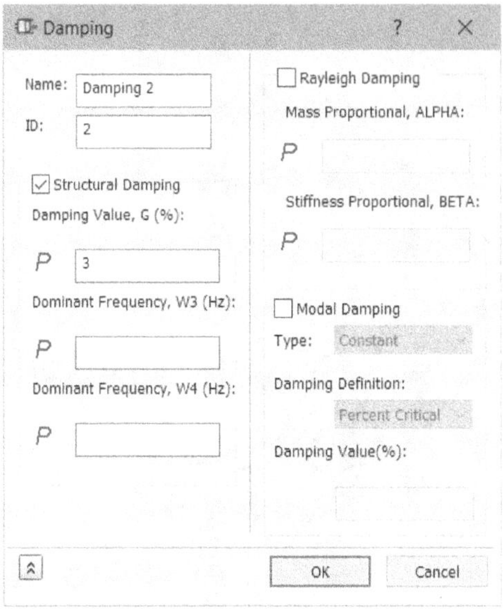

Figure-16. Damping value for practical

- Double-click on **Modal Setup** option from the **Subcases** node in **Nastran Model Tree**. The **Modal Setup** dialog box will be displayed.
- Specify the parameters as shown in Figure-17 and click on the **OK** button. Note that here we want to find out 10 natural frequencies between 10 to 200 Hz if possible.

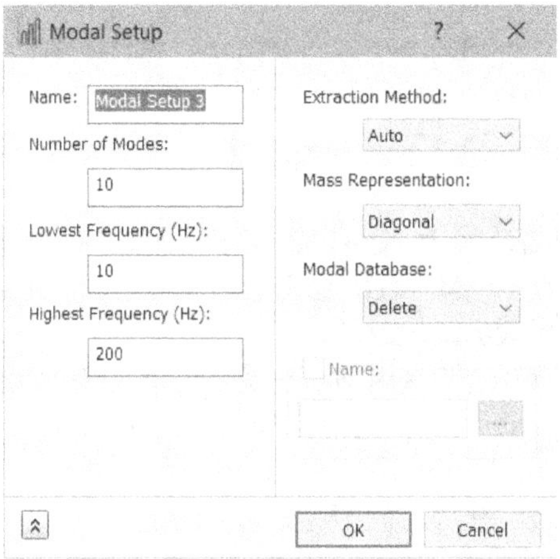

Figure-17. Modal Setup parameters specified

- Double-click on **Dynamics Setup** option from the **Nastran Model Tree**. The **Dynamics Setup** dialog box will be displayed.
- Specify the **Discrete Frequencies** and **Frequency Range** options as shown in Figure-18.
- After setting the parameters, click on the **OK** button from the dialog box.

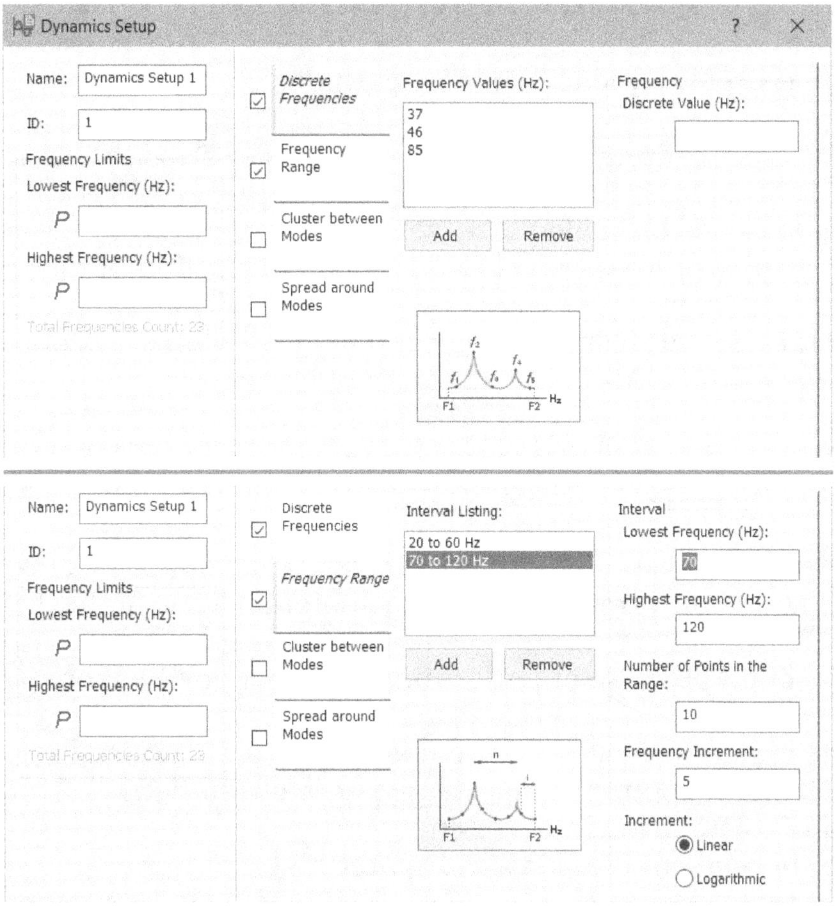

Figure-18. Dynamics Setup options specified

- Since all the other parameters are already specified by duplicating, click on the **Run** button to run the study. Once the results are loaded, you need to check for stresses and displacements near force operating frequency 85 Hz and other natural frequencies which are approximately 37 and 46 Hz. You can also check the **Maximum Displacement Magnitude Versus Frequency** XY Plot to find the frequency at which maximum displacement is happening.

SELF ASSESSMENT

Q1. What is the use of Frequency Response Analysis?

Q2. What are the types of Frequency Response Analysis? Describe each of them briefly.

Q3. In the **Dynamics Setup** dialog box, select the .... check box if you want to specify values of frequencies explicitly for excitation of model.

Q4. In the **Dynamics Setup** dialog box, select the .... check box to define range of frequencies to be used for excitation of system.

Q5. In the **Dynamics Setup** dialog box, **Cluster between Modes** check box is to be selected to define parameters related to frequency distribution. (True/False)

Q6. In the **Dynamics Setup** dialog box, **Spread around Modes** check box is to be selected to define different frequency range clusters. (True/False)

Q7. What is the main purpose of performing a Frequency Response Analysis?

A. To determine maximum temperature changes in a structure
B. To find structural response under steady state oscillation
C. To analyze fluid flow through a system
D. To compute thermal conductivity of a material

Q8. When should Direct Frequency Response Analysis be preferred?

A. For thermal conduction studies
B. When high computational efficiency is needed for large models
C. When response is required at discrete frequencies under high frequency excitation
D. When analyzing vibration of small models

Q9. Which of the following is a key benefit of Modal Frequency Response Analysis?

A. It calculates stress values for individual bolts
B. It is more computationally efficient for large models
C. It finds the maximum temperature at all time steps
D. It ignores damping completely

Q10. What mathematical expression represents displacement when damping causes phase shift?

A. D = amplitude × sine(angle)
B. D = amplitude × cosine(angle + φ)
C. D = amplitude × sine(angle + φ)
D. D = amplitude × sine(φ)

Q11. What does the Discrete Frequencies checkbox allow you to do during setup?

A. Automatically generate a frequency range
B. Add specific frequency values to be analyzed
C. Apply random load values
D. Ignore damping effects in vibration

Q12. When is the Logarithmic radio button used in frequency increment options?

A. When equal spacing between points is needed
B. When the model has a constant stiffness
C. When frequency range to be analyzed is large
D. When only a single frequency is defined

Q13. In Modal Frequency Response Analysis, what does the Cluster between Modes option enable?

A. Apply random loads between nodes
B. Define damping values for clustered nodes
C. Set frequency clusters between natural modes
D. Identify phase angle at each point

Q14. What is the impact of setting Bias Factor to a value greater than 1?

A. Frequencies are evenly distributed
B. Frequencies cluster near the starting value
C. Frequencies cluster near the ending value
D. No clustering occurs at all

Q15. What is the purpose of selecting the Spread around Modes checkbox?

A. To calculate spread of temperature
B. To find range of damping ratios
C. To generate frequencies near each natural mode
D. To apply loads at every mode

Q16. What does the Number of Points Spread per Mode setting control?

A. Number of damping values used
B. Frequency points around each natural frequency
C. Number of constraints applied
D. Number of parts in a simulation

For Student Notes

Chapter 9

Random Response Analysis

Topics Covered

The major topics covered in this chapter are:

- ***Introduction***
- ***Performing Random Response Analysis***
- ***Defining Dynamic Setup Parameters***
- ***Setting PSD Output Control***
- ***Defining Summation Method for Structural Response***
- ***Performing Shock/Response Spectrum Analysis***
- ***Defining Shock Spectrum Curve***

INTRODUCTION

The Random Response analysis is performed when the model is under vibrational conditions such as earthquake, ocean waves hitting, wind pressure fluctuations on aircraft and tall buildings, acoustic excitation due to rocket and jet engine noise. In such vibrational conditions, exact values of frequencies of excitation are not known but you know the mean value, standard deviation, and probability of exceeding a certain value.

PERFORMING RANDOM RESPONSE ANALYSIS

The procedure to perform random response analysis is given next.

- Open the part on which you want to perform random response analysis and start **Autodesk Inventor Nastran**. Linear static analysis will activate automatically.
- Click on the **Edit** button from the **Analysis** panel of **Autodesk Inventor Nastran** tab in the **Ribbon**. The **Analysis** dialog box will be displayed.
- Select the **Random Response** option from the **Type** drop-down. The options related to random response will be displayed.
- Click on the **PSD Output Control** button from the **Dynamic Options** area to define output control parameters for nodes and elements. The **Output Control** dialog box will be displayed; refer to Figure-1.

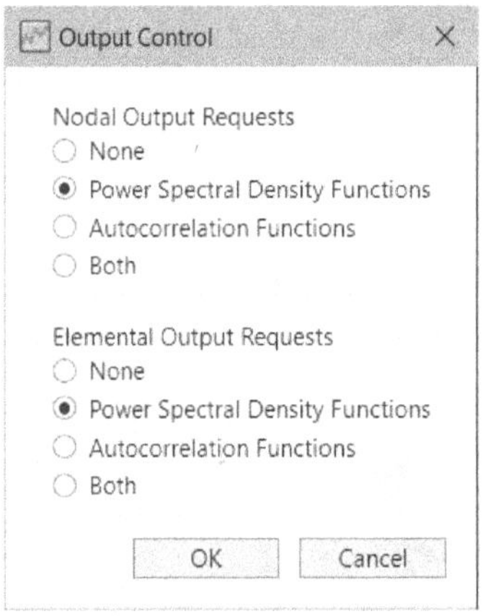

Figure-1. Output Control dialog box

- Select the **Power Spectral Density Functions** radio button to check distribution of peaks and lows of vibrational energy as function of frequencies. Select the **Autocorrelation Functions** radio button to check similarity in pattern of frequencies using a time series. Select the **Both** radio button to use both functions in output. Set desired radio buttons from the dialog box and click on the **OK** button.

Note that rather than using fix values of frequency at various time steps, random vibration analysis takes help of Statistics and Probability functions to determine vibrational loads on the model. This happens by using the correlation functions and Power Spectral Density functions. Check the QR Codes given next. If you have checked videos of the given QR codes then you can understand that Autocorrelation function finds the degree of similarity between a given time series and a lagged version of itself over successive time intervals. It's conceptually similar to the correlation between two different time series, but autocorrelation uses the same time series twice: once in its original form and once lagged one or more time periods.

- Specify desired parameters in the **Analysis** dialog box and click on the **OK** button.
- Set desired parameters for damping, modal setup, loads, and constraints as discussed earlier.
- Double-click on **Dynamics Setup** option under **Subcase 1** node. The **Dynamics Setup** dialog box will be displayed.
- Click on the **New Table** button in **Random Analysis Options** area of the dialog box. The **Table Data** dialog box will be displayed; refer to Figure-2.

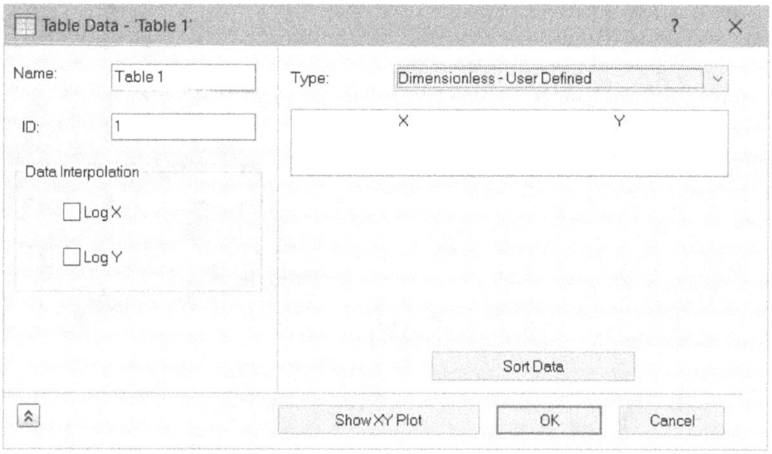

Figure-2. Table Data dialog box

- Select the **PSD (Acceleration) vs. Frequency** option from the **Type** drop-down if you want to specify acceleration for each specified frequency value. Select the **PSD (Force) vs. Frequency** option from the **Type** drop-down if you want to specify force for each specified frequency value; refer to Figure-3. Scan the QR code 1 below to learn basics of spectrums and their practical application. Note that when specifying PSD, you are defining the values against frequency not the time. But all the measurements that we take for vibrations are with respect to time. So, here Fourier Transform function is playing big role in background to generate force versus frequency function. Check the QR code 2 below to know how Fourier Transform works in an interesting way.

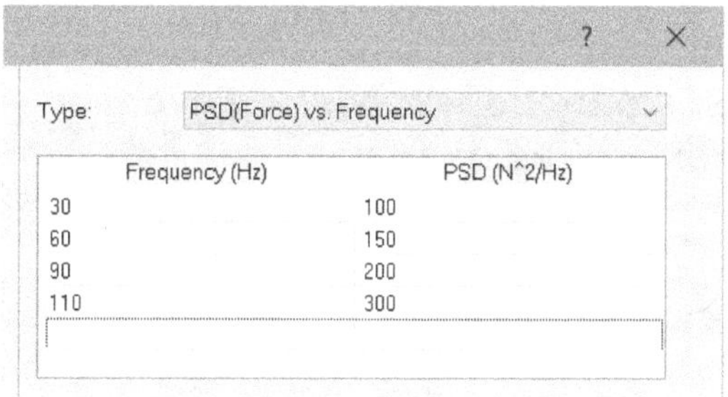

Figure-3. Specifying force vs frequency values

1 2

- After setting desired values, click on the **OK** button from the **Table Data** dialog box.
- Set other parameters in the **Dynamics Setup** dialog box as discussed earlier and click on the **OK** button from the dialog box.

- Click on the **Run** button from the **Solve** panel and perform the analysis. Once the analysis is complete, the results will be displayed; refer to Figure-4.

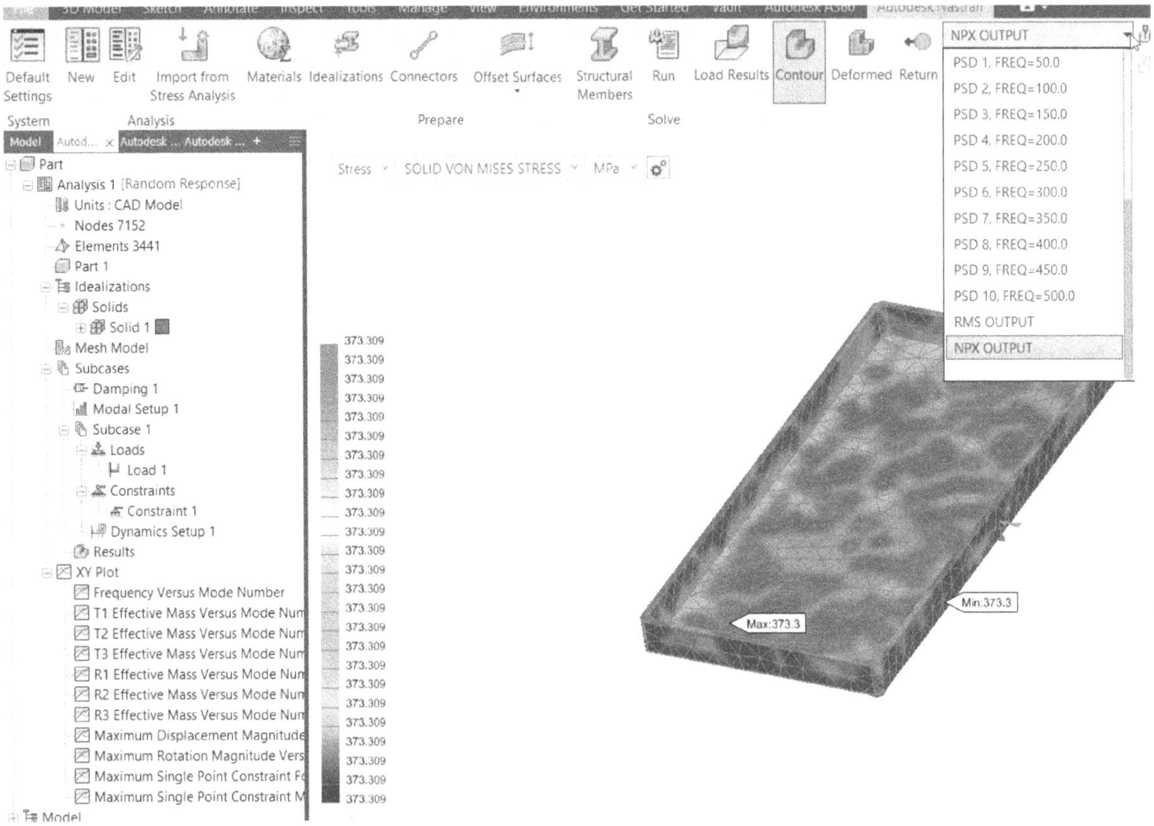

Figure-4. Result of random response analysis

- Select desired frequency from **Results** drop-down in **Results** panel to check the results at that specific frequency.

PERFORMING SHOCK/RESPONSE SPECTRUM ANALYSIS

The Shock/Response Spectrum analysis is performed when there is a shock load on the model (also called impulse load) and you want to check the results in the form of a stress frequency band. The procedure to perform this analysis is given next.

- Open the model on which you want to perform shock analysis and start Autodesk Inventor Nastran environment.
- Click on the **Edit** button from the **Analysis** panel of **Autodesk Inventor Nastran** tab in the **Ribbon**. The **Analysis** dialog box will be displayed.
- Select the **Shock/Response Spectrum** option from the **Type** drop-down of the dialog box.
- Click on the **Options** tab to specify parameters for spectrum. The options will be displayed as shown in Figure-5.

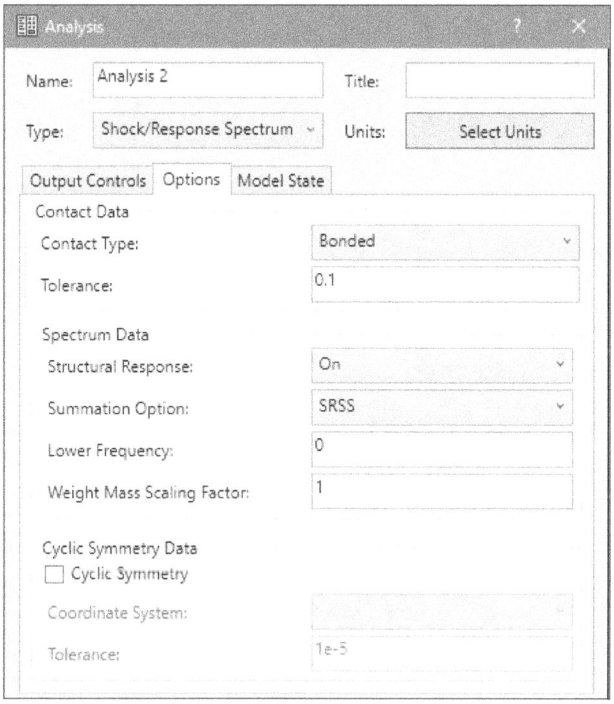

Figure-5. Response Spectrum options

- Select the **On** option from the **Structural Response** drop-down if you want to include structural response of shock as well as along with modal response.
- Select desired option from the **Summation Option** drop-down to define how modal results will be combined. Select the **ABS** option if you want to add absolute values of modal results in the analysis result. Select the **SRSS** option (Square Root of Sum of Squares) if you want to add squares of modal results and square root the final value. Select the **NRL** option (Naval Research Laboratory) if you want to combine ABS and SRSS methods to get final result. Select the **CQC** option (Complete Quadratic Combination) from the drop-down if you want to use the quadratic combination formula.
- Specify desired value of lower frequency and weight mass scaling factor in respective edit boxes for the analysis. Weight mass scaling factor is used to define factor by which specified weight of model will be converted to mass.
- After setting desired parameters, click on the **OK** button from the dialog box.
- Double-click on the **Dynamics Setup** option from the **Subcase** node to define parameters related to dynamic loading. The **Dynamics Setup** dialog box will be displayed; refer to Figure-6.

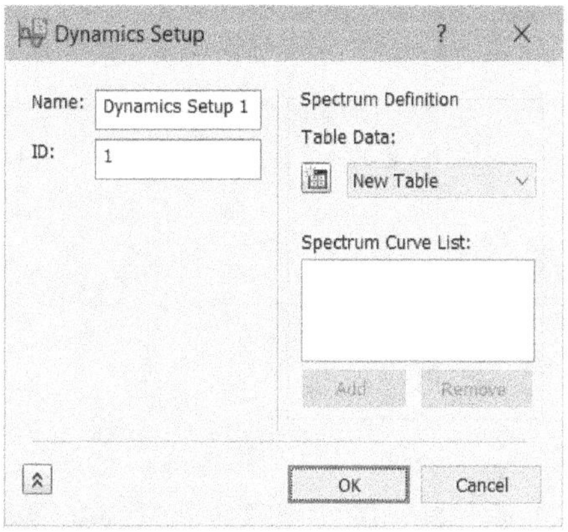

Figure-6. Dynamics Setup dialog box

- Click on **Define New Table** button from the **Table Data** area. The **Table Data** dialog box will be displayed; refer to Figure-7.

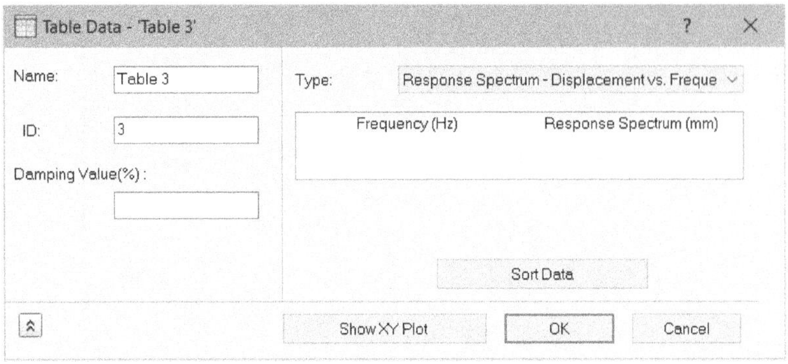

Figure-7. Table data for response spectrum

- Select the **Response Spectrum-Acceleration vs. Frequency** option from the **Type** drop-down and set desired parameters for response spectrum; refer to Figure-8.

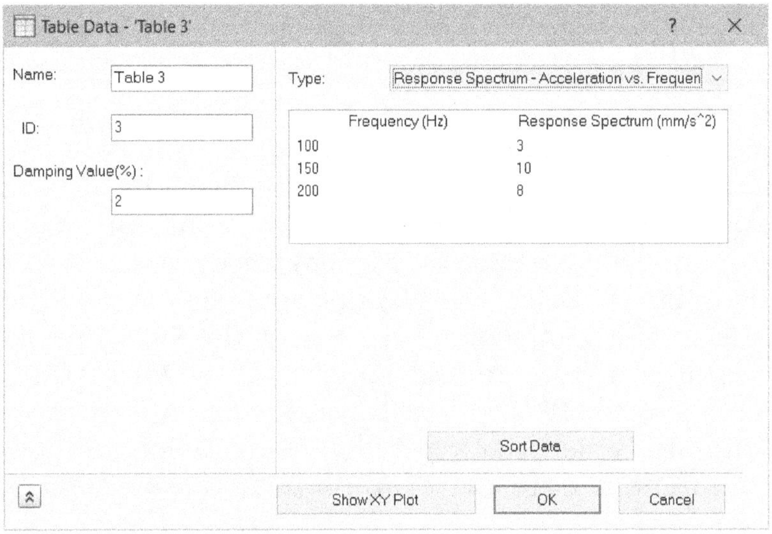

Figure-8. Parameters for response spectrum

- Click on the **OK** button from the dialog box.
- Select the newly created table data from the **Table Data** drop-down and click on the **Add** button. The selected spectrum curve table will be added in the **Spectrum Curve List** box; refer to Figure-9.

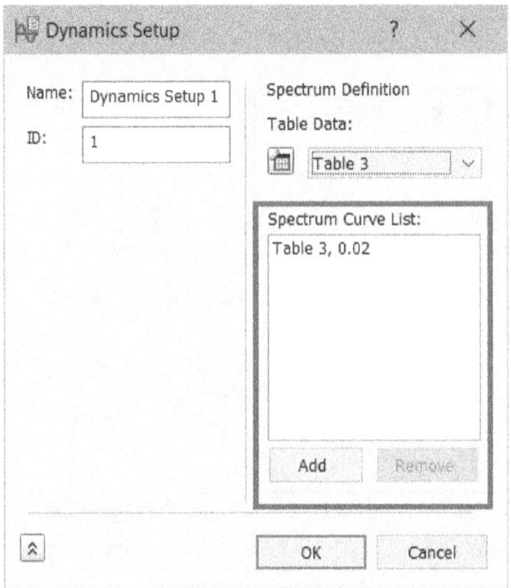

Figure-9. Spectrum curve added

- After setting desired values, click on the **OK** button from the **Dynamics Setup** dialog box.
- Click on the **Constraints** tool from the **Setup** panel. The **Constraint** dialog box will be displayed with Response Spectrum constraint types.
- Select desired check boxes from the dialog box to define how model will be constrained during the analysis.
- Set the other parameters as discussed earlier and click on the **Run** tool from the **Solve** panel of **Ribbon**. The analysis result will be displayed; refer to Figure-10.

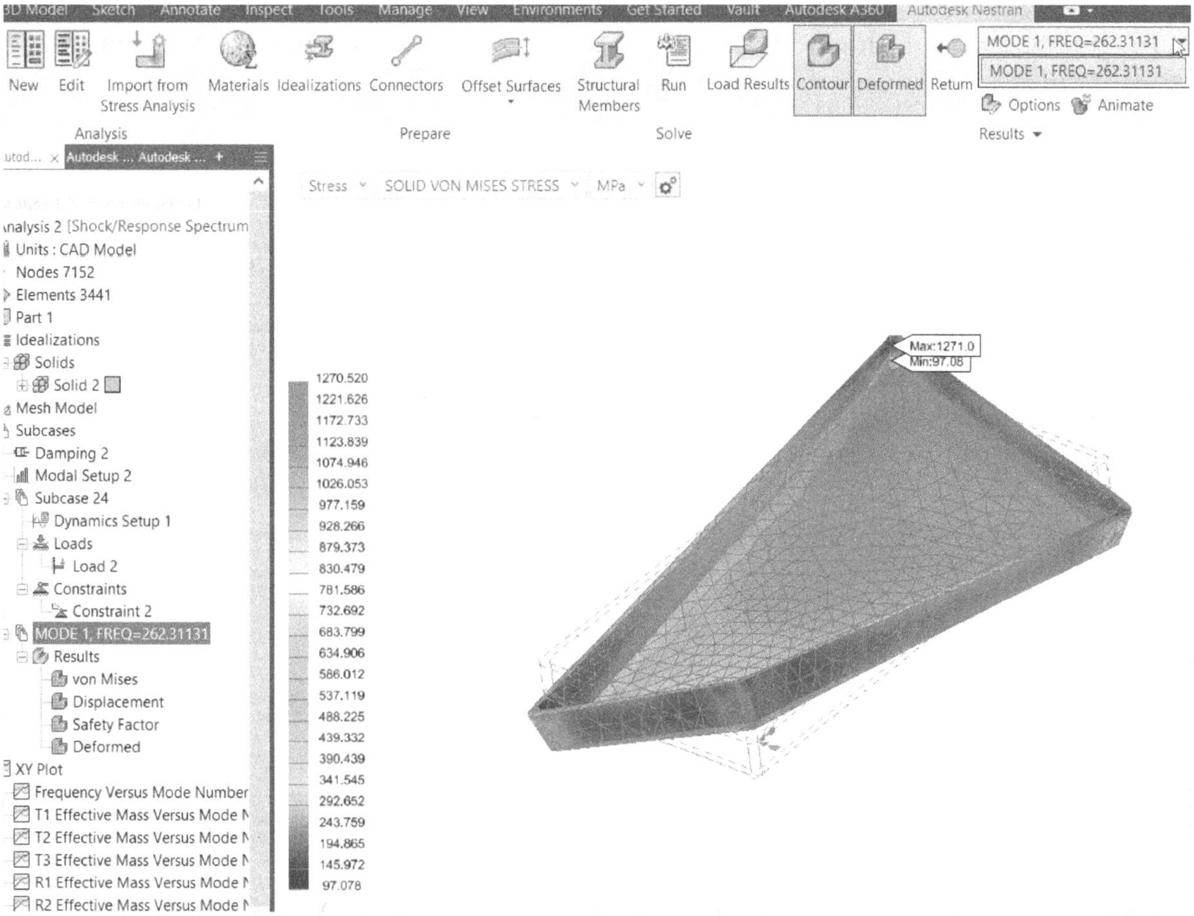

Figure-10. Result of shock analysis

SELF ASSESSMENT

Q1. Describe the conditions for performing Random Response Analysis.

Q2. What is the objective to perform Shock/Response Spectrum Analysis?

Q3. In the **Table Data** dialog box, select the .... option to specify acceleration for each specified frequency value.

Q4. In the **Analysis** dialog box, select the .... option if you want to add absolute values of modal results in the analysis result.

Q5. In the **Analysis** dialog box, select the **NRL** option (Naval Research Laboratory) if you want to combine .... and .... methods to get final result.

Q6. What is the main use of Random Response analysis in Autodesk Inventor Nastran?

A. To calculate static loads
B. To determine vibrational loads under known frequencies
C. To analyze vibrational conditions using statistical data
D. To measure temperatures in thermal analysis

Q7. Which button must you click to define output control parameters for nodes and elements during Random Response analysis?

A. Dynamics Setup
B. Output Manager
C. PSD Output Control
D. Frequency Control

Q8. What does the Autocorrelation Function evaluate in a random response context?

A. Power of frequency waves
B. Difference between time and frequency data
C. Similarity within a time series across time lags
D. Fixed values of frequency

Q9. Which function does Fourier Transform help to generate in the background during PSD setup?

A. Time vs. Force
B. Frequency vs. Acceleration
C. Force vs. Frequency
D. Acceleration vs. Time

Q10. What does PSD (Force) vs. Frequency setup allow you to define?

A. Acceleration at every time step
B. Force values for each frequency
C. Mass at a specific frequency
D. Vibration energy over time

Q11. What is the primary purpose of Shock/Response Spectrum analysis?

A. To detect material flaws
B. To study results of a model under shock loads
C. To reduce noise levels
D. To calculate thermal expansion

Q12. Which Summation Option in Shock/Response Spectrum combines absolute values of modal results?

A. CQC
B. NRL
C. SRSS
D. ABS

Q13. What does the NRL method do in Shock/Response Spectrum analysis?

A. Ignores both ABS and SRSS
B. Combines SRSS and CQC
C. Uses only SRSS
D. Combines ABS and SRSS methods

Q14. What type of table must be selected when defining a new shock response spectrum table?

A. PSD vs. Time
B. Response Spectrum-Acceleration vs. Frequency
C. Load vs. Displacement
D. Force vs. Time

Q15. In Shock/Response Spectrum analysis, what is the function of the Weight Mass Scaling Factor?

A. To increase the frequency
B. To define how much load to apply
C. To convert specified weight into mass
D. To limit acceleration

FOR STUDENT NOTES

Chapter 10

Fatigue Analyses

Topics Covered

The major topics covered in this chapter are:

- ***Introduction***
- ***Performing Multi-axial Fatigue Analysis***
- ***Defining Fatigue Setup Parameters***
- ***Performing Vibration Fatigue Analysis***

INTRODUCTION

Fatigue analyses are performed to check the effect of cyclic loading and unloading of component for specified duration under specified load. The damage caused in any component due to cyclic loading-unloading is cumulative. It is different from sudden failure due to excessive loads or buckling because the load being applied on component is well within safe range. It is the repetition of loading-unloading that causes failure in long run. For performing fatigue analyses, S-N curve is the basic requirement of material to be analyzed; refer to Figure-1. Here, S is strength and N is number of cycles. This S-N data is provided by your material manufacturer or you need to obtain it by experiment. Note that there is a region in S-N curve called Infinite Life because its life is much higher to find out. There are two types of fatigue analyses available in Autodesk Inventor Nastran viz. Multi-Axial Fatigue and Vibration Fatigue. A multi-axial fatigue analysis is performed to check fatigue under structural loads like force, pressure, moment, and so on. A good article on material fatigue and video can be check by scanning QR codes given below. The Vibration Fatigue analysis is performed to check model under cyclic vibrational loads. The procedures to perform these analyses are discussed next.

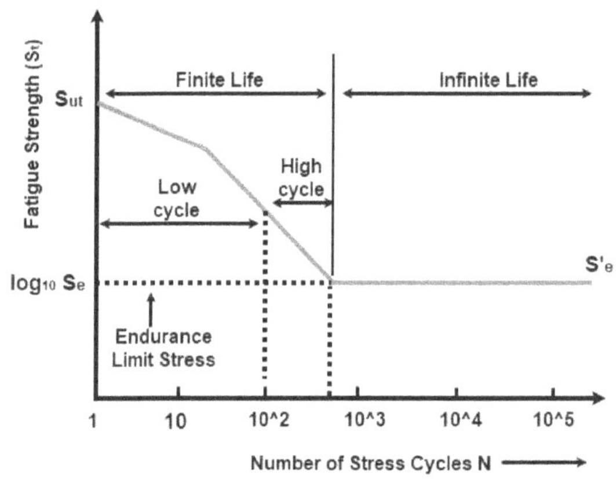

Figure-1. S-N curve for steel

PERFORMING MULTI-AXIAL FATIGUE ANALYSIS

The Multi-axial fatigue analysis is performed when a structural load is applied and removed from the model in cycles for long period of time. The procedure to perform multi-axial fatigue analysis is given next.

- Open the model on which you want to perform multi-axial fatigue analysis and start **Autodesk Inventor Nastran** environment. Linear static analysis will be activated automatically.
- Click on the **Edit** button from the **Analysis** panel of **Autodesk Inventor Nastran** tab in the **Ribbon**. The **Analysis** dialog box will be displayed.
- Select the **Multi-Axial Fatigue** option from the **Type** drop-down and set desired parameters.
- Click on the **OK** button from the dialog box. The parameters for fatigue setup will be displayed; refer to Figure-2.

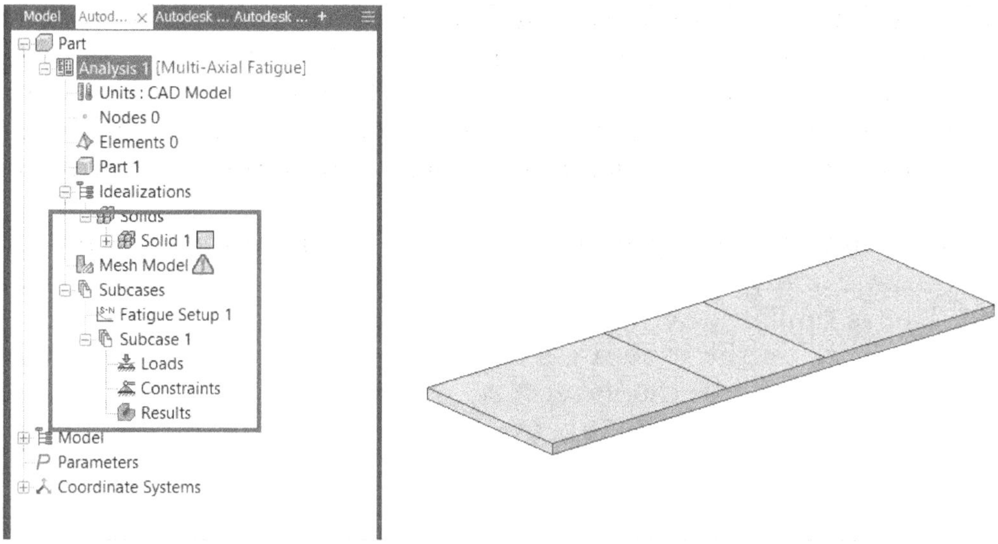

Figure-2. Parameters for multi-axial fatigue

Fatigue Parameters

- Double-click on **Fatigue Setup 1** option from **Subcases** node in **Model Tree**. The **Fatigue Setup** dialog box will be displayed; refer to Figure-3.

Figure-3. Fatigue Setup dialog box

- Select desired option from the **Approach** drop-down. Select the **Stress-Life** option if you want to use SN data of material for calculating fatigue deformation. Select the **Strain-Life** option from the drop-down if you want to use EN data of material for calculating fatigue deformation.
- Select desired option from the **Method** drop-down to define how life of part will be calculated. For example, select the von Mises option to use Von Mises stress values of analysis result as factor to define life of part.
- Specify desired value of loading threshold (percentage) in **Threshold** edit box.
- Specify desired value of fatigue study duration (in number of cycles) in the **Event Duration** edit box. Each cycle consists of one time load and unloading of acting loads. Based on specified event duration, an average life will be calculated.
- Specify desired value in **Time Conversion Factor** edit box to define the conversion of default time unit which is second to desired unit.

- Select desired option from the **Signed Stress Invariant** drop-down to specify the stress or strain used in the life calculation method should be signed or not. If you select **Yes** option from the drop-down then both positive and negative stress values will be considered in analysis. If you select the **No** option then only positive values will be considered. On selecting the **Auto** option, the value is automatically decided.
- Set desired parameters as required and click on the **OK** button from the dialog box.
- Note that fatigue analysis need a material which has fatigue material properties activated. This is similar to activating nonlinear properties of material as discussed in Chapter 3. Click on the **Materials** tool from the **Prepare** panel of **Ribbon**. The **Material** dialog box will be displayed.
- Select desired material using **Select Material** button in the dialog box as discussed earlier and then click on the **Fatigue** button from the **Analysis Specific Data** area of **Material** dialog box. The **Fatigue** dialog box will be displayed; refer to Figure-4. Specify the values of fatigue parameters in the dialog box and click on the **OK** button. Note that you can specify either S-N Data or E-N Data for the material.

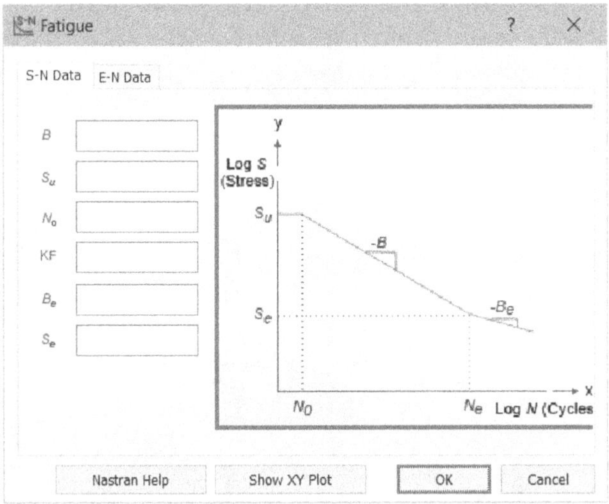

Figure-4. Fatigue dialog box

- Set the other parameters like idealization, load, constraint, and click on the **Run** button from the **Solve** panel. The result of analysis will be displayed; refer to Figure-5.

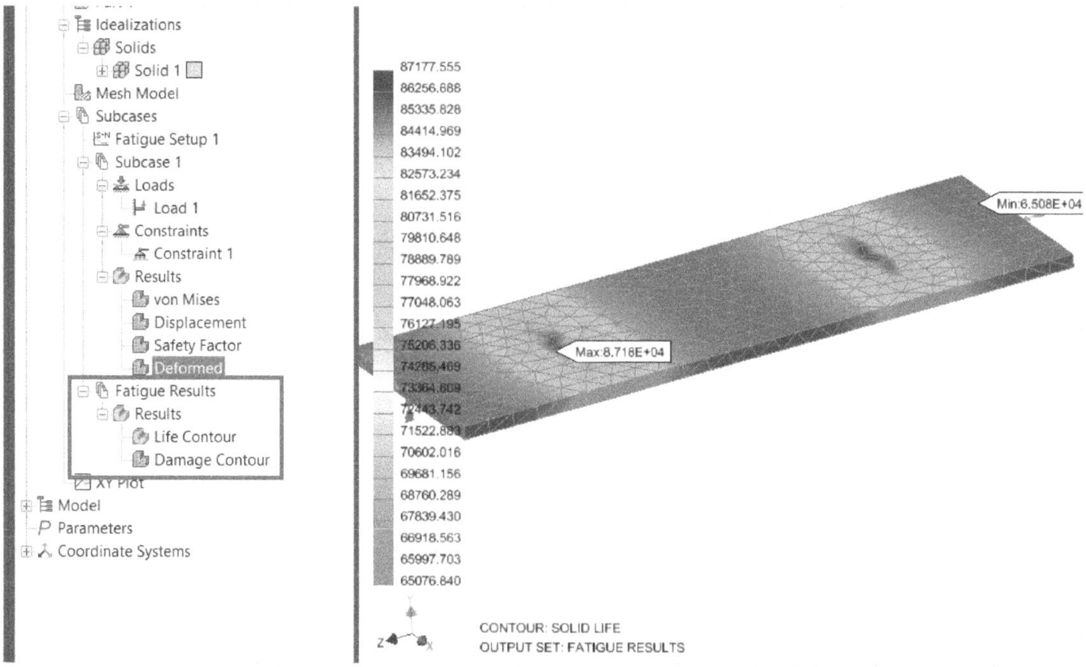

Figure-5. Fatigue analysis result

- Double-click on desired option in **Results** node. The respective result will be displayed.

PERFORMING VIBRATION FATIGUE ANALYSIS

The vibration fatigue analysis is performed when there is continuous loading and unloading of vibrational excitation. The procedure to perform this analysis is given next.

- Open the part on which you want to perform vibrational fatigue analysis and start Autodesk Inventor Nastran environment.
- Click on the **Edit** button from the **Analysis** panel of **Autodesk Inventor Nastran** tab in the **Ribbon**. The **Analysis** dialog box will be displayed.
- Select the **Vibration Fatigue** option from the **Type** drop-down. The options related to vibrational fatigue analysis will be displayed.
- Set the other parameters as discussed earlier and click on the **OK** button from the dialog box. The options for vibrational fatigue analysis will be displayed as shown in Figure-6.

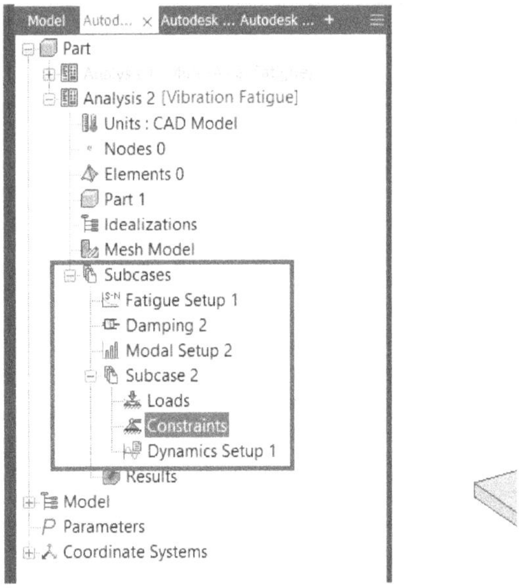

Figure-6. Options for vibration fatigue analysis

- Double-click on the parameters under **Subcases** node as discussed earlier and set desired values.
- Click on the **Run** button after setting all the parameters. The results will be displayed; refer to Figure-7.

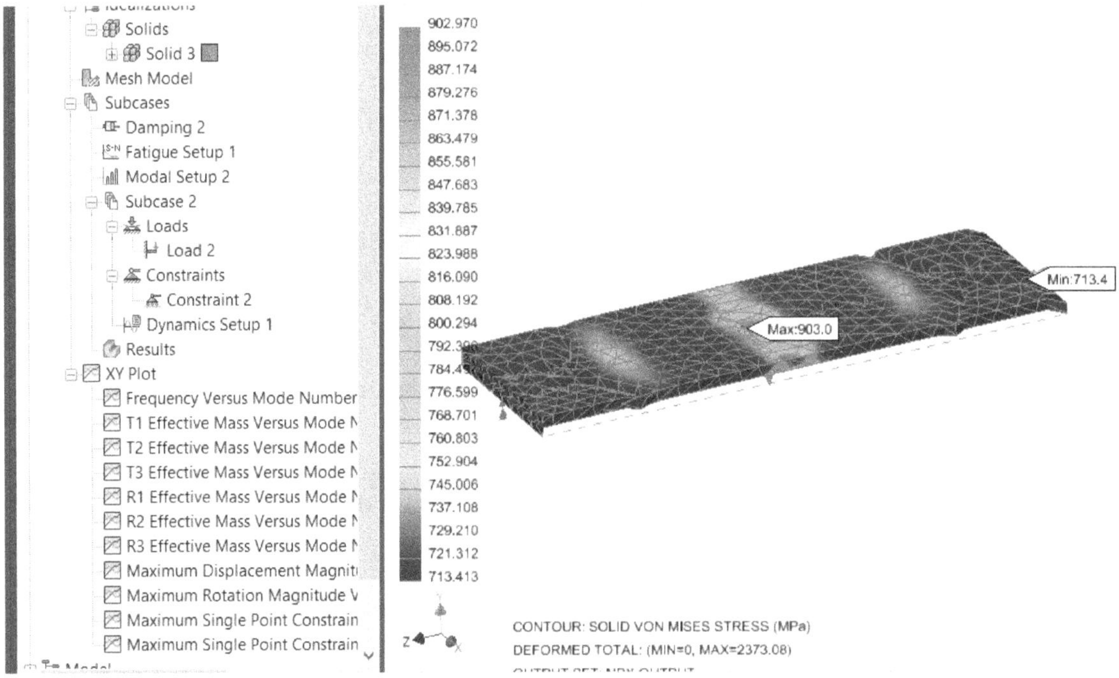

Figure-7. Result of vibration fatigue analysis

SELF ASSESSMENT

Q1. Why is Fatigue Analysis performed?

Q2. How many types of Fatigue Analysis are available to perform in Autodesk Inventor Nastran? Describe them briefly.

Q3. In **Fatigue Setup** dialog box, select the .... option if you want to use S-N data of material for calculating fatigue deformation.

Q4. The .... analysis is performed when there is continuous loading and unloading of vibrational excitation.

Q5. In **Fatigue Setup** dialog box, specify the value in **Threshold** edit box to define the conversion of default time unit. (True/False)

Q6. What is the primary reason for failure in components undergoing fatigue?

A. Excessive load applied once
B. Sudden buckling due to instability
C. Cumulative damage from repeated loading and unloading
D. Inadequate material strength

Q7. What does the S-N curve represent in fatigue analysis?

A. Stress and strain curve of material
B. Strength vs notch sensitivity
C. Strength vs number of cycles
D. Speed vs normal force

Q8. What is the meaning of the "Infinite Life" region in an S-N curve?

A. Component fails after infinite stress
B. Component does not fail within measurable cycles
C. Component is permanently deformed
D. Component is instantly destroyed

Q9. Which type of fatigue analysis is used to check cyclic structural loads?

A. Modal Fatigue
B. Multi-Axial Fatigue
C. Buckling Fatigue
D. Static Load Fatigue

Q10. When would you use the Vibration Fatigue analysis?

A. For sudden shocks and impacts
B. When model fails under thermal stress
C. Under cyclic vibrational loading
D. When static pressure is high

Q11. What is automatically activated when you open the model in Inventor Nastran for fatigue analysis?

A. Vibration module
B. Buckling analysis
C. Linear static analysis
D. Material setup

Q12. What does selecting the “Stress-Life” option in fatigue setup use for analysis?

A. E-N Data
B. Buckling coefficient
C. Strain-Rate curve
D. S-N Data

Q13. What does the “Signed Stress Invariant” option control?

A. Whether only compressive stress is used
B. Whether both positive and negative stresses are considered
C. Direction of strain
D. Number of cycles in the load

Q14. What must be activated in the material properties to perform fatigue analysis?

A. Static yield point
B. Thermal coefficients
C. Fatigue properties
D. Poisson’s ratio

Chapter 11

Heat Transfer Analyses

Topics Covered

The major topics covered in this chapter are:

- ***Introduction***
- ***Performing Linear Steady State Heat Transfer Analysis***
- ***Performing Nonlinear Steady State Heat Transfer Analysis***
- ***Performing Nonlinear Transient Heat Transfer Analysis***

INTRODUCTION

Thermal analysis is a method to check the distribution of heat over a body due to applied thermal loads which in turn can be used to check expansion of part due to heat. Note that thermal energy is dynamic in nature and is always flowing through various mediums. There are three mechanisms by which the thermal energy flows:

- Conduction
- Convection
- Radiation

In all three mechanisms, heat energy flows from the medium with higher temperature to the medium with lower temperature. Heat transfer by conduction and convection requires the presence of an intervening medium while heat transfer by radiation does not.

The output from a thermal analysis can be given by:

1. Temperature distribution.
2. Amount of heat loss or gain.
3. Thermal gradients.
4. Thermal fluxes.

This analysis is used in many engineering industries such as automobile, piping, electronic, power generation, and so on.

Important terms related to Thermal Analysis

Before conducting thermal analysis, you should be familiar with the basic concepts and terminologies of thermal analysis. Following are some of the important terms used in thermal analysis:

Heat Transfer Modes

Whenever there is a difference in temperature between two bodies, the heat is transferred from one body to another. Basically, heat is transferred in three ways: Conduction, Convection, and Radiation.

Conduction

In conduction, the heat is transferred by interactions of atoms or molecules of the material. For example, if you heat up a metal rod at one end, the heat will be transferred to the other end by the atoms or molecules of the metal rod.

Convection

In convection, the heat is transferred by the flowing fluid. The fluid can be gas or liquid. Heating up water using an electric water heater is a good example of heat convection. In this case, water takes heat from the heater. Every medium has its limitation to transfer the heat energy. This limitation is mathematically represented by **Convection Heat coefficient** $Q_{convection}$.

$$Q_{convection} = hA(T_s - T_f)$$

Here, **h** is heat transfer coefficient and its unit is $W/m^2.k$

T_s is the temperature of the surface.

T_f is the temperature of the surrounding fluid.

A is the area of surface.

Radiation

In radiation, the heat is transferred in space without any matter. Radiation is the only heat transfer method that takes place in space. Heat coming from the Sun is a good example of radiation. The heat from the Sun is transferred to the earth through radiation.

Thermal Gradient

The thermal gradient is the rate of increase in temperature per unit depth in a material.

Thermal Flux

Thc Thermal flux is defined as the rate of heat transfer per unit cross-sectional area. It is denoted by q.

Bulk Temperature

It is the temperature of a fluid flowing outside the material. It is denoted by Tb. The Bulk temperature is used in convective heat transfer.

Film Coefficient

It is a measure of the heat transfer through an air film.

Emissivity

The emissivity of a material is the ratio of energy radiated by the material to the energy radiated by a black body at the same temperature. Emissivity is the measure of a material's ability to absorb and radiate heat. It is denoted by e. Emissivity is a numerical value without any unit. For a perfect black body, $e = 1$. For any other material, $e < 1$.

Stefan–Boltzmann Constant

The energy radiated by a black body per unit area per unit time divided by the fourth power of the body's temperature is known as the Stefan-Boltzmann constant. It is denoted by s.

Thermal Conductivity

The thermal conductivity is the property of a material that indicates its ability to conduct heat. It is denoted by K.

Specific Heat

The specific heat is the amount of heat required per unit mass to raise the temperature of the body by one degree Celsius. It is denoted by c.

Note that you should be able to answer the following questions before performing thermal analysis using the Autodesk Inventor Nastran software:

1. **Heat transfer through a solid body is referred to as**

a. Conduction b. Convection c. Radiation d. Generation

2. **The temperature gradient is defined as**

a. Temperature rate of change per unit length
b. Heat flow through a body
c. Temperature rate of change per unit volume
d. Temperature rate of change per unit area

3. **Heat flux is defined by**

a. The amount of heat generated per unit volume
b. The heat transfer rate per unit area
c. The amount of heat stored in a control volume
d. The temperature change per unit length

4. **Heat transfer between a solid body and a fluid is referred to as**

a. Conduction b. Convection c. Radiation d. Generation

5. **Which behavior best describes a material with a high thermal conductivity compared to a material will a smaller thermal conductivity?**

a. Temperature change is smaller through the solid
b. Heat flux is higher through the solid
c. Thermal resistance is lower through the solid
d. All of the above

6. **The convection coefficient is related to**

a. The rate that heat is transferred between a solid and fluid
b. The rate that heat is transferred between two solids
c. The emissive power of the material
d. The heat generation capability of the material

7. **The amount of heat transferred by radiation is directly related to**

a. The Stephan-Boltzmann constant
b. The surface temperature
c. The emissivity of the material
d. All of the above

8. **If no heat is transferred to or from a surface, it is referred to as**

a. Isothermal b. Exothermal c. Adiabatic d. Isobaric

9. **When all temperatures are in equilibrium, the problem is assumed to be**

a. Transient
b. Steady-State
c. Laminar
d. None of the above

10. **Which of the following terms is not part of the energy balance for heat transfer?**

a. Generated energy
b. Stored energy
c. Energy into the system
d. Energy destroyed

There are three analyses available in Autodesk Inventor Nastran to perform thermal analyses; Linear Steady State Heat Transfer, Nonlinear Steady State Heat Transfer, and Nonlinear Transient Heat Transfer. These analyses are discussed next.

PERFORMING LINEAR STEADY STATE HEAT TRANSFER ANALYSIS

The linear steady state heat transfer analysis is performed when thermal conductivity of material do not depend on temperature and radiation is not applied. The procedure to perform linear steady heat transfer analysis is given next.

- Open the model on which you want to perform linear steady state heat transfer analysis and start Autodesk Inventor Nastran environment.
- Click on the **Edit** button from the **Analysis** panel of **Autodesk Inventor Nastran** tab in the **Ribbon**. The **Analysis** dialog box will be displayed.
- Select the **Linear Steady State Heat Transfer** option from the **Type** drop-down. The options will be displayed as shown in Figure-1.

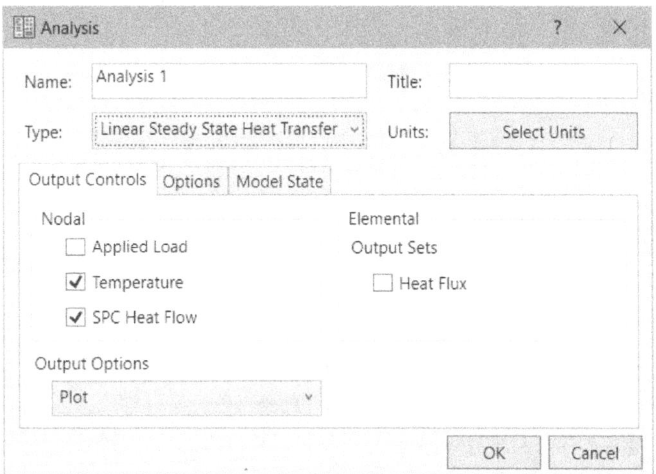

Figure-1. Linear Steady State Heat Transfer analysis options

- Select the **Applied Load** check box if you want to add applied load as output on nodes.

- If you want to generate heat flux as output on elements then select the **Heat Flux** check box from **Elemental** area of the dialog box.
- Click on the **Options** tab and select desired options from the **Contact Type** drop-down. Note that bonded option is used to perfectly transfer heat between assembled components.
- After setting desired parameters, click on the **OK** button from the dialog box. The options for linear steady state heat transfer analysis will be displayed; refer to Figure-2.

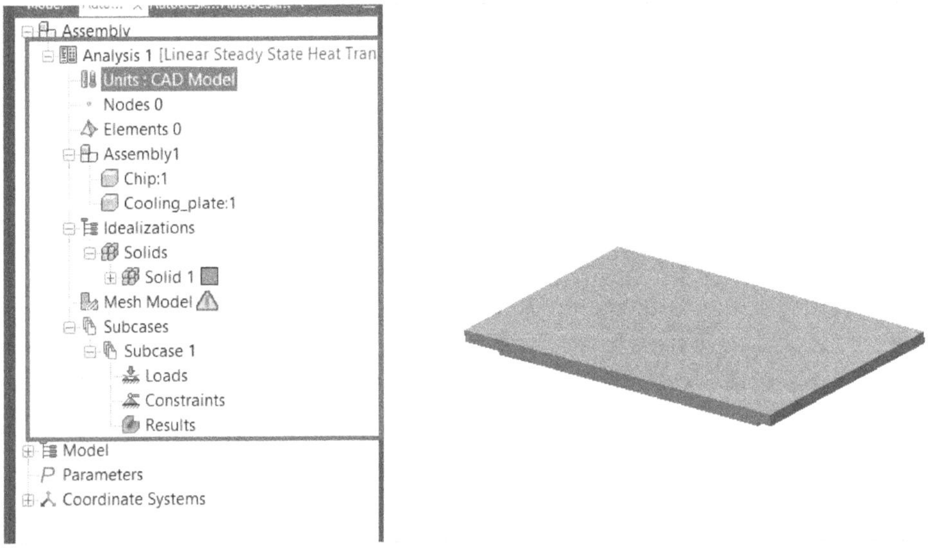

Figure-2. Options for linear steady state thermal analysis

- Click on the **Constraints** tool from the **Setup** panel of **Autodesk Inventor Nastran** tab in the **Ribbon**. The **Constraint** dialog box will be displayed; refer to Figure-3.

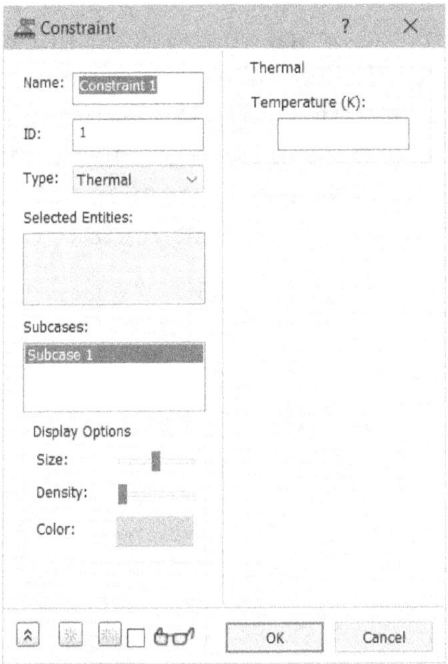

Figure-3. Constraint dialog box with thermal constraint

- Select the face/edge/vertex on which you want to specify fixed temperature.
- Specify desired value of temperature in the **Temperature (K)** edit box and click on the **OK** button.
- Click on the **Loads** tool from the **Setup** panel of **Autodesk Inventor Nastran** tab in the **Ribbon**. The **Load** dialog box will be displayed; refer to Figure-4.

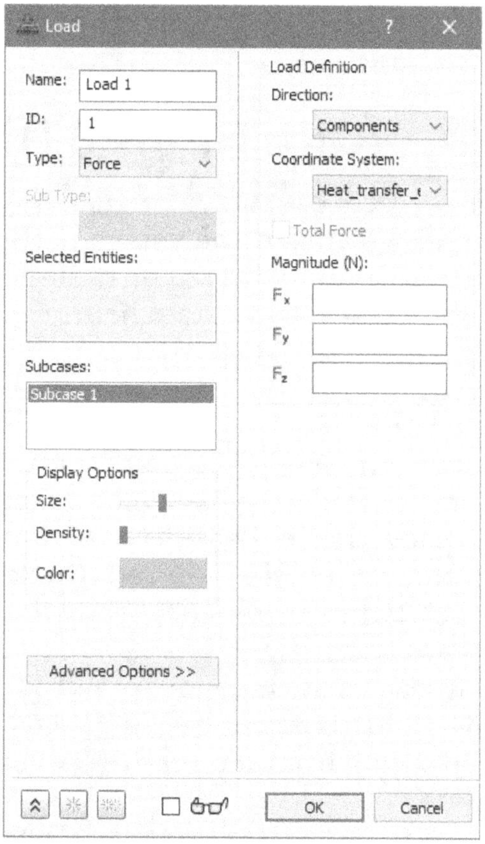

Figure-4. Load dialog box

- Select the **Heat Generation** option from the **Type** drop-down if you want to apply heat generation at selected body, face, edge, or vertex.
- Specify desired value of heat generation in the **Magnitude** edit box and click on the **OK** button. Similarly, set the other thermal loads like heat convection, heat flux, radiation, and other parameters.
- Set the other parameters as required and click on the **Run** tool from the **Solve** panel of **Autodesk Inventor Nastran** tab in the **Ribbon**. The results will be displayed; refer to Figure-5.

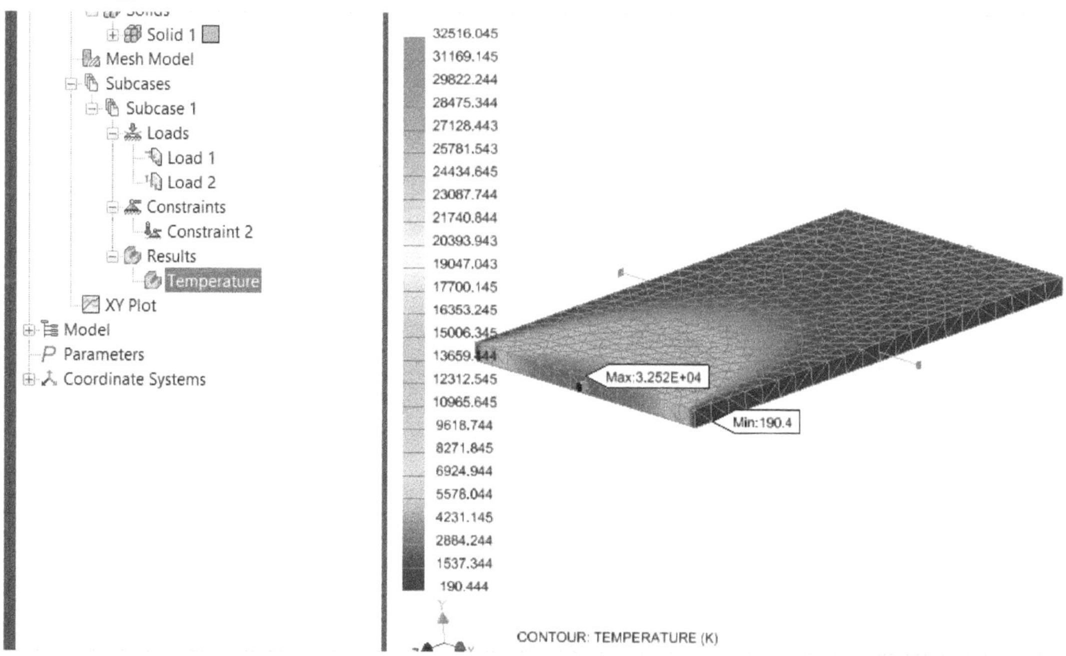

Figure-5. Thermal analysis result

Click on the **Options** tool from the **Results** panel and set desired parameters to check results.

PERFORMING NONLINEAR STEADY STATE HEAT TRANSFER ANALYSIS

The Nonlinear steady state heat transfer analysis is performed when either thermal conductivity of part changes with temperature or radiation is applied on the model. The procedure to perform nonlinear steady state heat transfer analysis is given next.

- Open the part on which you want to perform analysis and start Autodesk Inventor Nastran environment.
- Click on the **Edit** tool from the **Analysis** panel of **Autodesk Inventor Nastran** tab in the **Ribbon**. The **Analysis** dialog box will be displayed.
- Select the **Nonlinear Steady State Heat Transfer** option from the **Type** drop-down and set the other parameters as required. Click on the **OK** button from the dialog box. The options related to nonlinear steady state thermal analysis will be displayed.
- Click on the **Loads** tool from the **Setup** panel of **Autodesk Inventor Nastran** tab in the **Ribbon**. The **Loads** dialog box will be displayed.
- Select **Initial Condition** option from the **Type** drop-down and **Temperature** option from the **Sub Type** drop-down.
- Specify desired temperature value in the **Temperature** edit box and click on the **OK** button.
- Set desired thermal constraint and loads as discussed earlier.
- After setting desired parameters, click on the **Run** button from the **Solve** panel of **Autodesk Inventor Nastran** tab in the **Ribbon**. The analysis results will be displayed; refer to Figure-6.

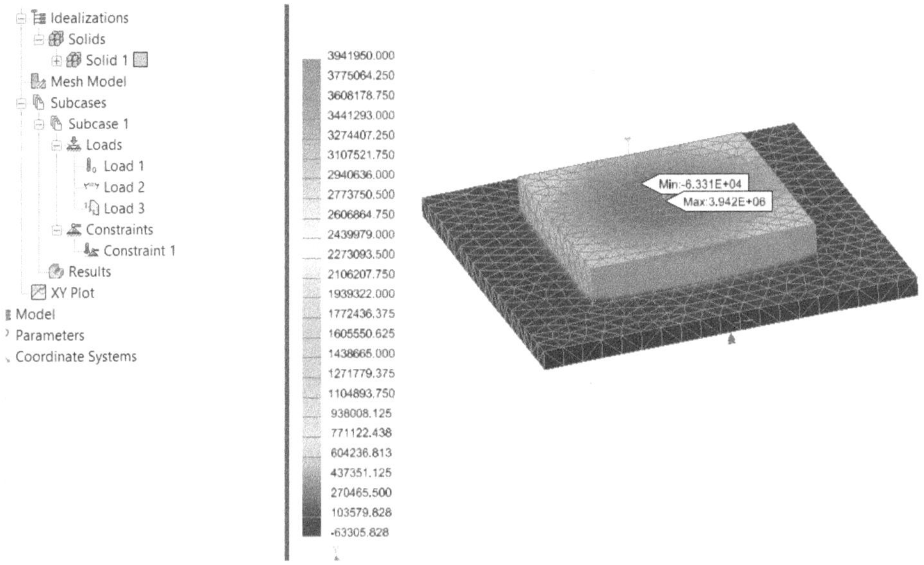

Figure-6. Nonlinear steady state thermal analysis result

PERFORMING NONLINEAR TRANSIENT HEAT TRANSFER ANALYSIS

Nonlinear transient heat transfer analysis is performed to check heat distribution at different time steps. The procedure to perform this analysis is given next.

- Open the part on which you want to perform the analysis and start **Autodesk Inventor Nastran** environment.
- Click on the **Edit** tool from the **Analysis** panel of **Autodesk Inventor Nastran** tab in the **Ribbon**. The **Analysis** dialog box will be displayed.
- Select the **Nonlinear Transient Heat Transfer** option from the **Type** drop-down and set the other options as required.
- Click on the **OK** button from the dialog box.
- Double-click on the **Time Step 1** option from the **Subcases** node. The **Time Step** dialog box will be displayed; refer to Figure-7.

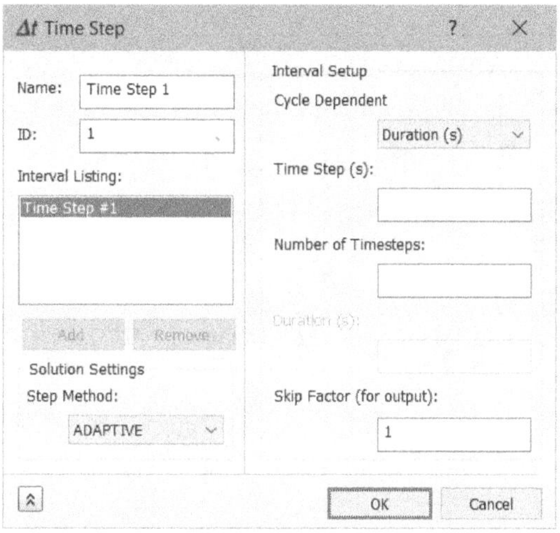

Figure-7. Time Step dialog box

- Specify desired time duration and time steps as required in the dialog box, and click on the **OK** button from the dialog box.
- Set the other parameters like idealization, load, and constraint.
- Click on the **Run** tool from the **Solve** panel. The analysis result will be displayed; refer to Figure-8.

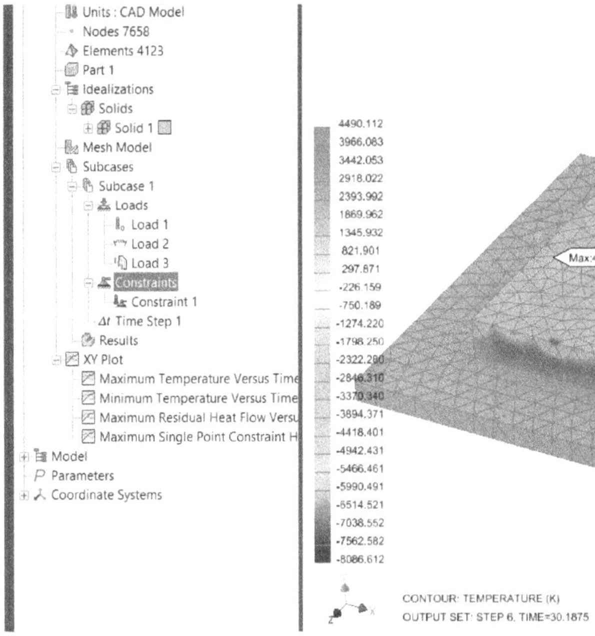

Figure-8. Result of nonlinear transient heat transfer analysis

Select desired time step from the **Results** drop-down in **Results** panel of **Ribbon**.

PRACTICE

Perform transient thermal analysis on the model with specified conditions as shown in Figure-9.

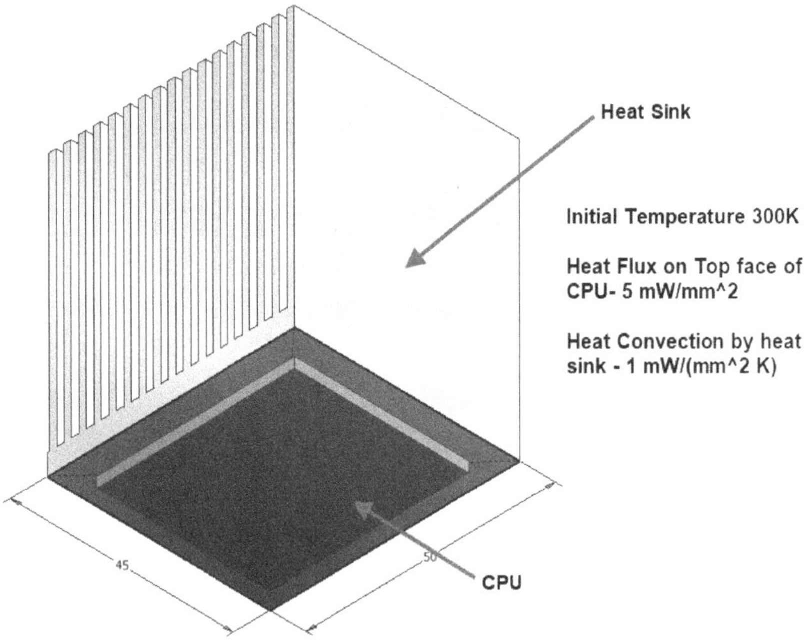

Figure-9. Model for Practice

PROBLEM 1

A metal sphere of diameter d = 35 mm is initially at temperature Ti = 700 K. At t=0, the sphere is placed in a fluid environment that has properties of $T\infty$ = 300 K and h = 50 W/m2-K. The properties of the steel are k = 35 W/m-K, ρ = 7500 kg/m3, and c = 550 J/kg-K. Find the surface temperature of the sphere after 500 seconds.

PROBLEM 2

A flanged pipe assembly; refer to Figure-10, made of plain carbon steel is subjected to both convective and conductive boundary conditions. Fluid inside the pipe is at a temperature of 130°C and has a convection coefficient of hi = 160 W/m^2-K. Air on the outside of the pipe is at 20°C and has a convection coefficient of ho = 70 W/m^2-K. The right and left ends of the pipe are at temperatures of 450°C and 80°C, respectively. There is a thermal resistance between the two flanges of 0.002 K-m^2/W. Use thermal analysis to analyze the pipe under both steady state and transient conditions.

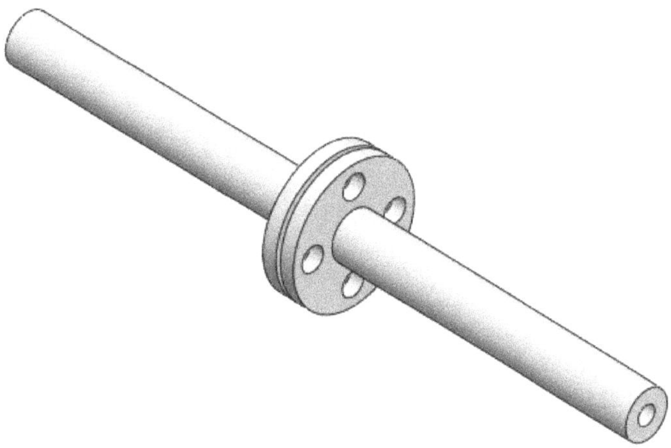

Figure-10. Flanged pipe assembly

SELF ASSESSMENT

Q1. Why is Heat Transfer Analysis performed?

Q2. How many types of analyses are available to perform Thermal Analyses? Describe them briefly.

Q3. In the **Analysis** dialog box, select the .... check box to generate heat flux as output on elements.

Q4. The Nonlinear steady state heat transfer analysis is performed when either .... of part changes with temperature or radiation is applied on the model.

Q5. In the **Analysis** dialog box, bonded option is used to perfectly transfer heat between assembled components. (True/False)

Q6. Nonlinear transient heat transfer analysis is performed to check heat distribution at different time steps. (True/False)

Q7. The amount of heat transferred by radiation is directly related to

A. The Stefan-Boltzmann constant
B. The surface temperature
C. The emissivity of the material
D. All of the above

Q8. If no heat is transferred to or from a surface, it is referred to as

A. Isothermal
B. Exothermal
C. Adiabatic
D. Isobaric

Q9. When all temperatures are in equilibrium, the problem is assumed to be

A. Transient
B. Steady-State
C. Laminar
D. None of the above

Q10. Which of the following terms is not part of the energy balance for heat transfer?

A. Generated energy
B. Stored energy
C. Energy into the system
D. Energy destroyed

Q11. Which of the following heat transfer mechanisms does not require a medium?

A. Conduction
B. Convection
C. Radiation
D. None of the above

Q12. What is the unit of the heat transfer coefficient used in convection?

A. J/kg.K
B. $W/m^2.K$
C. W/m.K
D. J/m^3

Q13. In conduction, heat is transferred through

A. Radiated waves in space
B. Flowing fluids
C. Interaction of atoms or molecules
D. Thermal energy generation

Q14. The formula Qconvection = hA(Ts-Tf) describes heat transfer through

A. Radiation
B. Conduction
C. Convection
D. Generation

Q15. Emissivity is

A. The ratio of heat transferred through convection
B. The rate of energy radiation in a material
C. A unit-based quantity used in thermal analysis
D. The measure of a material's ability to radiate heat

Q16. Which of the following Autodesk Inventor Nastran analyses should be used when thermal conductivity changes with temperature?

A. Linear Steady State Heat Transfer
B. Nonlinear Steady State Heat Transfer
C. Nonlinear Transient Heat Transfer
D. None of the above

Q17. Which heat transfer analysis is appropriate for observing temperature changes over time?

A. Linear Steady State
B. Nonlinear Steady State
C. Nonlinear Transient
D. Static Load

Q18. The Bulk Temperature (Tb) refers to

A. The temperature of the solid material
B. The average temperature of atoms
C. The fluid temperature surrounding the material
D. A fixed temperature in equilibrium

Q19. A perfect black body has an emissivity value of

A. 0
B. 0.5
C. 1
D. Less than 1

For Student Notes

Chapter 12

Explicit Analyses

Topics Covered

The major topics covered in this chapter are:

- ***Introduction***
- ***Performing Explicit Dynamics Analysis***
- ***Performing Explicit Quasi-Static Analysis***

INTRODUCTION

The Explicit dynamics analysis is performed when severe load is applied on the model for very short time (in milli- or micro-seconds) causing large deformation. Some of the examples where you should use explicit dynamic analyses are crash testing, metal forming, drop testing, explosion, on sports equipment, and so on.

The Explicit quasi-static analysis is used to analyze linear or nonlinear problems with time-dependent material changes like swelling in material, creep, viscoelasticity, and so on. The load is applied very slowing on the structure and the structure also deforms slowly. Note that effect of inertia is neglected for this analysis. The procedures to apply these analyses are discussed next.

PERFORMING EXPLICIT DYNAMICS ANALYSIS

The procedure to perform explicit dynamics analysis is given next.

- Open the model on which you want to perform explicit dynamics analysis and start Autodesk Inventor Nastran environment.
- Click on the **Edit** button from the **Analysis** panel in the **Autodesk Inventor Nastran** tab of **Ribbon**. The **Analysis** dialog box will be displayed.
- Select the **Explicit Dynamics** option from the **Type** drop-down and set other parameters as desired.
- Click on the **OK** button from the dialog box.
- Click on the **Materials** tool from the **Prepare** panel in the **Autodesk Inventor Nastran** tab of **Ribbon**. The **Material** dialog box will be displayed. (In this case, we are going to use special material from loaded material database generally found in C:\Program Files\Autodesk\Inventor Nastran 20xx\In-CAD\Materials folder). Click on the **Select Material** button from the dialog box. The **Material DB** dialog box will be displayed.
- Click on the **Load Database** button in the dialog box and select the nastran material database file as shown in Figure-1.

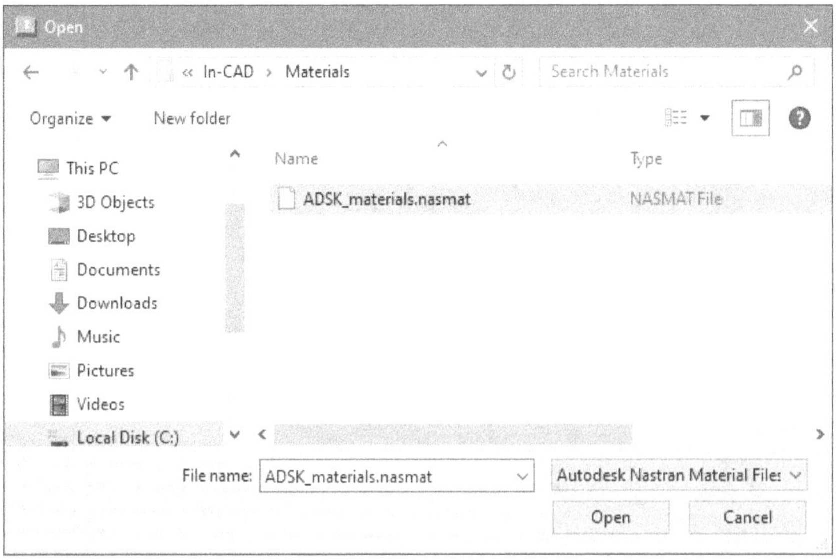

Figure-1. Nastran material database file

- Click on the **Open** button from the dialog box. The options in **Material DB** dialog box will be displayed as shown in Figure-2.

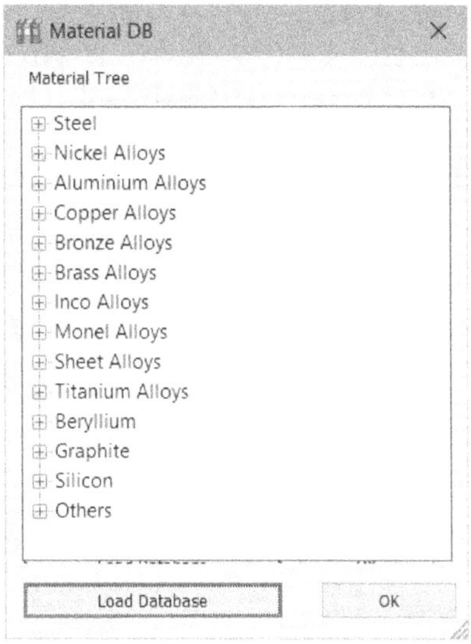

Figure-2. Nastran materials

- Select desired material from the dialog box (AISI Carbon Steel 1015 Hot Rolled in our case) and click on the **OK** button. The material will be selected for idealization. Click on the **OK** button from the **Material** dialog box.

Applying Shell Idealization

- Right-click on **Solid 1** from **Solids** node in **Idealizations** category and click on the **Edit** option from the shortcut menu. The **Idealizations** dialog box will be displayed. Note that your component is a flat object with same thickness then you can convert solid object idealization to shell.
- Select the **Shell Elements** option from the **Type** drop-down and specify desired thickness for shell element; refer to Figure-3.

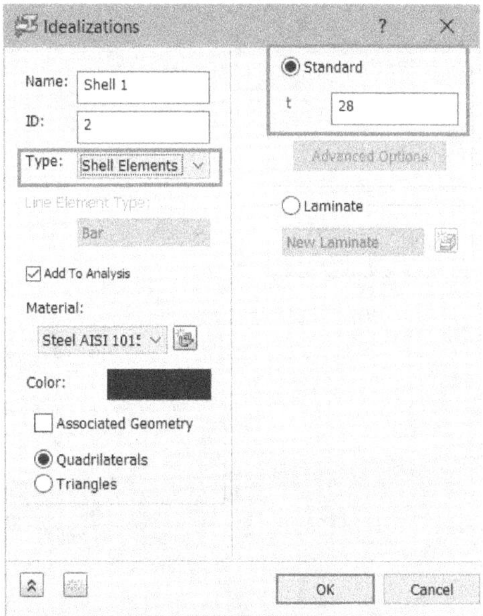

Figure-3. Specifying shell idealization

- Select desired element type whether quadrilaterals or triangles, and click on the **OK** button.
- Click on the **Constraints** tool from the **Setup** panel in the **Autodesk Inventor Nastran** tab of **Ribbon** and apply desired constraints.

Applying Impulse Load

- Click on the **Loads** tool from the **Setup** panel of **Autodesk Inventor Nastran** tab in the **Ribbon**. The **Load** dialog box will be displayed.
- Set the parameters as desired in the dialog box and click on the **Define New Table** button from **Transient Table Data** area of the dialog box. The **Table Data** dialog box will be displayed.
- For an impulsive load, the load should be applied for a small instance of time and then it should be zero. So, specify the parameters accordingly in the table; refer to Figure-4.

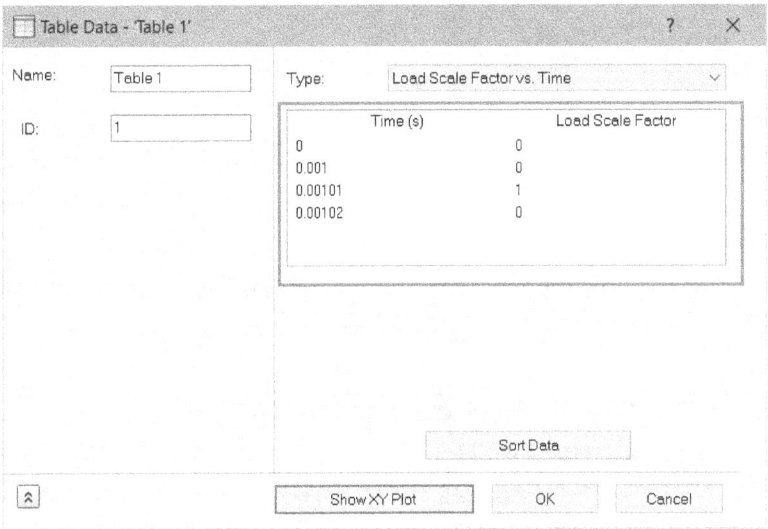

Figure-4. Table data specified

- Click on the **Show XY Plot** button from the dialog box to make sure the load is impulsive; refer to Figure-5.

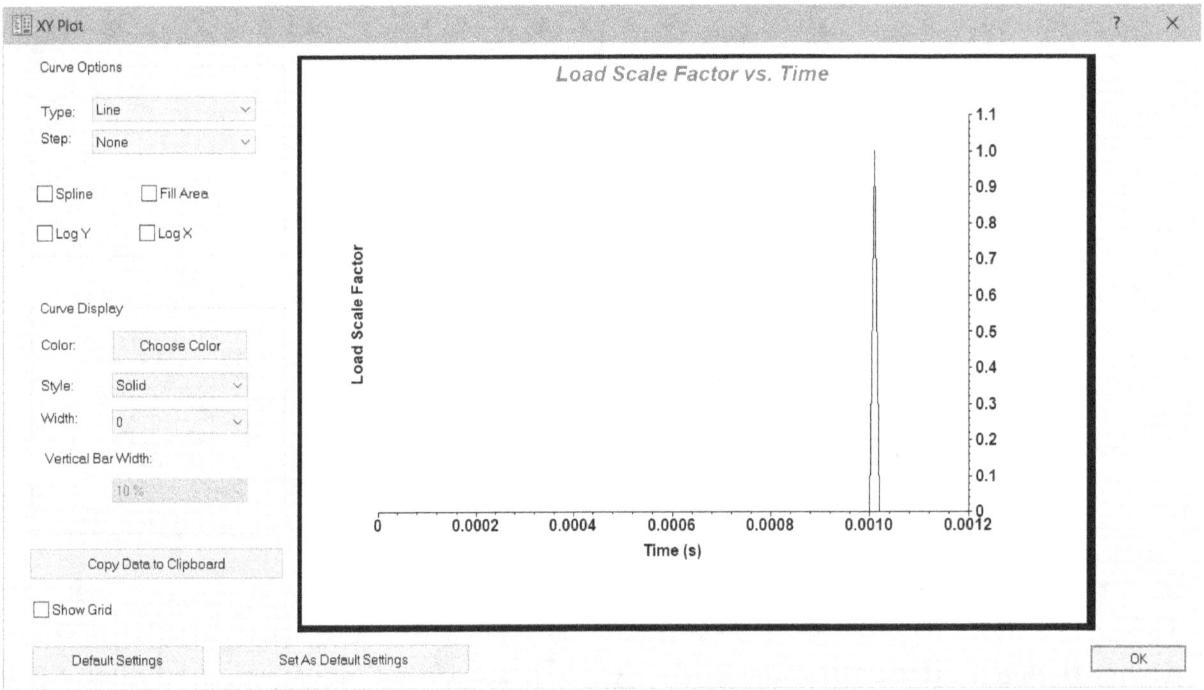

Figure-5. XY plot for impulsive load

- Click on the **OK** button from the **XY Plot** and then **Table Data** dialog boxes to apply the parameters.

- Specify the other parameters as desired in the **Load** dialog box; refer to Figure-6 and click on the **OK** button.

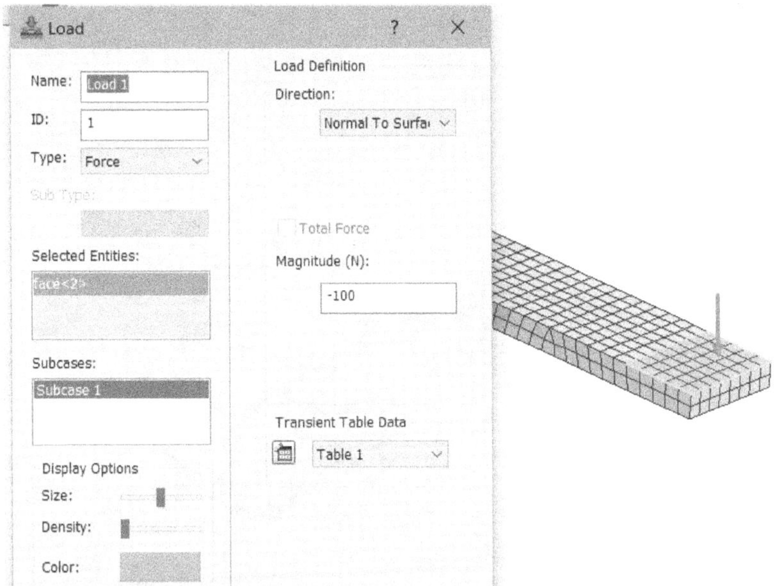

Figure-6. Applying impulsive load

- Click on the **Mesh Settings** button from the **Mesh** panel in the **Autodesk Inventor Nastran** tab in the **Ribbon**. The **Mesh Settings** dialog box will be displayed.
- Select the **Linear** option from the **Element Order** drop-down because we are using shell elements and **Parabolic** option is available only for solids in case of explicit analyses. Set the other parameters as desired and click on the **Generate Mesh** button.
- Click on the **OK** button from the dialog box to exit.
- Double-click on the **Dynamic Setup 1** option from the **Subcase** node. The **Dynamic Setup** dialog box will be displayed.
- Set the time duration, interval and other parameters for dynamic study; refer to Figure-7.

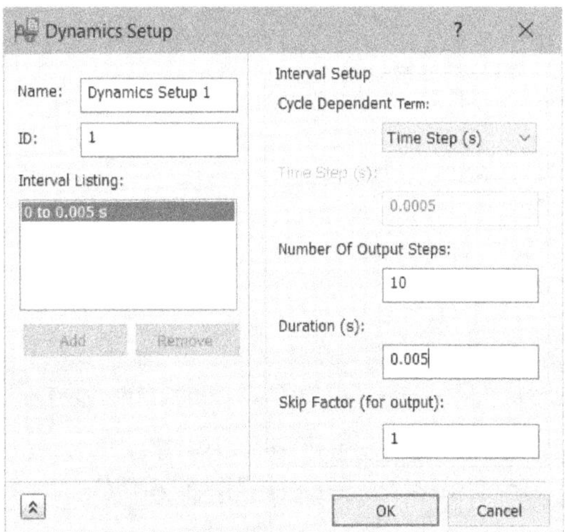

Figure-7. Dynamics Setup dialog box

- Click on the **OK** button from the dialog box to apply settings.
- Click on the **Run** tool from the **Solve** panel in the **Autodesk Inventor Nastran** tab of **Ribbon**. The result will be displayed.

- Select desired time point at which you want to check the results from the **Results** drop-down in the **Results** panel of **Ribbon**; refer to Figure-8.

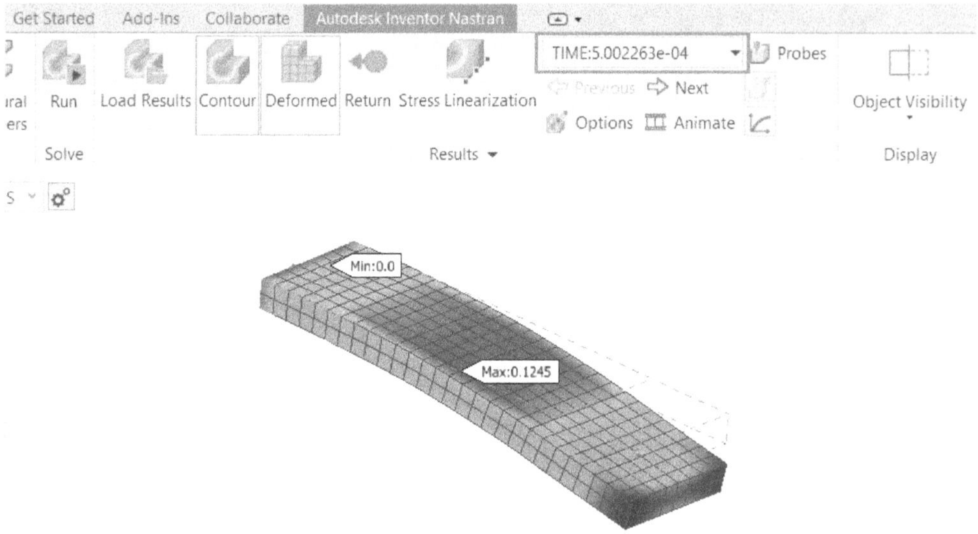

Figure-8. Time point selected for result

PERFORMING EXPLICIT QUASI-STATIC ANALYSIS

The procedure to perform a quasi-static analysis is given next.

- Click on the **New** tool from the **Analysis** panel in the **Autodesk Inventor Nastran** tab of **Ribbon**. The **Analysis** dialog box will be displayed.
- Select the **Explicit Quasi-Static** option from the **Type** drop-down and set the other parameters as desired; refer to Figure-9.

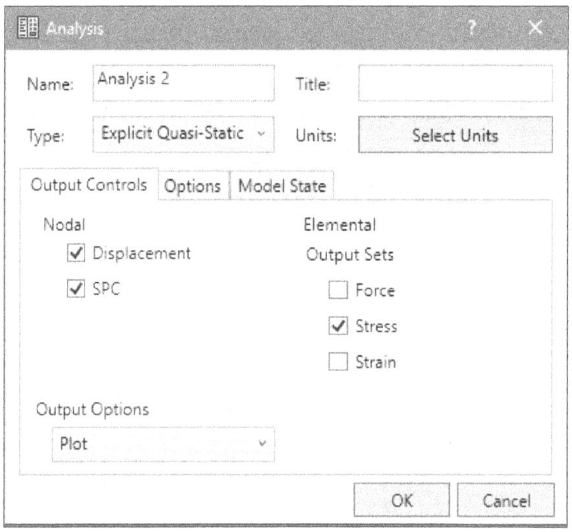

Figure-9. Options for explicit quasi-static analysis

- Click on the **OK** button from the dialog box. The parameters of analysis will be displayed in the **Model Browser**; refer to Figure-10.

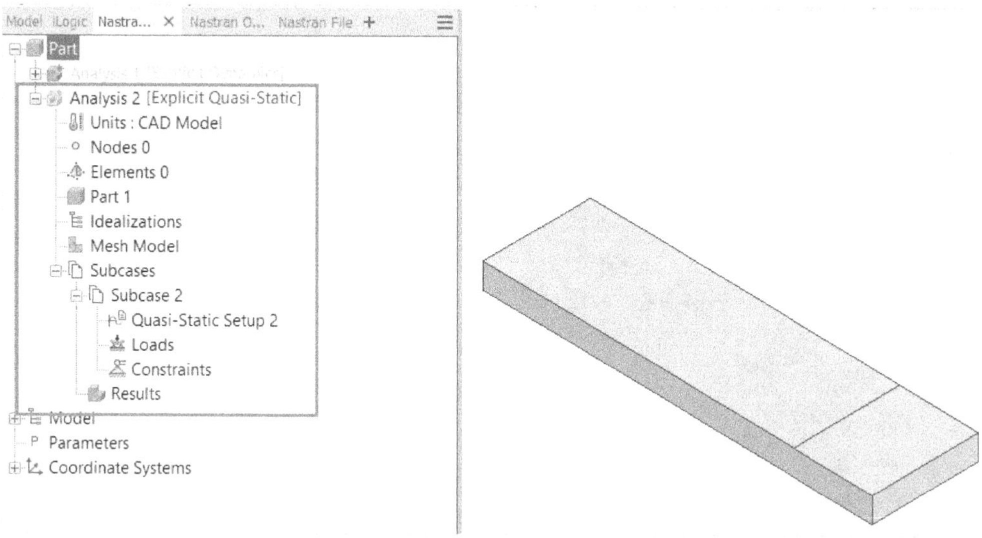

Figure-10. Parameters for explicit quasi-static analysis

- Double-click on **Quasi-Static Setup** option from the **Subcase** node in the **Model Browser**. The **Quasi-Static Setup** dialog box will be displayed; refer to Figure-11.

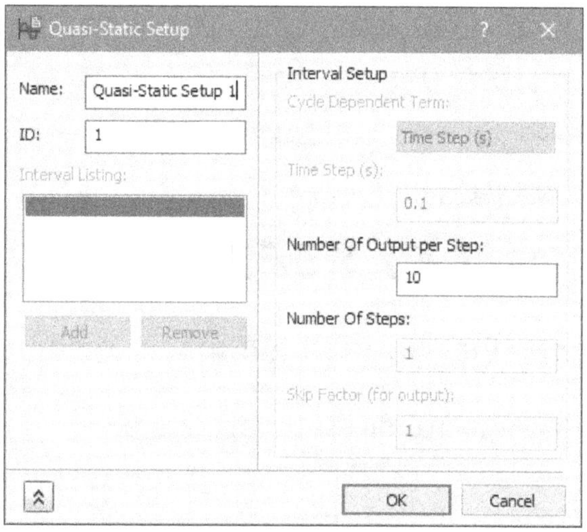

Figure-11. Quasi-Static Setup dialog box

- Set desired time period with time steps in the dialog box and click on the **OK** button.
- Set the other parameters as desired and click on the **Run** button to perform the analysis.

PRACTICE

In this practice, you will run the same study which we discussed earlier for Non-linear analysis in Chapter 3 but now you will use Explicit analysis to solve it; refer to Figure-12.

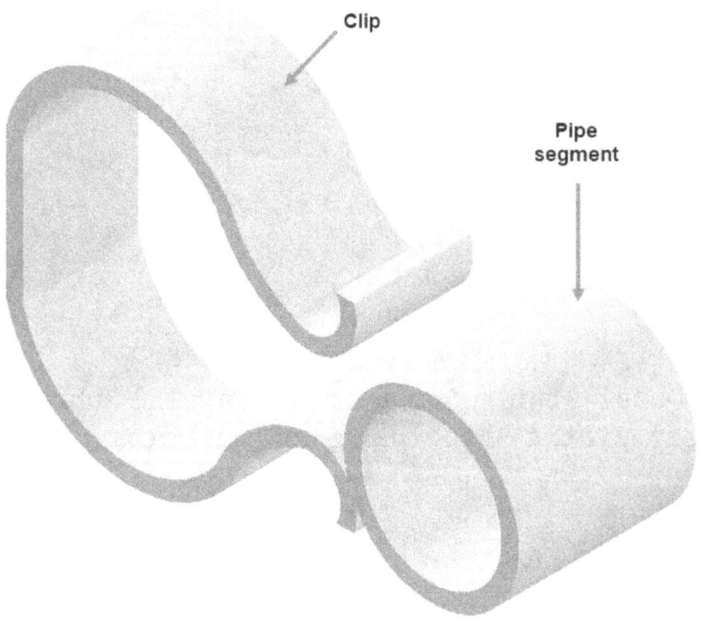

Figure-12. Nonlinear analysis model

SELF ASSESSMENT

Q1. Describe the conditions for performing Explicit dynamics analysis.

Q2. What is the use of Explicit quasi-static analysis?

Q3. In the **Load** dialog box, for an ...., the load should be applied for a small instance of time.

Q4. In the **Table Data** dialog box, click on the .... button to make sure the load is impulsive.

Q5. In the **Mesh Settings** dialog box, **Parabolic** option is available for both solids and shell elements. (True/False)

Q6. What is the primary condition that necessitates the use of explicit dynamics analysis?

A. Long duration and slow deformation
B. Sudden loads with large deformation over short time
C. Constant load application over time
D. Small deformation due to thermal expansion

Q7. Which of the following is not typically analyzed using explicit dynamic analysis?

A. Crash testing
B. Metal forming
C. Explosion simulations
D. Thermal conductivity

Q8. What is neglected in explicit quasi-static analysis?

A. Material properties
B. Deformation
C. Inertia effects
D. Load magnitude

Q9. During the material selection process for explicit dynamics, which action loads the material database?

A. Click on Show XY Plot
B. Select Shell Elements
C. Click on Load Database
D. Click on Define New Table

Q10. What must be selected when idealizing a flat component for shell elements?

A. Solid Elements with zero thickness
B. Shell Elements with specified thickness
C. Beam Elements
D. Thermal Elements

Q11. What kind of load is defined using a table that peaks quickly and returns to zero?

A. Constant Load
B. Static Load
C. Impulsive Load
D. Thermal Load

For Student Notes

Chapter 13

Fundamentals of FEA and Nastran

Topics Covered

The major topics covered in this chapter are:

- ***Introduction to FEA***
- ***General Description of FEA***
- ***Solving a problem with FEA***
- ***FEA V/s Classical Methods***
- ***FEA V/s Finite Different Method***
- ***Need for Studying FEM***
- ***Refining Mesh***
- ***Higher order element V/s Refined Mesh***
- ***FEA in Nastran***

INTRODUCTION

The finite element analysis is a numerical technique. In this method, all the complexities of the problems like varying shape, boundary conditions, and loads are maintained as they are but the solutions obtained are approximate. Because of its diversity and flexibility as an analysis tool, it is receiving much attention in engineering. The fast improvements in computer hardware technology and slashing of cost of computers have boosted this method, since the computer is the basic need for the application of this method. A number of popular brand of finite element analysis packages are now available commercially. Some of the popular packages are SolidWorks Simulation, NASTRAN, NISA, and ANSYS. Using these packages, one can analyze several complex structures.

The finite element analysis originated as a method of stress analysis in the design of aircraft. It started as an extension of matrix method of structural analysis. Today this method is used not only for the analysis in solid mechanics, but even in the analysis of fluid flow, heat transfer,electric and magnetic fields and many others. Civil engineers use this method extensively for the analysis of beams, space frames, plates, shells, folded plates, foundations, rock mechanics problems and seepage analysis of fluid through porous media. Both static and dynamic problems can be handled by finite element analysis. This method is used extensively for the analysis and design of ships, aircraft, space crafts, electric motors, and heat engines.

GENERAL DESCRIPTION OF THE METHOD

In engineering problems, there are some basic unknowns. If they are found, the behavior of the entire structure can be predicted. The basic unknowns or the field variables which are encountered in the engineering problems are displacements in solid mechanics, velocities in fluid mechanics, electric and magnetic potentials in electrical engineering, and temperatures in heat flow problems.

In a continuum, these unknowns are infinite. The finite element procedure reduces such unknowns to a finite number by dividing the solution region into small parts called elements and by expressing the unknown field variables in terms of assumed approximating functions (Interpolating functions/Shape functions) within each element. The approximating functions are defined in terms of field variables of specified points called nodes or nodal points. Thus in the finite element analysis, the unknowns are the field variables of the nodal points. Once these are found the field variables at any point can be found by using interpolation functions.

After selecting elements and nodal unknowns next step in finite element analysis is to assemble element properties for each element. For example, in solid mechanics, we have to find the force-displacement i.e. stiffness characteristics of each individual element. Mathematically this relationship is of the form

$$[k]_e \{\delta\}_e = \{F\}_e$$

where $[k]_e$ is element stiffness matrix, $\{\delta\}_e$ is nodal displacement vector of the element and $\{F\}_e$ is nodal force vector. The element of stiffness matrix k_{ij} represent the force in coordinate direction 'i' due to a unit displacement in coordinate direction 'j'. Four methods are available for formulating these element properties viz. direct approach, variational approach, weighted residual approach and energy balance approach. Any one of these methods can be used for assembling element properties. In solid mechanics variational approach is commonly employed to assemble stiffness matrix and nodal force vector (consistent loads).

Element properties are used to assemble global properties/structure properties to get system equations $[k] \{\delta\} = \{F\}$. Then the boundary conditions are imposed. The solution of these simultaneous equations give the nodal unknowns. Using these nodal values additional calculations are made to get the required values e.g. stresses, strains, moments, etc. in solid mechanics problems.

Thus the various steps involved in the finite element analysis are:
(i) Select suitable field variables and the elements.
(ii) Discretize the continua.
(iii) Select interpolation functions.
(iv) Find the element properties.
(v) Assemble element properties to get global properties.
(vi) Impose the boundary conditions.
(vii) Solve the system equations to get the nodal unknowns.
(viii) Make the additional calculations to get the required values.

A BRIEF EXPLANATION OF FEA FOR A STRESS ANALYSIS PROBLEM

The steps involved in finite element analysis are clarified by taking the stress analysis of a tension strip with fillets (refer Figure-1). In this problem stress concentration is to be studies in the fillet zone. Since the problem is having symmetry about both x and y axes, only one quarter of the tension strip may be considered as shown in Figure-2. About the symmetric axes, transverse displacements of all nodes are to be made zero. The various steps involved in the finite element analysis of this problem are discussed below:

Step 1: Four noded isoparametric element is selected for the analysis (However note that 8 noded isoparametric element is ideal for this analysis). The four noded iso-parametric element can take quadrilateral shape also as required for elements 12, 15, 18, etc. As there is no bending of strip, only displacement continuity is to be ensured but not the slope continuity. Hence displacements of nodes in x and y directions are taken as basic unknowns in the problem.

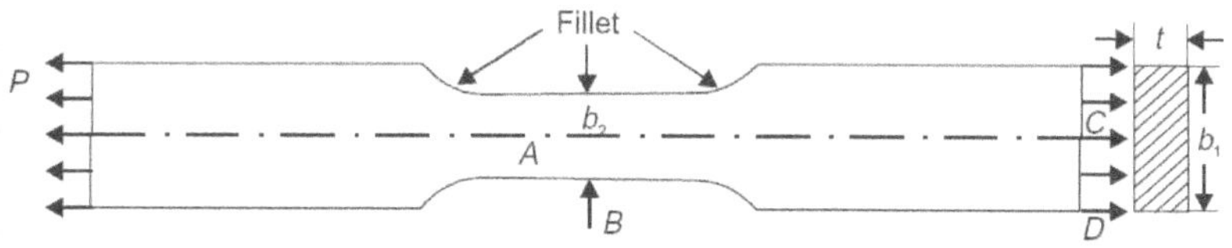

Figure-1. Tension Strip with Fillet

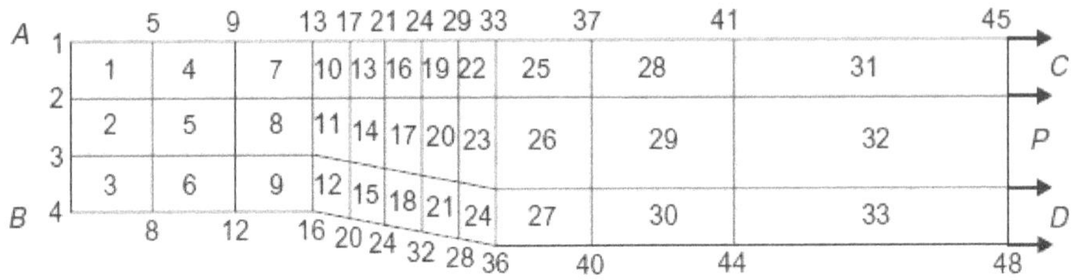

Figure-2. Descritization of quater of tension strip

Step 2: The portion to be analyzed is to be discretized. Figure-2 shows discretized portion. For this 33 elements have been used. There are 48 nodes. At each node unknowns are x and y components of displacements. Hence in this problem total unknowns (displacements) to be determined are 48 × 2 = 96.

Step 3: The displacement of any point inside the element is approximated by suitable functions in terms of the nodal displacements of the element. For the typical element, displacements at P are

$$u = \Sigma N_i u_i = N_1 u_1 + N_2 u_2 + N_3 u_3 + N_4 u_4$$

and

$$v = \Sigma N_i v_i = N_1 v_1 + N_2 v_2 + N_3 v_3 + N_4 v_4 \quad \ldots(1.2)$$

The approximating functions N_i are called shape functions or interpolation functions. Usually they are derived using polynomials.

Step 4: Now the stiffness characters and consistent loads are to be found for each element. There are four nodes and at each node degree of freedom is 2. Hence degree of freedom in each element is 4 × 2 = 8. The relationship between the nodal displacements and nodal forces is called element stiffness characteristics. It is of the form

$[k]_e \{\delta\}_e = \{F\}_e$, as explained earlier.

For the element under consideration, k_e is 8 × 8 matrix and δ_e and F_e are vectors of 8 values. In solid mechanics element stiffness matrix is assembled using variational approach i.e. by minimizing potential energy.
If the load is acting in the body of element or on the surface of element, its equivalent at nodal points are to be found using variational approach, so that right hand side of the above expression is assembled. This process is called finding consistent loads.

Step 5: The structure is having 48 × 2 = 96 displacement and load vector components to be determined.

Hence global stiffness equation is of the form

$$\underset{96 \times 96}{[k]} \quad \underset{96 \times 1}{\{\delta\}} = \underset{96 \times 1}{\{F\}}$$

Each element stiffness matrix is to be placed in the global stiffness matrix appropriately. This process is called assembling global stiffness matrix. In this problem force vector F is zero at all nodes except at nodes 45, 46, 47 and 48 in x direction. For the given loading nodal equivalent forces are found and the force vector F is assembled.

Step 6: In this problem, due to symmetry transverse displacements along AB and BC are zero. The system equation [k] {δ } = {F} is modified to see that the solution for {δ} comes out with the above values. This modification of system equation is called imposing the boundary conditions.

Step 7: The above 96 simultaneous equations are solved using the standard numerical procedures like Gauss elimination or Choleski's decomposition techniques to get the 96 nodal displacements.

Step 8: Now the interest of the analyst is to study the stresses at various points. In solid mechanics the relationship between the displacements and stresses are well established. The stresses at various points of interest may be found by using shape functions and the nodal displacements and then stresses calculated. The stress concentrations may be studies by comparing the values obtained at various points in the fillet zone with the values at uniform zone, far away from the fillet (which is equal to P/b_2t).

FINITE ELEMENT METHOD V/S CLASSICAL METHODS

1. In classical methods exact equations are formed and exact solutions are obtained where as in finite element analysis exact equations are formed but approximate solutions are obtained.

2. Solutions have been obtained for few standard cases by classical methods, where as solutions can be obtained for all problems by finite element analysis.

3. Whenever the following complexities are faced, classical method makes the drastic assumptions' and looks for the solutions:
(a) Shape
(b) Boundary conditions
(c) Loading

Figure-3 shows such cases in the analysis of slabs (plates).
To get the solution in the above cases, rectangular shapes, same boundary condition along a side and regular equivalent loads are to be assumed. In FEM no such assumptions are made. The problem is treated as it is.

4. When material property is not isotropic, solutions for the problems become very difficult in classical method. Only few simple cases have been tried successfully by researchers. FEM can handle structures with anisotropic properties also without any difficulty.

5. If structure consists of more than one material, it is difficult to use classical method, but finite element can be used without any difficulty.

6. Problems with material and geometric non-linearities can not be handled by classical methods. There is no difficulty in FEM.

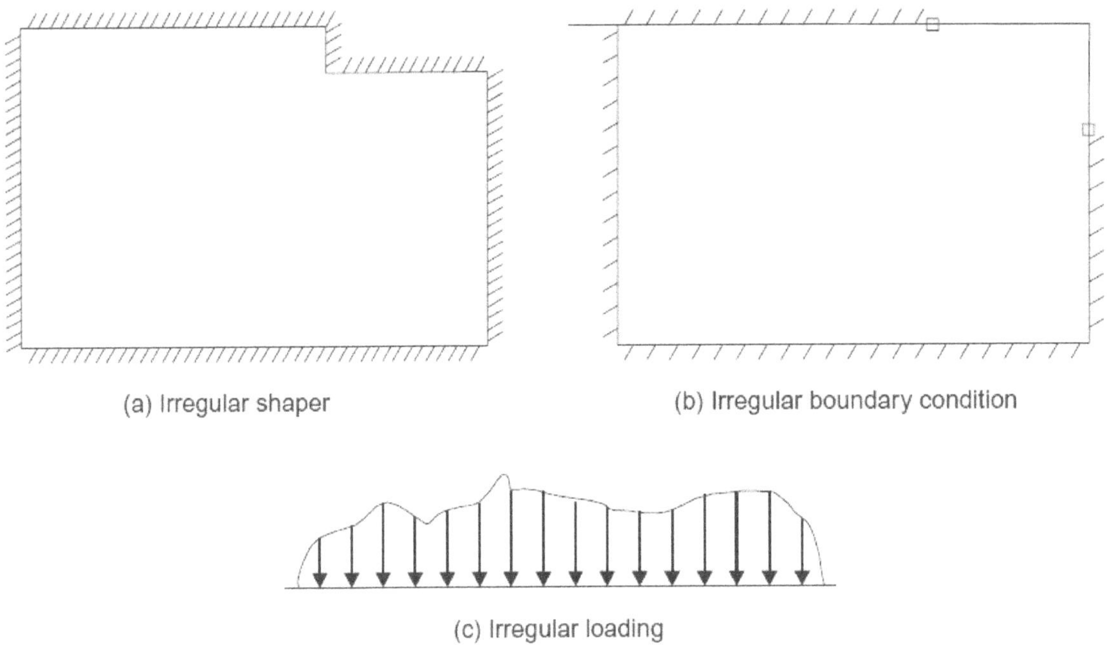

Figure-3. Analysis of slab

Hence, FEM is superior to the classical methods only for the problems involving a number of complexities which cannot be handled by classical methods without making drastic assumptions. For all regular problems, the solutions by classical methods are the best solutions. In fact, to check the validity of the FEM programs developed, the FEM solutions are compared with the solutions by classical methods for standard problems.

FEM VS FINITE DIFFERENCE METHOD (FDM)

1. FDM makes point wise approximation to the governing equations i.e. it ensures continuity only at the node points. Continuity along the sides of grid lines are not ensured. FEM make piecewise approximation i.e. it ensures the continuity at node points as well as along the sides of the element.

2. FDM do not give the values at any point except at node points. It do not give any approximating function to evaluate the basic values (deflections, in case of solid mechanics) using the nodal values. FEM can give the values at any point. However the values obtained at points other than nodes are by using suitable interpolation formulae.

3. FDM makes stair type approximation to sloping and curved boundaries as shown in Figure-4. FEM can consider the sloping boundaries exactly. If curved elements are used, even the curved boundaries can be handled exactly.

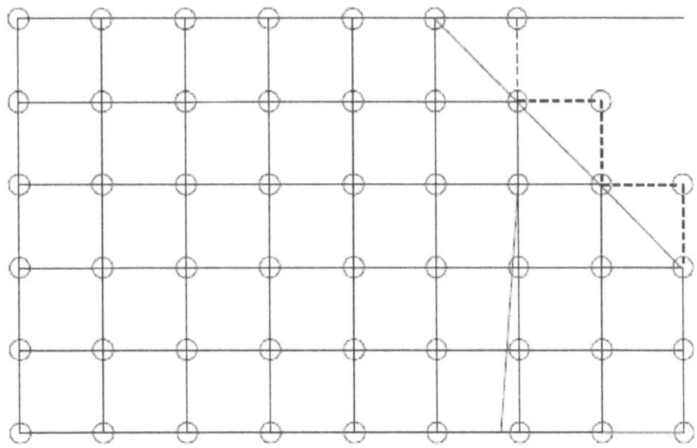

Figure-4. FDM approximation of shape

4. FDM needs larger number of nodes to get good results while FEM needs fewer nodes.

5. With FDM fairly complicated problems can be handled where as FEM can handle all complicated problems.

NEED FOR STUDYING FEA

Now, a number of users friendly packages are available in the market. Hence one may ask the question 'What is the need to study FEA?'.

The finite element knowledge makes a good engineer better while just user without the knowledge of FEA may produce more dangerous results. To use the FEA packages properly, the user must know the following points clearly:

1. Which elements are to be used for solving the problem in hand.
2. How to discretize to get good results.
3. How to introduce boundary conditions properly.
4. How the element properties are developed and what are their limitations.
5. How the displays are developed in pre and post processor to understand their limitations.
6. To understand the difficulties involved in the development of FEA programs and hence the need for checking the commercially available packages with the results of standard cases.

Unless user has the background of FEA, he may produce worst results and may go with overconfidence. Hence, it is necessary that the users of FEA package should have sound knowledge of FEA.

Warning To FEA Package Users

When hand calculations are made, the designer always gets the feel of the structure and get rough idea about the expected results. This aspect cannot be ignored by any designer, whatever be the reliability of the program, a complex problem may be simplified with drastic assumptions and FEA results obtained. Check whether expected trend of the result is obtained. Then avoid drastic assumptions and get more refined results with FEA package. User must remember that structural behavior is not dictated by the computer programs. Hence, the designer should develop feel of the structure and make use of the programs to get numerical results which are close to structural behavior.

One of the main concern for using FEA applications is selection of elements, in other words discretization. The process of modeling a structure using suitable number, shape, and size of the elements is called discretization. The modeling should be good enough to get the results as close to actual behavior of the structure as possible.

In a structure, we come across the following types of discontinuities:

(a) Geometric
(b) Load
(c) Boundary conditions
(d) Material.

Geometric Discontinuities

Wherever there is sudden change in shape and size of the structure there should be a node or line of nodes. Figure-5 shows some of such situations.

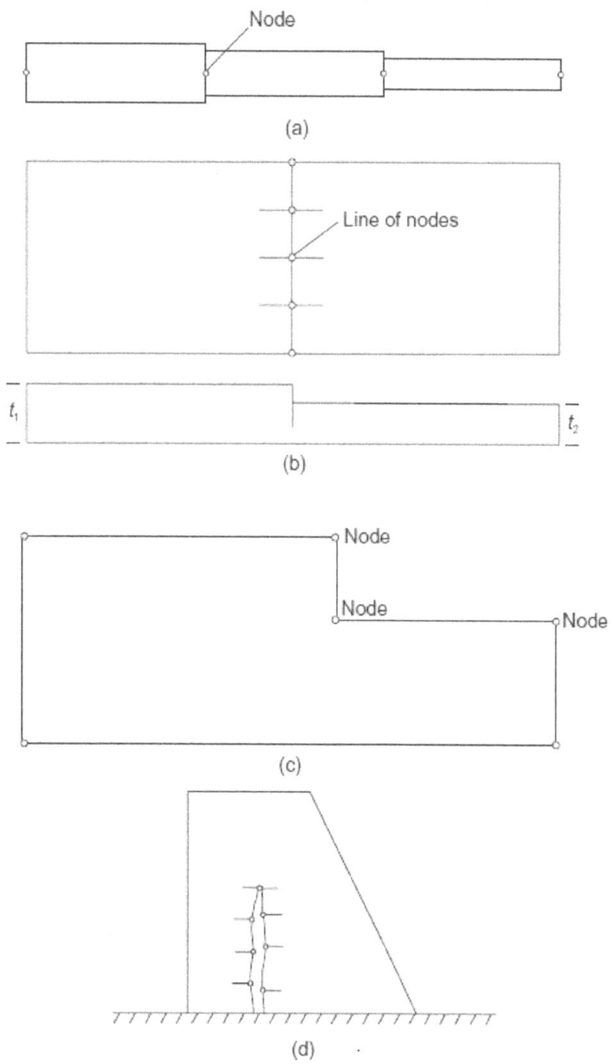

Figure-5. Geometric Discontinuity in the part

Discontinuity of Loads

Concentrated loads and sudden change in the intensity of uniformly distributed loads are the sources of discontinuity of loads. A node or a line of nodes should be there to model the structure. Some of these situations are shown in Figure-6.

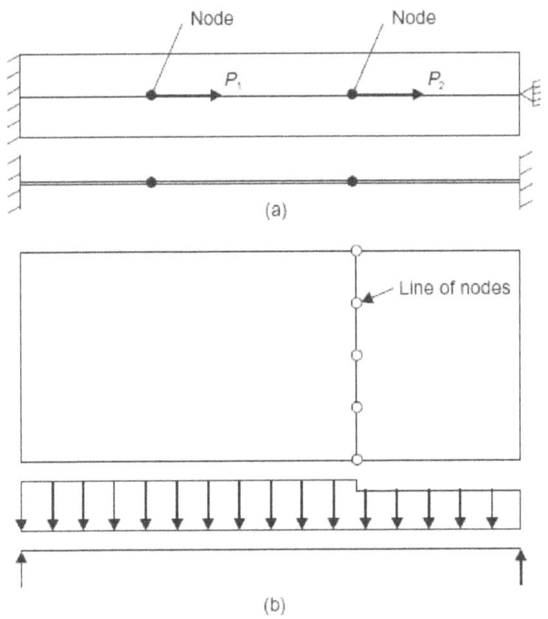

Figure-6. FEM Model and slab with different UDL

Discontinuity of Boundary conditions

If the boundary condition for a structure suddenly change then we need to discretize such that there is node or a line of nodes. This type of situations are shown in Figure-7.

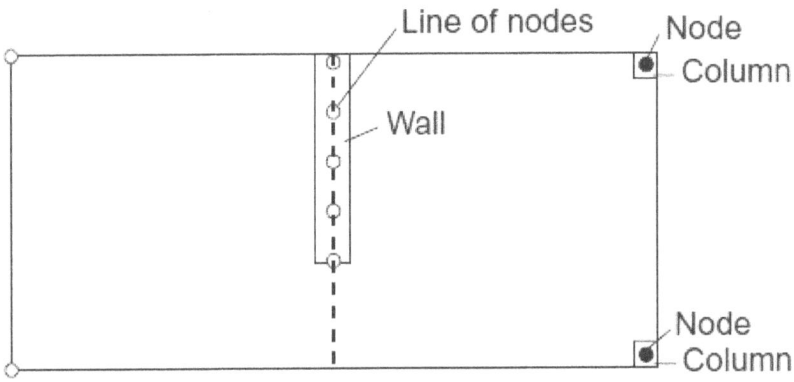

Figure-7. Slab with intermediate wall and columns

Material Discontinuity

Node or node lines should appear at the places where material discontinuity is seen; refer to Figure-8.

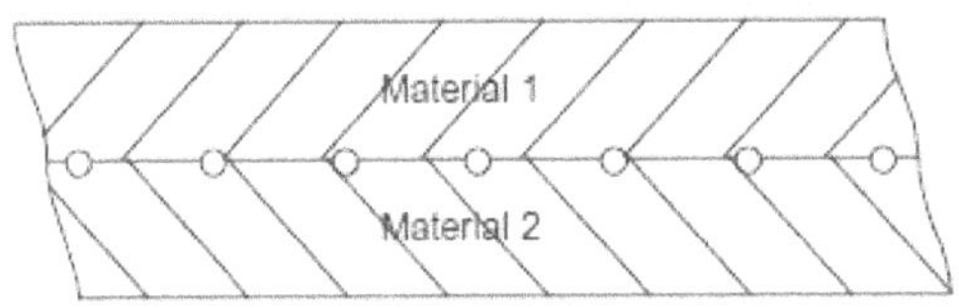

Figure-8. Material Discontinuity

REFINING MESH

To get better results the finite element mesh should be refined in the following situations:

(a) To approximate curved boundary of the structure
(b) At the places of high stress gradients.

Such a situation is shown in Figure-9.

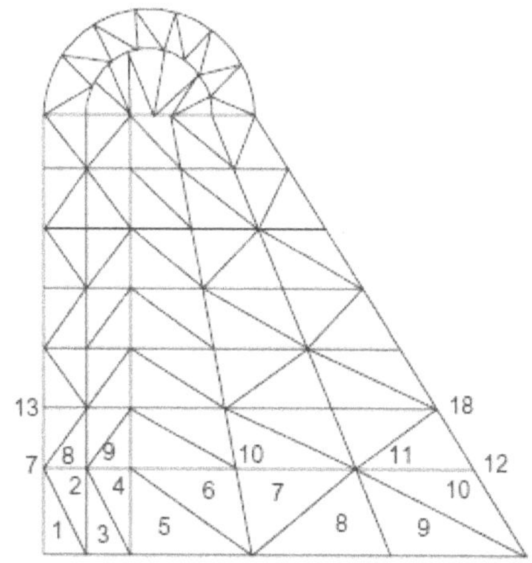

Figure-9. Refined mesh near curved boundary

Use Of Symmetry

Wherever there is symmetry in the problem, it should be made use. By doing so, lot of memory requirement is reduced or in other words we can use more elements (refined mesh) for the same capacity of computer memory. When symmetry is to be used, it is to be noted that at right angles to the line of symmetry displacement is zero.

HIGHER ORDER ELEMENTS V/S REFINED MESH

Accuracy of calculation increases if higher order elements are used. Accuracy can also be increased by using more number of elements. Limitation on use of number of elements comes from the total degrees of freedom the computer can handle. The limitation may be due to cost of computation time also. Hence to use higher order elements, we have to use less number of such elements. The question arises whether to use less number of higher order elements or more number of lower order elements for the same total degree of freedom. There are some studies in this matter keeping degree of accuracy per unit cost as the selection criteria. However the cost of calculation is coming down so much that such studies are not relevant today. Accuracy alone should be selection criteria which may be carried out initially on the simplified problem and based on it element may be selected for detailed study.

FEA IN NASTRAN

Earlier in this chapter, you have learned about how FEA works using mathematical formulae. When you solve any analysis in Inventor Nastran, the software follows a fixed pattern as shown by flowchart in Figure-10.

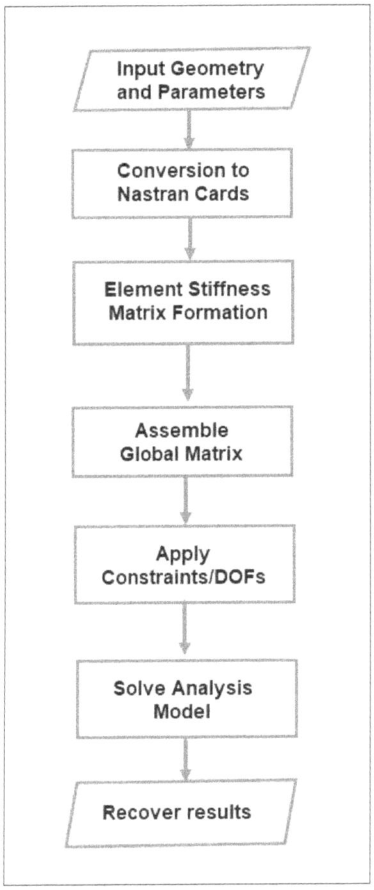

Figure-10. Nastran workflow

As the flowchart shows, all the geometric (1D, 2D, or 3D model) and various analysis related parameters like Modulus of elasticity, force value, torque value, etc. are converted into Nastran input entries called cards recognized by Nastran solver. Using the available parameters, element stiffness matrices are generated which act as input for Global Matrix solved by solver to each solution. Each of the steps involved in the process is discussed next.

Input Geometry and Parameters

This is the input step for Nastran solver. At this step, a specific set of information is collected by Nastran so that it can be later converted to Nastran cards. As you have seen through various chapters of this book earlier, you provide a 3D model with material properties which has loads and constraints defined as per the design problem. Any FEA solver that you encounter works on mathematical equations and not on graphics. Whatever 3D model you see on graphical screen is converted to elements and nodes by using various meshing techniques. This step is called discretization. These elements and nodes are collected as input for Nastran solver. It will collect various material properties like modulus of elasticity, thermal conductivity, electrical conductivity, and so on as input parameters depending on type of analysis to be solved. The load values and their types are also collected as input.

Conversion to Nastran Cards

At this step, all the geometric and design parameters are converted to Nastran cards. For example, nodes are converted to GRID, SPOINT, or EPOINT cards. There are various categories of Nastran cards which are discussed next.

Nodes

Nodes are points shared by various elements in the material. There are three cards available in Nastran to represent nodes. GRID, SPOINT, and EPOINT. GRID card is the primary node card used to represent standard structural node with 6 degree of freedom. SPOINT and EPOINT are special category node cards. SPOINT represents a scalar point with 1 DOF only. EPOINT represents extra node point for super elements or advanced cases.

Elements

Elements are used to define how the stiffness matrix will be formed for calculation. Various cards to represent structural elements are given in next table.

1D Elements (Line Elements)	
Card	**Description**
CROD	Simple axial rod (no bending)
CONROD	Rod with material defined directly
CBAR	Beam with bending + axial
CBEAM	Advanced beam (shear deformation included)
CBUSH	General spring/damper (6 DOF connection)
CELAS1–4	Scalar spring elements
2D Elements (Shell / Plate)	
Card	**Description**
CQUAD4	4-node shell (most common)
CQUAD8	8-node higher-order shell
CTRIA3	3-node triangular shell
CTRIA6	6-node higher-order triangle
CSHEAR	Shear panel element
3D Solid Elements	
Card	**Description**
CTETRA	Tetrahedral solid (4 or 10 node)
CHEXA	Hexahedral (brick) element
CPENTA	Wedge element
CPYRAM	Pyramid element

Various cards used to represent Mass are given next.

Mass Elements	
CONM1	Mass matrix
CONM2	Concentrated mass

Materials

These cards define the type of material and related properties in Nastran model.

Basic Structural Materials	
Card	**Description**
MAT1	Isotropic linear elastic (most common)
MAT2	Anisotropic (2D)
MAT8	Orthotropic (composites)
MAT9	Fully anisotropic (3D)
Thermal / Advanced	
Card	**Description**
MAT4	Thermal conductivity
MAT5	Thermal anisotropic
MATS1	Nonlinear material (plasticity)

Properties

The property cards define how elements use materials. They establish link between geometry and material.

1D Properties	
Card	**Description**
PROD	Rod property (area)
PBAR	Beam property
PBEAM	Advanced beam
PBUSH	Bush element property
2D Properties	
Card	**Description**
PSHELL	Shell thickness + material
PCOMP	Composite laminate
3D Properties	
Card	**Description**
PSOLID	Solid element property
Mass Properties	
Card	**Description**
PMASS	Mass property

Constraints/Boundary Conditions

The constraint cards define how structure is restricted when load is applied. Various cards used to define constraints are given next.

Basic Constraints (SPC)	
Card	**Description**
SPC	Single DOF constraint
SPC1	Multiple DOFs at once (most used)
SPCADD	Combine multiple SPC sets

Multi-Point Constraints (MPC)	
Card	**Description**
MPC	Equation-based constraint
MPCADD	Combine MPC sets
Advanced Constraint Types	
Card	**Description**
RBE2	Rigid body (independent → dependent nodes)
RBE3	Weighted interpolation (no artificial stiffness)
RBAR	Rigid connection
RSPLINE	Smooth constraint distribution

Loads

The load cards define different types of loads like Force, Moment, and so on in Nastran recognized terms.

Force Loads	
Card	**Description**
FORCE	Point force
FORCE1	Direction defined by nodes
FORCE2	Alternate directional input
Moment Loads	
Card	**Description**
MOMENT	Applied moment
MOMENT1, MOMENT2	Direction variations
Pressure Loads	
Card	**Description**
PLOAD	Pressure on surface
PLOAD2	Element-based pressure
PLOAD4	Most commonly used pressure load
Gravity / Acceleration	
Card	**Description**
GRAV	Gravity load
ACCEL	Acceleration load
Thermal Loads	
Card	**Description**
TEMP	Temperature at nodes
TEMPD	Default temperature
Load Combinations	
Card	**Description**
LOAD	Combine multiple loads
DLOAD	Dynamic loads

Element Stiffness Matrix Formation

At previous step, Nastran has converted geometry (nodes) into grids, it has assigned element type formed by nodes to appropriate category like CTETRA, CROD, etc. and similarly, other analysis parameters to respective cards in Nastran. At this step, Nastran combines these cards to form element stiffness matrix. An element stiffness matrix defines how much force is needed to move nodes of a specific element by given displacement. In equation form, it is given as:

$$\{F\}_e=[K]_e\{u\}_e$$

Where:

$[K]_e$ = **element stiffness matrix**
$\{u\}_e$ = nodal displacements
$\{F\}_e$ = nodal forces

The element stiffness matrix is formed using the equation:

$$[K]_e=\int B^T DB.dV$$

This equation combines the effect of deformation in element, what it is made of, and what is its total size. Here,

- B is the strain-displacement matrix which defines if a node moves then how does the element stretches or deforms. It depends on shape of element.
- B^T is the transpose of B matrix (rows become columns and columns become rows). It converts the deformation effects to forces. It is directly related to B matrix.
- D is material matrix and it defines if material is strained then how much stress develops in it. For 1D element like Rod, it is represented by E (Modulus of Elasticity). For 2D element, it is represented by 3x3 matrix and for 3d element, it is represented by 6x6 matrix. It depends on material type.
- $\int dV$ defines the integration of effect over volume for entire element. It depends on dimensions (1D, 2D, and 3D)

B (Strain-Displacement Matrix)

The Strain-Displacement matrix is calculated by formula **$\epsilon = B.u$**. Each term is discussed next.

Displacement

Assume that a node has moved by u_x, u_y, and u_z in X, Y, and Z directions, respectively. So **displacement** of node can be given as

$$u = \begin{bmatrix} u_x \\ u_y \\ u_z \end{bmatrix}$$

But in FEA, we also want to find out displacement at points in between the nodes. To do this, we use standard assumed functions called shape functions represented by N. Consider a case of 1D element where you want to find displacement u(x) as a function of x between two nodes Node 1 and Node 2; refer to Figure-11.

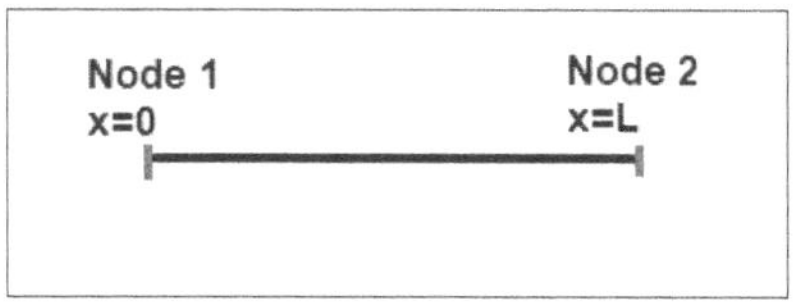

Figure-11. Nodes

Consider, u(x)=N1(x)u1+N2(x)u2

When x=0 then we are at node 1 and value of displacement u is u_1 so N1 becomes 1 and N2 becomes 0 to satisfy this condition.

When x=L then we are at node 2 and value of displacement is u2, so N1 becomes 0 and N2 becomes 1 to satisfy this condition.

If we assume that displacement varies linearly when going from Node 1 to Node 2 then

u(x)=a+bx

at x = 0, u(x) = u1 = a

at x= L, u(x) = u2 = a+bL = u1+bL

on rewriting this equation; b = (u2-u1)/L

which gives,

$$u(x) = u_1 + \frac{x}{L}(u_2 - u_1) \longrightarrow u(x) = \left(1 - \frac{x}{L}\right) u_1 + \left(\frac{x}{L}\right) u_2$$

Comparing it to our previous equation of u(x), we can say that

$$N_1 = 1 - \frac{x}{L}, \quad N_2 = \frac{x}{L}$$

Similarly, consider a 2D element with 3 nodes, then u(x,y) = a+bx+cy
This will give N1 (x,y), N2 (x,y), and N3 (x,y).

Similarly, 3D element with Tetrahedral shape will give 4 shape functions. General rule of assumption is:

Element	Assumed function
1D (2-node)	linear
1D (3-node)	quadratic
2D triangle	linear in x,y
3D tetra	linear in x,y,z

Some important properties of Shape function N are:

- Ni is equal to 1 at its own node. So, N1 is equal to 1 only at u1.
- Ni is equal to 0 at all other nodes. So, N1 is 0 at u2, u3, and so on.
- Sum of all Ni at a point is equal to 1. ∑Ni=1 So, at mid point of a 1D rod element, if N1 is 0.5 and N2 will be 0.5.

For different types of elements, the displacement function can be defined as

For 1D rod/bar element:

$$u(x) = \sum_{i-1}^{n} N_i(x)\, u_i$$

so 2-node element will be u(x)=N1(x)u1+N2(x)u2

in vector form: $u = [N_1 \quad N_2] \begin{bmatrix} u_1 \\ u_2 \end{bmatrix}$

For 2D element (Triangle/Quad):

$$u_x(x,y) = \sum_{i-1}^{n} N_i(x,y)\, u_{ix} \qquad u_y(x,y) = \sum_{i-1}^{n} N_i(x,y)\, u_{iy}$$

in vector form: $\mathbf{u} = \begin{bmatrix} u_x \\ u_y \end{bmatrix} = \begin{bmatrix} N_1 & 0 & N_2 & 0 & \cdots \\ 0 & N_1 & 0 & N_2 & \cdots \end{bmatrix} \begin{bmatrix} u_{1x} \\ u_{1y} \\ u_{2x} \\ u_{2y} \\ \vdots \end{bmatrix}$

For 3D element (Tetra/Hexa):

$$u_x(x,y,z) = \sum_{i-1}^{n} N_i(x,y,z)\, u_{ix} \quad u_y(x,y,z) = \sum_{i-1}^{n} N_i(x,y,z)\, u_{iy} \quad u_z(x,y,z) = \sum_{i-1}^{n} N_i(x,y,z)\, u_{iz}$$

in vector form: $\mathbf{u} = \begin{bmatrix} u_x \\ u_y \\ u_z \end{bmatrix} = \begin{bmatrix} N_1 & 0 & 0 & N_2 & 0 & 0 & \cdots \\ 0 & N_1 & 0 & 0 & N_2 & 0 & \cdots \\ 0 & 0 & N_1 & 0 & 0 & N_2 & \cdots \end{bmatrix} \begin{bmatrix} u_{1x} \\ u_{1y} \\ u_{1z} \\ u_{2x} \\ u_{2y} \\ u_{2z} \\ \vdots \end{bmatrix}$

Strain

Strain **ϵ** is calculated from change in displacement.

For 1D element, $\epsilon = \frac{du}{dx}$ since there is only one direction of deformation so there is no shear component.

For 2D element, there will be two normal strain (in x direction ϵ_x and y direction ϵ_y) and one shear strain (distortion γ_{xy}).

$$\epsilon_x = \frac{\partial u_x}{\partial x} \qquad \epsilon_y = \frac{\partial u_y}{\partial y} \qquad \gamma_{xy} = \frac{\partial u_x}{\partial y} + \frac{\partial u_y}{\partial x}$$

So the strain matrix becomes,

$$\epsilon = \begin{bmatrix} \epsilon_x \\ \epsilon_y \\ \gamma_{xy} \end{bmatrix}$$

For 3D element, there will be total three normal strains and three shear strains, one for each x, y, and z directions similar to 2D element. The strain matrix can be given as,

$$\epsilon = \begin{bmatrix} \epsilon_x \\ \epsilon_y \\ \epsilon_z \\ \gamma_{xy} \\ \gamma_{yz} \\ \gamma_{zx} \end{bmatrix}$$

B Matrix

To find out B matrix, we can use the equation:

$$\epsilon = B.u$$

Assuming a case of 1D element, from previous equations of displacement, we can write:

$$u_x = \sum N_i u_{ix}$$

If we apply differentiation on both sides then $\frac{\partial u_x}{\partial x} = \sum \frac{\partial N_i}{\partial x} u_{ix}$ and since $\epsilon_x = \frac{\partial u_x}{\partial x}$

So we can write, $\epsilon_x = \sum \frac{\partial N_i}{\partial x} u_{ix}$

If we compare this equation with our standard equation of B matrix **ϵ = B.u** then we can write B = ∑∂Ni/∂x

in vector form it gives: $\epsilon = \underbrace{\begin{bmatrix} \frac{dN_1}{dx} & \frac{dN_2}{dx} & \cdots & \frac{dN_n}{dx} \end{bmatrix}}_{B} \begin{bmatrix} u_1 \\ u_2 \\ \vdots \\ u_n \end{bmatrix}$ for 1D elements

For 2D Elements,

$$\begin{bmatrix} \epsilon_x \\ \epsilon_y \\ \gamma_{xy} \end{bmatrix} = \underbrace{\begin{bmatrix} \frac{\partial N_1}{\partial x} & 0 & \frac{\partial N_2}{\partial x} & 0 & \cdots \\ 0 & \frac{\partial N_1}{\partial y} & 0 & \frac{\partial N_2}{\partial y} & \cdots \\ \frac{\partial N_1}{\partial y} & \frac{\partial N_1}{\partial x} & \frac{\partial N_2}{\partial y} & \frac{\partial N_2}{\partial x} & \cdots \end{bmatrix}}_{B} \begin{bmatrix} u_{1x} \\ u_{1y} \\ u_{2x} \\ u_{2y} \\ \vdots \end{bmatrix}$$

For 3D elements,

$$\begin{bmatrix} \epsilon_x \\ \epsilon_y \\ \epsilon_z \\ \gamma_{xy} \\ \gamma_{yz} \\ \gamma_{zx} \end{bmatrix} = \underbrace{\begin{bmatrix} \frac{\partial N_1}{\partial x} & 0 & 0 & \cdots \\ 0 & \frac{\partial N_1}{\partial y} & 0 & \cdots \\ 0 & 0 & \frac{\partial N_1}{\partial z} & \cdots \\ \frac{\partial N_1}{\partial y} & \frac{\partial N_1}{\partial x} & 0 & \cdots \\ 0 & \frac{\partial N_1}{\partial z} & \frac{\partial N_1}{\partial y} & \cdots \\ \frac{\partial N_1}{\partial z} & 0 & \frac{\partial N_1}{\partial x} & \cdots \end{bmatrix}}_{B} \begin{bmatrix} u_{1x} \\ u_{1y} \\ u_{1z} \\ \vdots \end{bmatrix}$$

D (Material Matrix)

D is also called material matrix and defines relation between stress and strain. As you should be aware with the Hooke's Law which states **σ=E.ϵ**. Writing this in matrix form gives:

$$\sigma = \underbrace{[E]}_{D} \cdot \epsilon$$

For 1D elements

D is [E] because there are not directional components or forces.

For 2D elements

Strain ϵ is defined by

$$\epsilon = \begin{bmatrix} \epsilon_x \\ \epsilon_y \\ \gamma_{xy} \end{bmatrix}$$

Stress σ is defined by

$$\sigma = \begin{bmatrix} \sigma_x \\ \sigma_y \\ \tau_{xy} \end{bmatrix}$$

For calculating normal stresses σ_x and σ_y, we will use the formulae:

$$\sigma_x = E\epsilon_x + (\text{effect of } \epsilon_y) \quad \sigma_y = E\epsilon_y + (\text{effect of } \epsilon_x)$$

The effect of ϵ_y and effect of ϵ_x values are calculated using Poisson ratio ν.

From basic mechanics, strain in x direction for 2D element can be given as:

$\epsilon_x = \frac{\sigma_x}{E} - \nu\frac{\sigma_y}{E}$, here negative portion is contraction in x due to stretching in y direction.

Similarly, strain in y direction can be given as:

$$\epsilon_y = \frac{\sigma_y}{E} - \nu\frac{\sigma_x}{E}$$

If we write it in matrix format then $\begin{bmatrix} \epsilon_x \\ \epsilon_y \end{bmatrix} = \frac{1}{E}\begin{bmatrix} 1 & -\nu \\ -\nu & 1 \end{bmatrix}\begin{bmatrix} \sigma_x \\ \sigma_y \end{bmatrix}$

If we invert this equation to get stress from strain then equation becomes: $\sigma = D.\epsilon$.

Inverse of $\begin{bmatrix} 1 & -\nu \\ -\nu & 1 \end{bmatrix}$ is $\frac{1}{1-\nu^2}\begin{bmatrix} 1 & \nu \\ \nu & 1 \end{bmatrix}$ so stresses are $\begin{bmatrix} \sigma_x \\ \sigma_y \end{bmatrix} = \frac{E}{1-\nu^2}\begin{bmatrix} 1 & \nu \\ \nu & 1 \end{bmatrix}\begin{bmatrix} \epsilon_x \\ \epsilon_y \end{bmatrix}$.

Expanding this stress matrix gives,

$$\sigma_x = \frac{E}{1-\nu^2}(\epsilon_x + \nu\epsilon_y)$$
$$\sigma_y = \frac{E}{1-\nu^2}(\epsilon_y + \nu\epsilon_x)$$

For calculating shear stress τ_{xy}, we will use the equation $\tau_{xy} = G.\gamma_{xy}$. Here, $G = \frac{E}{2(1+\nu)}$

So final equation of stress-strain relationship for 2D element is:

$$\begin{bmatrix} \sigma_x \\ \sigma_y \\ \tau_{xy} \end{bmatrix} = \underbrace{\frac{E}{1-\nu^2}\begin{bmatrix} 1 & \nu & 0 \\ \nu & 1 & 0 \\ 0 & 0 & \frac{1-\nu}{2} \end{bmatrix}}_{D}\begin{bmatrix} \epsilon_x \\ \epsilon_y \\ \gamma_{xy} \end{bmatrix}$$

For 3D elements

If we extend the same logic of 2D to 3D element then

$$\begin{bmatrix}\sigma_x\\ \sigma_y\\ \sigma_z\\ \tau_{xy}\\ \tau_{yz}\\ \tau_{zx}\end{bmatrix} = \underbrace{\frac{E}{(1+\nu)(1-2\nu)}\begin{bmatrix}1-\nu & \nu & \nu & 0 & 0 & 0\\ \nu & 1-\nu & \nu & 0 & 0 & 0\\ \nu & \nu & 1-\nu & 0 & 0 & 0\\ 0 & 0 & 0 & \frac{1-2\nu}{2} & 0 & 0\\ 0 & 0 & 0 & 0 & \frac{1-2\nu}{2} & 0\\ 0 & 0 & 0 & 0 & 0 & \frac{1-2\nu}{2}\end{bmatrix}}_{D}\begin{bmatrix}\epsilon_x\\ \epsilon_y\\ \epsilon_z\\ \gamma_{xy}\\ \gamma_{yz}\\ \gamma_{zx}\end{bmatrix}$$

Note that D is not node dependent and it is uniform for material. While deducing the matrix for D, we have assumed material to be isotropic which means same load required in any of the directions for same amount of deformation. With change in material property, there will be change in this D matrix.

Now, we have B matrix, D matrix, and B^T is just transpose of B matrix. Let's put everything together in stiffness matrix

For 1D element:

$$[K]_e = \int_0^L B^T DB\, A\, dx$$

On substituting parameters,

$$[K]_e = \int_0^L \begin{bmatrix}\frac{dN_1}{dx}\\ \frac{dN_2}{dx}\end{bmatrix} E \begin{bmatrix}\frac{dN_1}{dx} & \frac{dN_2}{dx}\end{bmatrix} A\, dx$$

On expanding this equation,

$$[K]_e = \int_0^L AE \begin{bmatrix}\frac{dN_1}{dx}\frac{dN_1}{dx} & \frac{dN_1}{dx}\frac{dN_2}{dx}\\ \frac{dN_2}{dx}\frac{dN_1}{dx} & \frac{dN_2}{dx}\frac{dN_2}{dx}\end{bmatrix} dx$$

Which gives,

$$[K]_e = \frac{AE}{L}\begin{bmatrix}1 & -1\\ -1 & 1\end{bmatrix}$$

Here, A is cross-section area of rod element and L is length of rod element. We have used two nodes but there can be multiple nodes in the element.

Similarly, **Element stiffness matrix for 2D elements** can be given by:

$$[K]_e = \int_A B^T DB\, t\, dA$$

which produces matrix of size (2n × 2n). Here t is thickness of plate.

Element stiffness matrix for 3D elements can be given by:

$$[K]_e = \int_V B^T DB\, dV$$

which produces matrix of size (3n × 3n).

Note that Nastran or any FEA solver does not perform integration directly. It converts these integration equations to finite summation equations. Which means:

For 1D, equation is $[K]_e = \sum_{i=1}^{n_{gp}} B_i^T EB_i\, w_i\, |J_i|\, A$

For 2D, equation is $[K]_e = \sum_{i=1}^{n_{gp}} B_i^T DB_i\, w_i\, |J_i|\, t$

For 3D, equation is $[K]_e = \sum_{i-1}^{n_{gp}} B_i^T D B_i \, w_i \, |J_i|$

When converting integration equation to summation problem, solver picks smart points inside the element called gauss points. For example, hexa (brick) element has 8 gauss points, quad elements have 4, and linear tetra elements have 1 gauss point. So exact solver workflow is

1. Choose Gauss points
2. For each Gauss point:
   - Compute B
   - Compute Jacobian (J)
   - Compute contribution: B^T D B × w × |J|
3. Sum all contributions

-> Gives element stiffness matrix

Nastran Cards for Elemental Stiffness Matrix

At root level, Nastran only knows the parameters (cards) that are stored in its programming library. Nastran does not know what is D and what is B in our final equation. It knows GRID, MAT1, CTETRA etc. So, when we convert our final equation of elemental stiffness matrix to Nastran cards, for a 3D Tetrahedral element example then it should look like:

$$[K]_e = \sum_{i-1}^{n_{gp}} \left[B_i(\text{GRID, CTETRA})^T \cdot D(\text{MAT1}) \cdot B_i(\text{GRID, CTETRA}) \cdot w_i(\text{element}) \cdot |J_i(\text{geometry})| \right]$$

Note that in this equation w_i is weight of that gauss point in total integration and $|J_i|$ is the Jacobian determinant which converts local coordinate system of deformed element to real coordinate system based on GRID geometry.

To solve this equation, Nastran does following in the background:

1. Read GRID to get node coordinates
2. Read element to get connectivity between nodes
3. Read MAT1 to build D matrix which defines material properties
4. Read property to get Area A or thickness t in case of 1D and 2D elements.
5. For each Gauss point:
   - Compute B from geometry
   - Compute Jacobian |J|
   - Compute contribution: B^T D B × w × scaling
6. Sum all contributions → Ke

Force Matrix

Earlier, you have worked on Displacement matrix and elemental stiffness matrix. The next piece of puzzle is Force/load matrix. The force/load that you apply on model is divided into smaller portions as per the number of elements and then further divided as per the number of nodes in the elements. There are many types of forces that work on the body during analysis like shown in next table:

Type	Example
Point force	Bolt Load
Pressure	Wind, Fluid
Body force	Gravity
Thermal	Expansion
Constraint reaction	Supports

At any point in the body, the applied force can be represented as f(x,y,z). The net force on a node is combination of all the applied forces $\{F\}=\{F\}_{point}+\{F\}_{pressure}+\{F\}_{body}+\{F\}_{thermal}$. All these forces are calculated differently in Nastran. For example, for point forces there is no need of integration and they can be independently added based on direction components whereas calculating pressure force will require integration.

Point Force (FORCE card)

The point force is represented by following piece of code in Nastran:

FORCE SID G CID F N1 N2 N3

Here FORCE parameter defines that it is a point force. SID defines the load case/set ID of the force which is replaced by a value. G defines node number in grid on which force is being applied. CID defines coordinate system ID being used for calculating components of force. Generally 0 is used for global coordinate system and non-zero numbers define local coordinate systems. F is a scalar value which defines actual value of point force. N1, N2, and N3 values define direction of force vector in X, Y, and Z.

Example code:

```
GRID 1 0 0 0 0
FORCE 10 1 0 1000 1 1 0
```

Here, force is defined for Node 1 in the GRID. FORCE card means point force is being applied. It is a part of load set 10 at node 1 with global coordinate system applicable. Value of force is 1000 and it is acting along bisector of X axis and Y axis which means at 45° in XY plane. Note that Nastran does not have a unit system internally for calculation. Units are automatically converted to same level by CAD software. This code is internally converted to Force matrix by Nastran using following steps:

1. Find normalize direction using formula: $\vec{n} = \frac{(N1, N2, N3)}{\sqrt{N1^2 + N2^2 + N3^2}}$. For our example it will be $\vec{n} = \left(\frac{1}{\sqrt{2}}, \frac{1}{\sqrt{2}}, 0\right)$.

2. Multiply it by Magnitude which is 1000 in our case. This gives us

$$\vec{F} = 1000 \cdot \left(\frac{1}{\sqrt{2}}, \frac{1}{\sqrt{2}}, 0\right) = (707, 707, 0)$$

3. In matrix for this gives force on Node 1 : $\{F\}_1 = \begin{bmatrix} 707 \\ 707 \\ 0 \end{bmatrix}$

Surface Load like Pressure (PLOAD / PLOAD4 cards)

The nodal force due to pressure is calculated by the formula: $\{F\}_e=\int_S N^T p dS$ which translates to $\{F\}_e = \sum_{i=1}^{n_{gp}} N_i^T \, p \, w_i \, |J_i|$ when converted to finite sum equation. So, in background Nastran runs following loop:

```
for each element face:
    for each Gauss point:
        evaluate N
        compute surface Jacobian
        compute contribution
    sum → element force vector
```

Similarly, other forces are calculated to form an elemental force matrix.

$$\{F\} = \sum_e \{F\}_e^{pressure} + \sum_e \{F\}_e^{body} + \sum \{F\}_{point} + \sum \{F\}_{thermal}$$

System now solves for unknown {u} for element. Once, {u} for each element is known, the system assembles global matrix.

Global Matrix

Global matrix is assembled by combining individual elemental matrices in their order in the body.

Global u

Global u matrix will show degree of freedom for all the nodes in the form of 3 x n matrix like

$$\{u\} = \begin{bmatrix} u_{1x} \\ u_{1y} \\ u_{1z} \\ u_{2x} \\ u_{2y} \\ u_{2z} \\ u_{3x} \\ u_{3y} \\ u_{3z} \\ u_{4x} \\ \vdots \end{bmatrix}$$

Global K

Global stiffness matrix is represented by:

$$[K] = \begin{bmatrix} K_{11} & K_{12} & K_{13} & \cdots & K_{1n} \\ K_{21} & K_{22} & K_{23} & \cdots & K_{2n} \\ K_{31} & K_{32} & K_{33} & \cdots & K_{3n} \\ \vdots & \vdots & \vdots & \ddots & \vdots \\ K_{n1} & K_{n2} & K_{n3} & \cdots & K_{nn} \end{bmatrix}$$

where, $K_{ij} = \sum_{e=1}^{n_{elem}} \sum_{p=1}^{n_e} \sum_{q=1}^{n_e} K_e(p,q)\ \delta_{i,g_e(p)}\ \delta_{j,g_e(q)}$

Global Force

Similarly, global Force matrix F can be given as:

$$\{F\} = \begin{bmatrix} F_1 \\ F_2 \\ F_3 \\ \vdots \\ F_n \end{bmatrix}$$

where, $F_i = \sum_{e=1}^{n_{elem}} \sum_{p=1}^{n_e} F_e(p)\ \delta_{i,g_e(p)} + F_i^{ext}$

Applying Constraints to Global Matrix

At this step, Nastran starts to reduce the size of global matrix by apply restrictions to degree of freedom which in turn remove rows and columns from matrices. There are two type of constraints Single Point Constraint (SPC) and Multi Point Constraint (MPC).

Single Point Constraint

The Single Point Constraint defines degree of freedom for a node without relating it to other nodes. For example node 1 in GRID can move in u_x and u_y but cannot move in u_z. Starting with real system [K]{u}={F}, assume following is a 3DOFs problem for our analysis:

$$\begin{bmatrix} 10 & -5 & 0 \\ -5 & 10 & -5 \\ 0 & -5 & 5 \end{bmatrix} \begin{bmatrix} u_1 \\ u_2 \\ u_3 \end{bmatrix} = \begin{bmatrix} 0 \\ 10 \\ 0 \end{bmatrix}$$

Applying SPC, we constraint $u_1 = 0$, first row and column becomes null and our problem is reduced to

$$\begin{bmatrix} 10 & -5 \\ -5 & 5 \end{bmatrix} \begin{bmatrix} u_2 \\ u_3 \end{bmatrix} = \begin{bmatrix} 10 \\ 0 \end{bmatrix}$$

Multi Point Constraint

The Multi Point Constraint defines relation between degrees of freedom for multiple nodes. Assume in same previous example of SPC, if we constraint $u_1 = u_2$ then {u} matrix becomes:

$$\{u\} = \begin{bmatrix} u_2 \\ u_2 \\ u_3 \end{bmatrix}$$

which means only independent DOFs are u2 and u3. After replacing u1 with u2 and solving the original matrix, we will get reduced matrix as:

$$\begin{bmatrix} 5 & -5 \\ -5 & 5 \end{bmatrix} \begin{bmatrix} u_2 \\ u_3 \end{bmatrix} = \begin{bmatrix} 0 \\ 0 \end{bmatrix}$$

Solution

After applying constraints, we get equation $[K_{ff}]\{u_f\}=\{F_f\}$. Here, K_{ff} is reduced global stiffness matrix (only free DOFs), u_f is unknown displacement vector, and F_f is reduced force vector. Generally K_{ff} matrix is symmetric ($K = K^T$), sparse (mostly zeros), and positive definite (for stable structure). There properties allow us to select Sparse Direct Solver.

The solver factorizes [K] to $[L][L]^T$. Here [L] is lower triangular matrix and $[L]^T$ is its transpose. Now two equations are solved to get unknown u; Forward substitution and Backward substitution.

Forward substitution: $[L]\{y\}=\{F\}$, solves for intermediate vector {y}
Backward substitution: $[L]^T\{u\}=\{y\}$, solves for final displacement {u}

Summary

Start with the model definition: nodes (GRID) define geometry, elements (CTETRA, CQUAD4, CROD) define connectivity, materials (MAT1) define D, and properties (PSHELL, PSOLID, PROD) define thickness/area.

From this, each element uses shape functions N and their derivatives to build the strain–displacement matrix B, and then computes its stiffness using numerical integration: $[K]_e=\sum B^T D B w|J|$

All element stiffness matrices are then assembled via DOF mapping into the global sparse matrix [K], while loads (FORCE, PLOAD, GRAV, etc.) are converted into the global force vector {F}.

Next, constraints (SPC/MPC) are applied, which remove or relate DOFs, reducing the system to: $[K_{ff}]\{u_f\}=\{F_f\}$

This reduced system is then solved using a sparse direct solver (Cholesky factorization) to obtain displacements {u}. Finally, results are recovered at element level using: $\epsilon=Bu$, $\sigma=D\epsilon$ along with internal and reaction forces, completing the analysis.

SELF ASSESSMENT

Q1. What is Finite Element Analysis?

Q2. What are the basic unknowns in the engineering problems through which the behavior of entire structure can be predicted?

Q3. Name the steps which are involved in the Finite element analysis.

Q4. Each element stiffness matrix is to be placed in the global stiffness matrix appropriately. This process is called ....

Q5. In element analysis problems, ... method can handle structures with anisotropic properties without any difficulty.

Q6. The process of modeling a structure using suitable number, shape, and size of the elements is called ....

Q7. In Geometric discontinuities of structure, when there is not any change in shape and size of the structure there should be a node or line of nodes. (True/False)

Q8. In the analysis of elements, accuracy of calculation can be increased by using less number of elements. (True/False)

Q9. What does Finite Element Analysis (FEA) primarily deal with?

A. Exact solutions to simple problems
B. Approximate solutions to complex problems
C. Exact solutions to boundary conditions
D. Approximate solutions only to heat transfer problems

Q10. What was the original application of Finite Element Method?

A. Electrical field analysis
B. Fluid flow analysis
C. Aircraft stress analysis
D. Ship design analysis

Q11. What is the correct order of steps in the Finite Element Analysis?

A. Discretize → Select field variables → Solve equations → Impose boundary conditions
B. Select field variables → Discretize → Select interpolation functions → Assemble properties → Impose boundary conditions → Solve → Post-process
C. Discretize → Assemble → Interpolate → Solve → Visualize
D. Select interpolation functions → Discretize → Impose boundary conditions → Assemble → Solve
Q12. The interpolating functions used in FEA are also called:

A. Integration functions
B. Boundary functions
C. Shape functions
D. Transfer functions

Q13. In a typical 4-node quadrilateral element with 2 DOF per node, what is the size of the element stiffness matrix?

A. 4 × 2
B. 8 × 8
C. 2 × 2
D. 6 × 6

Q14. What is the purpose of assembling global stiffness matrix?

A. To approximate the solution region
B. To get local stresses
C. To prepare the system equation $[k]\{\delta\} = \{F\}$
D. To interpolate shape functions

Q15. Which numerical method is commonly used for solving the simultaneous equations in FEA?

A. Euler's method
B. Choleski's decomposition
C. Simpson's rule
D. Lagrange interpolation

Q16. In comparison to FDM, FEM is better at:

A. Handling only node point values
B. Approximating only straight boundaries
C. Ensuring continuity at node and element edges
D. Requiring more nodes for accuracy

Q17. What is discretization in FEA?

A. The process of solving boundary conditions
B. Modeling using a suitable number and shape of elements
C. Applying loads to a structure
D. Writing the system equations

Q18. What types of discontinuities require special attention during discretization?

A. Only geometric
B. Only boundary conditions
C. Geometric, load, material, and boundary conditions
D. None

Q19. Why is symmetry used in FEA models?

A. To increase computation time
B. To eliminate boundary conditions
C. To reduce memory requirements and refine the mesh
D. To reduce the number of loads

Practice Questions

Topics Covered

The major topics covered in this chapter are:

- ***Practice Questions***

PROBLEM 1

Sometimes, we see people fighting and in some extreme cases, fighting with the help of Baseball bats. We are not here to discuss concepts of fighting but once the fighting is over, everybody is busy to see effect of baseball bat on humans. Due to unknown elastic property of human body, we can not perform analysis to find effect of baseball bat on humans, but here we can check the effect of force exerted on the baseball bat due to some freaks; refer to Figure-1.

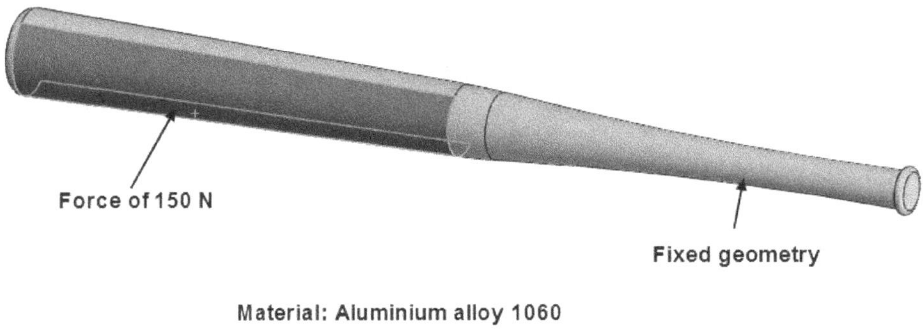

Figure-1. Problem 1

We assume it to be a static analysis. Check whether the bat will break or not.

PROBLEM 2

The wall of a house is 7 m wide, 6 m high and 0.3 m thick made up of brick. The thermal conductivity of brick is k = 0.6 W/m.K. If the inside temperature of wall is 16 °C and outside temperature is 6 °C then find out the heat lost from inside wall to outside wall in a steady state condition. The model is given in Figure-2.

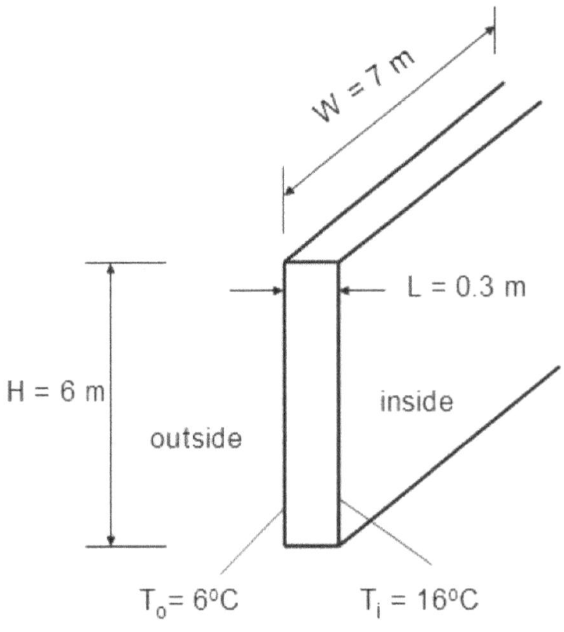

Figure-2. Problem 2

Note that to perform this thermal analysis, you need to create a new material with thermal properties as follow:
Thermal Conductivity = 0.6 W/(m.K)
Specific heat = 1214 J/(kg.K)
Mass density = 2405 kg/m^3

PROBLEM 3

An axial pull of **35kN** is applied at the ends of a shaft as shown in Figure-3. If the material is **Alloy Steel** then find the total elongation in the shaft.

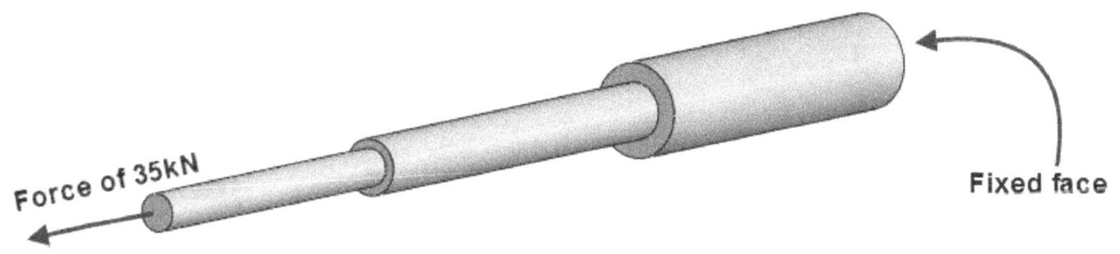

Figure-3. Problem 3 shaft

PROBLEM 4

A cast iron link is required to transmit a steady tensile load of 45kN. The initial boundary conditions are given in Figure-4.

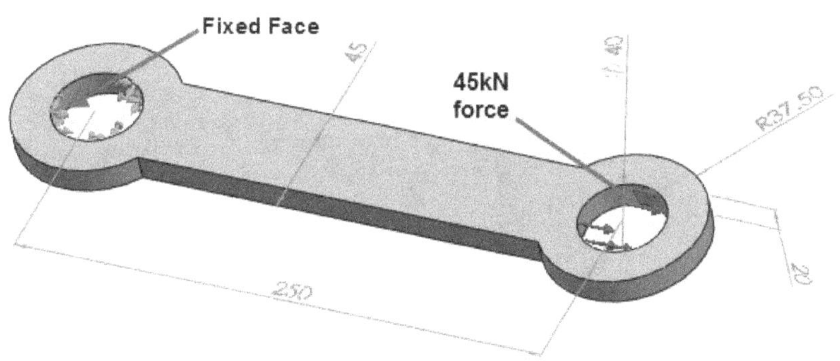

Figure-4. Problem of link

Find out the optimum thickness of link so that factor of safety is 3.

PROBLEM 5

A part of car jack assembly is displayed in Figure-5 with its boundary conditions. Optimize the assembly with respect to material cost. Note that all the contacts are no penetration as you find in a real car jack.

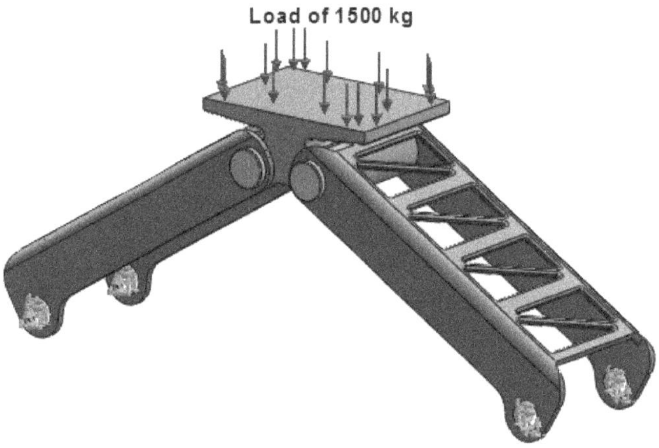

Figure-5. Problem 5

PROBLEM 6

An assembly of cooling fins and CPU is displayed in Figure-6 with boundary conditions. The bulk temperature is 300K and operating temperature band for CPU is 304K to 354 K. Check if fins are enough to dissipate the heat. If not then perform modifications in fin to dissipate heat. Note that fins and heat sink are perfectly bonded for heat transfer.

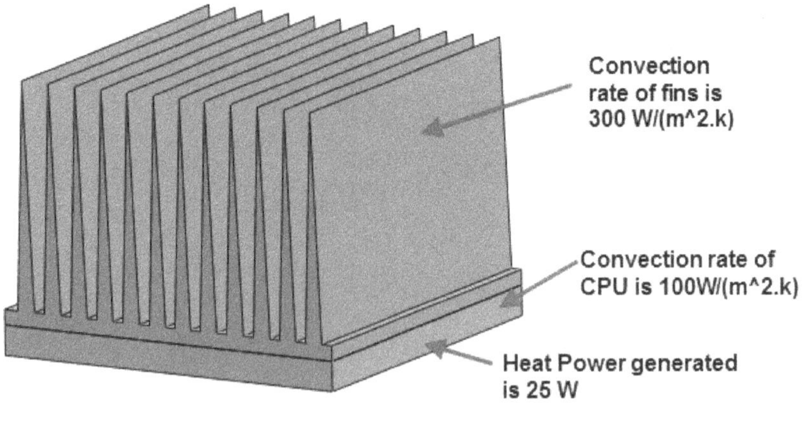

Figure-6. Problem 6

Index

Symbols

2D triangular shell elements 2-66
3D tetrahedral solid elements 2-66

A

Advanced Mesh Settings dialog box 2-67
Advanced Options button 2-45, 2-63
Advanced Settings button 7-5
Analysis dialog box 3-2
Animate button 2-77
Animate tool 2-82
Animation Options tab 2-76
Anisotropic 3D option 2-16
Anti-Sym button 2-24
AntiSymmetry area 2-43
Applying Contacts 3-8
Associated Geometry check box 2-21
Automatic plot updating check box 2-5
Auto tool 2-60

B

B 13-16
Bar option 2-25
Beam option 2-25
Bearing Load option 2-50
Bending check box 2-22
bisections for each increment 3-22
B Matrix 13-19
Body Temperature option 2-53
Bolt option 2-36
Bonded option 2-61
Bottom Fiber edit box 2-22
Brittle option 2-17
Buckling Analysis 1-4
Bulk Temperature 11-3

C

Cable option 2-32
Centroidal option 2-7
Choleski's decomposition 13-5
Cluster between Modes check box 8-9
Coefficient of Friction edit box 2-63
Cohesive Zone Model 2-65
Compressive Limit (MPa) edit box 2-14
Conduction 1-9, 11-2
Connector dialog box 2-30
Connectors tool 2-30
consistent loads 13-4
Constraint dialog box 2-41
Constraints/Boundary Conditions 13-14
Constraints tool 1-14, 2-41
Contact Parameters dialog box 2-63
Contact Type drop-down 2-8, 2-61, 11-6
Contour Options check box 2-74
Convection 1-9, 11-2
Convection Coefficient vs. Temperature option 2-55
Convection option 2-54
Convergence criteria and error tolerances option 3-21
Convergence Settings dialog box 2-70
Convergence Settings tool 2-70
Coordinate System dialog box 6-9
Coordinate Systems option 6-9
Corner option 2-7
Coupled option 4-4
CQC option 9-5
Crash option 2-3
Create AVI button 2-77
Creating New Material 2-11
creep analysis 3-14
Crushable Foam option 2-17
cycle 1-4
Cyclic Symmetry check box 2-8
Cylindrical option 6-10

D

Damping 4-2
Damping coefficient edit box 2-24
Damping Coefficient edit box 2-13
Damping dialog box 6-3
Data Type drop-down 2-7
Default Settings tool 2-2
Define New Table button 2-46, 2-54
Deform Options check box 2-74
Degrees of Freedom area 2-43
Delay (msec) edit box 2-5
Dependent Term drop-down 7-6
Design View drop-down 2-9
Diagonal option 4-4
Direct Frequency Response analysis 8-2
Direct Frequency Response Analysis 1-7
Direct Frequency Response option 8-2
Direct Transient Response Analysis 1-7, 6-2
Disable option 2-61
Discontinuity of Boundary conditions 13-10
Discontinuity of Loads 13-9
Discrete Frequencies check box 8-5
Displacement 13-16
Displacement option 2-74
Display button 2-77
Display Labels check box 2-4
Display Nodes check box 2-4
Display Options node 2-3
Distributed Load option 2-47
divergence conditions 3-21
Download Local Help link 2-3
Dynamic Analysis 1-4
Dynamics Setup dialog box 6-4, 8-4

E

Edit tool 2-9

Elastic Modulus (MPa) edit box 2-13
Elasto-Plastic (Bi-Linear) radio button 2-12
Element properties 13-3
Elements 13-13
Element Size edit box 2-67
Elements option 2-4
Element Type Default option 4-4
Emissivity 11-3
Enforced Motion option 2-52
Event Duration edit box 10-3
Explicit dynamics analysis 12-2
Explicit quasi-static analysis , 1-9
Explicit Quasi-Static option 12-6
Extraction Method drop-down 4-4

F

Failure Theory drop-down 2-14, 2-24, 2-65
Fatigue button 2-12
Fatigue Setup dialog box 10-3
FCS 2-24
Film Coefficient 11-3
Find Thin Bodies tool 2-39, 2-83
FINITE DIFFERENCE METHOD 13-6
finite element analysis 13-2
Fluid Depth Direction area 2-48
FORCE card 13-23
Force check box 2-7
Force Matrix 13-22
Force option 2-44
Fraction of Max Allowable Penetration edit box 2-64
Free button 2-43
Frequency Range check box 8-6
Frequency Response Analysis 1-7
Frictional Stiffness for Stick edit box 2-64
Frictionless option 2-42
From Output option 2-58

G

Gausselimination 13-5
Generate Mesh tool 1-16, 2-68
Geometric Discontinuities 13-8
Global Force 13-25
Global K 13-24
Global Ply button 2-24
Global Refinement radio button 2-70
global stiffness equation 13-4
Global u 13-24
Gravity option 2-49
Grounded Spring check box 2-33

H

Hardening Rule drop-down 2-18
H Axis radio button 2-82
HCS 2-24
Heat Flux check box 2-7, 11-6
Heat Flux option 2-57, 2-59
Heat Generation option 2-57, 11-7
HILL option 2-24
HOFF option 2-24
Hooke's Law 1-2
Hydrostatic Load option 2-47
Hyperelastic option 2-16

I

Idealizations tool 2-19
Impact Analysis 1-8
Impact Analysis option 7-4
Impact Event Parameters dialog box 7-5
Impact Setup option 7-4
Import from Stress Analysis tool 2-9
Impulse Load 12-4
Include Drilling DOF (CQUADR/CTRIAR) check box 2-22
Initial Condition option 2-52
Installed Local Help radio button 2-3
Isotropic option 2-13
Iterations before stiffness update edit box 3-21

L

Laminate radio button 2-22
Lanczos Iteration option 4-4
large displacements 3-14
Linear Buckling Analysis 1-5, 5-3
Linear Buckling option 5-3
Linear Equation Based option 2-45
Linear option 2-67
Linear Static Analysis 1-2, 3-2
Linear Steady State Heat Transfer option 11-5
Line Elements option 2-25
Line search tolerance 3-21
Load dialog box 2-43
Loads 13-15
Loads tool 1-15, 2-43
Local Refinement radio button 2-70

M

Manual tool 2-61
Mass density edit box 2-13
Mass Representation drop-down 4-4
Material dialog box 2-10
Material Discontinuity 13-10
Material Matrix 13-19
material nonlinearity 3-15
Material Orientation dialog box 3-22
Material Orientation option 3-22
Materials 13-14
Materials tool 1-13, 2-10, 2-83
Max Allowable Adjustment Ratio edit box 2-64
Max Allowable Penetration edit box 2-64
Max Allowable Slip edit box 2-64
Max Element Growth Rate edit box 2-67
Max Radial Activation Distance edit box 2-64

Max. Strain option 2-24
Max. Stress option 2-24
Max Triangle Angle edit box 2-67
MCT option 2-24
Membrane-Bending check box 2-22
Mesh Control tool 2-69
Meshing 2-66
Mesh Settings tool 2-66
Mesh Table button 2-68
Mesh Table dialog box 2-68
Mesh Troubleshooter tool 2-71
MidPlane Offset Distance (mm) check box 2-22
Midsurface dialog box 2-39
Midsurfaces tool 2-39
Min Feature Angle edit box 2-68
Min Triangle Angle 2-67
Modal Database drop-down 4-4
Modal Frequency 8-7
Modal Frequency Response analysis 8-2
Modal Frequency Response Analysis 1-8
Modal Frequency Response option 8-7
Modal Setup dialog box 4-3
Modal Setup option 4-3
Modal Transient Response Analysis 1-7, 6-2
Modal Transient Response option 6-5
Model State tab 2-8
Modes Analysis 4-7
mode shape 4-2
Moment option 2-46
Mullins Coefficients check box 2-16
Multi-axial fatigue analysis 10-2
Multi-Axial Fatigue Analysis 1-8
Multi-Axial Fatigue option 10-2
Multi Point Constraint 13-25

N

Nastran cards 13-13
natural frequencies 4-2
Neo-Hookean option 2-16
Neutral Axis Offset area 2-27
New Laminate button 2-22
New tool 2-6
Nitinol option 2-16
NN button 2-81
nodal points 13-2
noded isoparametric element 13-3
nodes 13-2
Nodes 13-13
Nodes option 2-4
Nonlinear Buckling Analysis 1-6
Non-Linear Buckling Analysis 5-5
Nonlinear Buckling option 5-5
Nonlinear button 2-17
Nonlinear Elastic radio button 2-12
Nonlinear Material Data dialog box 2-11
Nonlinear Setup dialog box 5-6
Nonlinear Static Analysis 1-3
Nonlinear Static Parameters dialog box 3-19
Nonlinear steady state heat transfer analysis 11-8, 11-12
Nonlinear Transient Response Analysis 1-7, 6-2
Nonlinear Transient Response option 6-7
Normal Modes analysis 4-2
Normal Modes Analysis 1-4, 4-3
No Rotation button 2-43
No Translation button 2-43
NRL option 9-5, 9-8
NSM edit box 2-22
Number of Frames edit box 2-5
Number of Modes edit box 4-4
Number of Points in the Range edit box 8-6
Number of Timesteps option 6-4

O

Object Visibility drop-down 2-82
Offset Bonded option 2-61
Offset Surface dialog box 2-38
Offset Surfaces tool 2-38
Orthotropic 2D option 2-15
Orthotropic 3D option 2-16
Oscillate option 2-5
Output Options drop-down 2-7

P

Parabolic option 2-67
Parameters dialog box 3-25
Parameters option 3-24
Part View check box 2-75
Penetration Surface Offset (mm) edit 2-63
Penetration Type drop-down 2-63
Perform PPFA Calculation check box 2-12
Pin option 2-42
Pipe option 2-25
plasticity problems 3-14
Plastic radio button 2-12
PLOAD / PLOAD4 cards 13-24
Plot dialog box 2-73
Plot option 2-7
Ply Option 2-23
Point on Fluid Surface area 2-48
Poisson's Ratio edit box 2-14
Post-Processing option 2-4
PPFA button 2-12
Pressure option 2-49
Prestress Normal 4-7
Prestress Normal Modes option 4-7
Prestress static analysis 3-13
Prestress Static Analysis 1-3
Principal Stress option 2-14
Probes toggle button 2-78
Progressive Ply Failure Analysis Data 2-18
Projectile Translation Vector selection box 7-4
Project Midside Nodes check box 2-68
Properties 13-14
PSD (Acceleration) vs. Frequency option 9-3
PSD Output Control button 9-2
Punch and Plot option 2-7

Punch option 2-7

Q

Quadratic option 2-45
Quadrilaterals radio button 2-21
Quality Midside Adjustment drop-down 2-68
Quasi-Static Setup dialog box 12-7

R

Radiation 1-9, 11-3
Radiation option 2-56
Random Response analysis 9-2
Random Response Analysis 1-8
Random Response option 9-2
Rayleigh Damping check box 6-4
Reference Temperature edit box 2-13
Refinement Factor edit boxes 2-71
Refinement Ratio check box 2-67
Refinement Threshold edit box 2-71
REFINING MESH 13-11
Remote Force option 2-49
Report Generation option 2-6
resonance 1-4, 4-2
resonant frequencies 4-2
Response Analysis 8-7
Response Spectrum option 2-42
Rigid Body option 2-35
Rigid check box 2-15
Rigid(Explicit) option 2-43
Rod option 2-31
Rotational Force option 2-51
Rotation Angle edit box 2-27
Run button 2-72

S

Safety Factor Plot area 2-5
Saint-Venant torsional constant 2-27
Save dialog box 2-77
Section View check box 2-74
Select Units button 2-7
Separation/No Sliding option 2-61
Shear Limit (MPa) edit box 2-14
Shear Modulus (MPa) edit box 2-14
Shell Elements option 2-20
Shell Idealization 12-3
Shock/Response Spectrum analysis 9-4
Shock/Response Spectrum Analysis 1-8
Show XY Plot button 2-56
Simulation 1-2
Single Point Constraint 13-25
Sliding/No Separation option 2-61
SMC option 2-24
SME option 2-24
Solid Idealization 2-20
Solid Tetrahedral element 2-20
Solver tool 2-65
Sparse Direct Solver 13-26
Specific Heat 11-3
Specify Min/Max check box 2-74
Spectrum Curve List box 9-6
Spherical option 6-10
Spread around Modes check box 8-10
Spring option 2-33
SRSS option 9-5
Static Analysis , 1-2
Steady State Thermal Analysis 1-9
Stefan–Boltzmann Constant 11-3
Stiffness check box 2-33
Stiffness Factor edit box 2-63
Stiffness update method drop-down 3-21
Strain 13-18
Strain check box 2-7
Strain-Displacement Matrix 13-16
Strain Energy check box 2-7
Strain-Life option 10-3
Strength Ratio drop-down 2-24
Stress check box 2-7
Stress Classification Line 2-80
Stress-Life option 10-3, 10-7
Stress Linearization 2-80
Stress Linearization tool 2-80
Stress option 2-74
Stress Recovery Coefficients area 2-27
Structural Members dialog box 2-41
Structural Members tool 2-41
Structural option 2-42
Subcase dialog box 3-24
Subcase option 3-24
Subspace Iteration option 4-4
Suppress Short Features edit box 2-68
Surface Contact dialog box 2-61, 2-65
Sym button 2-24
Symmetric Contact option 2-63
Symmetry area 2-43

T

Table Data dialog box 2-54
Temperature Dependence check box 2-54
Temperature (K) edit box 11-6
Temperature option 2-53
Tensile Limit (MPa) edit box 2-14
Thermal analysis , 1-9
Thermal check box 2-15
Thermal Conductivity 11-3
Thermal Exp. Coeff. edit box 2-14
Thermal Flux 11-3
Thermal Gradient 11-3
Thermal option 2-42
Thickness edit box 2-21
Time Conversion Factor edit box 10-3
Time Step dialog box 11-9
Time Step(s) option 6-4
Tolerance edit box 2-8
Top Fiber 2-22
Transient response analysis 6-2

Transient Response Analysis 1-6
Transient Thermal Analysis 1-9
Transverse Shear 2-22
Triangles radio button 2-21
TSAI option 2-24

U

Units dialog box 2-7
Unsymmetric Contact option 2-63
Upper Jacobian Ratio Bound edit box 2-68
Use Of Symmetry 13-11
Use Plane Strain Element Type check box 2-22

V

Variable Load Definition check box 2-45
Vector drop-down 2-74
Vector Options 2-76
Verbose option 2-3
Vibrational Fatigue 1-9
Vibration Fatigue Analysis 10-5
Viscoelastic option 2-17
Visibility Options tab 2-77
von Mises Stress option 2-14

W

Weld Damage Model area 2-63
Weld Failure Model 2-65

X

XY Plot node 4-8

Y

Yield Limit (MPa) edit box 2-14

Ethics of an Engineer

- Engineers shall hold paramount the safety, health and welfare of the public and shall strive to comply with the principles of sustainable development in the performance of their professional duties.
- Engineers shall perform services only in areas of their competence.
- Engineers shall issue public statements only in an objective and truthful manner.
- Engineers shall act in professional manners for each employer or client as faithful agents or trustees, and shall avoid conflicts of interest.
- Engineers shall build their professional reputation on the merit of their services and shall not compete unfairly with others.
- Engineers shall act in such a manner as to uphold and enhance the honor, integrity, and dignity of the engineering profession and shall act with zero-tolerance for bribery, fraud, and corruption.
- Engineers shall continue their professional development throughout their careers, and shall provide opportunities for the professional development of those engineers under their supervision.

OTHER BOOKS BY CADCAMCAE WORKS

Autodesk Revit 2027 Black Book
Autodesk Revit 2026 Black Book

Autodesk Inventor 2027 Black Book
Autodesk Inventor 2026 Black Book

Autodesk Fusion 360 Black Book (V 2701.1.18) Part I and Part II
Autodesk Fusion 360 PCB Black Book (V 2701.1.18)

AutoCAD Electrical 2027 Black Book
AutoCAD Electrical 2026 Black Book

SolidWorks 2026 Black Book
SolidWorks 2025 Black Book

SolidWorks Simulation 2026 Black Book
SolidWorks Simulation 2025 Black Book

SolidWorks Flow Simulation 2026 Black Book
SolidWorks Flow Simulation 2025 Black Book

SolidWorks CAM 2026 Black Book
SolidWorks CAM 2025 Black Book

SolidWorks Electrical 2026 Black Book
SolidWorks Electrical 2025 Black Book

SolidWorks Workbook 2022

Mastercam 2023 for SolidWorks Black Book
Mastercam 2022 for SolidWorks Black Book

Mastercam 2026 Black Book
Mastercam 2025 Black Book
Mastercam 2024 Black Book

Creo Parametric 12.0 Black Book
Creo Parametric 11.0 Black Book
Creo Parametric 10.0 Black Book

Creo Manufacturing 12.0 Black Book
Creo Manufacturing 11.0 Black Book
Creo Manufacturing 10.0 Black Book

ETABS V22 Black Book
ETABS V21 Black Book
ETABS V20 Black Book

Basics of Autodesk Inventor Nastran 2027
Basics of Autodesk Inventor Nastran 2026
Basics of Autodesk Inventor Nastran 2025

Autodesk CFD 2027 Black Book
Autodesk CFD 2026 Black Book

FreeCAD 1.0 Black Book
FreeCAD 0.21 Black Book
FreeCAD 0.20 Black Book
FreeCAD 0.19 Black Book

LibreCAD 2.2 Black Book

Tinkercad Black Book

Ansys Discovery 2025 Black Book

NX 2506 Black Book

www.ingramcontent.com/pod-product-compliance
Lightning Source LLC
LaVergne TN
LVHW080021210926
848481LV00011B/3079
* 9 7 8 1 7 7 4 5 9 2 1 8 2 *